Introduction to Land Law

Introduction to Land Law

Third Edition

Roger J. Smith

Magdalen College, Oxford

PEARSON

Harlow, England • London • New York • Boston • San Francisco • Toronto • Sydney
Auckland • Singapore • Hong Kong • Tokyo • Seoul • Taipei • New Delhi
Cape Town • São Paulo • Mexico City • Madrid • Amsterdam • Munich • Paris • Milan

Pearson Education Limited
Edinburgh Gate
Harlow CM20 2JE
United Kingdom
Tel: +44 (0)1279 623623
Web: www.pearson.com/uk

First published 2007 (print)
Second edition published 2010 (print)
Third edition published 2013

© Pearson Education Limited 2007, 2010 (print)
© Pearson Education Limited 2013 (print and electronic)

ISBN: 978-1-4082-9346-1 (print)
        978-1-4082-9348-5 (PDF)
        928-1-292-00058-9 (etext)

British Library Cataloguing-in-Publication Data
A catalogue record for the print edition is available from the British Library

Library of Congress Cataloging-in-Publication Data
A catalog record for the print edition is available from the Library of Congress

10 9 8 7 6 5 4 3 2 1
17 16 15 14 13

Print edition typeset in 9.5/13pt ITG Giovanni Std by 35
Print edition printed and bound in Great Britain by Henry Ling Ltd., at the Dorset Press,
Dorchester, Dorset

NOTE THAT ANY PAGE CROSS REFERENCES REFER TO THE PRINT EDITION

Brief contents

Contents

CONTENTS

Join over 5,000 law students succeeding with MyLawChamber

Visit **www.mylawchamber.co.uk** to access a wealth of tools to help you develop and test your knowledge of Land Law, strengthening your understanding so you can excel.

 The Pearson eText is a fully searchable, interactive version of *Introduction to Land Law*. You can make notes in it, highlight it, bookmark it, even link to online sources – helping you get more out of studying and revision. The Pearson eText is linked to the learning tools you'll find in MyLawChamber.

- Interactive multiple choice questions to test your understanding of each topic
- Practice exam questions with guidance to hone your exam technique
- Weblinks to help you read more widely around the subject and really impress your lecturers
- Glossary flashcards to test yourself on legal terms and definitions
- Legal newsfeed to help you read more widely, stay right up to date with the law and impress examiners
- Legal updates to help you stay up to date with the law and impress examiners

 Case Navigator provides in-depth analysis of the leading cases in land law, improving your case-reading skills and understanding of how the law is applied.

 Explore the world of **Virtual Lawyer** and develop your skills in answering legal problem questions as you apply your knowledge of the law to a range of interactive scenarios.

Use the access card at the back of the book to activate mylawchamber. Online purchase is also available at **www.mylawchamber.co.uk/register**.

Lecturers Teach your course, your way.

MyLawChamber is a powerful teaching tool which you can use to assess your students, and improve their understanding.

 Make the interactive Pearson eText a 'live' teaching resource by annotating with your own commentary, links to external sources, critique, or updates to the law and share with your students.

 Set quizzes and mini-assessments using the bank of over 500 multiple-choice questions to gauge your students' understanding.

 Use Case Navigator, a case reading resource we offer in conjunction with LexisNexis, to assign student seminar work.

 Virtual Lawyer is an engaging way to help your students develop their problem-solving skills through scenario-based learning.

For information about teaching support materials, please contact your local Pearson sales consultant or visit **www.mylawchamber.co.uk**.

The regularly maintained mylawchamber site provides the following features:

- Search tool to help locate specific items of content.
- Online help and support to assist with website usage and troubleshooting.

Case Navigator access is included with your mylawchamber registration. The LexisNexis element of Case Navigator is only available to those who currently subscribe to LexisNexis Butterworths online.

Preface to third edition

Inevitably, the passing of a few years means that new and important cases have emerged. This new edition incorporates the leading decisions over the past three years – including those of the Supreme Court in *Manchester CC* v *Pinnock* (human rights) (Extract 2.3.1), *Jones* v *Kernott* (family home) (Extract 8.2.3) and *Mexfield Housing Co-operative Ltd* v *Berrisford* (leases).

As with previous editions, the text outlines the main principles and rules in each topic, whilst going into detail where the law is most controversial and interesting – the issues which most law courses concentrate upon. In previous editions, these fuller analyses were placed at the end of each chapter. This has been changed in the third edition, so that they are found within the relevant discussion in the chapter. This leads to a more natural ordering of the material within each topic.

A novel feature of this edition is that the cases discussed (and also some other materials) contain references to extracts in the author's *Property Law: Cases and Materials* (fifth edition, 2012). As an example, page 127 mentions '*Lloyds Bank plc* v *Rosset* (Extract 10.2.28)'. Chapter 10 of *Cases and Materials* contains that extract, quoting two pages from the case.

Preface to first edition

This text is written to introduce students to fundamental principles of land law. Over the years, land law has gained a reputation as a difficult subject. In part this is because much of it is statutory, in part because it contains a fair amount of detail and in part because students are usually unfamiliar with dealings with land. These factors can mask the reality that land law raises numerous interesting issues, most of which are socially and economically important.

The approach adopted in the text is first to explain the general role and rules of each topic and then to consider a few specific issues in more detail. These last issues have been chosen as those which are most controversial and which frequently appear in examination questions. Leaving aside the five introductory sections (in Part 1), each section is divided into three. First, there is a quite short introduction, considering the nature and importance of the topic. Next, a section 'Main issues and rules' summarises the essential rules and principles. It is usually impossible to contribute to the most interesting questions before understanding these rules and principles. Finally, the 'Critical and controversial issues' section goes into rather more detail on selected issues. The object here is to demonstrate how land law topics raise interesting, important and challenging questions. They are approached at a level of depth similar to that of land law texts, though without heavy citation of supporting authorities. Throughout the text, footnote references have been kept to a minimum. The guiding principle has been to cite those cases and statutory provisions which students are most likely to be expected to be familiar with. Of course, not every institution places emphasis on the same issues and authorities.

No prior knowledge of land law is expected of readers, though a general understanding of the law of contract and the use of cases is assumed. The book is designed for students who are about to embark on the study of land law or who wish to read a short description of an individual topic before embarking on a chapter in a mainstream text. I am grateful for the guidance provided by those who have read draft sections. In particular, I should thank Zoë Botterill and Cheryl Cheasley at Pearson Education, who have between them read the entire text. They have enabled me to avoid many infelicities, though remaining defects are entirely my responsibility.

Roger J. Smith

Note: Where a word is emboldened in the main text, this indicates that it is a first/significant occurrence of a **Glossary term** (please refer to the Glossary).

Guided tour

Under section 146, the landlord must serve notice of the breach on the tenant. If the breach is remedied, then this bars forfeiture. If the breach has not been remedied within a reasonable time, the court has a discretion to give relief. If the court allows forfeiture, then this is conclusive. Unlike non-payment of rent, there is no scope for relief thereafter.

Before going into detail as to the operation of section 146, an initial and rather difficult question is how far it applies if there is forfeiture out of court. This is usually described as peaceable re-entry. It is quite clear that notice must be served before any sort of re-entry (peaceable or by court order) and that remedying the breach precludes re-entry. More difficult is whether the court possesses a statutory discretion to order relief after peaceable re-entry. The problem is that section 146(2) (15.4.11) confers discretion: 'Where the landlord is proceeding . . . [to enforce forfeiture]'; the use of the present tense ('is proceeding') might seem to rule out cases where forfeiture has been completed. However, the House of Lords in *Billson v Residential Apartments Ltd*[17] (15.4.1) thought it unacceptable that a landlord could be better off by employing peaceable re-entry. Such a limit on the statutory discretion would encourage direct action by landlords, which might have public order consequences. Accordingly, the section was given a bold construction so as to apply to peaceable re-entry.

The notice

The notice must specify the breach, require it to be remedied and require compensation to be paid (if the landlord wants compensation). Specifying the breach is crucial, as it is this that has to be remedied.

It is necessary to require the breach to be remedied only if remedy is possible. It is widely recognised that some types of breach are irremediable, but deciding which breaches are irremediable has caused considerable difficulty. The leading authority of *Rugby School (Governors) v Tannahill*[18] (15.4.12) involved premises used as a brothel,

The text is fully **cross-referenced** to Roger Smith's *Property Law: Cases and Materials* book, directing you to original source extracts and further commentary for a fuller understanding. Use these two books together for the perfect combination to deepen your knowledge.

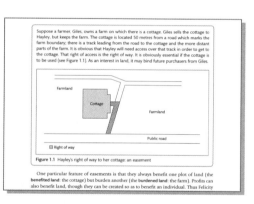

Suppose a farmer, Giles, owns a farm on which there is a cottage. Giles sells the cottage to Hayley, but keeps the farm. The cottage is located 50 metres from a road which marks the farm boundary; there is a track leading from the road to the cottage and the more distant parts of the farm. It is obvious that Hayley will need access over that track in order to get to the cottage. That right of access is the right of way. It is obviously essential if the cottage is to be used (see Figure 1.1). As an interest in land, it may bind future purchasers from Giles.

Figure **1.1** Hayley's right of way to her cottage: an easement

One particular feature of easements is that they always benefit one plot of land (the **benefited land**: the cottage) but burden another (the **burdened land**: the farm). Profits can also benefit land, though they can be created so as to benefit an individual. Thus Felicity

Figures and diagrams are used to strengthen your understanding of legal processes in land law.

---

law case), Mummery LJ thought that it might never be resolved. Most cases can be decided by applying more specific arguments, especially section 3 on interpreting legislation. This is particularly relevant in land law, as so many of the principles are enshrined in legislation.

CRITICAL ISSUE

Human rights in the enforcement of property rights

The past decade has seen a highly controversial series of cases on the inter-relationship between property rights and human rights. The problems have turned on the application of Article 8: respect for homes. If an owner of land (in most cases, a landlord) seeks to enforce their property rights to evict a trespasser or tenant, can the defendant occupier rely on the argument that the land constitutes their home and that any loss of the home has to be justified in terms of proportionality? Although eviction is nearly always undertaken following a court order, the possession actions are usually very brief. If the court were to look in detail at questions of proportionality in every case, this would cause significant added costs and delays within the judicial system.

Most of the problems have arisen when local authorities are exercising their powers as landlords. Local authorities are, of course, clearly public authorities and so Article 8 clearly applies to them. A series of House of Lords decisions[7] held that Article 8 does not qualify an owner's right to obtain possession. However, decisions of the European Court of Human Rights[8] took the opposite view, insisting that the occupier should have the

[6] [2004] ICR 1634 at [44]–[46].
[7] *Harrow LBC v Qazi* [2004] 1 AC 983; *Kay v Lambeth LBC* [2006] 2 AC 465; *Doherty v Birmingham City Council* [2009] 1 AC 367.
[8] See especially *McCann v UK* [2008] 2 FLR 899 and *Kay v UK* [2011] HLR 13. Cases arising from other jurisdictions took the same approach.

Critical Issues are highlighted throughout the text, introducing you to topical issues and debates and outlining the important key arguments you should consider during your studies.

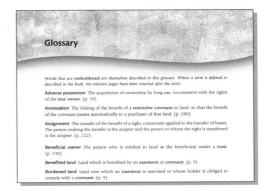

Alan has both an expensive house, Giant Gables, and a smaller adjoining one, Cosy Cottage. He is selling Cosy Cottage and is concerned about how its use and appearance might affect Giant Gables. Accordingly, Alan requires the purchaser, Brian, to promise (i) not to use Cosy Cottage for any purpose other than a family home and (ii) to paint it every five years. Nine years later, Brian sells Cosy Cottage to Caroline.

When we consider possible issues as between Alan and Brian, these can be dealt with under normal contract principles: there is little or no need for any special land law. However, it is the effect of these arrangements on Caroline which is more interesting. Contract will not suffice: the burden of contracts affects nobody save the parties. This is unaffected by the Contracts (Rights of Third Parties) Act 1999 (20.15), as that relates only to the benefit of contracts. For Caroline to be bound by the burden of the covenant, Alan will need to be able to assert an interest in land.

The promise to use Cosy Cottage only as a family home is what lawyers describe as a **restrictive covenant**. It has been recognised as an interest in land since 1848 and so can bind Caroline. She will, for example, be unable to use Cosy Cottage as a shop. The promise to paint is a **positive covenant**: the difference between restrictive and positive covenants is based on whether expenditure (or work) is required. Positive covenants have never been recognised as interests in land. It follows that Caroline is bound by the family home promise, but has no obligation to paint.

This distinction between restrictive and positive covenants is further considered in Chapter 17. As we will see, it is by no means obvious that the distinction between restrictive and positive covenants can be justified today. This is one example of a controversial issue arising in land law.

Examples help you to understand the law by showing you how it works in everyday life.

A **glossary** located at the back of the book can be used throughout your reading to clarify unfamiliar terms.

Glossary

Words that are emboldened are themselves described in this glossary. Where a term is defined or described in the book, the relevant pages have been inserted after the entry.

Adverse possession The acquisition of ownership by long use, inconsistent with the rights of the **true owner**. (p. 39)

Annexation The linking of the benefit of a **restrictive covenant** to land, so that the benefit of the covenant passes automatically to a purchaser of that land. (p. 280)

Assignment The transfer of the benefit of a right, commonly applied to the transfer of leases. The person making the transfer is the *assignor* and the person to whom the right is transferred is the *assignee*. (p. 222)

Beneficial owner The person who is entitled to land as the beneficiary under a **trust**. (p. 130)

Benefited land Land which is benefited by an **easement** or **covenant**. (p. 9)

Burdened land Land over which an **easement** is exercised or whose holder is obliged to comply with a **covenant**. (p. 9)

Visit **www.mylawchamber.co.uk** to access a wealth of tools to help you develop and test your knowledge of Land Law, strengthening your understanding so you can excel.

 mylawchamber

 The Pearson eText is a fully searchable, interactive version of *Introduction to Land Law*. You can make notes in it, highlight it, bookmark it, even link to online sources – helping you get more out of studying and revision. The Pearson eText is linked to the learning tools you'll find in MyLawChamber.

- Interactive multiple choice questions to test your understanding of each topic
- Practice exam questions with guidance to hone your exam technique
- Weblinks to help you read more widely around the subject and really impress your lecturers
- Glossary flashcards to test yourself on legal terms and definitions
- Legal newsfeed to help you read more widely, stay right up to date with the law and impress examiners
- Legal updates to help you stay up to date with the law and impress examiners

 Case Navigator provides in-depth analysis of the leading cases in land law, improving your case-reading skills and understanding of how the law is applied.

 Explore the world of **Virtual Lawyer** and develop your skills in answering legal problem questions as you apply your knowledge of the law to a range of interactive scenarios.

Use the access card at the back of the book to activate mylawchamber. Online purchase is also available at **www.mylawchamber.co.uk/register**.

Acknowledgement

We are grateful to all the lecturers who reviewed this text and contributed to its development, including:

Dr Janine Griffiths-Baker, University of Bristol

Dr Antonia Layard, Cardiff University

Shan Cole, University of Glamorgan

Ben Mayfield, Lancaster University

Table of cases

Table of legislation

Part 1

Introduction to land law

1   Introducing land law

The first five chapters – all quite short – are designed to introduce the reader to some basic land law principles. Land law contains many new ideas and technical terms and the first objective is to survey the scene. This survey is likely to provoke numerous questions about how these ideas work out: these will be considered in subsequent chapters.

What is land law?

Most transactions relating to land are based on contract. A simple example would be a contract to clean the windows of a house. There is no need for a special body of law to deal with disputes regarding window cleaning: the law of contract provides the answers. What is special about land law is that it allows somebody to be affected by an obligation when contract cannot apply.

> I agree that Malcolm can possess my house for a year at a rent of £1,000 a month (a **lease** or tenancy). A week later, I sell and transfer the house to Nicola. As between Malcolm and Nicola, there is no contract. However, because a lease is an interest in land it will bind Nicola, who will have to allow Malcolm to possess it for the full year.

Land law is concerned with those rights and interests relating to land which can affect purchasers: these are what we call interests in land, or **proprietary interests**. The many controversial policy issues concerning the extent and effect of interests in land will form the basis of much of this text.

The way in which the law draws lines as to what is an interest in land is illustrated by the following example, taken from the law relating to **covenants** (promises in formal witnessed documents called **deeds**).

Alan has both an expensive house, Giant Gables, and a smaller adjoining one, Cosy Cottage. He is selling Cosy Cottage and is concerned about how its use and appearance might affect Giant Gables. Accordingly, Alan requires the purchaser, Brian, to promise (i) not to use Cosy Cottage for any purpose other than a family home and (ii) to paint it every five years. Nine years later, Brian sells Cosy Cottage to Caroline.

When we consider possible issues as between Alan and Brian, these can be dealt with under normal contract principles: there is little or no need for any special land law. However, it is the effect of these arrangements on Caroline which is more interesting. Contract will not suffice: the burden of contracts affects nobody save the parties. This is unaffected by the Contracts (Rights of Third Parties) Act 1999 (Extract 20.1.5), as that relates only to the benefit of contracts. For Caroline to be bound by the burden of the covenant, Alan will need to be able to assert an interest in land.

The promise to use Cosy Cottage only as a family home is what lawyers describe as a **restrictive covenant**. It has been recognised as an interest in land since 1848 and so can bind Caroline. She will, for example, be unable to use Cosy Cottage as a shop. The promise to paint is a **positive covenant**: the difference between restrictive and positive covenants is based on whether expenditure (or work) is required. Positive covenants have never been recognised as interests in land. It follows that Caroline is bound by the family home promise, but has no obligation to paint.

This distinction between restrictive and positive covenants is further considered in Chapter 17. As we will see, it is by no means obvious that the distinction between restrictive and positive covenants can be justified today. This is one example of a controversial issue arising in land law.

What issues arise in land law?

Our principal concern is with interests in land – interests capable of binding purchasers. What exactly are these interests? They are summarised in the following section, in order to aid familiarity with the terminology of land law. The various interests provide the basis of the chapters in Parts 3 and 4. The list of interests in land has been fine-tuned over many centuries and most of the categories are well settled, though their detailed rules still give rise to litigation. However, some categories continue to provoke controversy as to whether they are (or should be) interests in land. This is especially true of **licences**, permission to do something on land (Chapter 15), and positive covenants (Chapter 17). These still developing areas mark the outer boundaries of land law.

Some interests have attracted specific and extensive rules as to how they operate; these will be considered in the relevant chapters. A good example is provided by tenancies (often called leases). Suppose Harriet has a tenancy of a house from Ian for a year. Can she complain if the cooker stops working or there is a problem with the drains? Chapter 14 is devoted to the way in which the landlord and tenant relationship operates. We shall see that she can complain about the drains, but not normally the cooker.

A particular feature of interests in land is that there is a large body of law on how they are created. This is dealt with in Part 2. They normally require writing and the more important interests have to be created by a formal witnessed document, called a deed. One example is that the transfer of land requires a deed. These requirements are generally described as **formality** rules. As interests in land are increasingly being entered on computerised registers, these formality rules are likely to give way to requirements of **electronic registration**. We shall ask the important question why land transactions require special formalities.

Formality rules have the potential to give rise to unfairness.

> Suppose Rachel orally agrees to sell a vacant house to Sally and agrees that Sally can immediately start work on renovating the house. After Sally has done a lot of work on the basis of Rachel's assurance that the house will be hers, Rachel denies any obligation to sell, arguing that contracts to sell land have to be in writing. This would enable Rachel to take the benefit of Sally's renovation. Although Rachel is correct that such contracts require writing, it would be quite unfair for her to rely on the absence of formality when she has encouraged Sally's expenditure. The courts will find a way of avoiding formality requirements and therefore rule in Sally's favour.

Property rights sometimes arise without any form of agreement. Two situations will be studied. The first is where one person has **adverse possession** of land: this means possessing it without the owner's permission. The rules changed in 2002 legislation, but prior to 2002 the adverse possessor became owner after 12 years. The second situation relates to **fixtures**: objects fixed to land which become part of it. An example is where Richard builds a house including a few of Simon's bricks: the bricks are now part of Richard's house and are no longer owned by Simon.

We have seen that the nature of an interest in land is that it binds later purchasers of the land. However, that does not mean that interests in land always bind purchasers. This competition between earlier and later interests raises **priorities** questions (Chapter 10). In the modern law, most land is registered (the owner is described as **proprietor**). Whether an interest affects purchasers usually depends on whether it has been entered on the register. Let us return to the example where Brian promised Alan not to use his house other than as a family home: a restrictive covenant. It was noted that this is an interest capable of binding the purchaser, Caroline. To be more precise, we should say that Caroline will be bound only if the restrictive covenant has been entered on the register. The fact that it is an interest in land does Alan no good if he doesn't protect it. There is a constant tension between the needs of interest holders and the needs of purchasers. This is why priority disputes give rise to controversy. One example is where Alan has failed to protect his interest, but Caroline is well aware of it anyway. Should Caroline still be able to claim priority as a result of Alan's failure to protect? As we shall see, it seems that she still wins.

Interests in land

In this section, mention will be made of the most important interests in land. Nearly all of them feature in later sections of the text; the present purpose is to explain some of the technical terms encountered in land law.

We will divide interests into two categories. The first (we will call it 'splitting ownership') covers what may be described as ownership or enjoyment rights. These involve full enjoyment of the land: living in a house, using an office or leasing out land and receiving rent from a tenant. The second category involves more limited and specific rights. They do not involve full enjoyment, but confer rights which may be exercised against the owner. A good example is provided by Alan's restrictive covenant, discussed above. Alan has an interest against the owner (Brian), but it would be strange to describe them as sharing ownership.

Splitting ownership

There are two ways in which ownership may be split. Most simply, ownership may be shared by two people at the same time. Felicity and George may buy a house as their home and become joint owners of it. We say that they have **concurrent interests**.

Alternatively, two or more people can enjoy land successively: **successive interests**.

> Larry could say in his will that land is to go 'to my widow Martha for life and thereafter to my son Norman'. This means that the land can be enjoyed by Martha for her life, but thereafter will be Norman's. If it is a house, it means that Martha can live in it for her lifetime. Alternatively, if the land has been rented out by Larry, Martha will receive the rents. In neither case will Norman be able to claim anything while Martha is alive, but after she dies he will be the sole owner. We say that Martha's right is **in possession** (signifying present enjoyment) and Norman's is **in remainder** (signifying future enjoyment).

A rather odd feature of English land law is that it does not recognise ownership as an interest. Instead, it recognises **estates**. The nature of the estate is that it establishes the time for which the interest is enjoyed. Two forms of estate recognised in the modern law are the **life estate** and the **fee simple**. We say that Martha has a life estate: this is quite natural terminology as she has the benefit of the land for her life. Norman has a fee simple, which has no time limit. The fee simple is much closer to what we might view as ownership.

The simplicity of having two estates (whether in possession or remainder) is impaired by the fact that conditions can be applied to them. Two examples may be given.

> The first example is a condition precedent. Thus I could say 'to my son Richard if he obtains an Upper Second class degree by the age of 25'. This gives Richard what we describe as *contingent* fee simple: he gets it only if he obtains the degree. It becomes obvious that it is

difficult to talk about anybody as 'the owner' in this example. It might be reasonable to refer to Norman as having deferred ownership in the previous example, but the contingent nature of Richard's interest makes it difficult to describe him as owner.

The second example is a condition subsequent. Thus I could say 'to Salman on condition that he never takes up smoking'. This means that Salman has an interest in possession, but will lose it should he ever start to smoke. When an interest is limited in this way, it is called a *qualified* interest.

In most situations there is no such qualification; the interest is then described as *absolute*. Qualified interests attract a morass of complex and largely outdated rules. There are two forms: *conditional* interests and *determinable* interests (these are briefly described in Chapter 11).

Let us return to the proposition that English land law does not recognise ownership. The reader might respond that millions of people buy homes expecting to own them: how can this be reconciled with the ideas just outlined? The point is a good one. However, the answer is that a fee simple may, in practical terms, be the same as ownership. We have already seen that the fee simple is fairly close to ownership as it may last indefinitely. If it is both in possession (not in remainder or contingent) and absolute (not qualified), then it is as close to ownership as makes no difference. Technically, a person buying a house is purchasing a **fee simple absolute in possession**. As we see in Chapter 3, the fee simple absolute in possession has played a central role in land law since reforming legislation in 1925.

These estates are ones recognised in medieval times: they are called **freehold estates**. A different sort of estate (still splitting the use of land by time) is the lease or tenancy. Rachel might lease her house to Sarah for one year at a monthly rent of £800. Sarah (described as tenant or lessee) then has a lease from Rachel (the landlord or lessor). She has a *leasehold estate*. Leases can be created for as long or short a period as the parties want.

It might be asked why, after several centuries, we continue to have these categories of leasehold and freehold estates. Leasehold estates exist where there is a specified maximum length of time (such as five years), whereas freehold estates exist where the length is indeterminate (fee simple) or the termination date is unknown (life estate). That definition offers no clue as to why they are different categories. More important is the fact that rent is nearly always payable if there is a lease, whereas the holder of a life estate almost never pays for it. The reason is that life interests are normally created by the owner (slipping into colloquial language) for the benefit of family members: illustrated by the example involving Martha and Norman. By contrast, leases are usually commercial transactions with no element of gift.

The payment of rent means that the landlord, Rachel in our example, continues to benefit from the land even though it is Sarah who is occupying it. We still say that Rachel has a fee simple absolute in possession. It is in possession because she is able to claim the rent: there is no need for her to have an immediate right to physical possession. Perhaps more important is the position of a purchaser. Although many purchasers want to occupy land and would not be interested in purchasing Rachel's interest, there are good numbers of purchasers who view land as a source of income rather than occupation. Such purchasers will be very happy to purchase from Rachel, knowing that they will be receiving rent from Sarah.

In contrast, almost no purchaser wants to buy land subject to a life interest; there is no rent and the date of termination of the life interest is unknown. Because it is undesirable to render land incapable of sale, the law sets out to ensure that it is always possible to purchase the fee simple absolute in possession. Upon sale, the holders of other freehold estates (including life interests) cease to have an interest in the land. These ideas are outlined in Chapter 3 and further explored in Chapter 14.

Other interests in land

There is quite a long list of interests in land, but we will concentrate on those which are most commonly encountered.

Mortgages

Suppose Gillian and Harry are buying their first house. It is almost inevitable that they will need a loan from a bank or building society to cover most of the cost. A simple loan of a large amount to two young people with no assets would be very risky for the lender – there is a good chance the sum would not be repaid. However, a mortgage over the house makes the transaction viable. It means that if Gillian and Harry are unable to pay then (as a last resort) the house can be sold to pay off the loan. This makes lenders more willing to lend money.

The mortgage is the principal example of a security interest. Unlike other interests, security interests don't involve use of the land or impose obligations as to land use. They simply operate in the background to ensure that loans are repaid. Their status as interests in land means that any purchaser from Gillian and Harry is bound by their mortgage: the lender can still have the property sold. In practice, sale receipts are used to pay off mortgage loans – it is exceptional for a mortgage to be enforced against a purchaser.

Easements and profits

These two interests are closely related, with very similar rules applying to them. They enable the benefits of land to be split, though in a form very different to concurrent and successive interests.

Let us take the **profit** of fishing as an example. Suppose Ed sells Felicity fishing rights over a river on his land. Ed's land may provide him with a number of practical benefits: living in a house, farming a field and fishing from the river. Just one of these benefits, the right to fish, has been sold to Felicity. However, Felicity isn't the owner of the river: Ed can still use it for swimming or boating.

Easements similarly involve a right to use land, though (unlike profits) not to take things from it. The best-known example is a right of way.

Suppose a farmer, Giles, owns a farm on which there is a cottage. Giles sells the cottage to Hayley, but keeps the farm. The cottage is located 50 metres from a road which marks the farm boundary; there is a track leading from the road to the cottage and the more distant parts of the farm. It is obvious that Hayley will need access over that track in order to get to the cottage. That right of access is the right of way. It is obviously essential if the cottage is to be used (see Figure 1.1). As an interest in land, it may bind future purchasers from Giles.

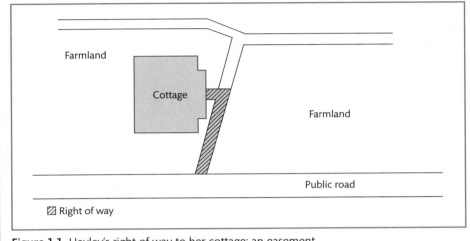

Figure 1.1 Hayley's right of way to her cottage: an easement

One particular feature of easements is that they always benefit one plot of land (the **benefited land**: the cottage) but burden another (the **burdened land**: the farm). Profits can also benefit land, though they can be created so as to benefit an individual. Thus Felicity could enjoy the right to fish either as an individual or as owner of neighbouring land. If she enjoys it as a neighbour, the benefit will pass automatically to anybody she sells her land to.

Restrictive covenants

We encountered restrictive covenants earlier, in the example where Brian promised Alan to use his house only as a family home. Restrictive covenants are rather like easements, in that they involve two plots of land. However, most easements involve a right to do something on a neighbour's land, as with a right of way. In contrast, a restrictive covenant is a right to stop a neighbour from doing something.

Restrictive covenants are commonly insisted upon by a person who is selling part of a large plot.

Let us return to the example of Giles selling a cottage and retaining the farm. Giles may be concerned that the purchaser (Hayley) will rebuild the cottage as an office block, rendering the farm less attractive (and less valuable). He might then insist that Hayley promises not to develop the cottage. The price which Hayley is prepared to pay for the cottage will be affected by any significant obligations which Giles insists upon.

It has been noted earlier that positive obligations are not recognised as interests in land. They may be fully effective contracts between the parties to the obligation, but will not bind any later purchaser of the land involved.

Estate contracts

> Ursula contracts to sell her house to Vera. A day later, Ursula receives a higher offer from Will. She decides to forget about Vera and proceeds to transfer the land to Will. Normally, contracts affect only the contracting parties (Ursula and Vera). However, a contract for an interest in land has long been treated as creating an immediate property interest: it is called an **estate contract**. Provided that Vera has registered her estate contract and is able and willing to pay the agreed purchase price, she can claim the house from Will.

The estate contract enhances the position of buyers such as Vera, who can sell their existing homes without fear of their intended new home ending up with a rival purchaser. More generally, it helps ensure an orderly system of land purchase, limiting the temptation to accept higher offers.

Estate contracts cover more than contracts to buy the land: they include contracts for leases or mortgages. Another form of estate contract is an **option**.

> Jake pays Ivy £35,000 for an option to buy Ivy's house for £200,000 within the next six months. This means that Jake has a choice whether or not to buy the house. If it is worth more than £200,000, then it makes sense for him to buy. Should the value fall to, say, £175,000 then it would not make financial sense for Jake to buy – though he would lose the £35,000 he has paid. It should be stressed that Ivy has no right to force Jake to buy: this is what distinguishes an option from a normal sale agreement. Because an option is an interest in land, it can bind any purchaser from Ivy.

Why have a list of interests in land?

The law contains a list of recognised interests (the more important ones being listed above): landowners are not allowed to create new ones outside those categories. One reason for this is that too much flexibility would make the purchase of land more complex, as purchasers would have no clear idea of what rights they should be looking out for. If extensive obligations were to be imposed on purchasers, that might also mean that owning the land could become less attractive. In turn, that might impede the most useful and economically beneficial use of land.

Why have the individual interests listed above been recognised? The courts have made what are essentially pragmatic decisions based on the utility of the right, whether its operation is reasonably certain and whether transactions with land would be impeded if purchasers were to be bound.

This does not mean that the list is fixed for all time. Individual interests (such as easements) are developed over time. One modern example of an easement is a right to park a car. This is a development of easements rather than a completely new interest. It may be possible for the law to develop completely new interests, though this is much more controversial. As mentioned earlier, there has been debate in the past 50 years whether to recognise positive covenants and licences (permission to enter and remain on land).

Questions to consider

1. Is it accurate to say that land law is simply all the law that relates to land?

2. What are the main issues that arise in land law?

3. Are there good reasons for the law to recognise a wide range of interests in land?

4. Can the owner of land create whatever interests in land he or she wishes? If not, why not?

Further reading

Honoré, A M (1961) 'Ownership' in *Oxford Essays in Jurisprudence*, First Series, ed. A G Guest, Chapter 5.

Visit **www.mylawchamber.co.uk** to access tools to help you develop and test your knowledge of land law, including interactive multiple choice questions, practice exam questions with guidance, weblinks, glossary flashcards, legal newsfeed and legal updates.

2 Trusts and equitable interests

Much of modern English land law derives from a strange duality in the legal system. Today we think of a single court system applying legal rules. Until the 1870s, it was quite different: different courts operated different principles and sometimes reached different results. The original courts were generally described as common law courts. The Lord Chancellor exercised a separate jurisdiction. This was intended to avoid some of the technicalities and inflexibility found in the common law courts. The guiding principle for the Lord Chancellor was to follow the dictates of conscience: in short, to produce a fair result. In the course of time, this was recognised as a court: the Court of Chancery. It sounds like a recipe for anarchy, but in fact the results fitted together well. The body of rules established by the Court of Chancery is generally described as **equity**.

Although the separate courts have disappeared, equity survives. For example, legislation and books refer to equitable interests in land (those earlier recognised by the Court of Chancery) and legal interests in land (those recognised by the common law courts). It sounds terribly confused, but it will be seen in both this and the following chapter that the distinction between legal and equitable rights performs a useful function in the modern law.

In this chapter we consider the most important examples of equitable interests.

The trust

Suppose that Martin owns land (rented out to tenants). Martin is going abroad for a few years and wants his young daughter, Natasha, to receive the rents. He transfers the land to a friend, Oliver, on the express basis that Oliver is to hold the property for Natasha's benefit. The common law courts would say that Oliver was the owner. No direct relationship existed between Oliver and Natasha and accordingly she had no remedy if Oliver kept the rents for himself. The Lord Chancellor, observing that this was quite unfair, told Oliver that he might indeed own the land, but he was under a duty to apply the rents for Natasha's benefit.

This example illustrates the **trust**: the most significant development arising from the Court of Chancery. We say that Oliver is a trustee and Natasha is a beneficiary under the trust. It is significant to note that equity does not deny Oliver's ownership; rather, it qualifies what

Oliver can do with the benefits from the land. This means that Oliver can deal with the land. For example, he can enter into fresh leases if the original tenants leave. In functional terms, we can say that Oliver, as trustee, is managing the land for the benefit of Natasha. The trustee status of Oliver differs from that of a normal manager or agent in that he owns the land: he does not have to refer back to the absent Martin when difficult decisions have to be made.

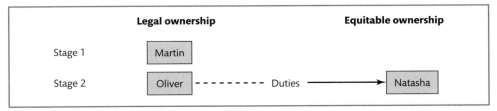

Figure 2.1 Operation of the trust

Figure 2.1 shows how the trust operates in the example above. One point to note is that Martin's ownership is complete without any element of trust. Where there is no trust, the legal owner enjoys the full benefits from the land. It is only where there is a trust that the legal owner (then a trustee) is manager without a right to keep the benefits from the land for himself.

A later (but still many centuries old) development was to say that Natasha's rights would affect purchasers from Oliver. However, not every purchaser would be bound: the Chancery courts required the conscience of the purchaser to be affected. This would apply if the purchaser was aware of the trusts or should have been aware of them. Such a purchaser was described as having notice of the trusts. Once purchasers could be bound, lawyers began to regard beneficiaries such as Natasha as having a form of equitable ownership. The common law courts might say that Oliver is owner, but the Court of Chancery regarded Natasha as the owner. It has been accepted for over 400 years that in any conflict the Court of Chancery has precedence: this means that Oliver cannot insist on his common law rights against Natasha.

The resulting position has been found very useful. It enables land to be efficiently managed by the trustee for the beneficiary, while recognising that the real economic value of the land is vested in the beneficiary. Recognising the beneficiary as having an equitable interest in land makes the trust a safe vehicle for settlors such as Martin to use: there is less risk of Oliver destroying Natasha's rights. Contrast the dangers if Natasha had a remedy only against Oliver. Oliver might simply transfer the land as a gift to his son Peter. Oliver might open himself up to personal liability in damages, but that is of little comfort to Natasha if Oliver is bankrupt and cannot pay. With an interest in land, Natasha can readily bring a claim against the current landowner, Peter. It might be added that all forms of property can be held under trusts, so Martin could just as easily transfer shares to Oliver on trust.

Other equitable interests; remedies

The trust is not the only development arising from the Court of Chancery. The Lord Chancellor developed other principles which were based on what good conscience required: the fairness of the situation mattered more than legal form. Unsurprisingly, this meant that equitable principles were far more flexible than common law principles. One consequence of this was that it was easier for the Court of Chancery to develop new interests in land. The restrictive covenant mentioned earlier provides an example (see Chapter 1).

Another very important right developed by the Lord Chancellor was the **mortgage**. Originally, the lender obtained the legal fee simple absolute in possession as security for repayment of the loan (though the borrower would still occupy the land). The Lord Chancellor ensured that, whatever the document said, the borrower could get the land back if the debt was repaid: this is the equitable right to redeem, giving the borrower the *equity of redemption*. The structure of modern mortgages is different, but there is still an equitable right to end a mortgage by paying off the loan.

In addition, the Court of Chancery would give different remedies. The standard common law remedy is money damages, whereas Chancery might order that an agreement be carried out (**specific performance**) or that some wrong should not be done (injunction). This is important as regards contracts to sell land (estate contracts). The fact that the seller could be ordered to transfer the land to the purchaser meant that Chancery viewed the purchaser as being the person really entitled to the land, even before a specific performance order. This is backed up by the saying that equity treats as done that which ought to be done. It was on this basis that estate contracts were accepted as equitable interests in land.

Another point relating to remedies is that a transaction can sometimes be attacked by an equitable remedy.

Suppose that Terry agrees to sell two of three fields to Vera. Their lawyers draw up the sale documents, but mistakenly they include all three fields in the transfer. Neither Terry nor Vera spots this. These facts give rise to the contractual remedy of **rectification** for mistake: the court will order that the transfer be amended to exclude the third field. The point of interest to us is that Terry will have an equitable right to the field even before the court order.

This type of right is often described as an *equity* rather than an equitable interest, though it can bind purchasers.[1]

Equitable interests in the modern law

The common law courts and the Court of Chancery were fused into a single court (the High Court) by the Judicature Acts 1873–1875. This has not affected the principles discussed above. The courts still say that Oliver is the legal owner holding on trust for Natasha. It is difficult to believe that the trust would have arisen without the twin common law and equitable jurisdictions, but it survives without them.

Whether the difference between legal and equitable rights is justified outside the context of trusts is more questionable. Indeed, the past century has seen some convergence of

---

[1] Equities are briefly considered below (p. 117).

legal and equitable rules. One example is that equitable rights and remedies are generally said to be discretionary: they are available only if the claimant is acting fairly. By contrast, there is no such limit on the exercise of legal rights. There may still be some truth in this, but the cases reveal that the differences are diminishing. In particular, a person acting unfairly is likely to find that they cannot always enforce even legal rights.

We have seen that the major difference between legal and equitable interests is that equitable interests affect purchasers only if they have notice. In the modern law, nearly all interests require entry on a register before they can affect purchasers. This applies to both legal and equitable interests. This forces us to ask whether it remains relevant to describe the restrictive covenant (to take one example) as an equitable right. Just like a legal right, it will bind a purchaser if, but only if, it is protected on the register. Yet the registration rules themselves distinguish between legal and equitable rights. In particular, they are entered on the register in different ways; the different forms of entry have differing effects. It is less clear that these differences should survive in the future.

It may be concluded that the trust, which is deeply imbedded in modern land law, requires a continuing distinction between legal and equitable rights. Outside that context, the future role of a special category of equitable rights is becoming controversial.

Questions to consider

1. What was the Court of Chancery? Does it matter that it no longer exists?

2. What is a trust?

3. Apart from the trust, what does it mean to say that an interest is equitable?

Further reading

Baker (1977) 93 LQR 529: The future of equity.

Everton (1976) 40 Conv (NS) 209: 'Equitable interests' and 'equities' – in search of a pattern.

Millett, P J (1998) 114 LQR 214: Equity's place in the law of commerce.

Visit **www.mylawchamber.co.uk** to access tools to help you develop and test your knowledge of land law, including interactive multiple choice questions, practice exam questions with guidance, weblinks, glossary flashcards, legal newsfeed and legal updates.

 mylawchamber

3 Legislative reform: 1925 to 2002

A particular feature of land law is that so much of it has been affected by legislation, more than in subjects such as contract or torts. One reason for this is that many land law principles date back to the Middle Ages and had accumulated complex and antiquated rules. By the end of the nineteenth century, the need for reform was acute.

Apart from clearing up the clutter from the past, a major objective has been to make it easy to purchase (or take a lease or mortgage) land. Having a wide range of interests in land may be fine for the holders of the interests, but can cause problems for purchasers. These problems are twofold. The first is that the process of buying land may be lengthy and complex, as the purchaser may have to deal with a multitude of people and undertake elaborate checks (especially reading long and complex documents) before it is safe to proceed. The second category of problem is that the purchaser cannot be confident about acquiring the land free of undiscovered interests, despite taking time and trouble over the purchase.

Apart from land purchase being slow and expensive, purchase might be impossible if agreement could not be reached with all those with successive or concurrent interests in the land. A simple example is where land is given to Andrew for life and thereafter to Betty. If Betty were an infant, it might well be impossible to buy the land. The result could be inefficient land use: a cost to the country, as well as the individuals involved.

English property law was significantly restructured by a series of statutes in 1925. Though a fair proportion of the 1925 legislation has been amended and re-enacted in recent years, much has survived to the present day, as have nearly all the basic ideas. It might be added that the 1925 reforms themselves had roots in the previous half-century: not all of the legislation was new in 1925.

Part of the purpose of the 1925 legislation was to get rid of unnecessary complexities and rules that land law had accumulated over the centuries. This backwards-looking material need not detain us. The range of interests in land is barely affected by the legislation. The central changes are to the form in which interests exist and how they will affect purchasers.

A strategy for estates

We start with the question: what interests do purchasers want to buy? In order to facilitate land transactions and, thereby, efficient land use, we need to ensure that purchasers can readily purchase those interests. We start with freehold estates (life interests and the fee simple) and then move on to leasehold estates (tenancies).

Freehold estates

Nearly all purchasers want to buy 'the land'. We have seen that ownership of land is not, technically, recognised by English land law. The closest right is the fee simple absolute in possession. This is what purchasers want to buy. Virtually nobody wants to purchase life estates or remainders: their length is uncertain and they are simply not what purchasers are looking for. It follows that a central objective is to ensure that there is always somebody with the fee simple absolute in possession and that a purchaser can safely purchase from that person.

The 1925 legislation

That central objective explains section 1 of the Law of Property Act 1925, which states that the only legal freehold estate that can exist today is the fee simple absolute in possession. This means that there will always be somebody with a fee simple absolute in possession: it is this person that a purchaser of the freehold will deal with. Life interests and remainders can still exist, but only as equitable interests under a trust.

If the law were simply to limit the number of legal estates, purchasers would still have to discover equitable interests and negotiate with their holders. Suppose Richard and Sally hold on trust for Andrew for life and thereafter for Betty. Without further provisions, a purchaser would almost certainly have notice of Andrew and Betty's equitable interests and therefore be bound by them. Purchasers do not want to be bound by life interests or remainders and so they would have to ascertain that Andrew and Betty approved the sale. Purchase of land would be made no easier.

To avoid these problems, the legislation entitles the trustees (Richard and Sally) to sell the legal fee simple free of interests under trusts. These interests then take effect against the proceeds of sale held by the trustees, not against the purchaser. This means that a purchaser can deal with just Richard and Sally and can ignore the beneficial interests of Andrew and Betty (whether or not the purchaser knows about them). Richard and Sally might, for example, buy Marks & Spencer shares with the proceeds of sale: Andrew will now have a life interest in the shares and will be entitled to the dividend income from them.

This shifting of interests from the land to the proceeds of sale is called **overreaching**. So far we have been considering **successive interests**. However, it was thought that concurrent interests might also pose problems for purchasers (this is further discussed in Chapter 12). In order to avoid similar problems for purchasers, there is again a trust and the equitable concurrent interests can be overreached.

Figure 3.1 illustrates the split in legal and equitable rights for successive and concurrent ownership. The concurrent interests example shows Richard and Sally as trustees and Carla and Davina as beneficiaries. We shall see later (in Chapter 12) that it many cases

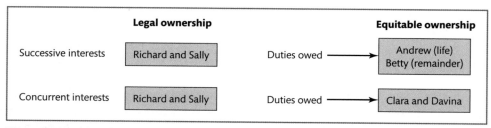

Figure 3.1 Legal and equitable rights for successive and concurrent ownership

Carla and Davina will be trustees as well as beneficiaries. Odd as it may seem, they then appear on both sides of the illustration: as trustees and as beneficiaries.

The Trusts of Land and Appointment of Trustees Act 1996 (TLATA)

Under the 1925 legislation, there is a trust whenever there are successive and concurrent interests. The object of TLATA is to regulate how that **trust of land** operates. For example, it tells us what powers the trustees have and whether the beneficiaries have rights to occupy the land. Very importantly, it gives the court discretion to settle any disputes regarding the land. Let us return to the example involving Richard and Sally as trustees and Andrew and Betty as beneficiaries. There may be disagreement as to whether the land should be sold. Whether there is disagreement between Richard and Sally or between them and the beneficiaries, the court can decide what should happen.

Though some of these issues had been dealt with by the 1925 legislation, TLATA introduces much more comprehensive rules. It provides the focus of Chapter 12.

Leasehold estates

Leasehold estates do not pose the same problems as freehold estates such as life interests and remainders. Experience shows that purchasers are happy to buy leases and to buy land that is subject to a lease.

Suppose that Fast Food Ltd wants to open an outlet in Bristol. It wants to have a lease because it doesn't have the resources to purchase a fee simple; anyway, it does not want a long-term commitment to any particular plot of land. It would be happy either to take a lease from a landlord for, say, five years or to purchase a lease from an existing tenant. Suppose Gourmet Meals Ltd has a lease of a restaurant from Megaproperty Ltd (the landlord) for ten years and wants to leave after five years. Fast Food will be perfectly happy to take over Gourmet Meals' lease, making a payment to Gourmet Foods if the rent is below current market levels. This is an example of a sale of a lease.

Many purchasers buy land as an investment, intending to receive rent from tenants rather than to occupy the land. This means that it is quite easy for Megaproperty to find a purchaser for the freehold of the restaurant, despite the lease of Gourmet Meals (or Fast Food).

There are two reasons why buying land subject to a lease is very common, whereas buying land subject to a life interest is rare. The first is that life tenants do not pay rent: invariably, life interests are created by individuals making gifts of their property to other family members. In contrast, a purchaser from Megaproperty will receive rent. The second reason is that a purchaser knows how long the lease will last. Even if the rent is below current rental levels, the purchaser can calculate the cost of this over the duration of the lease and negotiate for a lower purchase price to take account of it. With a life interest, nobody knows how long the life interest holder will live: any purchaser would be taking a gamble.

This shows that land can readily be sold despite the fact that the purchaser is bound by a lease. The 1925 legislation recognises this by allowing a leasehold estate to be legal – technically labelling it as a 'term of years absolute'. We therefore have two types of ownership right that are commonly bought and sold: the fee simple absolute in possession (whether or not subject to a lease) and the lease.

Registration of title

In the modern law, the great majority (nearly 95 per cent) of houses and other plots of land are registered. This means that there is a register that identifies the relevant plot of land and who owns it. The system may come close to covering all land within the next decade. Registration makes it much easier to buy and sell land. For **unregistered land** (the 5 per cent not yet registered), purchasers have to read through documents transferring the land from one person to another – these are the **title deeds**. This can be a lengthy process and doesn't guarantee that the seller owns the land. By contrast, the registration system identifies who has the fee simple absolute in possession and, most importantly, guarantees that information. This makes the purchase of land simpler and safer; there are no longer any title deeds. It is also possible to register leases, which assists the purchase of leases. The system dates back to the nineteenth century, but is today governed by the Land Registration Act 2002.

Land registration is studied in later chapters, but one point to note is that the 2002 legislation makes provision for a fully computerised system. The registers are already held in electronic form, but e-conveyancing would enable sale to take place purely electronically (without documents and signatures). A separate point is that the guarantee of title provided by registration makes it easier to talk about ownership of land. If Sarah is registered as proprietor (the word the system uses) of the fee simple absolute in possession, then we might as well say that she owns the land.

A strategy for interests other than estates

Overreaching does not make sense for non-estate interests. Suppose Rachel has a right of way over Tim's land in order to gain access to her house, which is 50 metres away from the public road. If Tim sells his land to Ursula, it is essential that Rachel should be able to have access over the land now owned by Ursula. To give a right equivalent to a right of way over the purchase price paid to Tim would be nonsensical.

An interim solution: land charges legislation

The Land Charges Act 1925 (Extract 9.6.3) (re-enacted in 1972 with only minor changes) required certain listed interests to be registered. It applies only until title to the land is registered, so today it applies only to the 5 per cent not yet registered. The listed interests bind purchasers only if they are registered. What interests are within this scheme? The answer – rather oversimplified – is that most equitable interests (but not equitable estates) have to be registered. These include equitable mortgages, estate contracts and restrictive covenants.

It might be noted that the 1925 legislation leaves little scope for the old doctrine of notice (whereby equitable interests bound purchasers who knew about them or ought to have known about them). If the interest is a successive or concurrent interest (estate) under a trust then it will usually be overreached and not affect a purchaser at all. Most other types of equitable interest have to be entered on the land charges register before a purchaser can be bound. If they were not registered then they do not bind purchasers, even if they are aware of the unregistered interest.

The modern solution: registration of title

Once the fee simple absolute in possession or lease has been registered, the land charges scheme ceases to apply. This means that land charges, as described above, will soon become obsolescent. Instead, the interests have to be protected on the land registers.

There may be some surprise that there are two different registration systems. In part, this is because they operate quite differently. Registration of title (often described as land registration) uses a separate register (computer file today) for each plot of land. This requires every plot to be identified and mapped. This time-consuming exercise is a major reason for the delay in rolling out land registration. By contrast, land charges are registered by reference to the name of the owner. That system is simple, but it is prone to human error and is widely regarded as much inferior to registration of title. One obvious point is that land charges doesn't tell the purchaser who is entitled to the fee simple absolute in possession: to discover this, the title deeds have to be inspected.

Once title is registered, the basic principle is that all interests have to be entered on the register before they can affect purchasers. This applies as much to legal rights as to equitable rights. There are some exceptions, which are called **overriding interests**: these bind purchasers without any register entry. This controversial category includes both legal and equitable interests. One example is a legal lease not exceeding seven years. It may be justified as it would be too much trouble to register short leases, which will normally be obvious to purchasers. Another example is that those in *actual occupation* do not need to protect their interests. This applies mainly to equitable interests. Its rationale is that a sensible purchaser should inspect the land and make inquiries of occupiers, as well as looking at the register.

It may be noted that we register the fee simple and lease in order to facilitate their sale. Technically, it is these estates rather than the land which are registered; there may be more than one register for a single plot of land. Other interests are unlikely to be bought and sold; these other interests are entered on the register of the relevant fee simple or lease. The register is designed to provide purchasers of a fee simple or lease with a comprehensive picture as to what rights will bind them. That comprehensive picture is, of course, rendered incomplete by overriding interests.

One consequence of these rules is that it is less relevant to draw distinctions between legal and equitable interests today: entry on the register is what counts. Nevertheless, some registration provisions apply only to legal interests. One example is the lease not exceeding seven years mentioned above: this is an overriding interest only if it is a legal lease.

Commonhold: a new estate?

Commonhold was introduced by the Commonhold and Leasehold Reform Act 2002 (Extract 17.1.1). Commonhold will not feature in later chapters and is therefore dealt with here at fuller length than the topics above.

Commonhold is designed for properties with a high degree of interdependence. In particular, flats require careful management. To take an obvious point, flats depend on the roof being sound. If the roof leaks water, this will affect them all – not just the flat which includes the roof. This means that there has to be somebody responsible for undertaking work such as roof maintenance and, in appropriate cases, clear obligations on the individual flat-holders to share the cost.

If the flats are held by tenants with short leases (a year, for example), there is no problem. The landlord will undertake the repairs and their anticipated cost will be factored into the rent. The problems arise when people wish to purchase flats rather than lease them. The major stumbling block is that positive obligations do not bind purchasers of the fee simple. If the owner of the top-floor flat promises to repair the roof or to contribute towards the cost of repair, this promise could not be enforced against any purchaser of that flat.

The result was that owning (holding the fee simple absolute in possession) flats was not practicable. Instead, the universal practice was to lease flats on very long leases (perhaps 99 years), the tenants paying a purchase price (close to the freehold value) and a nominal or very low rent. The landlord would undertake repairs and charge them to the tenants. It should be explained that positive obligations can be enforced against later purchasers of leases: a very different rule than applies for the fee simple.

The leasehold solution ran into criticism for two reasons. First, it failed to give effect to the aspirations of very many people to own their flats. Second, there was dissatisfaction with the repairs being undertaken by landlords and the charges for them. Commonhold is designed to remedy these problems.

The commonhold scheme is complex and space permits only a brief description. Each individual flat or unit will be owned in fee simple, though with some special rules applying to it. There will be a *commonhold association* (CA), which is responsible for running the commonhold scheme. This scheme will include the individual units and common areas such as stairs, lifts and gardens. The CA, a company controlled by the owners of the units, will own these common areas in fee simple.

There are two particularly important aspects of commonhold. The first is that the owners of the units, through the medium of the CA, control the management of the land: deciding when a roof is to be repaired or an old lift replaced, for example. The involvement of the unit-holders is thought likely to result in more effective management. The second is that the CA can enforce obligations (positive and negative) against the current owners of the units. These obligations arise from the *commonhold community statement*, which sets out the obligations of both the CA and the unit owners. Positive obligations will bind purchasers, although this is normally not allowed for freehold estates.

The term 'commonhold' might indicate that it is a new form of estate, different from freehold and leasehold estates. Strictly speaking, this is not the case. Commonhold involves the fee simple absolute in possession (whether of individual units or the common areas). Rather than being a new estate, commonhold is a system of management for blocks of flats and other interdependent properties. Yet this fee simple is subject to special rules inapplicable outside commonhold: thus there are some detailed limits on what transactions can be entered into by the unit-holders and the CA. In substance, commonhold may be regarded as a different form of landholding.

How popular is commonhold? It is unlikely to apply to existing developments, given that unanimity is required for conversion to commonhold. Its use is likely to be limited to new developments. Though a few large developments are using commonhold, by early 2008 the pitifully small number of 14 commonholds had been registered.

Conclusions

We have seen that legislation over the past century has made significant changes to land law. However, much of land law retains its origins in a mixture of common law and equitable principles, though large areas are dominated by legislation. We have identified here a number of areas in which legislation is particularly important. Many other aspects of land law are affected by legislation, sometimes in very important respects. These will be observed as we look at individual topics in later chapters.

Questions to consider

1. Why did the law relating to estates require reform in the nineteenth century? How has the law dealt with this area?

2. What is the role of registration in dealing with property interests?

3. Why was commonhold introduced? How successful has it been?

4. What are the main ideas underpinning commonhold?

Further reading

Clarke, D [2002] Conv 349: The enactment of commonhold: problems, principles and perspectives.

Roberts, N [2002] Conv 341: Commonhold: a new property term – but no property in a term?

Rudden, B (1994) 14 OxJLS 81: Things as things and things as wealth.

Smith, P F [2004] Conv 194: The purity of commonholds.

van der Merwe, C G and Smith, P (2005) 'Commonhold – a critical appraisal', in *Modern Studies in Property Law*, Vol 3, ed. E. Cooke, Chapter 11.

Visit **www.mylawchamber.co.uk** to access tools to help you develop and test your knowledge of land law, including interactive multiple choice questions, practice exam questions with guidance, weblinks, glossary flashcards, legal newsfeed and legal updates.

4   Land and other property

We will consider here how and why land law is different from the law relating to other forms of property. We will concentrate on comparing land with chattels: objects other than land. These include jewellery, cars, boxes of chocolates and vast numbers of other items. There are also forms of intangible property (e.g. rights of action, such as a right to sue for debt), but these will not be considered.

The range of proprietary interests recognised

The previous chapters reveal a wide range of interests in land. Our first comparisons concern estates and ownership. Estates do not apply to property other than land. Instead, we recognise ownership: it is entirely accurate to say that Jane owns a box of chocolates. Suppose I want Kerry to be able to hang my painting in her house for her lifetime. I cannot create a life estate in her favour, but I can create a trust over the painting so that Kerry has an equitable life interest. Another clear proposition is that two people can own property concurrently: Betty and Carla could buy a pony together and jointly own it. It seems likely that the equivalent of leases (hiring) applies to chattels, though the question of its proprietary status has not been finally settled.

The range of other interests in chattels is restricted. There are, for example, no true equivalents of easements, restrictive covenants and estate contracts. The value and utility of land frequently depend on rights over adjoining land: this explains easements and restrictive covenants. The same cannot be said for chattels. Indeed, we prize the ability to buy chattels free from obligations: it encourages commerce. Although the law encourages the easy sale of land, some delays required for checking the register and making other enquiries are regarded as acceptable. By contrast, I do not expect to have to undertake inquiries as to whether somebody else has a claim to a necklace I am buying in a shop. One form of interest that is recognised in chattels is the mortgage. A right to sell a valuable sculpture, for example, if a debt is not repaid would be a useful form of security. However, there are detailed rules designed to protect purchasers from the borrower (mortgagor), when the purchaser is unaware of the mortgage.

In summary, the narrower range of interests in chattels may be explained by the lesser need for them and the greater significance accorded to very easy transfer of ownership of chattels.

The significance of possession

We talk about estates being in possession, but possession of the land itself is less significant. Possession of chattels is important in two contexts. The first is that a gift of chattels can be made by handing them over. This is not possible for land. Second, a person who finds a chattel gains ownership rights to it.

> Brian finds a ring on a street, dropped by Alison a few hours earlier. He takes it home, intending to take it to the police. That night, Charlie breaks into Brian's house and takes the ring. Brian can reclaim the ring from Charlie: his finding it confers rights on him that are superior to those of anybody else, except Alison. Alison could claim the ring from either Brian or Charlie. Brian's rights are especially important if the true owner, Alison, is never discovered.

Gift and finding have led to much analysis as to the true meaning of possession. There are no direct equivalents for land. One of the few contexts in which possession becomes relevant is that of adverse possession (dealt with in Chapter 6).

Formalities

Statute requires most transactions with land to be in writing, with a formal deed being required for most legal estates and interests. Save in exceptional cases, no such rules apply for chattels. Contracts for interests in land also must be in writing, whereas contracts to sell chattels can be oral. Indeed, ownership of chattels usually passes by virtue of a contract of sale: the purchaser becomes owner when the contract says he does. These contracts may be oral, though large commercial contracts will almost invariably be in writing.

Why do we have special rules for land? A mixture of reasons may be given. Many of the rules go back centuries, to a time when land was by far the most important form of asset. Today, the point can be made that for many individuals their home is their most important asset. It is a good thing that they have to sign a document before entering into transactions with it, as this reduces the risk of ill-considered commitments. Next, possession of chattels is generally linked with ownership. This does not apply to land, when the person occupying it may well have limited rights to it: a tenant under a short lease or the holder of a life interest provide examples. Furthermore, many interests are not at all apparent from inspecting the land. It is therefore unsurprising that writing is essential so that we can establish with certainty what rights exist and what their terms are.

Registration

Having a large number of interests in land demands a system whereby they can be registered. A large proportion of houses will be bound by mortgages and restrictive covenants and have the benefit of easements. There is a need for straightforward purchase procedures. In turn, this requires certainty as to what interests exist. Registration provides that certainty. Further, registration plays an important role in recording and simplifying the often complex documentation used in land transactions. No similar system operates for chattels generally. It is unsurprising that there is no register of ownership of boxes of chocolates!

Land as a home

The growth of owner-occupation over the past century means that there are particular concerns as to how land law impacts on the family home. This is encountered in several different areas. One area concerns disputes as to ownership of a family home vested in the name of just one spouse or partner. Another area covers the rules applicable when creditors and mortgagees seek to have the family home sold, in order to get loans repaid. In addition, a large part of the modern legislation relating to leases has centred on protecting tenants' homes. In all these areas, the law recognises that people living on land deserve particular protection. A home is more significant than an investment.

Land and the 1925 legislation

In general terms, the legislation sought to abolish special rules for land where these were unnecessary. Let us take one example. Before 1925, land would pass directly under a will to the new owner. By contrast, all other assets would pass to those selected by the deceased as executors (or **personal representatives**). These persons would pay any debts and then pass the assets on as required by the will. In 1925, the special rules for land were abolished. Today, all assets, including land, pass to the executors on death.

Much of the 1925 legislation applies only to land. In part, this is because land transactions are complex and the legislation seeks to shorten them. It was common for transfers of land to contain many complex standard terms. The 1925 legislation ensures that these standard terms are implied. The result is that transfers are shorter and easier to read. This applies only to land because it was only in land transfers that such terms were common. Another point is that many provisions apply to specific interests, such as leases and easements. These interests are interests in land, not chattels, so inevitably the provisions apply only to land.

A rather different point is that land has several unique features. Quite apart from its intrinsic value, the fact that it is immoveable sets it aside. This is very important as regards mortgages. A feature of the mortgage is that the borrower (mortgagor) retains possession of the premises. This would be fraught with danger if there were a mortgage of, say, a diamond ring. There is a danger that the owner of the ring might lose it or sell it. If sold, there is every risk that the purchaser will never be traced. Some of these dangers may be countered by insurance, but this does not provide a complete answer. In a mortgage of land, it is trivially easy to know where the land is! Entry of the mortgage on the register of title will rule out any unauthorised dealing with the land. There is also the separate consideration that land has a relatively stable value: it provides good security for a loan. These factors together mean that mortgages of land are especially common and, in turn, attract detailed statutory regulation.

Conclusions

Some of the principles studied in this text are applicable to all forms of property. However, many of the topics studied are, for good practical reasons, unique to land. This is true of formalities and registration, as well as particular interests such as easements. Even where principles covered in land law apply to other property, they often attract special rules where land is involved. A good example is the trust. All forms of property may be held under a trust, but we shall see later that land law makes special and extensive use of the trust. Largely because trusts of land are very common, we have modern legislation governing how they work: the Trusts of Land and Appointment of Trustees Act 1996. This deals, for example, with rights to occupy the land – scarcely an important issue for other forms of trust assets. It is not surprising that land law requires treatment as a distinct area of law.

Questions to consider

1. Are there good reasons why land (but not other property) should be subject to special rules?

2. Should the aim of the law be to maximise or minimise the differences?

Further reading

Harris, J W (1987) 'Legal doctrine and interests in land', in *Oxford Essays in Jurisprudence*, Third Series, eds J M Eekelaar and J Bell, Chapter 8.

Honoré, A M (1961) 'Ownership' in *Oxford Essays in Jurisprudence*, First Series, ed. A G Guest, Chapter 5.

Visit **www.mylawchamber.co.uk** to access tools to help you develop and test your knowledge of land law, including interactive multiple choice questions, practice exam questions with guidance, weblinks, glossary flashcards, legal newsfeed and legal updates.

5 Human rights

The role of human rights in English cases has dramatically increased since the Human Rights Act 1998 (the 1998 Act) (Extract 2.1.1). Until then, cases had to be heard by the European Court of Human Rights in Strasbourg, based on the European Convention for the Protection of Human Rights and Fundamental Freedoms. Now that the 1998 Act enables human rights to be argued in English courts, the interest in human rights, together with litigation, has expanded fast. Land law is no exception.

In assessing human rights, one of the problems is that we are still working out when Convention rights will impact on principles of land law. Nevertheless, there have been some important decisions in the past few years. These give useful guidance and emphasise just how important human rights can be.

Here we consider the general principles of human rights as relevant to land law. The application of these principles to specific areas of land law will be considered in later chapters: an understanding of the relevant areas of law is essential before sense can be made of most human rights litigation.

Convention rights

The European Convention is incorporated into the 1998 Act and forms the basis upon which claims may be brought. Perhaps the most obviously important provision for land law is Article 1 of the First Protocol (Extract 2.1.1). This provides: 'Every natural or legal person is entitled to the peaceful enjoyment of his possessions. No one shall be deprived of his possessions except in the public interest . . .' Clearly, the State cannot confiscate assets, unless justified by the public interest. A clear example of public interest is where land is compulsorily purchased for the site of a new hospital: the owner cannot complain of deprivation of possessions. Even then, however, the payment of compensation will be an important factor in assessing whether the public interest defence operates. It is usually said that the interference with Convention rights must be proportionate to any legitimate end being pursued; it is not necessarily a defence that there is some public interest. Whether compensation is payable is very relevant in deciding questions of proportionality.

It might be thought that, leaving aside compulsory purchase (and a few criminal law rules, such as confiscation of drugs), confiscation of assets is no part of English law. That would be wrong. Numerous examples can be found when property rights are terminated by law. Three examples are given. Before recent reforms, a person who occupied land without the permission of the owner (an 'adverse possessor') could defeat the true owner after 12 years: the adverse possessor became the new holder of the fee simple. This is a clear example of the law terminating ownership. The Strasbourg court in *JA Pye (Oxford) Ltd v United Kingdom*[1] (Extract 2.1.2) (as is seen in Chapter 6) was split on whether the adverse possession rules, as they applied before the reforms, were inconsistent with Convention rights. A majority held that there was no breach of human rights.

A second example is provided by registration of title.

> Suppose Carla owns a plot of land. Because of a mistake some years previously, Brian (unaware of the mistake) is registered as the first **proprietor** of the plot. The Land Registration Act 2002 provides that Brian is the proprietor: Carla is relegated to claiming compensation. The courts have said that the loss of Carla's ownership is acceptable, a result more readily reached because of the availability of compensation for Carla. There is a legitimate public interest in settling issues of land ownership: this is achieved by guaranteeing Brian's title as proprietor. It is especially important that people should be able to rely on the register when buying land: this ensures safe and inexpensive land transfer.

The third example is based on the law relating to leases. We will see (in Chapter 14) that a landlord can terminate ('forfeit') a lease if the tenant is in breach of its terms. Is the tenant deprived of his possessions (the lease)? Two factors are likely to provide a defence to the landlord. First, **forfeiture** operates by virtue of a term inserted by the parties. English law simply enforces what the parties have agreed. The second point is that the courts almost always have a discretion whether or not to allow forfeiture. If the tenant can remedy the breach, forfeiture will not normally be allowed. Even though no compensation is payable on forfeiture (despite the lease often being a valuable asset), there is a viable public interest defence. Its basis is that landlords need an effective remedy against tenants who fail to comply with obligations, coupled with the court's discretion in favour of deserving tenants.

These three examples show that we need to think carefully about long-established rules of land law. There are, of course, other examples. Returning to land registration, many interests in land (such as contracts to buy land – estate contracts) have to be registered before they can affect purchasers. When an unregistered right fails, is this a deprivation, especially as no compensation is payable in this example? *Pye* treated adverse possession as a control of use rather than a deprivation. The same is likely to apply in the registration context: registration rules represent a necessary control over interests (determining the exact circumstances in which purchasers are affected by proprietary claims) rather than outright deprivation. Both control and deprivation are within Article 1. However, where no compensation is paid, control is easier to justify than deprivation. Justifying the registration rules should be relatively straightforward.

---

[1] (2007) 46 EHRR 1083; see below (p. 47). It was litigated in Strasbourg because the facts predated the 1998 Act.

Two other Convention rights are particularly likely to impact on land law. The first is Article 8 (Extract 2.1.1): 'Everybody has the right to respect for his private and family life, his home . . .' This is subject to controls necessary for factors such as health, safety, security and the rights and freedoms of others. Article 8 is particularly relevant for land law in so far as it protects homes. It has, as will be seen later,[2] been used to challenge rules whereby land can be sold following bankruptcy. A number of other legal rules may be attacked for inadequately recognising the importance of homes. However, it is likely that most rules adequately take into account the significance of people's homes and balance this against other objectives being pursued. Modern legislation frequently sets out to protect homes. One example is that since 1970 we have had rules restricting the right of mortgage lenders to take possession (almost invariably as a prelude to sale), where there is a reasonable prospect of arrears being paid.

The last Convention right to be mentioned is the Article 6 (Extract 2.1.1) right to 'a fair and public hearing' in the determination of rights and obligations. In the land law context, this is most likely to apply if rights are exercised out of court. In some circumstances, leases can be forfeited and lenders can sell mortgaged land without court proceedings. Might these be open to attack? Court proceedings are nearly always required to oust a person in possession, but this does not cover every case. For example, if a borrower fails to pay mortgage instalments and then leaves the mortgaged property, then the lender can sell it to recover the unpaid loan. A recent attempt to use human rights in similar circumstances failed.[3]

Enforcement of Convention rights

If a statute is inconsistent with human rights then the courts are to interpret it so as to make it consistent. If that is not possible, the courts cannot strike it down but must issue a declaration of incompatibility.[4] For other legal rules, inconsistency means that the courts are obliged to amend them so as to comply with human rights.[5]

A major debate has arisen as to whether the 1998 Act has a *horizontal* as well as *vertical* effect. All agree that the State (more accurately 'public authorities', as defined by section 6) is obliged to comply with human rights; this is what is meant by vertical effect. What is less clear is whether Convention rights can be enforced by an individual against another individual: horizontal effect.

Let us take the adverse possession case of *Pye* as an example. This was brought against the Government in Strasbourg, where all issues are vertical (defendants are always governments). However, in English courts one individual may be claiming against another individual. For human rights to be effective in such litigation, it is necessary for human rights to have horizontal effect. If there were no horizontal effect then (for

---

[2] See below (p. 172). It is not settled whether such a challenge will succeed.

[3] *Horsham Properties Group Ltd* v *Clark* [2009] 1 WLR 1255, (Extract 21.4.33), below (p. 310) (the claim was based on Article 1 rather than Article 6).

[4] 1998 Act, ss 3 and 4.

[5] 1998 Act, s 6.

example) Convention rights could not prevent an individual from relying on adverse possession. These issues simply do not arise at Strasbourg, where all disputes are vertical.

Three factors combine to indicate some level of horizontal effect. Most obviously, as *Pye* shows, rights which individuals exercise against each other can place the Government in breach of Convention rights. This is not a horizontal effect, but can mean that reform of the law will follow. Next, a common effect of breach of Convention rights is that legislation is interpreted so as to make it compliant with human rights (section 3). This interpretation must apply whether the litigation happens to involve an individual or a public authority. The legislation cannot have different meanings for different parties. Accordingly, where legislation is involved, a Convention-compliant interpretation will be applied as between individuals. A similar analysis operates where a non-statutory rule is challenged on human rights grounds: the rule will be made Convention-compliant regardless of whether a public authority is involved.

The third factor is the most radical and controversial. Courts are public bodies required to comply with human rights. It is argued that when courts enforce rights of individuals, they are bound to ensure that Convention rights are complied with. Otherwise, the court is failing in its duties under the 1998 Act. It is unclear whether the argument will be accepted, as few cases have even mentioned the problem. Though it was discussed in *X v Y*[6] (Extract 2.2.1) (not a land law case), Mummery LJ thought that it might never be resolved. Most cases can be decided by applying more specific arguments, especially section 3 on interpreting legislation. This is particularly relevant in land law, as so many of the principles are enshrined in legislation.

Human rights in the enforcement of property rights

The past decade has seen a highly controversial series of cases on the inter-relationship between property rights and human rights. The problems have turned on the application of Article 8: respect for homes. If an owner of land (in most cases, a landlord) seeks to enforce their property rights to evict a trespasser or tenant, can the defendant occupier rely on the argument that the land constitutes their home and that any loss of the home has to be justified in terms of proportionality? Although eviction is nearly always undertaken following a court order, the possession actions are usually very brief. If the court were to look in detail at questions of proportionality in every case, this would cause significant added costs and delays within the judicial system.

Most of the problems have arisen when local authorities are exercising their powers as landlords. Local authorities are, of course, clearly public authorities and so Article 8 clearly applies to them. A series of House of Lords decisions[7] held that Article 8 does not qualify an owner's right to obtain possession. However, decisions of the European Court of Human Rights[8] took the opposite view, insisting that the occupier should have the

CRITICAL ISSUE

---

[6] [2004] ICR 1634 at [44]–[46].

[7] *Harrow LBC* v *Qazi* [2004] 1 AC 983; *Kay* v *Lambeth LBC* [2006] 2 AC 465; *Doherty* v *Birmingham City Council* [2009] 1 AC 367.

[8] See especially *McCann* v *UK* [2008] 2 FLR 899 and *Kay* v *UK* [2011] HLR 13. Cases arising from other jurisdictions took the same approach.

opportunity to raise issues of proportionality. Indeed, that had been the approach of minority judges in the earlier House of Lords cases. Though the Strasbourg court considered that it would be unusual for the local authority decision to be overturned, there needs to be a way to challenge it. The House of Lords responded by broadening the scope of judicial review of the local authority decision, whilst leaving the possession application itself untouched by Article 8.

In the remarkable decision of the Supreme Court in *Manchester City Council* v *Pinnock*[9] (Extract 2.3.1), the three earlier House of Lords cases were overruled. The Strasbourg court has prevailed, the Supreme Court observing that the Strasbourg analysis has been consistent over several years and that it cannot be criticised as failing to appreciate the position in English law. The result is that the courts now accept that it is open to an occupier to raise a defence based upon Article 8.

What does this mean in practice? The courts have made it very clear that there will be few cases in which an Article 8 defence will be arguable (let alone succeed). The expectation is that local authorities will be exercising statutory powers in an appropriate manner; the court should respect the balancing of public and private interests that parliament has entrusted to local authorities. Though *Pinnock* rejected a 'very highly exceptional' test, preferring instead to stress proportionality, the fact remains that very few cases are likely to succeed. The more recent cases tend to make more use of the language of 'very highly exceptional' – it may not be the test, but it encapsulates the rarity of successful defences. One particular factor is that there are several statutory schemes under which local authorities lease houses and flats. Especially where local authorities are operating these schemes, the courts are reluctant to interfere.[10] Sometimes, these schemes confer no discretion on the court once the local authority has reached a decision to terminate a tenancy and seek possession. This is made consistent with Article 8 by allowing (as had been developing before *Pinnock*) a broadly based judicial review of the local authority decision to seek possession. Again, the chances of a successful challenge are small.

Leaving aside patently irrational local authority decisions, can we predict when an Article 8 defence will succeed? Much depends upon the particular context, but some statutory schemes provide a significant level of security for occupiers. If the local authority seeks to bypass that security on a technical basis, then there is a real risk that Article 8 will operate. The Strasbourg case of *McCann v UK*[11] provides an example. We shall see in Chapter 13 that, where a couple hold a lease together and it is a periodic tenancy (such as a weekly tenancy), then either party can terminate the lease by giving notice to the landlord. If the couple break up, then the local authority landlord may persuade the person who leaves to give notice – with the effect that the lease comes to an end. This can be seen as unfair on the remaining tenant, given that the local authority would otherwise have had no basis for terminating the tenancy. It was on that basis that *McCann* held there to be a breach of Article 8. However, that conclusion is not inevitable

---

[9] [2011] 2 AC 104; it was a unanimous nine judge court.

[10] In *Hounslow LBC* v *Powell* [2011] 2 AC 186 the Supreme Court considered the application of *Pinnock* to a number of such schemes.

[11] [2008] 2 FLR 899.

– there may be good reasons why the remaining tenant should not keep possession, as where the premises are far too large for one person and the local authority offers alternative accommodation.

All these cases involve local authority claimants. Does Article 8 apply to a private owner? This, of course, raises the question of horizontal effect discussed above. If Article 8 does apply, then this could be a very significant constraint upon the exercise of property rights – quite possibly the most important consequence of horizontal effect in land law. Indeed, going too far in applying Article 8 runs the risk of contravening the protection of the owner's property rights in the First Protocol, Article 1 (Extract 2.1.1). *Pinnock* restricted its analysis to public sector housing, but recognised that conflicting views as regards private owners are found in the English cases and at Strasbourg. An extension to private owners would pose some problems. Much of the present law is based upon the role of local authorities in balancing various claims upon limited resources. None of that applies to private owners. Nor can judicial review apply to them. The idea that property rights have to be exercised in a proportionate manner is not one which fits English property law at all well.

However, two points may be made regarding private owners. The first is that it is quite clear (regardless of the *Pinnock* point) that Article 8 can be used to challenge a legal rule or principle. A well known example, mentioned above, concerns the statutory rules relating to the sale of family homes following bankruptcy of a co-owner. If those rules can be successfully attacked (which is not clear), that will clearly affect private owners. *Pinnock* relates to owners' decisions to exercise valid legal rights. In the bankruptcy setting, not only the right to seek sale can be challenged but also the decision of the trustee in bankruptcy in the individual case to sell. It is the latter challenge which might flow from *Pinnock*. If it does, then Article 8 arguments may become important in a multitude of cases.

The second point is that there are several areas in which the court has to exercise a statutory discretion before possession can be obtained of a home. These include trusts of land and applications by mortgagees. Where those discretions apply, it is almost unthinkable that there could be a breach of Article 8 – the fact that the land is the home of the person opposing sale is almost certain to be taken into account in the exercise of the discretion. However, there are many cases where discretion will not assist. Thus the two examples just considered will protect beneficiaries under trusts and borrowers, yet there may well be other family members whose home the land is – the discretion may well not protect them. Other decisions by owners involve no element of court discretion, as where a landlord seeks to recover property at the end of a lease. The law chooses to protect a person's home in certain situations, though there is no general recognition of a home as being sufficient to challenge the exercise of property rights. It remains to be seen how this fits the new human rights environment.

CRITICAL ISSUE

Assessing human rights in land law

The potential for human rights to intrude into land law disputes is immense. Whenever looking at rules and principles (however basic and obvious), we have to bear in mind the possibility of a human rights challenge. We have already seen a wide range of situations (in quite different areas of land law) in which human rights may feature.

What is more difficult to assess is in how many of these areas Convention rights will be successfully deployed. Is reliance on human rights any more than a last-ditch argument in otherwise hopeless cases, used more for its nuisance value than for any real chance of success? That would be to diminish its impact to an unjustified extent, but the reality is that few challenges to land law principles have succeeded. Many cases that have gained attention have subsequently been overruled. One point to bear in mind is that many land law rules (including much legislation) replicate what parties normally specify. When the parties are free to exclude these rules, it will be difficult to challenge them on human rights grounds.[12] Subject to one point, it may be predicted that human rights will play an increasingly important role, but that it is unlikely that large swathes of land law will have to be rewritten as a result. That qualification is that a broad application of Article 8 to private owners could have a revolutionary impact on the ability of owners (and other holders of property interests) to exercise their rights. Nevertheless, experience in the local authority setting indicates that the impact may be limited to exceptional, rather than everyday, circumstances.

[12] *Horsham Properties Group Ltd v Clark* [2009] 1 WLR 1255, (Extract 21.4.33) below (p. 310): mortgagees' power of sale.

Questions to consider

1. What difference did the human rights legislation in 1998 make?

2. Which human rights are likely to be important for land law?

3. What is meant by horizontal effect? When is it likely to be important?

4. If a landowner has rights to the land, is their enforcement qualified by human rights principles?

5. How much of land law is likely to be affected by human rights?

Further reading

Bamforth, N C (2001) 117 LQR 34: The true 'horizontal effect' of the Human Rights Act 1998.

Buxton, R (2000) 116 LQR 48: The Human Rights Act and private law.

Harpum, C (2000) 4 L&T Rev 4 and 29: Property law – the human rights dimension.

Howell, J (2007) 123 LQR 618: The Human Rights Act 1998: land, private citizens, and the common law.

Wade, H W R (2000) 116 LQR 217: Horizons of horizontality.

Visit **www.mylawchamber.co.uk** to access tools to help you
develop and test your knowledge of land law, including
interactive multiple choice questions, practice exam questions
with guidance, weblinks, glossary flashcards, legal newsfeed
and legal updates.

Use **Case Navigator** to read in full some of the key cases referenced in
this chapter with commentary and questions:

JA Pye (Oxford) Ltd v *United Kingdom* (2007) 46 EHRR 1083

Part 2

Acquiring interests and binding purchasers

6 Adverse possession and fixtures

Nature and importance

In Part 2 we look at the creation and transfer of interests in land. Many rules are specific to land; these frequently give rise to challenging questions. Most interests will be created (or transferred) by somebody with an interest in land: derivative acquisition. A simple example is where the holder of the fee simple creates a lease. However, interests sometimes arise without being created by anybody: original acquisition. Two forms of original acquisition are considered in this chapter: adverse possession (when ownership is obtained by possessing land for a period of years) and fixtures (property attached to land becomes part of the land).

Justifications for adverse possession, especially in the light of human rights arguments, are considered below. However, it has a much reduced application following the Land Registration Act 2002 (LRA or 2002 Act). Fixtures will be seen to raise few difficult points of principle.

Adverse possession

Introduction

For centuries, English law has recognised that possessing land adversely to the owner (i.e., without permission) gives rise to a claim to the land. We shall see that, odd as it may seem, the adverse possessor is viewed as having a fee simple at an early stage. This means that there are two fees simple for the same plot, one held by the original owner (the **true owner**) and the other by the adverse possessor. Initially, the fee simple of the true owner prevails and the adverse possessor can be evicted. However, until the 2002 Act the true owner lost his title after 12 years. After 12 years the land really did belong to the adverse possessor.

> Richard owns a house and an adjoining paddock, which he uses for a pony. When Richard is sent abroad by his employer, he leases the house to Sally. The lease does not include the paddock, which is no longer used. Tamara owns another house adjoining the paddock. Seeing that it hasn't been used for a couple of years, Tamara incorporates the paddock into her garden. She fences it so that the only access is from her house and cultivates it as part of her garden. Fifteen years later, Richard returns. When he attempts to reclaim the paddock, he will discover that Tamara now owns it; his ownership has been extinguished and he has lost the paddock without compensation.

Adverse possession has long been regarded with a degree of suspicion – it can be viewed as a form of land theft, especially as the adverse possessor need not be in good faith. The law was revolutionised by the 2002 Act. Adverse possession has a much limited importance for nearly 95 per cent of the titles that are registered. We shall see that, under the 2002 Act, adverse possession operates only if there is a boundary dispute between neighbours or the owner does not bother to assert his title when notified of a claim. Many cases before the legislation involved local authorities that had failed to evict trespassers. Their conduct was explicable because they own thousands of properties: administrative inefficiency was the consequence of having overworked staff. Today, adverse possession would fail in such cases, as it also would in Tamara's claim.

After looking at justifications for adverse possession, we will consider two core issues: what counts as adverse possession and what the effect of adverse possession is. The first issue is the same for both registered and unregistered land. However, the old law on the effect of adverse possession has largely disappeared in registered land: no longer are the true owner's rights lost after 12 years' adverse possession.[1] The 2002 Act is so important that we will consider it first.

Justifications for adverse possession; human rights arguments

How can we justify the drastic effect of taking away the rights of the true owner after 12 years? Even though adverse possession has been rendered largely toothless for registered titles, this question remains important for unregistered land. A number of points can be made:

(i)   The law frequently bars claims that have not been pursued within a limited period: six years for breach of contract, for example. This avoids stale claims, which can be difficult to assert and defend. These arguments are not compelling as regards adverse possession. As ownership is proved from documents (or the register), the true owner's rights are easily proved: there is no danger from stale claims. We could justify stopping a claim for trespass against the adverse possessor many years ago:

[1] LRA, s 96.

that claim would require old acts of trespass to be proved. However, it does not follow that ownership should be taken away.

(ii) It is said to be wrong for owners to sleep on their rights: if they want to keep them, they should assert them without allowing decades to pass. This point seems to carry little weight by itself, though it may be an aspect of the previous and following points. Furthermore, adverse possession sometimes arises without any fault on the part of the owner, as when (exceptionally) it is not obvious to the owner.

(iii) The effect on the adverse possessor may provide a more promising justification. Individuals are prone to treat the position on the ground as representing legal rights.

> Frances has occupied land for 15 years. She is likely to treat the land as belonging to her. The law frequently attempts to bring strict legal rights into line with practical reality. Frances may have spent money on the land and feel unfairly treated if after decades the owner can return and reclaim the land. However, we should remember that estoppel may protect Frances if, for example, the true owner's conduct has led Frances to believe that the land does belong to her. There is then no need to rely on adverse possession.

A related argument is that adverse possession encourages efficient land use. If the owner has no apparent use for the land, it may be preferable that somebody else uses it effectively.

> Eric is a farmer. He makes no use of a field which is too wet for his cattle to graze. Frances, a neighbour, starts to make use of the field. Initially, she does minor acts such as collecting fallen branches and grazing a goat when the land is dry. Over several years, she incorporates the field into her farm. Fifteen years later, Frances wants to improve the drainage of the field so that it can be put to good use. She contacts Eric. Although he is unwilling to come to any agreement with Frances, he takes no steps to recover the land. It would be madness for Frances to spend money on the field if Eric could claim it back. If we did not allow adverse possession, then the land would not be used to its full potential. Indeed, without Frances's wrongful (if relatively innocuous) actions it wouldn't be used at all.

(iv) Most convincing is the argument that ownership of land frequently is less than certain. Adverse possession plays an important role in removing that uncertainty, thereby simplifying purchase of land. There are commonly technical defects in ownership. This may be because relevant deeds have been lost or improperly signed and witnessed; it is also common for the boundaries to be imprecisely or inaccurately described. Because old claims are defeated by adverse possession, we can be confident that no claims to ownership can survive 12 years' possession by the seller. When land is sold, the seller has to provide documents going back just 15 years in order to prove ownership.[2] Suppose there is a defect in a deed 30 years

---

[2] More fully described below (at p. 116).

ago, with the result that Xavier, rather than the seller, was the owner. Xavier's claim will be defeated by virtue of adverse possession. Without adverse possession, purchasers would have to inspect documents much older than 15 years, just in case such a defect were to exist.

This last point constitutes a powerful argument, but its strength today is minimal for registered land. The register guarantees ownership: there is no uncertainty needing to be cured by adverse possession and no deeds which have to be investigated. However, the argument remains strong for unregistered land.

In the 1990s, the Law Commission investigated adverse possession as part of their reforms of registered land. They concluded[3] that these justifications for adverse possession were insufficient to justify keeping it (unchanged) for registered land. In particular, the effects of adverse possession can be viewed as disproportionate in that it deprives the owner of ownership without any compensation. Their proposals led, of course, to the 2002 Act.

The human rights challenge

The same factors as impressed the Law Commission led to challenges to adverse possession on human rights grounds. The relatively narrow scope of this challenge should be noted: it applies only to registered land and then only to adverse possession before the 2002 Act. The following observations apply only in that narrow context.

Strauss QC held in *Beaulane Properties Ltd* v *Palmer*[4] that adverse possession was inconsistent with Article 1 of the First Protocol of the European Convention on Human Rights (deprivation of possessions) (Extract 2.1.1). More significant is the decision of the European Court of Human Rights in *JA Pye (Oxford) Ltd* v *United Kingdom*[5] (Extract 4.2.3). *Pye* followed on from a decision in the English courts described later:[6] it was heard in Strasbourg because the facts predated the human rights legislation. Though a bare majority (a four to three majority) initially reached the same conclusion as *Beaulane*, this was soon reversed by the Grand Chamber (ten to seven majority).

Though the outcome was that the challenge to adverse possession failed, the judges accepted that Article 1 was engaged. Adverse possession was treated as a control of use, rather than a deprivation; this is because it sets out to regulate land ownership. Though both control and deprivation are caught by Article 1, control is more readily shown to be consistent with human rights. It is a fair observation that the differences between the judges were largely based on the extent of the margin of appreciation allowed to legislatures to settle national legal structures. All the judges thought the 2002 reforms well justified, but the majority concluded that this was not enough to condemn the law prior to 2002. It should be stressed that there has never been any prospect of challenging adverse possession as it operates in unregistered land or in registered land after 2002.

---

[3] Law Com No 271, paras 14.1–4; see also Law Com No 254, paras 10.5–19.
[4] [2006] Ch 79.
[5] (2007) 46 EHRR 1083, reversing (2005) 43 EHRR 43.
[6] *JA Pye (Oxford) Ltd* v *Graham* [2003] 1 AC 419 (Extract 4.2.2) (see p. 47, below).

Is adverse possession justified today?

We will consider this question first as regards registered land, given its prevalence today. As will be seen, adverse possession will operate only if the owner fails to object or the true owner and adverse possessor are neighbours. Even where the parties are neighbours, the adverse possessor must reasonably believe that the land is theirs.

This establishes a reasonable balance between, on one side, the rights of the owner and, on the other, the need to encourage efficient land use and to recognise boundaries on the ground. It is unfortunate that what counts as adverse possession is so complex: all the old rules still apply to registered land. However, the analysis of the House of Lords in *Pye* allows a broader scope for adverse possession. That might be criticised, but this matters little now that the 2002 Act restricts the circumstances in which adverse possession operates.

For unregistered land, adverse possession can be justified as helping to establish ownership. The impact of *Pye* in the House of Lords may render its application unreasonably wide, but this is of limited importance given the small (and reducing) numbers of unregistered titles.

Adverse possession under the Land Registration Act 2002

Schedule 6 establishes a three-stage process: application by the adverse possessor (who we will call Sylvia), objection by the owner (who we will call Olivia) and further application by Sylvia.

The flow chart illustrated in Figure 6.1 summarises the process described below.

Application by the adverse possessor

After ten years of adverse possession, Sylvia can apply to the land registry to be registered as proprietor (paragraph 1) (Extract 4.2.4). Ten years is, of course, less than the traditional period of 12 years.

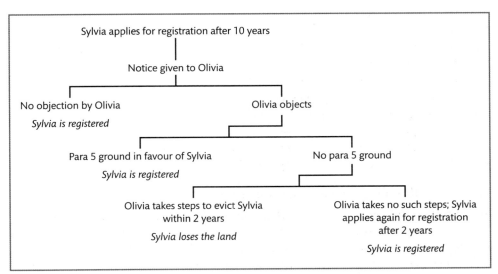

Figure 6.1 Adverse possession under the LRA 2002

CRITICAL ISSUE

The ten years must be the ten years immediately before the application. It is common for disputes to arise when the owner 'wakes up' and retakes possession. Should Olivia retake possession, Sylvia is allowed up to six months to make an application.

The immediate effect of the paragraph 1 application is that the land registry notifies Olivia. Unless Olivia responds, paragraphs 3 and 4 (Extract 4.2.5) provide for Sylvia to be registered as proprietor. This means that an owner who fails to express an interest in retaining the land loses it. If Olivia has no use for the land and does not respond, adverse possession is justified because it enables the land to be used efficiently by Sylvia.

However, if Olivia has simply overlooked the adverse possession or previously did not want to make a fuss, then she can object to Sylvia's application. We move to the second stage.

Objections by the owner

In most cases, an objection by Olivia will block Sylvia's application (paragraph 5). However, paragraph 5 (Extract 4.2.5) provides for three circumstances in which Olivia's objection fails and Sylvia will be registered as proprietor.

The first two are situations in which adverse possession is not strictly necessary. They are included because the legislation sets up a convenient procedure for resolving disputes and it is useful to employ that procedure. The two situations are (i) where Sylvia will succeed because she has an independent right to register (perhaps under a contract to buy the land) and (ii) if she can assert an **estoppel**. An example of the latter would be if Olivia had encouraged Sylvia to build on the land on the supposition that she could keep it.

Much more interesting is the third circumstance. It applies when Olivia and Sylvia are neighbours. If Sylvia reasonably believed that the disputed land belonged to her, then she can overcome Olivia's objection and get herself registered. This is the only true example of adverse possession operating under paragraph 5. It is clear that this has limited application: the great majority of adverse possession claims under the previous law did not involve neighbours (or, if they did, no reasonable belief of entitlement).

Why does the 2002 Act allow adverse possession in the third circumstance? The reason is that boundaries on the ground are frequently different from what appears in plans. This may be because the plans were inaccurate to start with (common in new building developments) or a previous owner established the physical boundary in the wrong place. Even registry plans provide no more than the 'general boundary' – not a guaranteed boundary. Especially when a purchaser has bought land on the reasonable assumption that it includes the disputed area, it seems appropriate to recognise the position on the ground as it has existed over a lengthy period.

Further application by the adverse possessor

Suppose that Olivia has objected to Sylvia's application and Sylvia is unable to establish any of the three circumstances for her to be registered. That does not mean that Olivia receives more than temporary protection. Unless Olivia has, within two years, taken proceedings to evict Sylvia, paragraph 6 (Extract 4.2.6) permits Sylvia to make a further application to the land registry. This time Sylvia will automatically succeed and be registered as proprietor. The policy is to protect only those owners who really want to recover their land. If Olivia takes proceedings within the two-year limit, she can be sure of recovering her land. Otherwise, efficient land use points to Sylvia's being the best person to own and manage the land.

Overall, it can be concluded that adverse possession will apply only in situations in which either the owner cannot be bothered to take action (despite notification by the land registry) or boundaries are disputed. The latter, of course, also requires Sylvia reasonably to believe that the land is hers. Are there any circumstances in which Olivia could justifiably feel aggrieved by a successful adverse possession claim? One example will be considered.

Adverse possession may succeed because a land registry notification has not reached Olivia. This may happen if she has moved from the relevant property and has not notified the land registry of a new address. If she never receives the notice, no objection can be lodged and inevitably Sylvia will be registered as proprietor. Depriving Olivia of owner-ship without compensation could be seen as draconian. She might be able to claim **rectification** of the register under statutory powers under the registration scheme.[7] Though rectification is available if there has not been sufficient adverse possession, there is no authority relating to the receipt of notices.

When is there adverse possession?

Adverse possession, as described in this section, must be proved before a claim can be brought for either registered or unregistered land. There is a mountain of authority, though much of it is specific to the facts of the particular case. Most of the really difficult questions have become obsolescent now that the effects of adverse possession have been heavily restricted by the 2002 Act. This justifies a relatively short discussion of the principles.

There are three essential ingredients in proving adverse possession. There must be acts of possession, there must be an intention to possess and the possession must be adverse (without consent).

Possession

Not every act of **trespass** counts as possession. There must be the sort of conduct that indicates an ownership claim by the adverse possessor. Taking over a house and living there would plainly suffice. Many cases involve farmland. This can pose more difficult-ies, as it can be used for a range of activities. One useful test is whether the claimant has fenced the land. Fencing is not essential, but it is a strong indicator that the claimant is asserting ownership by excluding everybody from the land.

The nature of the land is also important. Some land is barely suitable for any use, perhaps because it floods frequently. In *Red House Farms (Thorndon) Ltd* v *Catchpole*,[8] the claimant had been shooting over an island in a river. Such conduct would not normally suffice as adverse possession: more would be expected of somebody asserting ownership. However, the island was of little or no use for agricultural purposes and adverse possession succeeded – shooting was as much as could be expected.

[7] See below (p. 138).
[8] [1977] 2 EGLR 125.

Cases where people boldly go on to a stranger's land and start using it as their own are relatively few. More often, land isn't being actively used by the owner and the adverse possessor (often an adjoining landowner) begins to use it in minor ways. Over the years, the use increases. The influential decision of Slade J in *Powell* v *McFarlane*[9] provides a good example. The claimant, aged 14, lived with grandparents who were farmers. The defendant owned a field nearby which was poor agricultural land and unused apart from some Christmas trees on it. The claimant began to cut and remove hay from the field. After making limited repairs to the fencing, he began to graze the family cow Kashla there. In later years, he made more extensive use of the land in connection with his business as a tree surgeon, including erecting a noticeboard on it and storing wood and vehicles on it from time to time. Slade J held that the original activities were insufficient: they showed trespass rather than a claim to ownership. It was possible that the later activities did constitute adverse possession, but they had not continued for the required period of 12 years. The fact that the claimant was aged 14 at the start made it more difficult to prove intention to possess at that time.

A final point is that if the true owner continues to make active use of the land, then this is inconsistent with adverse possession. On the other hand, it does not matter if the claimant uses part of the land and the owner the rest: this is the typical scenario for boundary disputes.

Intention to possess

Intention to possess (sometimes encountered in its Latin form: *animus possidendi*) is not found in the legislation. However, the courts have always treated it as an ingredient in determining whether there is sufficient possession, especially in circumstances where (as in *Powell*) the facts do not clearly show possession.

The requisite intention will be easily shown where the claimant believes they have ownership. Disputed boundaries often involve such belief; this fits the continued application of adverse possession in such cases after the 2002 Act. More difficult are cases such as *Powell*, where claimants know that the land does not belong to them. To require the claimant to show an intention to own would mean that they would have to intend to repel the true owner. Only the more outrageous cases of adverse possession would pass that test!

The modern test is that the adverse possessor must intend to possess the land to the exclusion of others: one reason why fencing the land is treated as so significant. Most explicit is the Court of Appeal in *Buckinghamshire CC* v *Moran*[10] (Extract 4.2.8), in which Slade LJ required 'an intention for the time being to possess the land to the exclusion of all other persons, including the owner with the paper title'. It does not matter that the claimant accepts that any future assertion of rights by the true owner cannot be resisted. In *Moran*, the claimant had incorporated a vacant plot (being held by the local authority for a possible future road) into his adjoining land. Access by the local authority was originally through a gate in a fence, but the claimant used a lock and chain to prevent entry. The adverse possession claim succeeded.

[9] (1977) 38 P&CR 452.
[10] [1990] Ch 623.

Adverse

Consent by the true owner prevents possession being adverse. Problems are most likely to arise where it is claimed that an initial consent does not cover later actions, especially where use of the land by the adverse possessor has changed over the years.

This is illustrated by the leading recent authority on adverse possession: *JA Pye (Oxford) Ltd v Graham*[11] (Extract 4.2.10). Graham initially had a licence to cut hay and graze animals on a number of fields. When the licence expired, Graham requested its renewal, but Pye refused (without evicting Graham). Despite his further offers to continue the licence being ignored, Graham began to make full use of the land as if the owner. Pye had no access to the fields and made no use of them. The House of Lords held that the original licence had terminated and that from that time Graham's use was adverse.

The true owner can stop time running by giving the occupier permission to remain there: this stops the possession from being adverse thereafter. It is particularly useful if the true owner wants to prevent adverse possession, but without taking immediate steps to evict the possessor.

Time also stops running if the possessor acknowledges in writing the rights of the true owner. This is a statutory rule, but even an unwritten acknowledgement might make it difficult to show the necessary intention for adverse possession.

In many of the difficult cases (including *Powell*, *Moran* and *Pye*), the owner had no present use for the land. This is most likely for unbuilt land with no significant farming value. Let us see how this operates.

Suppose that Sylvia takes possession of Olivia's land, in circumstances in which Olivia has no present use for the land. Olivia makes no objection: Sylvia's cultivating the land or using it for storing things is likely to be seen as innocuous conduct that it is not worth objecting to. In these circumstances, Olivia may well be taken aback if she is told that she should have evicted Sylvia and that her failure to act means that she has lost the land.

These arguments have at times impressed the courts. At one stage, it was thought that Olivia impliedly consents to Sylvia's possession, such that it is not adverse. However, this rather artificial idea was rejected by the Limitation Act 1980[12] (Extract 4.2.12) and need not be further considered. More generally, there were a few indications that there could not be adverse possession if Sylvia's acts were consistent with the future intended use by the owner.

The decisions in *Powell*, *Moran* and (in particular) *Pye* reject any special rule for true owners with no present use for the land. The tests for possession and intention to possess must be applied free from any artificial rules. If one can say that Sylvia is in possession and intends to possess (in the sense described above) then adverse possession operates. If Sylvia intends to use the land on a purely temporary basis, then it will be difficult for her to prove the necessary intention.

The cases mentioned in the above example simplify the law and may be welcomed for doing so. However, they also considerably widen the circumstances in which adverse

[11] [2003] 1 AC 419.
[12] Schedule 1, para 8(4) (Extract 4.2.12).

possession can be proved. Is that good policy? We have seen that the 2002 Act set out to narrow the effect of adverse possession: a response to the criticism that adverse possession operates in an unreasonably wide manner. The claimants in each of these three cases would fail today, if title were registered. The real continuing significance of the cases is that they make it relatively easy to gain title by adverse possession in unregistered land.

The effects of adverse possession

We have already seen many of the effects of adverse possession when we investigated the provisions for registered land in the 2002 Act. However, there are a few additional points to consider.

Before adverse possession is completed

Suppose Sylvia is in adverse possession of Olivia's land. After five years, Timothy dispossesses Sylvia, so that he is now the adverse possessor. Assuming that Olivia is still taking no interest in the land, what rights does Sylvia have against Timothy?

The law treats Sylvia as having a fee simple from the beginning, though it is inferior to Olivia's fee simple. It might be thought odd that two people have a fee simple in the same plot, but it illustrates the relativity of title accepted by English property law. It means that Sylvia can evict Timothy, whose claim is clearly inferior to hers (until he has been there for the full period for adverse possession).

When considering adverse possession as against Olivia, can we add together the periods of occupation of Sylvia (there for five years) and Timothy so that there is effective adverse possession against her once Timothy has been there for seven more years (five years under the 2002 Act)? If Sylvia had transferred her rights to Timothy, then it is clear that the two periods could be added together. However, in our example Timothy took possession away from Sylvia. The unregistered land rule was that the two periods could again be added together, but the 2002 Act requires Timothy to start from the beginning. The other rules mentioned earlier in this section are unaffected by the 2002 Act.

After adverse possession is completed

For unregistered land, the title of the original owner is extinguished after 12 years. The adverse possessor has a new title (Sylvia's fee simple as described above) and is not treated as the holder of the former owner's title. In registered land, we apply the rules in the 2002 Act (the three-stage process). If the claim succeeds, the adverse possessor is simply registered as proprietor.

Whether title is registered or not, the general rule is that the adverse possessor will be bound by all proprietary interests (such as easements) in the land. This applies whether they are legal or equitable and whether or not they are entered on the register.

Adverse possession operating against tenants

Suppose Norman has leased land to Olivia for 15 years. A year into the lease, Olivia is dispossessed by Sylvia. How does adverse possession operate after Sylvia has been there for 12 years? One initial point is that Norman is unaffected: adverse possession operates only against those whose interests are in possession. Time runs against future interests (including landlords) only when they are in possession. It follows that Norman can recover the land after the 15-year lease has ended.

Taking unregistered land first, Sylvia gets a new title: she does not obtain Olivia's lease. If she had obtained the lease, she would be treated as a tenant of Norman and therefore liable on the covenants in the lease. These results cannot apply to Sylvia because she has a new title; she cannot, for example, be liable for rent. This was established in the seminal decision in *Tichborne* v *Weir*[13] (Extract 4.2.19). Though the result appears inconvenient, it confers limited benefit upon Sylvia. Unless she complies with the covenants (including payment of rent), Norman can terminate the lease by forfeiting it.[14]

Turning to registered leases (which are much more common today), the outcome is quite different. Sylvia will be registered as proprietor of the lease (rather than a fee simple) and will be able to sue and be sued on the covenants. This looks by far the simpler and most appropriate outcome.

Another problem arises after Sylvia has gained title by adverse possession. Can Olivia surrender the lease to Norman, so as to bring it to an end? If she could do so, then Norman could rely on his fee simple (now conferring immediate rights to the land) to recover the land from Sylvia. The main problem is whether Olivia has a lease to surrender after adverse possession is complete. We will start with the position for unregistered land.

The House of Lords in *St Marylebone Property Co Ltd* v *Fairweather*[15] (Extract 4.2.21) grappled with the problem. What is the status of the lease after the completion of adverse possession? It cannot be said to be held by Sylvia, as *Tichborne* establishes that the adverse possessor has a new and different title (a fee simple). It might seem attractive to treat the lease as destroyed by adverse possession. Unfortunately, that wouldn't work to Sylvia's advantage: it would enable Norman to take possession immediately. The only remaining possibility is for the lease to be extinguished as regards Sylvia (the normal effect of adverse possession), but to survive as regards Norman. That was the approach adopted by the House of Lords. They therefore concluded that Olivia could surrender the lease to Norman, whereupon Norman could recover the land. The result is widely viewed as odd, as Sylvia's rights are taken away by the agreement between Olivia and Norman.

In registered land, we have seen that the lease is vested in Sylvia if adverse possession is successful under the Schedule 6 procedures. As it is vested in Sylvia, only she can surrender the lease: the *Fairweather* analysis ceases to operate.

Fixtures

The law of fixtures deals with the fixing of moveable objects to land. Let us consider a very simple and typical sort of example.

[13] (1892) 67 LT 735.
[14] Forfeiture of leases is considered in Chapter 14.
[15] [1963] AC 510 (Lord Morris dissented).

> Frank, the owner of a house, installs a new and expensive bath in his bathroom. The bath is very clearly a **fixture** (applying principles considered below) and becomes part of the land. If he contracts to sell the house to Geraldine, then Geraldine is entitled to the bath. Frank cannot (in the gap between the contract and the later transfer to her) remove the bath and substitute a cheaper one. A contrasting example is wiring in an electric cooker. The degree of connection of electrical items such as cookers is not such as to make them fixtures. Even after Frank contracts to sell the land, the cooker can be removed and there is no need for him to provide any substitute. If Geraldine wants to acquire the cooker, she will need to specify this in the contract.

We will consider a number of issues relating to fixtures. The first concerns the circumstances in which status as a fixture is important (sale of the land has just been seen to be one example). Next is the question of when an object is a fixture – how and why do we distinguish between baths and cookers? Finally, we ask when fixtures can be removed. This is most commonly an issue when tenants have installed fixtures. Can they be removed when the lease ends?

■ The significance of fixtures

We shall consider three situations. The first two involve fixtures being installed by the owner of the land; the third involves installation by non-owners, tenants for example.

Fixtures installed by the owner of the land who owns the fixtures

The immediate effect of installing the fixture is small: the owner can remove it the following day! It becomes important when somebody else acquires an interest in the land, as in the above example when Geraldine buys from Frank. Similar reasoning applies if Frank leases the land to Harry: the fixture becomes part of the land to which Harry is entitled. Frank cannot remove it. Although the same applies to mortgages (whether before or after the installation), it is unrealistic to say that fixtures can never be removed. Otherwise, householders could not replace a cracked bath without consulting their building society! There is an implied permission for the owner (mortgagor) to remove fixtures in the normal course of the upkeep and improvement of houses.

Fixtures installed by the owner of the land who does not own the fixtures

Again, the fixture is part of the house and is owned by the owner of the land. The original fixture owner has lost it. That is the land law answer, though there may well be tort liability for wrongfully using the property of another.

Most cases have concerned objects hired to the owner of the land, usually in a business setting. The rules whereby objects become fixtures are frequently inconsistent with the wishes of the fixture owner. In *Re Samuel Allen & Sons Ltd*[16] (Extract 4.3.13), machinery was

---

[16] [1907] 1 Ch 575.

acquired under a hire purchase agreement.[17] The agreement stipulated that the seller of the machinery had a right to remove it. This right to remove was effective to bind a subsequent mortgagee of the land (the right to remove is a proprietary interest binding successors in title). Though a mortgagee would normally acquire the machinery as a fixture, this was effectively defeated by the right to remove.

Fixtures installed by non-owners of the land

Nearly all the cases have involved non-owners who are tenants under leases or (in the past) holders of life interests. The theoretical position is that the fixture belongs to the owner of the land. To make a gift of the fixture to the owner rarely meets the expectations of the parties. It also has the undesirable effect of discouraging improvement of the land. In response to these concerns, the law permits certain types of fixture to be removed (considered below).

When is there a fixture?

Unsurprisingly, fixing an object to the land provides the prima facie answer, the only issue being the degree of fixing required. In his classic analysis of the area in *Holland* v *Hodgson*[18] (Extract 4.3.2), Blackburn J starts by stressing the role of fixing the object. However, intention is also crucial. He provides these instructive examples:

1. A dry stone wall. With such walls, stones are placed on top of each other, without any fixing or cement. The nature of a wall, nevertheless, is such that it is intended to be permanent. This is a fixture, despite the stones not being connected to the land save by gravity;

2. An anchor embedded in the underwater soil to hold a ship steady. It is clear that the fixing is temporary, designed to benefit the ship and is readily undone. Despite the physical fixing, this is not a fixture and the shipowner does not lose ownership of the anchor.

A question that has given rise to constant difficulty is as to when intention will overcome a small amount of fixing. In *Holland* itself, machinery firmly nailed to a factory floor was held to constitute a fixture. The contrary conclusion is reached for carpets tacked to a floor. Although the situations look similar, carpets can very easily be removed. The test is sometimes said to be whether the fixing is designed to make the object part of the structure or to allow the object to be enjoyed. This might be useful for some decorative objects, but it provides little help on the facts of *Holland*.

The nature of the relevant intention was considered in *Melluish* v *BMI (No 3) Ltd*[19] (Extract 4.3.9). The House of Lords established that it is irrelevant whether or not an object was intended to be a fixture: the law determines what is a fixture. Intention is relevant

---

[17] Hire purchase is used for purchase on credit. Ownership of the object passes at a later stage when the purchase money has been paid. In the meantime, the buyer is a hirer of the object.

[18] (1872) LR 7 CP 328 at p. 335 (Exchequer Chamber). For the earlier law, see Luther (2004) 24 OxJLS 597.

[19] [1996] AC 454 at p. 473.

only in so far as it shows the purpose of fixing. Take the carpet example. Carpets are fixed to the floor to stop them from slipping, not for any purpose showing that they form part of the house.

Two factors may be of use in deciding some cases. It can happen that a loosely fixed object may be part of something else which is clearly a fixture. A simple example is provided by a toilet. The lid to the cistern can often be lifted off: it rests there by its weight alone. Yet it is obvious that it forms part of the toilet and nobody doubts that the toilet is a fixture. The second factor is whether any significant damage will be caused by removing the object. The courts are quick to conclude that there is a fixture if such damage is likely.

Among normal household objects, baths, cookers and carpets have been mentioned. *Botham* v *TSB Bank plc*[20] provides useful guidance as to how fixtures principles apply to many household objects. As well as baths, fitted kitchen units were treated as fixtures. These are objects that one expects to be part of houses, as well as being firmly fixed to the house. However, items such as cookers, refrigerators and washing machines (even if in fitted units) are not fixtures. They can readily be removed without significant damage and are not generally viewed as part of the house. Likewise, carpets, curtains and most light fittings were also held not to be fixtures.

So far we have considered what may be described as 'lightly fixed' objects. When, apart from dry stone walls, will objects be fixtures without being physically fixed to the land? There are few examples, though an interesting one is a house which rests on piles or pillars (a common building method in some parts of the world). More controversially, *D'Eyncourt* v *Gregory*[21] (Extract 4.3.4) held that unfixed objects such as carved figures and vases were part of the architectural design of a house and therefore fixtures. The theory looks sound, but the same result has very rarely been reached in later cases. The courts are reluctant to conclude that there is a fixture without some degree of fixing.

● Rights to remove fixtures

This section considers rights of tenants and life interest holders to remove fixtures, ignoring any express terms in the lease or **settlement**. Let us take two examples, in each of which there is a fixture. The first is a life interest holder who fixes tapestries to walls. The second is a shopkeeper tenant who fixes counters and display cabinets for his stock. In both cases, it would seem unduly generous to the owner of the land to allow him to make a windfall profit at the expense of the life interest holder or tenant. Equally seriously, occupiers would be discouraged from improving the land.

The courts have evolved rules whereby trade or ornamental fixtures can be removed; these rules apply to both examples just given. Trade fixtures are those fixed in the course of carrying out a trade and would cover the shopkeeper example. Tapestries would be ornamental fixtures. Relatively minor damage is not a problem, so long as it is made good. However, it should be noted that not all fixtures fall within the trade and ornamental

---

[20] (1996) 73 P&CR D1.
[21] (1866) LR 3 Eq 382.

categories. Suppose a tenant replaces the main window of a shop. This is an integral part of the premises and cannot be removed; it is called a 'landlord's fixture'.

A final point to remember is that the tenant can run two arguments. The first is that there is no fixture in the first place. If this succeeds, then the tenant can remove the object. Some earlier cases showed reluctance to find an intention to fix in the leasehold setting, but that probably does not survive the *Melluish* analysis of intention as discussed above. A tenant who fails in the first argument can fall back on the second: the right to remove trade or ornamental fixtures.

Assessing the law on fixtures

Every system of law has to deal with objects affixed to land. It is inconceivable that a house built on land could be viewed as a pile of bricks, separately owned and being capable of being reclaimed separately from the land. The more difficult questions are whether the courts employ the most appropriate tests for what counts as a fixture and whether the consequences are appropriate.

On the first point, the examples given in *Holland* demonstrate that the physical act of fixing cannot be determinative in all cases. Nevertheless, it has also been seen that the intention test is difficult to apply. To aid certainty, it seems preferable to concentrate on the level of fixing, allowing intention to come into play when there is a low level of fixing, easily undone.

So far as removal is concerned, the law seems to allow reasonable rights of removal by tenants and holders of life interests. These are persons who have most to lose from the law of fixtures. However, it has been observed that some objects (windows, central heating, lifts) cannot be removed. That seems reasonable on account of the damage involved, but it means that no compensation is payable. That outcome might be regarded as rather harsh, though it may be a comment on the law relating to leases as much as on the law relating to fixtures.

Questions to consider

1. What is adverse possession? Can it be justified today?

2. When will adverse possession lead to ownership of registered land? Is there much difference from the law before 2002?

3. What is required for adverse possession to be shown? What happens if the owner has no present use for the land?

4. Why may it be important whether there is a fixture?

5. What is the role of intention in deciding whether an object has become a fixture?

6. Can fixtures ever be removed?

Further reading

Adverse possession

Cobb and Fox (2007) 27 LS 236: Living outside the system? The (im)morality of urban squatting after the Land Registration Act 2002.

Dockray, M [1985] Conv 272: Why do we need adverse possession?

Radley-Gardner, O (2005) 25 OxJLS 727: Civilized squatting.

Wade, H W R (1962) 78 LQR 541: Landlord, tenant and squatter.

Fixtures

Guest, A and Lever, J (1963) 27 Conv 30: Hire-purchase, equipment leases and fixtures.

Luther, P (2004) 24 OxJLS 597: Fixtures and chattels: a question of more or less . . .

Visit **www.mylawchamber.co.uk** to access tools to help you develop and test your knowledge of land law, including interactive multiple choice questions, practice exam questions with guidance, weblinks, glossary flashcards, legal newsfeed and legal updates.

Use **Case Navigator** to read in full some of the key cases referenced in this chapter with commentary and questions:

JA Pye (Oxford) Ltd v *Graham* [2003] 1 AC 419

JA Pye (Oxford) Ltd v *United Kingdom* (2007) 46 EHRR 1083

7 Transfer and creation of interests in land

The importance of formalities

This chapter deals with interests created by the owner of the land: derivative acquisition. The most important question relates to the **formalities** required by statute before a **disposition** can be effective. It will be seen that writing is generally essential and that a special form of document – a deed – is required before most legal rights can be created. Formalities are required in order to guard against the casual (and possibly unintended) creation of interests, as well as to prevent the false assertion that an interest has been created. Nevertheless, formalities requirements can themselves be abused – the owner may deny an interest that he clearly intended to create.

Much of the interest in formality rules lies in how strictly they are enforced. Methods of avoiding the effects of formality rules are central to the following chapter on estoppel and the family home. Estoppel is the principle whereby a remedy is given to persons who have been led to assume that an interest exists and have, on that basis, acted to their detriment.

Many interests in land have to be registered before they can bind purchasers (this is considered in Chapter 10), but one aspect of registration will be considered here. Although implementation lies some years in the future, the Land Registration Act 2002 provides for the present formality rules to be replaced by the need to register electronically: without registration, nothing will be created. These electronic registration principles will have a huge impact on conventional formality ideas.

This chapter also considers the creation of trusts. Express trusts have to be in writing. Of particular interest to us will be two types of trust created by the courts: resulting and constructive trusts. Constructive trusts are imposed to avoid unconscionable (unfair) conduct by the owner. Resulting trusts have a more specific application. If a person transfers ownership without intending a gift, then the courts will say that the transferee holds on a resulting trust for the transferor.

A significant factor is that resulting and constructive trusts are effective without writing. Accordingly, these trusts can be employed both to assert an obligation and to avoid any formality problems. Their main rules are considered in this chapter. Perhaps their greatest importance for land lawyers lies in their application to the purchase of a family home, when the house is transferred to just one of a couple. A constructive trust enables the other partner to obtain an interest in the home in certain circumstances. This large topic is separately dealt with in Chapter 9.

The issues in this chapter are of vital importance to everybody dealing with land. The rules are designed to provide certainty for dealings with land and to avoid important obligations being entered into unwittingly. The reasons for formality obligations are further considered below. The consequence of failure to comply with formality requirements is that the transaction will fail. It is a common problem that individuals are unfamiliar with formality and registration requirements; their transactions may be ineffective as a result. It is important for students and lawyers to remember the impact of formality rules whenever they advise on the effects of what people have done, whatever area of land law (leases or easements, for example) is involved.

It should be added that we are concentrating on lifetime dispositions. On death, property passes by will. A will must be signed and also witnessed by two persons. As these rules are not specific to land, they will not be studied further.

The reasons for formality rules

This chapter is full of details of writing and deeds requirements. We need to be clear why we have such rules. The background position is that formalities are not generally required by common law or equity. Contracts can be entered into (or varied) orally and property can be sold or given away without writing. It makes no difference how valuable the contract or object is. If I were to own a £500,000 yacht, I could make a present of it (or contract to sell it) without any need for writing.

There are good reasons for requiring deeds for land transfers: for example, they provide certainty as to what is intended and limit the danger of entering into important transactions without giving them real thought. However, it must be remembered that formality requirements are themselves capable of causing injustice.

> Suppose that Rani is unaware of the law and simply signs a document transferring a house to her friend, Stephen, as a gift (we will see that this is not a deed). Stephen takes possession of the house and begins to update the wiring and plumbing. A year later they quarrel and Rani seeks possession of the land on the basis that, without a deed, there was no effective transfer. If she succeeds, Stephen loses his home and the money spent in improving it. Does the injustice he suffers outweigh the benefits that the formality rules are intended to produce? In severe cases, the courts may be able to neutralise such unfortunate effects of formalities. For example, Stephen may well be able to rely on estoppel. This makes formality rules more acceptable, but it inevitably leads to greater complications in the law and uncertainty as to exactly when the courts will intervene.

Especially because formality rules can themselves cause problems, it is important to understand why they are thought to play a useful role. We now turn to the arguments most commonly advanced.

Justifications

Avoiding fraud

The origins of our present rules lie in the Statute of Frauds 1677. The fraud contemplated is the false assertion that a transfer has been made or an obligation undertaken. In the above example this would be fraud by Stephen, if he had asserted a transfer by Rani which in fact had never taken place. If we require writing, then this risk is taken away (at least unless Stephen forged the document). Yet when the modern cases refer to fraud, it is usually the fraud of the person who tries to avoid an obligation by relying on failure to comply with formality requirements (fraud by Rani). There is little evidence in the modern law that obligations or dispositions are fraudulently asserted on a regular basis. Property other than land can be sold orally and given away by simply handing it over: there are few cases where sales or gifts have been fraudulently asserted.

The evidential function

Writing provides the best evidence of what the parties have agreed. The benefits of this are not limited to cases of fraud. There may be genuine uncertainty as to whether the parties had reached final agreement in a sale of land. Furthermore, the terms of an oral agreement or trust are likely to be shrouded in uncertainty. Putting them in writing will clarify exactly what was intended.

Consider an everyday contract for the sale of land. Without writing, the parties may be at odds as to when completion will take place, whether certain objects (whether or not fixtures) are included in the sale and whether the seller will be allowed to store surplus furniture on the land for a short period after sale.

The cautionary function

Many people believe, quite wrongly where land is not involved, that no liability can be incurred without writing. This can lead to their undertaking obligations without much thought. Writing cannot guarantee that an appropriate amount of thought is given to a transaction, but it helps to ensure that individuals appreciate that they are committing themselves. This becomes even stronger when we consider the requirements of deeds. The extra formality required (in particular, the need for a witness) renders it less likely that an obligation will be 'accidentally' undertaken. Indeed, it makes it more likely that a lawyer will be consulted, as the average person will not know how to create a deed. Having a lawyer limits the dangers of obligations being entered into without appreciating the consequences.

The channelling function

Formality requirements can help to ensure that the appropriate forms are used. This is most likely to apply if lawyers (or other professionals) are brought into the transaction. Where standard forms are used, they are unlikely to be ambiguous and they will cover all the common questions and problems that may arise from the transaction. Non-lawyers are, in contrast, likely to use wording which is difficult to interpret or include technical legal terms without understanding their significance. Formality rules cannot force people to use lawyers (nor should they), but there are good reasons to encourage people to take professional advice in suitable cases.

Contracts to sell land provide a good example. Lawyers invariably use a standard form of contract which sets out to deal with the many problems that may arise on the sale of land. These cover a host of circumstances that the buyer and seller are unlikely to think about, including detailed timescales and procedures for completion. Using a standard form enables the lawyers to concentrate on special terms which the parties have agreed (for example, that the seller is able to remove rose bushes of sentimental value).

Are the justifications convincing?

These justifications are persuasive: they are not silly points. Whether they are sufficiently convincing to justify our formality rules is another matter. Even when formality rules are not complied with, it is common for there to be no doubt that an obligation has been undertaken and what its terms are. This does not protect it from failure. We will see that many cases illustrate formality rules being used to get out of dispositions and obligations that have been deliberately undertaken.

The system works because the courts are prepared to use constructive trusts and estoppels to avoid the worst effects of the formality rules. It may be thought unfortunate that the courts have had to develop these principles without any guidance from the legislation establishing formality requirements. This has led to much uncertainty and litigation as to exactly when the courts will intervene.

A more specific question is whether we can justify having special rules for land transactions: the justifications above are not couched in terms specific to land. One point is that land transactions are inherently complex, partly because more varied interests can exist in land than in other forms of property. This means that several of the justifications carry greater force as regards land.

A second point is that, for many individuals, their home is their most important asset (both financially and as regards its role in their lives). The cautionary function, in particular, is very important in this respect. It may be true that some yachts and diamonds can be worth more than many small houses, but it would be wrong to overlook the significance of land, especially as a home.

A third point is that many land transactions can be undertaken without their being obvious from the land itself. In contrast, most sales and gifts of other objects are accompanied by a change in possession of the objects. Especially where no change in possession is involved (the wide range of interests in land makes this quite common), we can justify looking for some degree of corroboration from writing.

A final and rather different point is that modern land law is based on the entry of dispositions and contracts on the register. This would be far more difficult to operate if transactions could be entered into orally: how could the land registry be sure that an interest is valid? We shall see below that formalities are likely to be overtaken by electronic entries on the register. As the registration system applies only to land, it inevitably follows that these new electronic ways of creating and dealing with interests are unique to land.

Transfers of land

Nearly all sales of land take effect in two legal stages: a contract for the sale of land and the actual transfer or **conveyance** of land. One reason for this is that it takes time for the purchaser to make the necessary checks to ensure that there are no legal problems. The contract provides an assurance for both parties that the sale will go through and clarifies the obligations imposed on each party. If the contract is to bind purchasers, it must be registered (see Chapter 10).

The contract is not entered into as soon as a price is agreed. It is very unwise for a buyer to enter a contract until checks have been undertaken to ensure that the property has no problems. For example, it would be disastrous if a local authority had plans to demolish it in order to construct a new road. It has long been common to make all correspondence 'subject to contract'. This is effective to ensure that there is no contract, though writing requirements have since 1989 produce the same result (this is discussed below). Making enquiries and dealing with any problems is likely to take at least a month and can mean that the contract is not ready to be entered into until close to the transfer.

At the pre-contract stage, neither party can be sure that the sale will go through. This causes great problems if the seller pulls out in order to accept a higher offer from somebody else (gazzumping – common when house prices are rising) or the buyer pulls out in order to buy another house. This provides one of the main sources of criticism of the house-buying process.

Commonly there is a two- to three-month delay between a price being agreed and the final transfer (the stage often described as **completion**). This gap provides time for sellers to obtain alternative housing and buyers to find the necessary loan finance and to sell their existing homes. Nevertheless, the process is widely viewed as unnecessarily protracted. Attempts are being made to shorten the time period, mainly by ensuring that the seller provides all the essential information before a price is agreed.

Contracts for the sale of land

Section 2 of the Law of Property (Miscellaneous Provisions) Act 1989 (the 1989 Act) (Extract 5.2.3) requires contracts for the sale of land to be in writing, signed by both parties. This applies to all contracts to transfer or create legal interests, including contracts to transfer (assign) or create leases. It is different from previous legislation and establishes stricter formality requirements.

How does the 1989 Act apply to the typical house purchase? It is common for contracts to be drawn up in duplicate agreements: each contains detailed standard terms (two A4 pages of very small print) covering the sorts of points that can go wrong in a purchase transaction. Each party signs one of the duplicate agreements and gives it to the other: this is called exchange of contracts. The 1989 Act makes it clear that this procedure is as effective as if both parties signed a single document. However, the Court of Appeal in *Commission for the New Towns* v *Cooper (Great Britain) Ltd*[1] (Extract 5.2.9) held that it does not suffice simply to have a contract by correspondence.

> Suppose Andy writes to Beth, offering to buy her house for £175,000. Beth replies, accepting this offer. Although they have both signed documents, the 1989 Act is not satisfied: they have neither signed a single contract nor exchanged contracts containing all the terms.

The law takes this strict approach because we want parties to be well aware of what they are doing before they bind themselves to buy and sell land: this is more likely if the specified procedures are followed.

We will now consider in more detail what contracts are caught by the 1989 Act and what the writing must include. We also need to investigate the effect of failure to comply with the Act.

What agreements are caught?

It has been observed that all contracts for the sale or creation of legal interests are caught. Short leases provide an exception. We will see later that most leases not exceeding three years require no formalities. The 1989 Act provides that contracts for such leases similarly do not require writing. However, assigning such a lease does require writing.

Options have been held to require writing. Options are rights to buy (or, less commonly, sell) land. The exercise of the option gives rise to full contractual duties to buy and sell the land. The 1989 Act does not apply to the exercise of the option: that is a unilateral act by the buyer. It is only the initial creation of the option that has to be signed by both seller and buyer. More difficulty is posed by agency contracts.

> Andrew agrees with Brian that he will sell land to whomever Brian introduces. This will not be caught; instead, the 1989 Act will apply to the future contract between the introduced person and Andrew. On the other hand, it appears that a contract between Andrew and Brian to sell to Charlotte will be caught. This is because Charlotte's right to a conveyance derives directly from the Andrew–Brian contract.

Boundary agreements have also received attention. Suppose that the boundary between the gardens of two neighbours is unclear. If they agree that it should be in a certain place, this does not require writing. They are not consciously transferring land to each other but working out where the boundary line should fall. This seems a practical and acceptable solution to an everyday sort of problem.

What must the writing include?

The simple answer is that all terms must be included; otherwise the contract (not merely the omitted term) will be ineffective. This can cause substantial difficulty if, for example,

---

[1] [1995] Ch 259 at pp. 283–9 and 292–5.

the parties fail to tell their lawyers that they have agreed that the sale price includes the curtains. There is then every probability that the agreement produced by the lawyers will omit the curtains term and that the whole agreement may be void.

However, there are ways of getting around this sort of problem. The Law Commission thought that it might be possible to rectify the contract to include the missing term.[2] This is an application of normal contract principles whereby rectification can correct mistakes. It might apply to the curtains example, though not if the parties deliberately keep the term out of the written contract or believe that it is unnecessary to have it in writing.[3]

Another possibility is that there may be two separate contracts. Recent cases[4] have established that a single commercial agreement can be split into two parts: a contract for the sale of land and a separate contract (the latter not requiring writing). However, it is essential that the sale agreement is freestanding, in the sense that it is not conditional upon performance of the other contract. This can be achieved by a term which states that the land contract is the entire agreement between the parties (this does not prevent there being a separate contract unrelated to the land contract). The earlier example about curtains cannot be viewed as a separate contract, as they were to be included within the sale price.

A related point concerns collateral contracts, which the Law Commission thought to be separate. The collateral contract is best explained by an example.

Olivia orally agrees to sell her house to Pia, whose survey reveals rotten wood in the back door. Pia tells Olivia that she will not proceed with the purchase unless the door is replaced. Olivia agrees, but none of this finds its way into a later written contract to sell the house. In this example we may say that there is a separate collateral contract: Pia agrees to enter a contract to buy the house if Olivia undertakes to replace the door. The collateral contract certainly refers to the contract of sale, but can still be seen as separate. On that basis, there is a valid written contract to sell the house and a valid oral contract for the door to be replaced.

Separate and collateral contracts reveal obvious tensions in this area. The courts are unwilling to water down the statutory requirement that all the terms be in the written contract. At the same time, they are reluctant to allow unmeritorious attempts to avoid liability, simply because some insignificant aspect of the parties' agreement has not found itself into the written contract. They are also aware that sale of land is frequently a small part of a larger commercial deal. To insist that the entire deal is part of the land contract would be unrealistic.

Failure to comply with the 1989 Act

Without the necessary writing there is no contract. The pre-1989 law took a more relaxed approach in allowing enforcement by a person who had undertaken acts of *part performance*

---

[2] Law Com No 164, para 5.6 (this report led to the 1989 Act).
[3] *Francis v Berndes Ltd* [2012] 11 EG 94.
[4] The most recent are *North Eastern Properties Ltd* v *Coleman* [2010] 1 WLR 2715 (Extract 5.2.8) and *Keay* v *Morris Homes (West Midlands) Ltd* [2012] 1WLR 2855.

to the knowledge of the other. Although part performance does not survive the 1989 Act, there is scope for slightly similar doctrines. If a person is allowed to act to their detriment on the supposition that there is a valid contract, they may bring a claim based upon a constructive trust or estoppel. These remedies require proof of detriment, which is more demanding than was part performance. This area is discussed in the following chapter. Suffice to say at this stage that the courts are wary about any widespread use of these remedies to circumvent the 1989 Act.

Transferring the land

We now move on to the completion stage: the time when the buyer pays the purchase price and acquires the land. The transfer document was traditionally called a conveyance, though for registered land we refer to transfers. An important consideration for registered land is that the transfer has to be registered before a legal title is obtained. Without registration, the purchaser obtains no more than an equitable right to the land.

For both unregistered and registered land, the Law of Property Act 1925 (LPA), section 52 requires transfers to be by **deed**. This is part of a wider rule that legal estates and interests in land must be created by deed. Without a deed, the transfer is ineffective to create a legal interest (unregistered land) or authorise registration (registered land). What is a deed? Traditionally, deeds had to be signed, sealed and delivered (they are sometimes called documents under seal). These rules were relaxed by section 1 of the 1989 Act (Extract 5.1.1). No seal is required, but a new rule is that the document must be witnessed by a person present at the time it is signed.

Given that a seal is no longer required, how do we tell whether a document is a deed? The 1989 Act states that 'An instrument shall not be a deed unless . . . it makes it clear on its face that it is intended to be a deed'. It seems unlikely that a document (even if witnessed) will be a deed unless it describes itself as a deed.

The requirements of signature and witnessing are moderately clear. But what is meant by requiring that it be delivered? 'Delivered' is a misleading word. It does not require physical handing over of the document to the other party. Rather, it means only an intention to be bound by the deed. However, a delivered deed may be conditional on some future event. A seller will usually sign the transfer in advance of completion, enabling the seller time to set about moving home while the lawyers finalise the legal details. The signing of the transfer does not immediately shift ownership. It is conditional on completion and does not take effect until that time.

Before leaving deeds, it might be added that they are useful in areas unrelated to land. For example, they can be used to create obligations (usually described as covenants). Deeds are especially useful because, unlike normal contracts, no consideration is required.

Creating interests in land

In this section we consider the formality requirements for creating interests such as leases and mortgages. We have already looked at estate contracts, which must be in writing.

Legal interests

LPA section 52 requires a deed. Without a deed there can at most be an equitable interest (based upon a contract, where there is one). Especially as regards leases, the need for a deed is commonly overlooked (by the parties and by students in answering problems!). However, the tenant will have an **equitable lease** if there was a contract for a lease which satisfies the 1989 Act writing requirements.

LPA section 54(2) provides an important relaxation of this deed requirement for short leases. Even oral leases are effective as legal estates if 'taking effect in possession for a term not exceeding three years . . . at the best rent which can be reasonably obtained without taking a **fine**'. The three-year maximum is straightforward, but it is not the only requirement. The first to consider is 'best rent . . . without taking a fine.' The best rent requirement usually causes no difficulty, as short leases are generally created at a full rent. The phrase 'without taking a fine' means that no capital sum must be paid.

Peter might lease a house to Queenie for two years with (i) a rent of £10,000 a year; or (ii) £1,000 paid now and £9,500 a year rent; or (iii) £19,000 paid now and no (or nominal) rent; or (iv) a rent of £3,000 a year. The final situation is outside section 54(2) because the rent is clearly not the best rent. The second and third situations also fall outside section 54(2) because the capital payments of £1,000 and £19,000 constitute fines. Only the first situation does not require a deed.

The final requirement for section 54(2) to apply is that the lease must take effect in possession. *Long* v *Tower Hamlets LBC*[5] (Extract 5.3.4) held that the lease must take effect in possession at the time it is created, with the three years being counted from that time. *Long* involved a lease to take effect in about three weeks' time. It would last (including those three weeks) for less than three years; under the pre-1925 law that would have meant that a deed was not required. However, James Munby QC held that since 1925, applying the clear wording of section 54(2), the lease must take effect immediately. The three-week delay was fatal to its being in possession.

However well justified by the statute, that result may be regarded as unfortunate – it is very common for leases to start a short time in the future. It gives rise to some very awkward distinctions.

Suppose Andy has a flat available for occupation from 1 September. In May he advertises it as available and reaches oral agreement that month with Bella (a student) for her to lease it for a year from 1 September. This could be interpreted in two ways. The first is that there is a lease to take effect from 1 September. In the absence of a deed, **Long** holds that this will be ineffective as a legal lease. Alternatively, they may agree that Andy will give Bella a lease on 1 September. This is a contract for a lease. As the lease will not exceed three years and, when

➡

[5] [1998] Ch 197.

> created, take effect in possession (it will be created and take effect on 1 September), neither lease nor contract requires any formality. These two possibilities (future lease; contract for a lease) will in practice be extremely difficult to distinguish, especially if there is no writing.

Why do we relax formality requirements for short leases? Three points spring to mind. Short leases (like the student lease Bella was taking) are frequently entered into without legal advice. Many people would be unaware of any requirement of a deed, so they would not use deeds. It would be unfortunate to make it difficult to create legal leases in this sort of situation, thereby penalising innocent parties such as Bella. Next, we shall see (in Chapter 13) that the courts sometimes imply leases from the payment of rent. This would be difficult if all leases had to be by deed. Finally, the presence of a full rent means that any future purchasers of the land, who are bound by the lease, will at least receive rent.

Do these points justify the recognition of oral leases? It may be proper not to require a deed, but should we not expect the parties to use writing? If we were to change the law in that way, short implied leases would need exemption.

Equitable interests

Declarations of trust will be separately considered later in this chapter. LPA section 53(1)(a) requires writing for all other equitable interests (including restrictive covenants and equitable **charges**).

Electronic conveyancing

The law on **land registration** was reformed by the Land Registration Act 2002, which will be studied in Chapter 10. A significant element of the reforms lies in the introduction of electronic registration (e-conveyancing). The new rules will apply to most land transactions: the word 'conveyancing' gives a misleadingly narrow impression. Generally, this book contains little about the mechanics of how land is sold. Nevertheless, e-conveyancing will have a significant and growing impact on the rules discussed in this chapter. Indeed, it will be seen that most of them will simply disappear and the remainder will apply only infrequently.

The introduction of e-conveyancing involves a lot of preparatory work: the 2002 Act did no more than provide an outline framework. In 2011, the land registry announced that it was ceasing, for the time being, work on the project. This was based upon the collapse in the volume of conveyancing, resulting from economic difficulties. This meant that it was too fraught a setting in which to introduce radical changes (especially as they would initially be optional). It is unclear how great the delay will be, but the subject is given a relatively brief treatment below. It might be added that the land registry is continuing to engage with electronic developments and, in particular, electronic applications – though this is less ambitious than e-conveyancing.

Before explaining what e-conveyancing involves, it is helpful to understand the current methods of transferring registered land.

> Vera is selling her house to William. At completion, Vera will execute a transfer of the land to William, who takes possession. William will send the transfer to the land registry to be registered. Once the land registry has checked that all is in order (it frequently isn't), William will be registered as proprietor. Only at that stage does William obtain the legal title.

Under e-conveyancing, there will be no transfer document and no application to the land registry. Instead, Vera's solicitor will directly instruct the land registry's computer to enter William as the new proprietor (as we describe the holder of the registered title). A press on the return button of a computer will replace all the pre-2002 stages. E-conveyancing is designed to speed and simplify the conveyancing process in a computerised age. It brings several welcome consequences, one being that it obliterates the 'registration gap' between completion and registration – this gap can at present cause real problems for purchasers.

E-conveyancing represents a radical change in how conveyancing is conducted and how the registration system operates. It was described by the Law Commission as a 'Conveyancing Revolution'.[6] Registered titles have been held in computerised forms for several years. By visiting the land registry website[7] and entering your postcode you can see whether your home is registered. If it is (nearly 95 per cent are), then you can get a copy of the register for £4.

In the years immediately after the 2002 Act, the initial stages consisted of designing the system and educating the legal profession. The plans involved no single 'big-bang' commencement. The land registry has already introduced online facilities for a few specific transactions (discharge of repaid mortgages, for example), with a significant extension to electronic mortgages (e-charges) in 2009. Despite the postponement of e-conveyancing, these developments may be expected to grow.

Electronic Communications Act 2000

This legislation covers a very wide sphere of activities, of which land transactions form a small part. Section 8 will enable transactions to be carried out electronically, replacing requirements such as writing. A statutory instrument would activate section 8 for contracts for the sale of land. This will remove the normal writing requirements imposed by the 1989 Act. We appear to use s 8 for these purposes (rather than the LRA provisions discussed below) because it can apply to both registered and unregistered land.

Land Registration Act 2002, section 91

Section 91 (Extract 5.3.7) is the provision under which all other e-conveyancing will be introduced. It permits dispositions to be undertaken in electronic form, with electronic

[6] The title of Law Com No 271. The proposals are summarised in paras 2.41–2.68 and discussed in Part XIII.
[7] http://www.landreg.gov.uk/

signatures being effective in the place of written signatures. The word 'dispositions' is broad, though it seems not to include contracts (hence the need for section 8 of the 2000 Act).

In the early years e-conveyancing is most likely to apply to charges, transfers and leases. When a disposition is undertaken in electronic form, the normal requirements of writing and deeds become unnecessary. Here we begin to see the impact on the rules discussed earlier: they become optional rather than compulsory for transactions to which e-conveyancing applies.

It was observed above that e-conveyancing will operate (as regards transfers) so as to pass ownership to the purchaser directly. This achieves more than replacing the present deed of transfer: the register is simultaneously changed so that the buyer is the registered proprietor. It may be best seen as a tripartite transaction involving buyer, seller and land registry. This is not obvious from the wording of section 91, which concentrates on making the electronic disposition as good as if it were by deed.

Land Registration Act 2002, section 93

The above provisions establish e-conveyancing as an option for those dealing with land. However, it is intended that e-conveyancing shall become the only way of dealing with land. This is authorised by section 93, but it will not be implemented until e-conveyancing has become established, solicitors are used to operating it and any flaws in the system have been ironed out.

Section 93 (Extract 5.3.7) provides that a disposition or contract 'only has effect' if created electronically and is communicated electronically to the land registry. There are three issues to consider: the scope of section 93, the effect of failure to use e-conveyancing and the effect of e-conveyancing on formality and other land law rules.

The scope of section 93

An initial point is that, unlike section 91, section 93 applies to contracts as well as dispositions. As with section 91, a statutory instrument will identify exactly what is covered. The list of interests will be especially crucial for section 93. It is easy to say that a transaction *may* be undertaken electronically (section 91), but quite different to say that it *must* be so undertaken (section 93). Suppose the scope of electronic e-conveyancing is (eventually) set very wide. As regards section 91, this causes almost no problems should few people choose to use it for a particular type of transaction. However, failure to use e-conveyancing when section 93 applies is disastrous: we shall see that the transaction fails completely.

The legislation provides no clue as to what dispositions will be excluded from the operation of section 93. However, the Law Commission has made suggestions.[8] They list four categories:

1. **Rights not requiring express grant.** These include rights by estoppel, implied and prescriptive easements and adverse possession. As no writing is required to create such rights, it would be utterly unrealistic to require them to be created electronically

[8] Law Com No 254, para 11.12.

and unjust to render them invalid. Indeed, some of them are created by the court or legislation rather than by any disposition between the parties; estoppel is one example.

2. **Dispositions taking effect by operation of law.** These cover death (passing to **personal representatives**) and bankruptcy (passing to the trustee in bankruptcy – the person who administers the assets of the bankrupt individual).

3. **Interests under trusts.** The general approach is that trusts are excluded from the register, though an entry can be made to ensure that the land is properly dealt with. It is most defensible that resulting and constructive trusts should operate without electronic creation. They are created by the courts and are exempt from writing requirements.[9] However, the category is not limited to those trusts.

4. **Overriding interest leases.** These are short leases, not exceeding seven years. As many leases not exceeding three years can be created without writing, frequently without solicitors being involved, it would seem wrong to insist on electronic registration.

This list shows that, apart from express trusts and short leases, all express dispositions are likely to be caught. Another way of looking at it is that whenever writing is presently required, e-conveyancing will usually become compulsory; express trusts form the only exception. This illustrates the huge scope that e-conveyancing is expected to have.

The effect of failure to use e-conveyancing

Present registration rules provide that an interest binds a purchaser only if it is protected on the register. However, it remains an interest in the land despite failure to protect it. Section 93 is quite different; it states that a disposition or contract 'only has effect' if e-conveyancing is used. Without e-conveyancing, there is no interest at all. In this respect the rules operate far more like formality rules than registration rules. Indeed, it appears that there are not even any contractual obligations between the parties.

It does not take too much imagination to realise that that there will be many occasions when the parties fail to use e-conveyancing. This is most likely if they do not use solicitors for the transaction.

Suppose Garry sells land to Harry. Garry transfers the land to Harry by a deed, in return for the purchase price. The transfer is ineffective because it is not an electronic transfer as required by section 93. It would be monstrous if Garry could keep the sale price and deny Harry any right to the land. One may predict the use of constructive trusts and estoppels (discussed in this and the following chapters) to avoid such unconscionable conduct by Garry.

The impact of e-conveyancing

E-conveyancing will obviously result in significant changes in the ways in which land transactions are undertaken. However, in this section we are more interested in its effect on legal principles. Two issues are now considered.

---

[9] LPA, s 53(2).

The first concerns the impact on land registration. This will be considered in Chapter 10, but one example is given here.

Andrew contracts to lease land to Briony, but then sells it to Clare (who registers the transfer). Briony has been allowed to occupy the land, but has not protected her estate contract on the register. Under present principles, we would say that Briony can assert her estate contract against Clare. This is because she has an interest in the land which is protected by virtue of her being in actual occupation of the land.[10] Under electronic conveyancing, section 93 will ensure that she has no interest at all. It follows that there is nothing that her actual occupation can protect; Clare can evict her.

The second issue returns to the concerns of this chapter: most of our formality rules can be forgotten. E-conveyancing will be limited to registered land, but by the time that section 93 is activated nearly all titles will be registered. Not only will the old requirements become optional (the effect of the 2002 Act and section 91), but the old methods of deeds and writing will be useless. This was seen in the above example concerning Harry and Garry: the use of a deed to transfer the land has zero effect.

Trusts

Express declarations of trust

The owner of any property can declare themselves a trustee. For land (but not other assets), LPA section 53(1)(b) requires the declaration to be evidenced in writing. Suppose that Sally owns a house, which she wants to be held on trust for her infant nieces Theresa and Ursula. She could transfer the land to trustees (the transfer requires a deed), declaring the trusts in the deed. Alternatively, she could simply sign a piece of paper along the lines: 'I hereby declare myself a trustee of 23 Acacia Avenue, Elsfield, for Theresa and Ursula.'

Trusts not requiring writing

LPA section 53(2) establishes that resulting, implied and constructive trusts can arise without any writing. These trusts are sometimes imposed in situations in which there is no element of avoiding formalities. Perhaps the best example of this is where a trustee makes a profit out of the position of trustee – as where a trustee receives a bribe for selling trust assets to the briber. Equity requires the trustee to hold the bribe on a **constructive trust** for the beneficiaries. It would frustrate the imposition of liability to say that there could be no trust as there is no writing.

Constructive trusts can be used where injustice would result if formality requirements were strictly insisted upon.

---

[10] LRA, s 29 and Sched 3, para 2.

Suppose George transfers land to his friend Harriet on the oral understanding that Harriet is to hold on trust for George's grandson Ivor. A few days later, Harriet has an argument with George and proceeds to deny any liability to Ivor, asserting that the land is hers. The courts are quite clear that it is fraudulent for Harriet to claim the land for herself, when it was only transferred to her because she agreed to hold for Ivor. To avoid such conduct (usually described as unconscionable conduct), the courts impose a constructive trust. This constructive trust gives effect to an obligation which lack of writing initially rendered ineffective. Although it avoids the normal effect of lack of formalities, it is justified by the objective of avoiding unconscionable conduct.

We should contrast the situation in which George simply tells Ivor that he is holding the land on trust for him. This oral declaration of trust is ineffective. This time, there is no unconscionable conduct if George changes his mind. We might feel that George has acted badly, especially as he has told Ivor, but (unlike Harriet) he has not benefited from inducing somebody to part with property. There is no constructive trust.

We will now turn to the situations in which resulting and constructive trusts are imposed, concentrating on situations relevant to formality issues. The application of trust principles to the family home setting is postponed to Chapter 9.

Resulting trusts

There is said to be a **resulting trust** when a transferee holds on trust for the transferor. An example of a resulting trust is where Brian transfers land to Cheryl so that she can manage it while he goes abroad for five years. Cheryl will hold the land on a resulting trust for Brian. LPA section 53(2) applies and the trust is effective without any writing.

Situations where resulting trusts operate

We will consider two further situations in which resulting trusts are encountered. The first is where money is handed over, rather than land.

Suppose Mary and Norman are buying a £240,000 house together as an investment. The purchase is organised by Norman and the house is registered in his name alone. However, Mary provides £160,000 towards the cost, Norman paying the other £80,000. Norman will hold the house on a resulting trust, giving Mary an equitable two-thirds share. We do not treat the money she provided as a gift (assuming no contrary evidence) and she obtains a proportionate share in the property purchased with it.

If the house is purchased as a family home, any trust will nearly always be what we call a common intention constructive trust. (These trusts are considered in Chapter 9.)

The second situation is where a trust is set up, but it does not, as lawyers say, exhaust the beneficial interest.

Suppose Peter transfers land to Quentin and Richard to hold for Sally for life and thereafter to Sally's children who reach the age of 21. Sally has children aged four and six. Sadly, both children die in a car crash a year later. Sally dies broken-hearted ten years later, not having had further children. It is plain that this situation has not been catered for: the trusts assume that at least one child will reach 21. There will be a resulting trust in favour of Peter: it is unthinkable that Quentin and Richard, chosen to be trustees, should themselves benefit from this oversight.

This second form of resulting trust is sometimes described as automatic. Even though Peter intended to get rid of the land completely, it will still result back to him. There is some controversy as to whether all resulting trusts should be based upon intention,[11] but this is best left to courses and books on trusts.

The presumption of resulting trust

Quite apart from this last point on automatic resulting trusts, a resulting trust is presumed whenever property (or money) is transferred to another without consideration. Returning to the example involving Mary and Norman, there is no need for Mary to prove that she did not intend a gift. A resulting trust is presumed and it is up to Norman to prove that a gift was intended.

This presumption against gifts looks rather surprising. When people transfer property to others, they usually expect the recipient to own it, not that the recipient holds on trust for them. Indeed, it is trivially easy to persuade the courts that handing over a box of chocolates to a friend at Christmas is a gift. The presumption of resulting trust is more understandable in two types of situation. The first is where the transferee is not a friend or relation. If a person transfers land to his bank manager, it is most unlikely that a gift is intended. It is most likely to be linked to the transferor's later telling the bank manager that he is to hold on trust for, say, the transferor's children.

The second type of situation is nicely exemplified by *Sekhon v Alissa*[12] (Extract 6.2.4). A mother gave her daughter £22,500 (a large sum in the early 1980s) to enable a house to be bought. The daughter argued that this was a gift and that any obligation owed to her mother was merely a moral one. Given that this was virtually all the mother's money and that she had two other children, Hoffmann J was able to find that no gift was intended. This did not require the application of presumptions, but the facts show how a presumption of a gift could often be inappropriate where valuable assets are at stake.

It remains to consider a statutory provision on resulting trusts. LPA section 60(3) enacts that 'a resulting trust for the grantor shall not be implied merely by reason that the property is not expressed to be conveyed for the use or benefit of the grantee'. Though this seems to exclude the presumption of resulting trust, a contrary view is that it was intended to deal with a different and highly technical aspect of the pre-1925 law.

---

[11] Megarry J in *Re Vandervell's Trusts (No 2)* [1974] Ch 269 uses the term automatic, supported by Lord Millett in *Air Jamaica Ltd v Charlton* [1999] 1 WLR 1399 at p. 1412 (PC) (Extract 6.2.2); contra Lord Browne-Wilkinson in *Westdeutsche Landesbank Girozentrale v Islington LBC* [1996] AC 669 at p. 708 (Extract 6.2.1).
[12] [1989] 2 FLR 94.

Its effect has never been settled. The fullest analysis is that of the trial judge in *Lohia* v *Lohia*,[13] who concluded that it does reverse the presumption of resulting trust. However, the Court of Appeal appeared unsure whether this was the correct answer[14] and the position remains unclear. In any event, section 60(3) applies only to the transfer of land (as in the Brian and Cheryl example). The great majority of cases in recent decades have involved the transfer of money rather than land (as does the Mary and Norman example). Those cases are unaffected by section 60(3) and the resulting trust presumption still applies.

A contrary presumption: advancement

In two situations, the presumption of resulting trust was replaced by the contrary presumption of advancement, whereby there was a gift. The first was where a father transfers property to children and the second was where a husband transfers property to his wife. Both seem to be based on the obligation of the transferor to maintain the transferee.

Both situations draw distinctions between men and women that are difficult to support today. It is no surprise that the presumption of advancement has been abolished by the Equality Act 2010, s 199.

Transfers for fraudulent purposes

> Suppose that Helen and Janet are living together in a house owned by Helen. Helen is in business and fears that her business may fail. She would probably then become bankrupt, whereupon the house would be sold to pay her debts. To avoid this, she transfers the house to Janet on the oral understanding that Helen is to remain the owner in equity. Should bankruptcy occur, Helen and Janet will treat Janet as the equitable owner so that the creditors cannot obtain the house. This is seen as fraudulent conduct: the plan is to disguise the parties' true intentions in a scheme designed to defeat the legitimate claims of creditors. Helen cannot argue both that it is her property (as against Janet, if they fall out) and that she has no interest in it (as against the creditors).

The question generally surfaces when the original owner (Helen, in the above example) attempts to claim the property back. The original approach is typified by *Tinker* v *Tinker*[15] (Extract 6.2.6), the facts of which were similar to our example (the parties were husband and wife). It was clear that the transfer was intended to put assets out of the reach of creditors. The Court of Appeal held that it would assume that the husband (the transferor) was not fraudulent and on that basis he could not deny that there was a gift to the wife. He could not reclaim the land.

The more modern approach derives from *Tinsley* v *Milligan*[16] (Extract 6.2.7). The case involved two women, like Helen and Janet. Their intention was that the transferor should be able to claim social security benefits, available only if she had no interest in the house.

---

[13] [2001] WTLR 101.
[14] [2001] EWCA Civ 1691 at [24], [25]; (2002) 16 *Trust Law International* 231.
[15] [1970] P 136.
[16] [1994] 1 AC 340.

The House of Lords held that if she had to rely on her fraudulent purpose, then she could not assert a claim to a beneficial interest. However, her transfer gave rise to a resulting trust, which enabled her to recover the land. Because that resulting trust was presumed, she did not have to rely on her fraudulent purpose.

This is a controversial decision because it places emphasis upon the presumption of resulting trust. It was criticised because if there were a transfer by a husband to wife (as in *Tinker*), then the transferee wife would win: the presumption of advancement would operate in the wife's favour. This contrast with the success of the transferor in *Tinsley* (and of transferor who is a wife) looked very odd – at least prior to the abolition of advancement. *Tinsley* has been heavily criticised by courts in other jurisdictions (and by some English judges), as well as by commentators. The Law Commission has proposed replacing *Tinsley*, regarding the abolition of advancement as insufficient.[17]

Constructive trusts

Constructive trusts are imposed in a variety of circumstances to avoid unconscionable or unfair conduct. We will deal only with examples that impinge on formality rules for land transactions.

Promises by a transferee in favour of the transferor

In *Bannister* v *Bannister*[18] (Extract 6.2.8), a purchaser orally agreed to hold on trust for the transferor (his sister-in-law) during her lifetime. The purchaser (transferee) paid considerably less than the land was worth with vacant possession. He later sought to evict the transferor. The oral trust fell foul of the writing requirement in LPA section 53(1)(b), but the Court of Appeal imposed a constructive trust based upon the transferee's fraudulent conduct: he was seeking to deny the obligation that had enabled him to buy the property very cheaply. It is not necessary that the transferee should have a fraudulent intent at the time of the transfer: a genuine intention to honour the oral trust is no defence. Instead, the law says that it would be fraudulent to assert, at whatever time, the legal title free of the oral trust. A change of mind by the transferee constitutes fraud.

The recognition of a trust in cases such as *Bannister* is relatively uncontroversial: virtually nobody would want the formality rules to facilitate such fraudulent conduct. However, the true nature of the trust has proved controversial. Although *Bannister* treats the trust as constructive, some cases say that the trust is an express one, enforced because of the fraud of the transferee. This reaches the same result, though by different reasoning. The constructive trust possesses the advantage that it is explicitly excluded from formality requirements by section 53(2); it has been used by the more recent cases.

Alternatively, could *Bannister* be explained as a resulting trust? Some similar situations could be explained that way. However, the resulting trust is less easy to apply when some specific right (the life interest in *Bannister*) is intended to be retained.

---

[17] Law Com No 320. *Stack* v *Dowden* [2007] 2 AC 432 (Extract 8.4.18) introduces a presumption of gift in joint transfers (as we will see in Chapter 9).
[18] [1948] 2 All ER 133.

Promises by a transferee in favour of a third party

Suppose that in *Bannister* the purchaser had agreed that the *transferor's sister* should have a life interest. Can that agreement be enforced? It seems clear that there is a constructive trust in favour of the sister. Again, it would be fraudulent for the transferee (purchaser) to be able to rely on the lack of writing in order to profit from the transfer.

However, this form of the trust raises additional questions. Should the trust be in favour of the sister or of the transferor? The sister is a volunteer and it may be said that it is the transferor who has been taken advantage of. Yet the courts have held that there is a trust for the third party (the sister).[19] One reason for this is that the oral trust may produce a benefit which can be enjoyed only by the third party. Suppose the transferor sells a house when emigrating, on the oral basis that her sister can reside in it. A right to reside will be worthless for the transferor who is now living abroad. The only effective remedy for the fraud is to recognise a trust in favour of the sister, which the sister can enforce.

The previous paragraph shows how the constructive trust avoids **privity** problems: normally only parties to agreements can rely on them. This should not concern us too much, as express trusts already constitute an exception to privity. If Andy transfers property to Brian on an express written trust for Carla, it has been clear from the inception of trust law that Carla is able to claim under the trust.

It is sometimes argued that, absent any express written trust, it would be preferable for the third party to claim under the Contracts (Rights of Third Parties) Act 1999 (Extract 20.1.5). It will be recalled that this Act enables third parties to enforce contract terms which are intended to be enforceable by them. It seems probable that a promise which gives rise to a constructive trust will also trigger the 1999 Act (and vice versa). However, it remains necessary to rely on the constructive trust if there is no enforceable contract between transferor and transferee (most obviously because of lack of formalities).

So far, we have considered who can sue. Two other difficult questions will be considered in Chapter 15, when we look at the use of constructive trusts to give effect to licences to use land. The first question relates to the nature of the promise by the purchaser. We will see that a promise to buy 'subject to' the rights of a third party does not normally mean that the purchaser promises to honour those rights. The second is whether the third party obtains a proprietary interest in the land.

The family home

The use of constructive trusts in the family home setting forms a large part of Chapter 9. In this section, we will outline a simple example of how the constructive trust operates.

Anna and Barry set up home together. They buy a house for £250,000, Barry providing £50,000 and Anna £20,000; a mortgage loan covers the remaining £180,000. There is a clear oral agreement between them that the legal title will be put in Anna's name (she deals with most of their financial affairs), but that it is to be held on trust for both of them equally. ➡

---

[19] One example is *Binions v Evans* [1972] Ch 359 (discussed at p. 246 below).

The courts will hold that there is a constructive trust to give effect to their common intention: it would be unconscionable for Anna to deny Barry any share after he has acted to his detriment by contributing to the purchase. This is different from the constructive trust categories considered above as the transferor (the person who sells to Anna) has not the slightest interest in who the beneficial owners should be. Resulting trust principles might seem relevant as regards Barry's £50,000, but they would give Barry a share proportionate to his contribution. This is not what Anna and Barry intend, so we use a constructive trust to give effect to their intention: equal shares on these facts.

Questions to consider

1. Why do we have formality rules for land transactions?

2. Why is there so much litigation regarding contracts for the sale of land? Are sensible results normally reached in this area?

3. What is meant by e-conveyancing? What difference would it make?

4. What are resulting and constructive trusts? Why do we distinguish between them?

5. What formality rules apply to trusts and equitable interests?

Further reading

Bright, S [2000] Conv 398: The third party's conscience in land law.

Gulliver, A G and Tilson, C J (1941) 51 Yale LJ 1: Classification of gratuitous transfers.

Harpum, C (2001) 'Property in an electronic age', in *Modern Studies in Property Law*, Vol 1, ed. E. Cooke, Chapter 1.

Hopkins, N (2006) 26 LS 475: Conscience, discretion and the creation of property rights.

McFarlane, B (2004) 120 LQR 667: Constructive trusts arising on a receipt of property *sub conditione*.

Pettit, P [1989] Conv 431: Farewell section 40.

Swadling, W J (2008) 124 LQR 72: Explaining resulting trusts.

Youdan, T G [1984] CLJ 306: Formalities for trusts of land, and the doctrine in *Rochefoucauld* v *Boustead*.

Visit **www.mylawchamber.co.uk** to access tools to help you develop and test your knowledge of land law, including interactive multiple choice questions, practice exam questions with guidance, weblinks, glossary flashcards, legal newsfeed and legal updates.

8 Estoppel

Nature and importance

Estoppel enables the courts to give effect to expectations. Like constructive trusts, it operates when an owner has acted unconscionably. In estoppel, the unconscionable conduct exists if the owner denies the expectation after having encouraged it, provided that the claimant has acted to their detriment. Estoppel is important for two principal reasons. First, it recognises obligations in situations where none would otherwise exist. Next, it plays an important role in circumventing formality requirements, bearing in mind that the creation of nearly every interest in land requires writing or (for legal interests) a deed.

Two examples illustrate how it works. The first is based on the influential nineteenth-century case of *Dillwyn v Llewelyn*[1] (Extract 7.2.1). A father wanted a son to live close to him and offered him a farm on which he could build a house. The son agreed and spent a very large sum on building. The transaction was recorded in a document, but this had no effect as the transfer of a legal estate requires a deed. After the father died, the son's rights were challenged by other relatives. Lord Westbury LC was emphatic that the son's expenditure, undertaken with the father's approval, gave the son an equitable right to the land. This is a good example of estoppel operating to avoid the formality requirement of a deed.

In the second example, Richard and Sally are neighbours. Sally is building a large garage, but does not realise that most of it is on Richard's side of the boundary. Richard is aware of this, but says nothing other than to tell Sally that her half-built garage looks nice. After it is finished, they quarrel and Richard says that Sally must either pull the garage down or allow him to use the part which is on his land. In this situation, the courts will say that Richard acquiesced in Sally's mistake as to the ownership of the relevant area of land. He will be prevented from asserting ownership of it. This second example shows how estoppel protects expectations regardless of whether a deliberate attempt to create property rights has been made.

[1] (1862) 4 De GF&J 517 (45 ER 1285).

Estoppel applies in many different areas – not just the property context. One example (far removed from land law) is that once a point has been settled in litigation between two persons, it cannot be challenged in other proceedings between them. Most students will have encountered the principle of promissory estoppel in the law of contract, based on the *High Trees* case.[2] Promissory estoppel operates as a defence. The estoppel we are dealing with here – proprietary estoppel – is much more powerful and has a positive effect. In *Dillwyn*, it didn't merely protect the son from being evicted but conferred a right to the fee simple. This is discussed later in this chapter.

Proprietary estoppel (which we will shorten to estoppel) has roots going back at least to the early nineteenth century. However, the area was overlooked for the best part of a century until it resurfaced in cases in the 1950s. Nearly all the cases in this chapter have been decided in the past 50 years, making it feel more modern than many areas of land law. Indeed, some of the features most discussed today (the remedy being the leading example) have emerged only in recent decades.

Three major issues are considered in this chapter. The first concerns the circumstances when an estoppel will arise. Two specific aspects of this – the use of estoppel to enforce promises and its use in sale negotiations – are discussed as Critical Issues below. The second major issue concerns the remedy which will be given when an estoppel has arisen. It cannot be assumed that effect will always be given to expectations. Suppose Arthur makes an oral (and therefore ineffective) gift of a house, worth £200,000, to Brenda. Brenda spends £3,000 replacing the central heating system. The courts may say that there is an estoppel because of her expenditure on the supposition that the house was hers. However, the benefit of a £200,000 house is so disproportionate to the £3,000 expenditure that the courts may well decide to give another remedy – perhaps the return of the money spent. This area has featured in several recent cases and will form another Critical Issue below.

The final issue to be considered relates to the proprietary effect of the estoppel: does it bind a purchaser from the person who encouraged the expectation and detriment? In *Dillwyn*, for example, the person bound was a relative entitled to the land under the father's will – not the father himself. Estoppel is almost completely derived from case law, but recent legislation confirms that successors in title can be bound by estoppel claims.

This is not the only chapter in which estoppel is mentioned. We will see in Chapter 9 that some of the rules relating to the acquisition of interests in the family home by constructive trusts are very similar to estoppel. Indeed, there are suggestions that the two areas should be integrated. However, they operate in rather different circumstances – almost none of the estoppel cases in this chapter involve a couple agreeing to be joint owners of the family home.

Estoppel also features in Chapter 15 on licences. A licence is a permission to enter or use land; it is thought not to be proprietary. Estoppel is especially interesting in that context because it gives effect to non-proprietary rights over land. If a licence protected by an estoppel binds purchasers, then that is a remarkable result. In the present chapter, we consider the simpler (and more typical) situation where there is an expectation of a

---

[2] *Central London Property Trust Ltd* v *High Trees House Ltd* [1947] KB 130.

conventional property right: fee simple (as in the examples at the beginning of this section), lease and easement being the most obvious rights.

When will estoppel arise?

The basic test

The traditional requirements for estoppel were laid down by Fry J in **Willmott v Barber**[3] over a century ago. Fry J identified five requirements (generally known as *probanda*). They may be summarised as follows, describing the owner as O and the claimant (the person who has acted to their detriment) as C:

1. C must have made a mistake as to his rights;
2. C must have expended money or done some act (not necessarily on O's land) because of the mistake;
3. O must be aware of his right (relevant to its being unconscionable to assert his title);
4. O must be aware of C's mistake;
5. O must have encouraged C's expenditure, either directly or by not asserting his rights.

It is easy to see that the two examples at the beginning of this chapter satisfy these requirements. However, there was a switch to a broader and less technical approach in **Taylors Fashions Ltd v Liverpool Victoria Trustees Co Ltd**[4] (Extract 7.1.1). The case was complex, but it involved an option for a tenant to renew the lease of a shop. Unknown to both tenant and landlord, the option had become void. The tenant (C) argued that detriment had been incurred in the belief (encouraged by the landlord, O) that the option was valid. The third of the probanda caused difficulty: O was unaware that the option was void. Oliver J held that the underlying test from the cases was whether 'it was unconscionable for the defendant to seek to take advantage of the mistake'. This rests the law on general unconscionability ideas, rather than the precise requirements articulated by Fry J. Although it is only a first instance decision, the judgment of Oliver J has been widely accepted and applied: the language of unconscionability is now common.

As Oliver J recognised, this does not mean that we can forget about the probanda. They illustrate the factors that lie at the heart of estoppel. We might say that there are three major components: the mistake made by C (the first of the probanda), detrimental reliance by C (the second of them) and responsibility on the part of O (the last three). Confirming this, the House of Lords in **Cobbe v Yeoman's Row Management Ltd**[5] (Extract 7.1.4) has recently stressed that more than unconscionability is required to prove estoppel. Though we will see that the impact of *Cobbe* has proved to be less dramatic than some thought, this point seems to survive.

---

[3] (1880) 15 Ch D 96.
[4] [1982] QB 133 (decided 1979). The application of the test to the facts is considered later in the text (p. 85).
[5] [2008] 1 WLR 1752; below (p. 82).

The mistake: assumptions and representations

The probanda refer to mistake: C has made a mistake as to rights in the land. The language of mistake can apply to some cases where there is a representation by O.

> David tells his new neighbour Erica that her house has an easement so that she can get access to the house over David's drive. Erica then builds a garage which can be accessed only from David's drive. Subsequently David denies that there is such an easement and in strict law it turns out that he is right. This is a case in which it is accurate to talk of a mistake by Erica.

However, the law does not stop there. The well-known decision in *Crabb* v *Arun District Council*[6] (Extract 7.2.2) provides a good illustration. Crabb reached an outline agreement with the Council for an easement of access, though it did not amount to a contract. Crabb started to use the access, encouraged by the Council's erecting substantial gates. There was alternative access through another part of Crabb's land. The crucial stage came when Crabb sold off this part, so that the only access to his remaining land was through the new gates. This sale was the detriment incurred by Crabb; he would not have sold the land unless he believed that there would be a right of way over the Council's land.

In these circumstances, the Court of Appeal held that Crabb could rely on estoppel: it was reasonable for him to believe that there would be an easement. An important point to note is that he cannot have thought there was already an easement: he was expecting (under the outline agreement) to pay for it. Rather, he reasonably thought that an easement had been promised in such circumstances that it would be unconscionable for the Council to refuse to grant the access.

This expansion from mistakes to expectations was probably inevitable. To try to distinguish between a person who believes he has a right and one who believes that there has been a promise to create a right would be almost impossible in practice. The two situations shade into one another and the average layman would not distinguish between them. This forms the basis for the following section.

The mistake: promises

Crabb shows how proprietary estoppel can be used to enforce promises. In this respect, it achieves far more than promissory estoppel achieves in non-land representations. Indeed, it seems to elevate proprietary estoppel to a role quite similar to contract – both are routes to acquiring equitable interests in land.

In this section, we will look at the general role of promises (especially promises to leave property on death) and the particular role of estoppel in sale negotiations. These areas were considered in some detail in two recent House of Lords cases: *Cobbe* v *Yeoman's Row Management Ltd*[7] and *Thorner* v *Major*[8] (Extract 7.1.5). These cases will be considered towards the end of this section.

[6] [1976] Ch 179.
[7] [2008] 1 WLR 1752.
[8] [2009] 1 WLR 776.

CRITICAL ISSUE

Not every promise in relation to land will attract proprietary estoppel.

> Fred agrees to sell his house to Gary for £180,000, but no formal written contract is entered into. Each assures the other that they can rely on the transaction going ahead. Relying on this, Fred rejects an offer from Harry of £220,000 (Harry deliberately offers more than market value, as he has a particular need for the house). Gary, who lives 60 miles away, gives up his present job in the expectation of buying Fred's house and finding a new job much closer to that house.
>
> Can either Gary or Fred use estoppel should the other try to get out of the agreement? The use of estoppel in the contract for sale context is considered in more detail below, but it seems possible that Gary would be able to assert an estoppel should Fred change his mind and refuse to sell – Gary would be asserting that he has a right to buy the house as they had agreed. But would Fred be able to use estoppel against Gary, if it were Gary who changed his mind and refused to buy? In this context, Fred is not claiming any right to land (he wants to sell it) and it is difficult to see how his claim could be articulated in terms of proprietary estoppel.

It is not easy to justify giving a remedy to Gary but not to Fred. This raises the difficult question whether proprietary estoppel is so different from other situations in which promises are made to persons who act to their detriment. However, this raises controversial questions about the use of estoppel as a sword (enforcing obligations), which are well outside the scope of this text!

Promises to leave property on death

A recurrent theme in recent cases is that one person (C) undertakes work or care for the landowner, O. O is sufficiently grateful that he promises to leave property to C in his will. The services performed by C are extensive and more than can be expected of an employee or friend. Things go wrong because either O dies without having changed his will, or O and C quarrel.

The early leading case of this type is *Gillett v Holt*[9] (Extract 7.1.3). Gillett worked on Holt's land for 40 years. Gillett was treated as a member of the family; he was paid less than his work merited and devoted himself entirely to advancing Holt's interests. The combination of these facts was enough to show detriment. There were several occasions (commencing 12 years after Gillett started work) on which Holt assured Gillett that he would inherit under his will.

Perhaps the major problem with this type of case is that wills are inherently revocable: people are free to decide who to leave their property to and frequently change their minds as the years go by. Accordingly, it is unsafe to count one's chickens simply because one has been named as a beneficiary under a will. Holt used these factors to assert that Gillett could not rely upon inheriting under the will. However, the Court of Appeal held that Holt had made very clear assurances that Gillett would inherit. Simply

[9] [2001] Ch 210.

being told about a person's plans for their will might well fall far short of an estoppel, but the facts involved clear and repeated assurances in front of witnesses. It was far more than a statement of present intention.

Another well-known case is ***Jennings v Rice***[10] (Extract 7.2.5), which is studied later in the context of remedies. Jennings (who had a full-time job) started working as a part-time gardener for Mrs Royal, then aged 66, in 1970. As she grew older, he undertook more tasks to help her. In the 1980s she stopped paying him, but made a number of assurances to him about inheriting the house and, more generally, 'being alright'. His help increased as she became more frail and, for four years until she died in 1997, he slept at her house to provide more security. Though their agreement was too uncertain for a contract, this was no obstacle to the court's finding that estoppel applied; he was awarded £200,000. It is another example of how estoppel provides a wider role than merely getting around failure to comply with formality rules.

Sale negotiations

Estoppel has been used by purchasers to try to get around two quite separate problems. The first is where there has been no final agreement – or any agreement is subject to contract and so (as seen in Chapter 7) unenforceable. The second is where section 2 of the Law of Property (Miscellaneous Provisions) Act 1989 (Extract 5.2.3) has rendered a contract for sale void because it is not in writing.

Subject to contract agreements

The courts are usually sceptical of estoppel being used where there is a 'subject to contract' arrangement. Most people dealing with land understand that making an arrangement subject to contract means that there is no binding obligation. This is illustrated by the Privy Council decision in ***Att-Gen of Hong Kong v Humphreys Estate (Queen's Gardens) Ltd***.[11] Following a subject to contract agreement to exchange properties, the Hong Kong government was allowed to take possession of 83 flats. The government incurred detriment in spending money on the flats and disposing of other properties that were being replaced. The owner of the flats then pulled out of the deal and reclaimed the property.

The Privy Council reasoned that the government knew what it was doing and was, essentially, gambling on the deal going through. Although the owner had acted so as to indicate that the transaction would go through, nothing had been said or done to indicate that it had passed beyond its subject to contract status or that the owner had abandoned the right to pull out of the transaction. The result may be regarded as tough on the government, but it may be justified as producing certainty when the phrase 'subject to contract' is used.

No final agreement

This was the issue in ***Cobbe***, which is discussed below.

[10] [2003] 1 P&CR 100.
[11] [1987] AC 114.

Agreements void for lack of writing

We have seen that section 2 of the 1989 Act requires agreements for the sale of land to be in writing. Can this requirement be avoided by estoppel, when the purchaser has incurred detrimental reliance? A background point is that before 1989, a person who partly performed a contract would be able to enforce it; part performance was quite easily proved. The 1989 Act abolished part performance. This leads one to doubt whether the somewhat similar estoppel principle can be applied.

The Law Commission, in its report leading to the 1989 Act, made it clear that estoppel can still be argued in appropriate cases. However, the Act departs in some respects from the Law Commission's proposals; it makes no reference to estoppel. By contrast, section 2(5) expressly states that constructive trusts survive the legislation.

The issue was fully discussed for the first time by the Court of Appeal in *Yaxley* v *Gotts*[12] (Extract 5.2.11). The buyer orally agreed to purchase the ground floor of a building being converted into flats. The consideration was that the buyer (a builder) would undertake building work on the other floors. The buyer duly did a large amount of work on all the floors, whereupon the seller pulled out of the deal. It looks like a classic estoppel scenario. However, the Court of Appeal was much vexed by the question of whether recognition of estoppel was consistent with the 1989 Act and the policy underpinning it. The judgments are difficult to assess because they stress that estoppel and constructive trusts overlap in their operation (as discussed in Chapter 9). One approach which emerges is that estoppel can be relied upon if the circumstances would also give rise to a constructive trust. It is unclear whether proprietary estoppel can be relied upon independently, though this is supported by Beldam LJ.

Subsequent cases did little to clarify the question, though most seemed content simply to rely on estoppel. However, *Kinane* v *Mackie-Conteh*[13] (Extract 5.2.12) appears to accept estoppel only when a constructive trust can be found. The facts involved an oral agreement for a mortgage, following which the lender had lent £50,000. This was held to give rise to an estoppel and constructive trust. This is interesting, as money will have been lent in virtually every case on oral agreements for mortgages. It seems that section 2 of the 1989 Act will have little if any effect in such litigation.

Assuming estoppel can apply in the section 2 context, what circumstances will justify a claim? Virtually every purchaser will incur some detriment, whether it be expenditure on legal fees and surveys or the sale of their existing homes. The courts are alert to the danger of section 2 being circumvented too readily. For example, in *Kinane*,[14] Neuberger LJ stated that the law must 'avoid regarding [section 2(5)] as an automatically available escape route from the rigours of section 2(1)'. It seems inevitable that a purchaser who can prove no more than some detriment, as mentioned above, will fail. There needs to be some assurance that, despite the absence of writing, an obligation is being undertaken.

---

[12] [2000] Ch 162.
[13] [2005] WTLR 345; see Arden LJ at [25]–[26] and (more explicitly) Neuberger LJ at [41]–[51].
[14] [2005] WTLR 345 at [40] (Extract 5.2.12).

Challenge in the House of Lords

There having been no House of Lords decision directly on proprietary estoppel for many decades, we now have two decisions within a year: *Cobbe v Yeoman's Row Management Ltd*[15] (Extract 7.1.4) and *Thorner v Major*[16] (Extract 7.1.5). Though fundamental issues were raised, it may be said at the outset that the outcome involves relatively few changes to the law as described above.

The context of *Cobbe* is that of sale negotiations where no final agreement has been reached. The parties were negotiating an agreement whereby Cobbe would obtain planning permission and then purchase the land. The price was calculated so that about half the uplift in the value, resulting from planning permission, would go to Cobbe. Cobbe then incurred substantial costs in time and money (valued between £100,000 and £200,000) in obtaining planning permission. At that point, the owner refused to proceed with the sale. The agreement was insufficiently certain and final to be a contract; in any event, it was not in writing.

The House of Lords held that estoppel was not proved on these facts, though a remedy allowing recompense for the value of Cobbe's services was allowed (not based on estoppel). The leading judgment was that of Lord Scott, who asked what right Cobbe thought he had. Given that he was well aware that there was no contract, he could scarcely claim that he thought he had a contractual right to the land. In truth, he had acted in the hope that the arrangement would go through. This is very similar to the subject to contract case of *Att-Gen of Hong Kong*. Accordingly, there was no basis for finding an estoppel. The major difficulty with this analysis is that this might be thought to bar a remedy whenever the representation takes the form of a promise – it will be rare for C to be able to claim that it was believed that a right existed. This problem most obviously applies to promises to leave property by will. It could represent a massive contraction in the scope of proprietary estoppel, though there is little recognition of such an effect in *Cobbe*.

It is unsurprising that this led to further litigation. The facts of *Thorner* are similar to those of *Gillett*: C worked on O's farm (O and C were cousins in *Thorner*), O giving C to understand that the farm would belong to C on O's death. The House of Lords had no hesitation in denying any 'apocalyptic' effect of *Cobbe*. It is plain that this leaves cases such as *Gillett* and *Jennings* intact. The real question in *Thorner* was whether there was a sufficient assurance on the part of C. This is essentially a factual issue, decided by Lord Walker on the basis that it was 'clear enough'.

How is *Cobbe* to be explained? Building on ideas of Lord Walker in *Cobbe*, *Thorner* stresses that different inferences can be drawn in family cases (or ones involving friends) as opposed to those involving businessmen. Whilst a businessman is readily seen to be taking a gamble in spending money in the hope that an arrangement will be implemented, those less used to business will not think in terms of legal categories and legal obligations. The facts of the two cases, of course, demonstrate the contrast.

It is not that there is a different rule applying to businessmen (or to expectations of contracts). This is a good thing, as the line between the two categories is not easy to

---

[15] [2008] 1 WLR 1752; McFarlane and Robinson [2008] LMCLQ 449.
[16] [2009] 1 WLR 776.

draw. The stress in subsequent cases has been on the nature of the promise rather than the status of the parties. Thus disputes relating to proposed contracts to sell land are treated as commercial, even though neither party is a businessman. The point is that the courts are sensitive to the danger of drawing the same inferences from different types of circumstances. Another way of looking at it is that businessmen invariably deal with precise legal categories such as contracts. In a family setting, it is common for a promise of a gift to be made. This would be completely foreign to a business transaction. We can still justify the estoppel in *Crabb*, which was in a business setting. Even though there was known to be no contract, the act of O in erecting gates for the right of way signified that they were committing themselves.

A few other aspects of these cases should be considered. In *Cobbe*, Lord Scott stressed the need for certainty as to what was promised. In *Thorner*, this was somewhat played down. It did not matter that bits of the farm might be sold off, so that the extent of the farm was left uncertain. However, in other contexts certainty may be more problematic. Thus Lord Walker in *Thorner* expresses some hesitation about *Re Basham*.[17] In that case the promise related to all the property of the deceased, not just a specific plot of land. On the other hand, failure to identify with certainty the type of right to be obtained by C, or the terms on which it would be obtained, was thought by Lord Walker not to cause problems (echoing views expressed in *Jennings*).

Turning to contracts which fail the writing requirements, this was a relatively minor element of *Cobbe*. However, Lord Scott thought that, by virtue of the terms of the 1989 Act, estoppel should not be used in such cases. This issue is not addressed by *Thorner*. Subsequent first instance cases have differed as to whether this really spells the end for estoppel arguments, though perhaps the best view, as expressed in *Whittaker v Kinnear*,[18] is that estoppel remains available. However, the availability of constructive trust arguments renders the debate of limited importance.

Detrimental reliance

Simply because O knows a mistake has been made does not mean that it is unconscionable to disappoint expectations. A rule as wide as that would make a mockery of formality requirements. C must undertake detrimental reliance before O's conduct can be regarded as unconscionable.

In many of the early cases, the detriment consisted of improving the land in question: the son's building a house in *Dillwyn* provides a good example. However, it has long been clear that other actions constitute detriment. Two examples will be selected from the cases. The first is undertaking work benefiting O or O's family, sometimes in the form of personal care services. This is illustrated by *Greasley v Cooke*[19] (Extract 7.1.6), in which Doris, a maid, worked in Arthur's house. Over time, she formed a relationship with one of his sons (Kenneth) and was assured by him and another son (Howard; the two sons owned the house) that she could stay there for life. She looked after the house and, in

---

[17] [1986] 1 WLR 1498.
[18] [2011] EWHC 1479 (QB).
[19] [1980] 1 WLR 1306.

particular, looked after a mentally ill sister of Kenneth. Some 30 years later (40 years since Doris arrived), Howard and Kenneth had both died, as had the sister. Arthur's family now sought to evict Doris, but the Court of Appeal had no hesitation in holding that Doris's actions sufficed as detriment – no improvement of the house or expenditure of money was required. The second example is *Crabb*. It will be recalled that the detriment lay in selling off land, which would leave Crabb's property landlocked without the claimed easement. The detriment contained no benefit for the owner at all.

Though expenditure readily constitutes detriment, expenditure within a family home can pose problems. This is because people living in homes naturally wish to improve the quality of the environment in which they live, regardless of having any property right. In some cases, the claimed detriment may be no more than an act of gratitude for the past benefit of living there. If rent-free accommodation is valued at £300 a month, then spending £1,000 on, say, carpets, in the course of a year may be difficult to justify as detriment. Alternatively, we might say that there is detriment, but (under principles considered below) no remedy is justified.

Coombes v Smith[20] (Extract 7.1.7) illustrates greater problems. Eileen and Robert, both already married to others, became lovers. When Eileen became pregnant, she left her husband and moved to a house provided by Robert. Although they discussed setting up home together, this never happened. Eileen left her job before the baby was born and thereafter undertook some decorating of the house – these were actions relied upon as detriment. When they quarrelled some 10 years later, Eileen claimed she was entitled to the house. Facts of this type are found in many cases, which makes it an interesting case. The judge treated Eileen's actions as being the natural actions of a woman in an unhappy marriage who wished to have a baby and live with her lover: there was no sufficient detriment for estoppel. It might be added that Robert accepted that she could stay there until the child reached 17: Eileen kept possession, but could not claim ownership.

The law here faces a difficulty. It seems hard to say that these sorts of facts cannot count as detriment, but to accept them as detriment would lead to representations being enforceable in a very large proportion of cases where people choose to live together. Similar conduct includes moving homes and giving up a job to be with another person. This can be seen as a benefit (emotional as well as having a home without payment) as much as a detriment (loss of existing accommodation and making it more difficult to re-enter employment later). There is no final resolution of those issues, though more recent cases have indicated a more generous approach than seen in *Coombes*.

Other cases involve doing work on the land (farming is an example in several cases).[21] Even though the claimant sometimes gets the benefit of free occupation of the premises, the courts have been prepared to find detriment. This can be based on either the amount of work done or the giving up of other routes to self-advancement. In any event, the courts can be taken as taking a broad and non-technical approach to detriment.

A rather different point concerns the element of reliance. Not only must there be detriment, but also it must be referable to the mistake or representation. *Taylors Fashions* provides

[20] [1986] 1 WLR 808 (Parker QC).
[21] These include *Gillett v Holt* [2001] Ch 210, discussed above (at p. 79). See also *Henry v Henry* [2010] 1 All ER 988 (PC).

an example of a claim's failing on this basis. The tenant of shop premises had installed a lift and argued that this was detrimental reliance on an expectation of being able to renew the lease. Oliver J was not much impressed by this. The lease had 18 years to run anyway, so the lift could be said to have been installed to benefit the shop during that period.

However, reliance is readily proved in the family home context. This emerges from *Greasley*. A factual difficulty was that Doris's conduct could be explained as much as resulting from her living with Kenneth as from the assurance that she could stay there for life. The Court of Appeal considered that reliance would be presumed: there was no need for Doris to prove why she undertook the detriment.

One type of situation requires a more subtle approach.

> Rose moves in with Simon and cares for Simon's elderly mother, Theresa. After a few years, Simon tells Rose (younger than him) that she has been so good that he will leave the house to her when he dies. Things remain exactly the same until Simon is killed in a car accident five years later. Simon has not made a will and the house passes to his brother, who seeks to evict Rose. On these facts, Rose did not change her conduct as a result of what Simon had said: her care for Theresa was the same before and after. The courts deal with this by saying that, had Simon later told her that she was not to get the house, Rose might well have been upset and stopped caring for Theresa. The reliance is thus related to Simon's not withdrawing the promise, rather than to the making of the promise.

The owner's responsibility

Without some responsibility for C's mistake, it is not unconscionable for O to deny C's claim. Most cases involve some sort of promise or representation. This is enough to establish responsibility. Even if there is a common mistake by O and C (so that O is not deliberately misleading C), the active role taken by O justifies finding him liable.

Mistake lay at the heart of *Taylors Fashions* (Extract 7.1.1). Oliver J held that estoppel operated even though the owner of the land was unaware (and so mistaken) that the option to renew a lease had been rendered void. It is interesting, however, that he considered that in cases of pure acquiescence (not involving any encouragement by O) it would be more difficult to show unconscionability if O were unaware of the true situation. On the facts of *Taylors Fashions*, there were two quite different claims. One was by the tenant who installed the lift (T1). The owner had not encouraged this and, indeed, could not object to it as T1 was entitled to make this sort of improvement. This (in addition to the reliance problems considered above) was relevant in rejecting the tenant's estoppel claim. A second claim was brought by tenants (T2) of an adjoining lease, the duration of which depended on T1's disputed option. The fact that the owner had dealt with T2 on the basis of T1's having an option was enough to establish the owner's responsibility: an estoppel was made out.

A rather different point is whether O must be aware of C's reliance. If the act of reliance is unexpected, then O may be able to argue that it is not unconscionable to deny C's claim. This was raised in *Crabb*, where the Council argued that it was unaware of Crabb's sale of part of the land. That was rejected on the basis that the Council was aware that he planned to sell off part: this general awareness sufficed. But is it necessary that C has any such knowledge?

> Richard tells Sally that a house is hers, but without executing a deed of gift. Richard then goes on an extended foreign visit for six months. While he is away, Sally spends large amounts of money in improving and extending the house. Is it not unconscionable of Richard to reclaim the house? Sally's conduct is what one might expect a person to do with a newly acquired house.

It may therefore be thought that a low level of awareness should suffice: no more than knowledge of circumstances in which some detrimental reliance is foreseeable. However, in situations in which there is simple acquiescence (no representation or encouragement) it will be rare for conduct to be unconscionable without knowledge of the detriment. The very essence of liability is based on standing by while the mistaken party expends money in the mistaken assumption. A person who knows only that person has made a mistake will not normally be acting unconscionably.

The remedy

In contract, remedies are designed to give effect to what has been promised. Does the same apply in estoppel? Giving effect to the promise is supported by the idea that O cannot unconscionably deny what C has been led to expect; it was also the usual outcome in the earlier cases. However, that must now be seen as too simplistic.

One uncontroversial point is that it will sometimes be impossible to give effect to the expectation. A good example is where the claimant is sharing a house with another person under an expectation of being able to stay there. Relationships may break down so that sharing becomes impossible. One extreme example is provided by *Baker* v *Baker & Baker*[22] (Extract 7.2.4). O accused C (his father) of molesting his children. The accusation was shown to be unjustified, but the damage to the relationship made it impossible for them ever to live in the same house again. This does not mean that no remedy is available; in *Baker*, a monetary payment was ordered.

Modern analyses are based on dicta of Scarman LJ in *Crabb* v *Arun District Council*[23] (Extract 7.2.2). Although it was not central to the issues in the case, he asserted that the remedy should be based on 'the minimum equity to do justice'. This moves the stress away from the expectation. This was illustrated by the reasoning in the well-known case of *Pascoe* v *Turner*.[24] On the breakdown of an affair (lasting over 10 years) in 1973, Pascoe told Turner that a house was hers. She spent a quarter of her capital on the house, though the expenditure was only £230. Nothing was in writing and subsequently Pascoe denied

---

[22] (1993) 25 HLR 408.
[23] [1976] Ch 179 at p. 198, discussed above (p. 78).
[24] [1979] 1 WLR 431.

that Turner had any right to the house. The court ordered the transfer of the fee simple (as had been promised), but this was only after much thought. The value of the fee simple far outweighed the detriment and the court was initially inclined to award some form of life interest to Turner. The fee simple was decided on only because she had expended a significant part of her capital and the history of Pascoe's 'ruthlessness' showed that Turner might be at risk if awarded anything less than the fee simple. The important point for us is that the court did not automatically give effect to the expectation.

The leading modern case is *Jennings v Rice*[25] (Extract 7.2.5). We have already seen that the claimant undertook care services for an elderly woman in the closing years of her life. The trial judge awarded £200,000 in circumstances where the house and furniture (what had been promised) were worth £435,000; £200,000 was chosen because it approximated to the value of the claimant's work, coupled with the fact that £150,000 would purchase an adequate house.

What makes *Jennings* important is that, for the first time, the court discussed in some detail the principles upon which remedies are given. It was accepted that it is far too simplistic to say that effect is given to expectations. On the other hand, any idea that the court has an unfettered ('palm tree') discretion was rejected. Aldous LJ stressed the need for proportionality and concluded that this provided a good basis for justifying an award of £200,000. Robert Walker LJ drew a distinction between two types of case. In the first, there is a clear agreement between the parties as to the terms involved. This will often be the case where estoppel is being used to get around the absence of formalities, especially in a commercial setting (though such cases may be less common after *Cobbe*). In these cases, the courts will normally award what has been promised. The second type of case is where the promise is unclear. *Jennings* is an example, as the old lady said the claimant would be 'alright'. In that type of case, the court has more of a discretion to decide what remedy is appropriate and will take the detriment into account.

A case can certainly be made for saying that both expectation and detriment are useful factors. In favour of expectation is the point that it is what the parties agreed. It can also be a lot easier to assess than the detriment. Suppose that in *Jennings* the house had been worth, say, £225,000. It would be much easier to award the house than trying to enter into a precise valuation of the services provided over many years. In many commercial settings the parties will have reached agreement, and then it makes sense to go along with that. Family settings are more likely to throw up cases of lack of proportionality simply because promises of gifts are common: businessmen do not normally promise gifts!

Detriment also has its merits as a factor. It is only when detriment is proved that the equity arises. How can it be equitable to give effect to a generous promise when there is a small amount of detriment? In *Sledmore v Dalby*,[26] C was O's son-in-law and had lived on O's land rent-free for 18 years (O's daughter died seven years before the dispute). C spent money on the basis of a promise (made 14 years before the dispute) that he could remain on the land. The Court of Appeal held that whatever equity had arisen from the expenditure (around £1,000 – quite a large sum in the 1970s) had been satisfied by the

---

[25] [2003] 1 P&CR 100, above (p. 80).
[26] (1996) 72 P&CR 196. Contrast *Suggitt v Suggitt* [2012] WTLR 1607, placing more emphasis on expectations and relying on a test of 'out of all proportion', rather than proportionality.

benefit of living on the land. It was a case in which the original detriment no longer justified any remedy.

The language of proportionality recognises that detriment is a significant factor. At a more theoretical level, it helps to distinguish the roles of contract and estoppel. Contract remedies give effect to expectations. If estoppel were to do the same, it might be seen as an improper circumvention of contract rules, especially regarding consideration. If issues of detriment and proportionality are to the fore in estoppel, this gives it a different and more justifiable role.

Is the distinction drawn by Robert Walker LJ (as to whether or not there is a clear agreement) as clear-cut as it seems? One could well imagine facts similar to *Jennings* in which the old lady is explicit that the house will be given in return for a continuation of care services. The promise is no longer uncertain. Would this mean that the claimant would receive the house, assuming the figures are the same as in *Jennings*? It seems likely that Robert Walker LJ would treat this as a disproportionate benefit, which should not be allowed. If the old lady unexpectedly died very soon after the promise, the detriment would be minimal and the benefit huge. This leaves open the question as to when an expectation will be regarded as disproportionate. The conclusion in *Jennings* that the expectation was disproportionate, when it was worth double the detriment, seems a quite tough application of the test.

We have seen that in *Cobbe v Yeoman's Row Management Ltd*[27] the House of Lords held that there was no estoppel. The lower courts had held otherwise and it remains instructive to observe what the Court of Appeal said about the remedy. Unlike *Pascoe*, *Jennings* and *Sledmore*, *Cobbe* arose in a commercial setting. Cobbe undertook work valued at £100,000 to £200,000 in obtaining planning permission. The terms of the arrangement were such that Cobbe would buy the land and develop it. In broad terms, half the expected profits would go to Cobbe. It was no longer feasible for Cobbe to buy the land, so the trial judge awarded Cobbe half the increase in the value of the property attributable to the planning permission. This was subsequently agreed to be £2m.

In the Court of Appeal it was argued that this was disproportionate: it was at least 10 times the detriment! The tension between expectation and reliance is laid bare by Dyson LJ: 'The difficulty with this area of law is that the two approaches are fundamentally different.' No wonder, then, that we have difficulty in weaving the two together in attempting to work out the effect of *Jennings*. Perhaps surprisingly, the Court of Appeal upheld the £2m award. A particular feature is that simply compensating for the detriment would leave the owner with a huge profit as a result of Cobbe's work. It seems likely that the House of Lords would have come to a different conclusion, had an estoppel been proved. When they considered the non-estoppel remedy of unjust enrichment, it was stressed that Cobbe's work simply unlocked the development potential of the land. It was not appropriate to view the profit as an enrichment from Cobbe's work.

The remedy awarded by the Court of Appeal in *Cobbe* (whether or not justified) illustrates how the courts generally opt for either detriment or expectation, rarely anything in between. It also exemplifies an instinct in favour of giving effect to expectations; this might be a guide to future developments.

[27] [2008] 1 WLR 1752, reversing [2006] 1 WLR 2964.

Estoppel as a proprietary claim

So far, we have considered estoppel as between O and C. What happens if O sells the land to P? There is no independent unconscionable conduct by P, so C will have to argue that the estoppel claim against O constitutes a proprietary interest binding P. A short introductory point is that estoppel claims are clearly equitable in nature: they are based on equitable principles and lie outside the legal interests listed in section 1 of the Law of Property Act 1925. They can bind purchasers of registered land only if protected by an entry on the register or an overriding interest. It is common for C to be in actual occupation.

The earlier cases

Successors in title have consistently been held bound by estoppels. *Dillwyn* is an early example, involving a person taking title under O's will. Nevertheless, a few cases and commentators expressed the contrary view.

Land Registration Act 2002, section 116

Section 116 enacts that 'for the avoidance of doubt', an equity by estoppel 'has effect from the time the equity arises as an interest capable of binding successors in title'. It is thought that the time the estoppel arises is when there is detrimental reliance. The section seems quite conclusive that estoppels constitute proprietary interests. Indeed, the way in which this is prefixed 'for the avoidance of doubt' shows that Parliament thought this to be the case already for unregistered land. Although section 116 applies only to registered land, it seems improbable that the position in unregistered land will be held to be different.

Is proprietary status appropriate?

If estoppel is seen as simply a way of avoiding formality rules, then it is easy to accept that it gives rise to a proprietary right. Take the facts of *Dillwyn*. The father assured the son that the land was his, whereupon the son built a house. This was an attempt to transfer the land, which equity was prepared to enforce. The result is an equitable right to a fee simple, rather similar to an equitable right under a contract.

However, it is not always as straightforward as this. We have seen that the courts do not always give effect to expectations. Suppose that Brenda is told that a house belongs to her. She spends £3,000 on replacing the central heating system. The courts may say that this is significant detriment, but that awarding ownership would be disproportionately generous. The courts might confer a life interest or monetary remedy instead. The obvious problem is that, before a remedy is given, it is difficult to know what it will be. When considering what rights qualify as interests in land, an important factor is whether they involve sufficient certainty so as not to cause purchasers unacceptable problems. It is far from clear that estoppels satisfy this requirement, even leaving aside the inevitable uncertainties arising from lack of writing. Nevertheless, section 116 appears to settle the question for the future, in favour of proprietary status.

A final point is that once the court has ordered a property right as a remedy, it is easy to accept that there is a proprietary right. If the court orders a life interest, we can readily say that there is an equitable life interest.

Non-proprietary expectations and remedies

The above reasoning is most readily applied where the underlying expectation and eventual remedy are both of a proprietary nature: fees simple and easements are good examples. However, it is much more difficult if the expectation is not proprietary. The most common example is an expectation of a licence (a permission to enter or remain on land). We will see that licences, when created by contract, do not bind purchasers. Similarly, a non-proprietary remedy will also cause problems. The best example is where (as in several recent cases) the courts give a monetary remedy. In the example of Brenda's central heating installation, the courts might well decide that Brenda should receive £3,000 compensation. If the land were to be sold before the court orders this remedy, would a purchaser be bound to pay the £3,000?

These questions have caused considerable difficulty: they form the context in which the proprietary status of estoppels is most controversial. They are fully discussed in Chapter 15, alongside other principles applying to licences. The orthodox (but not unchallenged) view is that it is the estoppel that binds purchasers, rather than an equitable right to a proprietary interest. If this is correct, it provides another reason for doubting whether estoppels deserve proprietary status. Not only is the remedy uncertain, but it is also difficult to explain why an estoppel, but not a contract, should have proprietary status.

Conclusions

Unlike most land law principles, much of estoppel is quite modern. Many of the principles date from its rediscovery half a century ago. That many of the rules are still being developed is one reason why it displays less certainty than other areas of land law. The stress on unconscionability means that it cannot be tied down in any precise way, as demonstrated by Lord Scott's failed attempt to do so in *Cobbe*. Indeed, it is designed to operate in contexts where strict property rules (especially as regards formalities) produce unacceptably unfair results.

Nevertheless, after *Thorner* the general principles as to when an estoppel will exist are tolerably clear. More difficult is the question of whether it is justified to have relatively generous and flexible rules operating for proprietary estoppel but not for other kinds of estoppel in other (more contractual) contexts. However, that tension has not led to serious questions or doubts as to proprietary estoppel, so these issues lie outside land law.

The remedy has given rise to substantial problems. The two basic approaches – satisfying expectations and recognising detriment – are fundamentally inconsistent, most clearly recognised by Dyson LJ in *Cobbe*. At the same time, it is clear that the courts exercise no palm-tree discretion: the remedy has to be fashioned applying legal principles. We appear to be moving towards a position whereby giving effect to expectations is the standard approach, at least where those expectations have been clearly articulated as part of an arrangement between the parties. On the other hand, this will quite often be disproportionately generous to the claimant relative to the detriment (most likely in the family setting, where an element of gift is involved). In such cases, we appear to switch to an analysis that places stress on the detriment as a measure of what should be awarded as a monetary remedy. It is difficult to avoid the conclusion that the courts have not sorted out exactly what estoppel is seeking to achieve. It is too facile to say that the courts are attempting to produce an equitable outcome: that begs the question as to what we regard as an equitable result.

Benefit and burden

This principle is similar to estoppel, but it applies unconscionability ideas in a slightly different manner. Its essence is that a person cannot insist on taking the benefit of an agreement without accepting the corresponding burden arising from it. The principle is best illustrated by taking two cases as examples.

In *ER Ives Investment Ltd v High*[28] (Extract 7.4.1), foundations of a block of flats were mistakenly placed on High's land. This was soon realised and it was agreed that the foundations could remain there. Because this restricted access to High's house, he was given a right of way across the back of the flats. Unfortunately, there was no formal grant of an easement. After the flats had been sold, the purchaser objected to the right of way. The Court of Appeal held that the purchaser had to accept the right of way if it wished the flats to remain on High's land. They could not both assert the benefit of the deal (foundations) and reject the burden (right of way).

Benefit and burden is not the same as estoppel. Although it can affect purchasers (as in *Ives*), this is by virtue of the purchaser's conduct in enforcing the agreement rather than because High had an interest in land. It appears to follow that the benefit and burden principle operates without any need for registration (in registration language, it can be seen as a personal obligation). In addition, it operates only as long as the benefit is asserted. The purchaser could tear the flats down and then deny the right of way. Needless to say, that is unlikely.

The second case is *Halsall v Brizell*[29] (Extract 7.4.2), which involved a large housing development. The developer was to maintain facilities such as roads and sewers and the first purchasers of each house agreed to contribute to the cost. The contribution obligation (a positive covenant) is not a proprietary right and so could not bind later purchasers of

[28] [1967] 2 QB 379.
[29] [1957] Ch 169.

those houses. A later purchaser of a house refused to pay. Upjohn J held that as long as he wished to use these facilities (roads, sewers), he had to pay. Obviously, the purchaser had no choice but to use these central facilities if the house was to be used.

The benefit and burden principle appeared to have a very high potential for enforcing obligations which would not normally bind a purchaser. These obligations might be non-proprietary (as in *Halsall*) or informal and unregistered (as in *Ives*). Suppose Rosalind sells a house to Sally, who promises to repair it. Sally later sells the house to Tony, who fails to repair. As in *Halsall*, the duty to repair is a positive obligation, not binding on purchasers. Could Rosalind say that Tony cannot rely on the transfer to show ownership while denying the duty to repair? Such a proposition was rejected in *Rhone v Stephens*.[30] There has to be some clear reciprocity as between the benefit and burden; furthermore, the purchaser has to exercise a choice in taking the benefit (not that there was much of a choice in either *Ives* or *Halsall*).

The facts of *Rhone* were unusual. The roof of a house also covered a cottage, the roof being supported by the cottage. The owner of both house and cottage sold the cottage, promising to repair the roof. It was held that a later purchaser of the house was not bound by that promise: there was insufficient reciprocity between the repairing obligation and the benefit of support for the roof.

It may be concluded that benefit and burden is a useful principle, applicable in a range of circumstances when normal property rules are of no help. However, it now seems to be limited to cases where each party is given directly reciprocal continuing benefits and burdens. Those cases will be relatively few.

[30] [1994] 2 AC 310 at p. 322.

Questions to consider

1. What is meant by estoppel?

2. Can estoppel be used to give effect to promises? Is estoppel useful apart from the promise cases?

3. Have recent decisions in *Cobbe* and *Thorner* changed the law to any significant extent?

4. How does the court decide what remedy to give?

5. Do estoppel claims bind purchasers? Why, if at all, should they be troubled by their doing so?

Further reading

Bright, S and McFarlane, B [2005] CLJ 449: Proprietary estoppel and property rights.

Davis, C J [1998] CLJ 522: The principle of benefit and burden.

Dixon, M (2010) 30 LS 408: Confining and defining proprietary estoppel: the role of unconscionability.

Gardner, S (2006) 122 LQR 492: The remedial discretion in proprietary estoppel – again.

Handley, K R [2008] Conv 382: Unconscionability in estoppel by conduct: a triable issue or underlying principle?

Mee, J (2008) 'The role of expectation in the determination of proprietary estoppel remedies', in *Modern Studies in Property Law*, Vol 5, ed. Cooke, Chapter 16.

Neuberger, Lord [2009] CLJ 537: The stuffing of Minerva's owl? Taxonomy and taxidermy in equity. [On estoppel following *Cobbe* and *Thorner*, stressing the contrast between commercial and domestic cases.]

Piska, N (2009) 72 MLR 998: Hopes, expectations and revocable promises in proprietary estoppel.

Robertson, A [2008] Conv 295: The reliance basis of proprietary estoppel remedies.

Visit **www.mylawchamber.co.uk** to access tools to help you develop and test your knowledge of land law, including interactive multiple choice questions, practice exam questions with guidance, weblinks, glossary flashcards, legal newsfeed and legal updates.

9 Ownership of the family home

Nature and importance

Whenever a couple (married or unmarried, with or without children) have a family home, questions may arise as to who owns it. Sometimes this may be settled by express written agreement between them, but often this does not happen. One of the parties may have taken the lead when the property was bought and had it put into his or her name. This is especially common where only that person is working. Alternatively, the house may have been owned by one of them before their relationship started. This is particularly common when it was owned in an earlier (failed) relationship.

Why should the non-legal owner have a claim? The answer will vary from case to case. They may have contributed part of the cost, paid some of the mortgage instalments, paid other household expenditure or borne responsibility for looking after the home and children. These activities may have carried on for a few months or several decades.

Although the discussion in this chapter concentrates on couples, most of the principles apply more generally. A quite common scenario is where a house is bought for parents and placed in the names of the parents or children. The other party may have contributed to the purchase and claim a share.

The financial significance of the home makes this a very important area. It is the most valuable asset of hundreds of thousands of families. Unsurprisingly, it has given rise to much litigation. Recently, the House of Lords has considered the area in *Stack* v *Dowden*[1] (Extract 8.2.1) and (as the Supreme Court) *Jones* v *Kernott*[2] (Extract 8.2.3). These are really important cases, as they support a more discretionary and less technical approach. However, the points they decide are quite specific and it remains to be seen just how far they change other principles previously established.

When does ownership become important? The most obvious answer is that the relationship between the couple may break down and they disagree as to who is entitled to what. A less obvious answer is that a third party may acquire an interest in the home.

---

[1] [2007] 2 AC 432.
[2] [2012] 1 AC 776.

Jane owns a house, burdened with quite a large mortgage. She meets Ken, who moves in with her. Soon after, she becomes pregnant and gives up work to look after the baby. Two other babies follow and she stays at home with them for the next eight years. As Jane now has no significant income, Ken pays all the mortgage instalments. Towards the end of the eight years, Jane succumbs to a gambling habit and borrows £50,000 from Limitless Bank, secured by a mortgage. Ken is quite unaware of this and Jane hides his existence from the bank. When the bank attempts to enforce its mortgage, a crucial question will be whether Ken has a share in the house binding the bank. On the facts, Ken's contribution is likely to lead to his having a share, which will bind the bank, preventing it from getting possession and selling the house. In this example, it does not matter that Jane and Ken are still (perhaps against the odds!) happily living together.

Where the parties are married, there has been since the early 1970s a statutory power[3] for the court to redistribute assets when the marriage breaks down. This means that it is unnecessary to work out the ownership of the home. It follows that ownership issues arise most frequently as regards unmarried couples, for whom there are as yet no equivalent statutory powers. However, the example involving Jane, Ken and the bank would arise even if they were married. The question there was as to who owned the house at the date of the mortgage. A court can adjust rights as between Jane and Ken, but it cannot do this retrospectively so as to affect third parties such as Limitless Bank.

Much of this chapter is devoted to discussing when the contributions of persons such as Ken give rise to shared ownership and how their shares are calculated. The courts initially relied on resulting trusts, but more recent cases (notably *Stack* and *Jones*) have rejected that and employed constructive trusts. Two general observations may now be made. The first is that trusts, a tool of financial management, seem ill-suited to the family-based problems under dispute. The courts may have had no other tool available, but it is scarcely surprising that the results have been widely condemned. The second is that the trust gives a proprietary right to persons such as Ken. The uncertainties of the present law are particularly unwelcome because land law seeks to provide certainty for those dealing with the land. We might accept uncertainty as between Jane and Ken, but it becomes less acceptable when the bank is involved. Indeed the law is widely thought to produce neither fair results for the parties nor certainty.

The main topics considered in this chapter include the operation of express written agreements, transfer into joint names at law, transfer into the name of one of the parties and the remedy that will be awarded. Finally, we consider the links between these principles and proprietary estoppel; it was observed earlier (Chapter 8) that the two areas substantially overlap. Nearly all the material under discussion has arisen over the past 40 years and it would be easy to describe the entire chapter as a Critical Issue. Four particular topics are so designated: joint names transfers, establishing the size of shares, the impact of *Stack* and *Jones* on single name transfers and the estoppel comparison.

---

[3] Matrimonial Causes Act 1973, s 24 (Extract 12.3.11).

Express declarations of trust

It will be seen later (Chapter 12) that co-ownership always involves a **trust of land**. This means that a couple who want co-ownership on the purchase of a house should execute a declaration of trust. Nearly always, this will be in the transfer document and thereby satisfy the need for writing.

We will consider two possibilities. In each of them, Charlotte starts with a half-share in a house, following a failed marriage. Her new partner, Dave, joins Charlotte in buying out her former husband's share; they fund this equally. Some years later, their relationship breaks down. In the first possibility, the legal title is transferred to Charlotte. In the second, it is transferred to Charlotte and Dave expressly on trust for them equally.

In the first possibility, there will be a trust under principles discussed in later sections. It is quite likely that the beneficial interests will reflect their contributions: Charlotte will have a three-quarters share (her original half, plus half the husband's share) and Dave a one-quarter share. That looks fair.

The second possibility mirrors the facts in **Goodman v Gallant**[4] (Extract 8.1.1). After a thorough review of the cases, the Court of Appeal concluded that the declaration of trust in the conveyance was conclusive: the parties each had a half-share. This result has the great merit of providing certainty and reducing litigation: everybody can rely on the words of the conveyance. Yet it may be seen as not entirely fair on Charlotte, who provided three-quarters of the money. That, however, is to take an unduly money-based approach. If Charlotte has formally declared that she wishes Dave to have a half-share, why should she not be held to that? One danger is that the lawyers may have failed fully to explain to Charlotte what she was agreeing to. Few people carefully read and understand all the documents they sign.

The result in *Goodman* has never been seriously challenged, though it can be side-stepped in limited circumstances. In particular, it can be avoided if there is a misrepresentation or mistake such that the conveyance does not represent the parties' true intentions. Suppose that Dave is contributing nothing, but that a lender tells Charlotte that the loan depends on there being a joint transfer to them, with a joint mortgage to the lender. The understanding between Charlotte and Dave is that the house is to belong to Charlotte alone; Dave's name is included solely to satisfy the lender. Any declaration of trust in such circumstances is plainly a mistake and the conveyance can be rectified, removing Dave's beneficial half-share. Probably, it is also possible to find a common intention to change the shares at a later stage. *Jones v Kernott* involved a change in intention, though there was no express declaration; the point is discussed later in this chapter.

---

[4] [1986] Fam 106.

Transfer into joint names

Suppose that, in the example concerning Charlotte and Dave, the transfer is into their joint names, without any mention of beneficial interests. The statutory forms require modern transfers to state the nature of the beneficial rights in the transfer. Though this may not always be complied with, it means that problems should arise infrequently in recent registered land transfers.

However, such a problem did arise in *Stack* v *Dowden*, in which the home had been bought before the transfer forms required beneficial interests to be specified. Traditional thinking had been that a transfer into joint names gives rise to a resulting trust reflecting contributions. However, the House of Lords (Lord Neuberger disagreeing) held that, where a family home is involved, the presumption should be of equal beneficial interests. This was felt best to match the intentions of the parties, who are unlikely to be thinking in terms of financial calculations when a joint names transfer is used. This is supported by the widespread use of a joint tenancy when beneficial interests are expressly declared. *Stack* was explicitly approved by the Supreme Court in *Jones* v *Kernott*.

However, it is possible to reverse this presumption by showing a common intention that the shares should be unequal. Though this was said to require very unusual circumstances, such a common intention was found on the facts in *Stack*. This was based on the almost total separation of the finances of the parties (other than the house), despite their living together for more than 20 years. On that basis a 65:35 split was upheld, reflecting their contributions. Critics have observed that such separation of finances is by no means rare, so the 'very unusual' case may be quite common.

Subsequently, the Court of Appeal in *Fowler* v *Barron*[5] (Extract 8.2.2) has shown that joint ownership will apply even if one person has paid all the cost of the house: far more extreme circumstances than in *Stack*. The court stressed that the separation of finances in *Stack* was lacking, so that the presumption of equal shares was to be applied. One problem in finding unequal shares in *Fowler* was in justifying any figure when one person has paid all: nobody argued that zero was appropriate.

Finally, *Jones* v *Kernott* illustrates that the common intention may arise at a later date (most likely after the couple separate), so that the shares cease to be equal. This is discussed later.

Transfer into a single name

This is the context of the great majority of the cases. As will be seen, *Stack* almost certainly liberalises the law in this area, as may *Jones*. Unfortunately, the extent of this is by no means clear – it remains necessary to consider the older ideas. An initial point is that *Stack* confirms that the starting point is that the land is owned solely by the legal owner: there is no general principle that a couple jointly own their home.

---

[5] [2009] 2 FLR 831.

Background and early developments

Almost always couples buy land with a large mortgage loan. A cash deposit will constitute a fairly small proportion of the cost, at least for first-time buyers.

A house is purchased in Gabriella's name. Her partner, Harry, pays part of the deposit. This clearly gives Harry a beneficial interest under a trust (originally aided by resulting trust thinking, though this no longer applies). What happens if, instead, Harry helps to pay the mortgage instalments? A very strict analysis might say that Gabriella has raised the purchase money on mortgage and has paid the entire cost: Harry gets nothing. That has always been seen as far too strict.

As soon as we recognise mortgage instalments as contributions giving a share, problems abound. Do we credit Harry with just the capital component of each instalment (usually very small, if anything at all)? What if Harry pays for the housekeeping so that Gabriella can afford the mortgage instalments? Our example is unusual in that it is the woman who is the major contributor. In most cases it is the man who has the legal title and the woman who is claiming a share. Frequently, she earns less than he does, especially if looking after children. An approach that stresses financial contributions is bound to favour men over women, given typical roles in families.

At one stage, it appeared that the courts might be developing a concept of family assets, sharing assets between the parties. That development was halted by the House of Lords in *Pettitt v Pettitt*[6] (Extract 8.4.11). A bare majority held that the cases had to be determined by conventional trusts concepts. There is no special family assets analysis, nor any judicial discretion. *Pettitt* is essentially backwards-looking: it rejects ideas put forward over the previous ten years.

The context of *Pettitt* – spouses – made the idea of family assets credible. It is less needed now their assets are subject to a statutory discretion. Family assets provides more of a challenge where unmarried couples are involved, as relationships can vary so much. Nevertheless, some modern thinking employs a very similar analysis for unmarried couples who share financial responsibilities – this lay at the heart of some of the reasoning in *Stack*.

Gissing v Gissing

Soon after *Pettitt*, the House of Lords in *Gissing*[7] (Extract 8.3.1) clarified the effect of their earlier decision and established principles to be applied in future cases. We will delay looking at its facts until we reach the issue of indirect contributions.

The essence of *Gissing*, still applied today, is that we look for a common intention. As everybody appreciates, couples buying their first home together rarely thrash out the details of their rights in detailed discussions regarding their shares. If they do, then it is

[6] [1970] AC 777.
[7] [1971] AC 886.

likely that the conveyance will contain an appropriate declaration of trust. We have seen that *Stack* and *Jones* confirm that the common intention takes effect through a constructive (not resulting) trust. This facilitates a more broad-brush approach and is much easier to apply where the shares are not based on financial contributions.

The courts will readily imply a common intention from their contributions to the purchase and to the mortgage. Many commentators have observed that this common intention is largely fictitious. It may indeed be appropriate for the law to recognise contributions, but common intention provides an insecure intellectual base. We will see that it has been widely criticised.

Alternatively, the courts may find that the parties have actually agreed what their shares should be: the express common intention. This cannot be effective without writing. However, if a party acts to their detriment on the basis of the common intention, then it would be unconscionable for the legal owner to deny an appropriate share.

There has been much discussion whether the cases should be explained as based upon resulting trusts or constructive trusts. The resulting trust applies readily to capital contributions, but is very difficult to apply to express common intentions. More generally, the resulting trust is prone to produce arithmetical solutions and is difficult to fit in with non-financial contributions. In *Stack*, the House of Lords was clear that, for both joint names and single names transfers, the constructive trust provides the most appropriate analysis so far as the family home is concerned.

⬤ Inferred and imputed intentions

CRITICAL ISSUE

Gissing fully accepts that the courts can draw inferences from the facts that the parties intended to share ownership. What was not permissible is for the courts to impose what they think to be a reasonable intention: an imputed intention. The freedom to find imputed intentions would enable the courts to impose results they think to be fair. Though one cannot rationally argue against fairness, there may be doubts whether such an interventionalist approach in property matters is justified.

In *Stack*, Lord Walker was critical of the old distinction between inferred intentions and imputed intentions. Lord Walker clearly thought that inferred intentions are largely fictitious and that it is more accurate to describe the intention as imputed. Lord Neuberger strongly disagreed and his views certainly reflect traditional analyses. Baroness Hale refers to inferred and imputed intentions, but without stressing the point.

Imputing intentions was central to *Jones v Kernott*. As we shall see, the Supreme Court accepts that intentions can be imputed when determining the size of the shares. However, the initial finding of a common intention (whether to change the shares from being equal, as in *Jones*, or to find an intention to share in single names transfers) is outside this freedom to impute shares.[8]

When we look at *Jones* in more detail, a bewildering variety of views are expressed. Apart from Lord Collins, all the judges seem to accept that inferring and imputing intentions are different, even if they may often reach the same result. Indeed, Lord Kerr is thoroughly

---

[8] See especially [2012] 1 AC 776 at [31] and [51] (Lord Walker and Lady Hale, delivering the leading judgment).

critical of imputing intentions, favouring a more direct imposition of a fair outcome. But it would be quite wrong to think that the judges agree with Lord Neuberger – they all want the freedom to impute intentions in the quantification of shares.

So far, one might suppose that imputing intentions has no role to place in finding a common intention in a single names transfer. Whilst that does appear to be the present position,[9] it might be unsafe to assume that it will remain unchallenged. To operate different bases for finding common intentions in different contexts does not make obvious sense. The thrust of *Jones* is to give more freedom to the courts to find fair results. In particular, the dicta of Lord Wilson seem more generally welcoming of imputing intentions. There is still much to play for!

Contributions and inferred common intentions

Direct financial contributions

A capital contribution to the purchase of a home virtually always gives rise to an inferred intention to share ownership. In theory, it could be a gift to the legal owner, but that conclusion is rarely reached. In **Midland Bank plc v Cooke**,[10] the husband's parents gave a wedding present of a 13 per cent contribution to the cost of buying a house. It was found to be a gift to both husband and wife. On that basis, the wife was able to claim a 6.5 per cent contribution to the purchase of the house (her only financial contribution). As we see later, the Court of Appeal went on to award her a half-share because they had agreed 'to share everything equally'. It is an irony that her half-share was based on her husband's parents' present.

Contributions to mortgage instalments also readily justify finding an implied common intention. However, this is not automatic: there has to be some consistency in the making of payments. It follows that contributing one or two instalments (perhaps for some short-term reason, such as the legal owner's illness) is very unlikely to count. In *Gissing*, Lord Diplock required the contributions to be 'regular and substantial'; this is supported by later cases.

Contributions are very readily proved when the couple maintain a joint bank account and the mortgage payments are made out of the account. The courts are likely to reason that the money in the account is jointly owned and that this results in contribution by both. In addition, the decision to have a joint account helps to prove a sharing of assets, and thereby a common intention. These factors were significant in the Privy Council decision in **Abbott v Abbott**[11] to uphold an order for equal beneficial ownership. The position where there is a joint account but the legal owner is the only person paying money into it does not appear to have been settled.

Indirect financial contributions

What is meant by an indirect financial contribution? It is best illustrated by an example.

---

[9] *Geary v Rankine* [2012] 2 FLR 1409 at [19] (Court of Appeal).
[10] [1995] 4 All ER 562; *Abbott v Abbott* [2008] 1 FLR 1451 (PC) involved similar facts.
[11] [2008] 1 FLR 1451.

Marion and Neill set up home together. Neill has savings of £50,000, which he puts into buying a house. He borrows £150,000 on mortgage and the house is registered in his name alone. Marion and Neill each earn (after tax) £1,300 a month. Neill pays the monthly mortgage instalments, amounting to £900. Marion pays household (food, electricity, council tax, etc) and car expenses, averaging £700 a month. They share personal expenses (including clothes, travelling and holidays). What these figures show is that Neill could not afford to pay the mortgage without the assistance provided by Marion: their core expenditure exceeds what Neill earns. The direct payment of mortgage instalments all comes from Neill. However, Marion can be said to make indirect contributions because her expenditure on the family enables Neill to pay the mortgage.

The wife in *Gissing* relied on making indirect contributions. She had bought some household equipment and paid for her clothes. Lord Diplock asked whether the wife's expenditure changed as a result of the house purchase and, in particular, made it possible for the husband to pay the mortgage instalments. However, the facts fell far short of satisfying these requirements.

Gissing might lead us to suppose that Marion would be able to claim a share. One can see the attraction of the argument that cases should not depend on the largely fortuitous question as to how a couple choose to divide family expenditure. However, doubts began to be expressed in the 1980s and then the House of Lords in *Lloyds Bank plc v Rosset*[12] (Extract 8.4.7) appeared to rule out indirect contributions, though without much reasoning. Nevertheless, a deputy judge in *Le Foe v Le Foe*[13] subsequently recognised relatively small indirect contributions. This was welcomed by commentators and the Law Commission.

Most important, however, are the dicta in *Stack v Dowden*. Both Lord Walker and Baroness Hale state (obiter) that the *Rosset* requirements are too strict. The analysis of Lord Walker shows that he is most concerned about the rejection of indirect financial contributions. It would be surprising, especially in the light of *Le Foe* and its support by the Law Commission, if *Rosset* were to survive on this point. Indeed, at County Court level indirect contributions have been assumed to count.[14]

However, indirect contributions are notoriously complex in their operation. The pre-*Stack* cases thought it necessary to show that the legal owner could not otherwise have afforded the mortgage instalments. A common scenario involves a couple with a child, where the mother works and contributes to expenditure when the child becomes older. While the child is young and the mother is at home, the father (legal owner) pays the mortgage and all other expenses out of his income. It is a struggle, but the couple cope. It is difficult to argue that the mother's later contributions while working are essential for the mortgage to be paid.

A further problem is that much depends on the wealth and earnings of the legal owner. The poorer the legal owner, the easier it is to prove that the indirect contributions assisted payment of the mortgage instalments. Most people would regard it as odd that

[12] [1991] 1 AC 107.
[13] [2001] 2 FLR 970 (Nicholas Mostyn QC).
[14] *Webster* v *Webster* [2009] 1 FLR 1240; a wide view of the effect of *Stack* was adopted.

the same contributions may give rise to a share in the home of a relatively poor partner but none in that of a wealthy partner. Indirect contributions can certainly be argued to have a useful role to play, but they are no panacea for all the family home difficulties.

Yet *Stack* might herald a more liberal approach to what counts as an indirect contribution: perhaps any sustained and significant contribution to family finances will suffice. This fits the modern approach (discussed below) to place considerable stress on how the couple share family obligations. This would make indirect contributions a much fairer and reliable route to finding a common intention.

Non-financial contributions

> Suppose a couple are living together. When the woman becomes pregnant with their second child, the man buys a house for them. The woman stays at home looking after the house and children for the next 12 years. After the relationship breaks down (after 19 years), does she have any right to the house?

These were the facts of **Burns v Burns**[15] (Extract 8.4.6). The Court of Appeal found no contribution to the purchase and dismissed the woman's claim. *Burns* represents a very financial approach to contributions.

> Consider two families, in both of which there are two young children. Andy and Briony decide that the children should go to a private nursery and that Briony should continue working. It takes all their joint income to pay the mortgage instalments, household and high nursery expenses. In the second family, George and Harriet decide that Harriet should stay at home to look after the children. As there are no nursery expenses, George can afford mortgage and household costs. Briony is very likely to have a good claim to a share in the house. Harriet, by contrast, clearly has no claim. Yet they have both contributed hugely to the family.

It cannot escape attention that it is almost always the mother who stays at home with the children and who loses out because such domestic activities are not recognised. More than any other, this area demonstrates the failure of a trusts-based system to cope with family circumstances. *Stack* takes a fresh approach to common intention and it is quite possible that this (coupled with the criticism of *Rosset*) could lead to a change in this area. Because the dicta are directed principally at the quantification of shares, we will postpone discussion until that area has been covered.

⬤ Express common intentions

As an alternative to implying a common intention from contributions, a court may find that the parties actually agreed that they should share ownership. This was given some prominence in *Rosset*.

---

[15] [1984] Ch 317.

By itself, a common intention is not enough: there has to be some sort of detriment before the lack of writing can be overcome. It is this which renders the conduct of the legal owner unconscionable, thereby justifying a constructive trust. Financial contributions, even if indirect, clearly constitute detriment; problems in showing detriment are likely only for express common intentions. Though extensive work on the premises (going beyond normal day-to-day activities) will be recognised, *Rosset* shows limits to this. A derelict house was being renovated. The wife spent much time supervising the work of the builders. The House of Lords regarded this as falling far short of what is required before an express agreement will be enforceable. Though some commentators have noted that detriment forms no part of the House of Lords analysis in *Stack*, it seems probable that it is still required.[16]

When will express intentions be relevant? If the parties explicitly agree to share ownership, they are most likely to put the house into joint names. Most express intentions in single name transfers will arise implicitly from conversations. In *Rosset*, the House of Lords stressed that the couple's intention to share the *home* did not suffice: there must be an intention to share *ownership*. When a couple refer to 'our home', this generally signifies no more than the house in which they live: the language would be appropriate if it were merely rented.

In *Rosset*, Lord Bridge explained two earlier cases as being based on express intentions. We will look at the first of these, *Eves* v *Eves*.[17] A young couple purchased a home, the man telling the woman that it could not be put in joint names because she was under 21. He later described this as an excuse to ensure that he had sole ownership. On the face of it, this looks more like an agreement that she should *not* have a share. However, it is treated as an agreement that she should have an interest, but that it is not possible for her to have a legal estate. Unless there was an underlying agreement that she should have an interest, it would have been wholly unnecessary to discuss legal ownership.

This analysis has been criticised by commentators on the basis that the intention as to equitable ownership did not really exist. It may be accepted that it is difficult (though not impossible) to spell out such an intention from conversations which conclude that no interest is given. Part of the criticism lies in the fact that the man clearly did not intend her to have an interest, so that there was no *common* intention. This criticism seems clearly misguided. Common intention (here, as in contract generally) is assessed on an objective basis. If the man gave the impression that she was to have a beneficial interest, then his private unspoken intentions are irrelevant.

The express common intention poses something of a paradox. If the parties have clearly agreed to share ownership then one's natural inclination is to give effect to their wishes. On the other hand, this approach readily descends into the farce of trying to remember 'the tenderest exchanges of a common law courtship', as Waite LJ has

---

[16] Numerous cases (most recently *Garwood* v *Ambrose* [2012] BPIR 996 (Ch) at [24]) assume that it is required, though without discussion of the arguments of Gardner (2008) 124 LQR 422 at p. 424 and Etherton [2008] CLJ 265 at p. 277.

[17] [1975] 1 WLR 1338. *Grant* v *Edwards* [1986] Ch 638 (Extract 8.6.1) is similar: property not put in the woman's name because of complications arising from her divorce proceedings.

described it. Now that *Stack* heralds a more generous approach to inferring intentions from conduct, it may be hoped that express intentions will be less relied upon.

Intentions after purchase: improvements

Suppose Sally is a successful solicitor who buys a house for herself, largely funded by a mortgage. Some years later she meets Terry, who moves in with her. She becomes pregnant and gives up work for the next ten years to look after her young children. During those ten years, Terry bears all the household expenses, including the mortgage instalments.

Sally obviously starts off as the sole owner. Any common intention can only commence later and will operate to effect a change of ownership. Yet Terry's contribution would clearly have given him an interest if they had bought the house as a family home. The situation is an increasingly common one, as people frequently own houses either as single persons (like Sally) or from a previous failed relationship.

A number of cases deal with this situation, but they fail to give authoritative and useful, practical guidance. In *Rosset*, Lord Bridge said that the common intention might arise 'exceptionally at some later date' (i.e., after purchase) and *Stack* recognises that it may change during a relationship. A later express common intention is plainly possible, but is likely to be difficult to prove. One would expect financial contributions to provide the best argument. Even then, the courts have shown a surprising caution in implying a common intention.

Jones v *Kernott* was based on a post-purchase common intention, but in very different circumstances. There was a transfer into joint names, which meant that (applying *Stack*) the parties held equal beneficial interests. When the relationship failed, the man left and thereafter made no contribution to the mortgage or other property expenses; the woman enjoyed sole occupation. Usually, such disputes relating to post-separation events are resolved using a process called accounting (see Chapter 12). However, in *Jones* this would have involved great complexity, as 13 years had elapsed between separation and the man's claiming his share. The court was able to find a common intention that the shares should be crystallised at a time two years into the separation when the parties cashed in an endowment life insurance policy. It is obvious that much depends upon the facts, but the case illustrates how shares can be changed if suitable evidence exists.

Improvements are considered in this section as they also occur after purchase. *Pettitt* held that minor DIY activities do not suffice. On the other hand, paying for significant improvements will probably give rise to an interest. In *Hussey* v *Palmer*[18] (Extract 8.4.1), a mother moved in with her daughter's family. She paid to have her daughter's house extended and lived in the new extension. Mother and daughter quarrelled and the mother moved out. The Court of Appeal held that a trust in the mother's favour arose in these circumstances.

Finding a trust is thought to be more difficult if the claimant personally carries out the work. However, there are indications that the claim will succeed if the work is of a type and extent as would normally be undertaken by a contractor. Again, one can see the preference for financial contributions. It is worth noting that improvements rarely occur

[18] [1972] 1 WLR 1286.

as the only reason for finding a common intention. If other factors prove a common intention, then improvements can be taken into account in deciding how large the share shall be.

Quantifying the shares

Once a common intention has been found, the further question arises as to what size the share should be. If the parties have agreed on the shares, that will settle the outcome, but other cases give rise to greater difficulties.

Resulting or constructive trust?

The question as to the type of trust is particularly important for quantification. In a resulting trust, the shares reflect the amount contributed by each party, though this need not demand a very precise mathematical calculation. The constructive trust is based on more general ideas of unconscionability. It is thought to provide greater freedom for the courts to fashion an appropriate remedy, as they are less tied to contributions.

Prior to *Stack* and *Jones*, the leading case was *Oxley* v *Hiscock*[19] (Extract 8.4.14). Chadwick LJ (delivering the only judgment) came down in favour of the constructive trust. An important plank in the reasoning is that the contribution need not determine the size of the shares. That approach is supported by *Midland Bank plc* v *Cooke*,[20] the case in which a wedding present constituted a 6.5 per cent contribution. Despite this small contribution, the Court of Appeal gave the wife a half-share in the house. Another justification for the use of constructive trusts relates to the express common intention. In *Eves*, the woman was awarded a one-quarter share. A resulting trust analysis for a case such as *Eves* is completely out of the question: there was simply no contribution upon which a resulting trust could be imposed.

The stress on constructive trusts was confirmed by *Stack* and *Jones*, as well as the Privy Council in *Abbott* v *Abbott*. It should be stressed that this applies as much to the single name transfer as to the joint names transfer in *Stack* itself. This need not mean that resulting trust ideas are to be completely forgotten: the parties' contributions are sometimes very significant in determining the outcome, as seen in *Stack*.

The role of common intention

In *Cooke*, Waite LJ stressed the nature of the relationship; this showed that the parties shared assets and expenditure. On that basis, he was able to find an intention of equal shares, even though the contribution to the purchase had been merely 6.5 per cent. The common intention approach was rejected in *Oxley*. In particular, to look for such an intention at the time of purchase was regarded as 'artificial – and an unnecessary fiction'.

---

[19] [2005] Fam 211.
[20] [1995] 4 All ER 562; above (p. 100).

Instead, *Oxley* adopted the test that the court will award such shares as are fair on all the facts.

Though *Stack* is generally very supportive of *Oxley*, this was one point upon which the *Oxley* analysis was rejected. It was thought inconsistent with the role of the court to apply such a judicial discretion based upon fairness. Instead the share should depend on the common intention of the parties, which may change after the date of purchase. This is, of course, what has to be proved to show that there is some sharing in single name transfers (described as the 'first hurdle' in *Stack*, before quantification issues become relevant).

The Supreme Court returned to the question in **Jones v Kernott**. All the judges recognised that it is not always easy to find a common intention relating to the quantum of shares. Yet if the parties have a common intention to share (or to vary shares), then there has to be some mechanism to determine those shares. If an actual or inferred intention can be found, then it should be given effect to. Otherwise, the court will impute an intention to the parties, based on what reasonable and just people would think. The Supreme Court is explicit that this approach applies for both joint and single name transfers. Though not admitted by Lord Walker and Lady Hale, *Jones* represents, in substance, a return to the fairness test articulated in *Oxley*. Indeed, Lord Kerr would have preferred a test directly based upon fairness and Lord Wilson was critical of the *Stack* comments on *Oxley*. The majority concluded that on the facts (described above) there was an inferred common intention that the man's share should be reduced to 10 per cent. However, Lords Kerr and Wilson thought it impossible to infer any such intention and that the appropriate approach was to impute an intention, whilst agreeing with the 10 per cent share.

How is common intention inferred?

Two dicta will be quoted. The first is from *Oxley*, approved in *Stack*:

> ... each is entitled to that share which the court considers fair having regard to the whole course of dealing between them in relation to the property. And, in that context, 'the whole course of dealing between them in relation to the property' includes the arrangements which they make from time to time in order to meet the outgoings (for example, mortgage contributions, council tax and utilities, repairs, insurance and housekeeping) which have to be met if they are to live in the property as their home.

The second is from Baroness Hale in *Stack*:

> Many more factors than financial contributions may be relevant to divining the parties' true intentions. These include: any advice or discussions at the time of the transfer which cast light upon their intentions then; the reasons why the home was acquired in their joint names; the reasons why (if it be the case) the survivor was authorised to give a receipt for the capital moneys; the purpose for which the home was acquired; the nature of the parties' relationship; whether they had children for whom they both had responsibility to provide a home; how the purchase was financed, both initially and subsequently; how the parties arranged their finances, whether separately or together or a bit of both; how they discharged the outgoings on the property and their other household expenses.

Though less restrictive than the traditional requirements, the factors stressed in *Oxley* are exclusively financial. This is illustrated by the decision on the facts. The house cost £127,000. H (Hiscock) and O (Oxley) provided £25,000 and £36,500 respectively from the sale of their previous houses. H provided a further £35,500 from his savings and the balance of £30,000 was provided by a mortgage. If one were to split the mortgage between them, a resulting trust analysis would give H a 59.6 per cent share. Using a constructive trust, the Court of Appeal decided that H was entitled to a 60 per cent share.

Though it is immediately obvious that financial contributions lay at the heart of assessing fairness, one element of the facts is very significant. The court treated the mortgage loan as equally provided by the parties, though there was no discussion as to how payments were made. This willingness to use ideas of sharing to split the mortgage between the parties may be very valuable, as the mortgage loan is frequently by far the greatest contribution to the purchase price. However, this works only if the claimant is working and thereby being able to contribute to family expenditure.

Turning to the dicta of Baroness Hale, these plainly take non-financial considerations into account. Yet it must be remembered that these dicta were in the context of a joint names transfer. Baroness Hale went out of her way to stress that the inferences to be drawn 'may be very different' in single name transfers. This is because of the presumption of equality in joint names transfers. In that context, to show unequal contributions comes nowhere close to rebutting that presumption. The factors she relies upon may go far to explain why equality makes sense in the context of the particular relationship. In the single name transfer, there is no presumption of equality. Once the first hurdle has been cleared, we know that the claimant will get some share, but no more than that.

It is difficult to assess just how much difference *Stack* makes. It may be that it remains appropriate in a single name transfer to start with a presumption of shares based on financial contributions (applying *Oxley*), but with freedom to move beyond that if the facts justify this. This may be seen in the earlier case of **Midland Bank plc v Cooke**, in which a sharing relationship led to shares being equal, and in the similar recent decision in **CPS v Piper**.[21] It may be relevant that both these cases involved spouses. Other cases display much more reluctance to favour equal shares, as seen in the recent decision in **Thomson v Hurst**.[22]

As indicated above, it may not be difficult to treat the mortgage as attributable to both parties where they both contribute to family expenses – that will go far towards equality in many cases. In particular, equality will be relatively straightforward if, as in *Abbott*, there is a joint bank account. However, in a significant number of cases one of the parties will have made a substantial capital contribution, most obviously when the house was already owned when the relationship commenced. It will take quite exceptional facts to justify equal beneficial shares in those circumstances.

CRITICAL ISSUE

---

[21] [2011] EWHC 3570 (Admin).
[22] [2012] 30 March (Court of Appeal).

The impact of *Stack* and *Jones* in single name transfers

We are not here interested in questions of calculation, but with the 'first hurdle' question as to whether there is a common intention at all.

Some aspects of these cases have already been considered. We have seen that a movement to imputing intentions could have a really radical effect, though at present imputed intentions seem limited to the quantification stage. When discussing indirect contributions, it was seen that *Rosset* was criticised by *Stack* as being too restrictive, though a balancing factor is that the House of Lords stressed that the starting point remains that a transfer into a single name gives that person sole ownership. The problem here is that few clues are given as to what this means – at least, outside indirect contributions.

Most helpful is Baroness Hale's analysis of common intention in the quantification context, often summarised as requiring a holistic view of the circumstances. It is easy to see that these dicta go way beyond the narrow stress on financial contributions found in *Rosset* and other earlier cases. Can these be used to bypass the earlier cases, especially *Burns* v *Burns* on non-financial contributions? Part of the problem is that Baroness Hale herself stresses that her dicta cannot readily be carried across into the single name context, a point repeated by Lord Walker and Lady Hale in *Jones*. As she states, things really are different where there is a transfer into joint names and a starting point of equality.

When we look at the cases in the years since *Stack*, none has offered a full analysis of the issues. Most judges have been content to summarise their understanding of *Stack* (and, more recently, *Jones*). However, a consistent picture is that the courts are citing Baroness Hale's dicta as applying to the 'first hurdle' issue for single names cases. Despite the caution of Baroness Hale, this is unsurprising. To say that the courts can take account of different factors, according to the stage of the enquiry, in deciding whether there is a common intention would seem very odd.

Stack tells what factors we can take into account, but what conclusions are to be drawn from them? There is little or no evidence that *Stack* is having any practical effect on the way single name cases are being decided. Several recent cases tell us that *Rosset* (together with the other earlier cases) remains authoritative in telling us what inferences should be drawn. Indeed, in *Thomson* v *Humphrey*[23] Warren J refers to *Burns* approvingly. This is significant, as it is the non-financial contribution cases which (though relatively rare) demonstrate the failure to provide for those who chose to stay at home to look after children. Nevertheless, it may be that we are still in the midst of a change in direction, a change which is encouraged by *Jones*. It may be unsafe to assume the courts will continue with the approach just described.

Reform

The deficiencies in the present law are all too obvious from the analyses above. The present law combines complexity and unpredictability in its application. Some of the worst

[23] [2010] 2FLR 107 at [29].

deficiencies may be removed by *Stack* and *Jones*, but the law remains in an uncertain state.

At least the law has sought to recognise rights of some of those who do not have the legal title. The trust may have been the only tool available for redistributing property rights and the common intention the most natural route into finding a trust. However, the trust is at heart a device for financial management, ill-suited for dealing with family issues. It may be better than nothing, but its use both subverts trust law principles and is an inadequate response to the needs of those sharing homes. In particular, the stress on common intention seems highly artificial. Even though *Stack* and *Jones* doubtless introduce greater flexibility, the cornerstone of the courts' analysis very clearly remains the common intention.

The problem lies in knowing what to put in its place. Some argue for an unjust enrichment basis, though this may not be easy to apply and would not normally produce an equality outcome. A few years ago, the Law Commission[24] attempted to produce a scheme for shared ownership of homes that would operate to the exclusion of intention. The attempt failed: quite unacceptable results followed from ignoring intention. In part, this was a result of a commendable attempt to include virtually all non-commercial relationships and to give effect to all forms of contribution.

It may be thought that, rather than using established legal categories such as trusts and unjust enrichment, we should look to family law principles as the way forward. These principles are almost always enshrined in legislation, rather than common law. Some countries have schemes for joint ownership of the family home, often described as community property. This was proposed a few decades ago for married couples in England, but this was never implemented. It isn't really needed for married couples, given the statutory discretion to redistribute assets on divorce. Other relationships take such a variety of forms that a single response may produce inappropriate results. People live together for short or long periods, with and without children. Sometimes one of the parties is married and living with their spouse. In other cases, they may be close friends or relatives, without any sexual relationship.

A more promising approach is to use the model of the statutory discretions available on marriage breakdown. Few argue in favour of simply copying those discretions to unmarried couples, as that would fail to recognise the real differences between the relationships. The Law Commission undertook a major review of the area, stressing the financial consequences of relationship breakdown.[25] They recommend that courts be given a discretion regarding cohabitants living in a joint household (most especially where there are children), applicable when their relationship breaks down. The discretion would include the reallocation of property rights.

The criteria to be applied would be quite different from those operating on divorce. Stress would be placed on economic advantages resulting from contributions and on economic disadvantages or sacrifices, but ignoring advantages and disadvantages operating only during the relationship. These proposals look valuable, though there is no likelihood of their being implemented in the near future.

---

[24] *Sharing Homes*: Law Com No 278.
[25] Law Com No 307 (2007).

Estoppel and constructive trusts

Over the past 20 years, many judges have commented on the similarity between these two legal doctrines. Each sets out to avoid unconscionable conduct. Each involves expectations: in **estoppel** we refer to representations or mistakes; in constructive trusts we refer to common intentions. Each requires the claimant to act to their detriment in order to show unconscionability.

It is therefore unsurprising that, as discussed below, the doctrines are converging. However, there are differences in the typical factual settings in which they arise. As regards the family home, the constructive trust has been used when the question is whether the parties should share ownership. Estoppels have arisen where somebody expects to have sole ownership or some other right (life interest or easement, for example); the context is rarely that of the acquisition of the property. The fact that they have been used in different factual situations doubtless explains why it took time for their similarities to receive attention.

Within the family home context, it would be wrong to think that constructive trusts and estoppel cover exactly the same ground. Two points might be made. Taking constructive trusts first, most of the law lies in when a common intention will be inferred (or imputed). There is no true equivalent of this in the estoppel framework. Indeed, it is the express common intention cases that have given rise to the comparisons being stressed. It is no accident that the first significant dicta on the comparison are found in *Grant v Edwards*[26] (Extract 8.4.13), one of the two pre-*Rosset* cases on express intentions. Next, an important aspect of estoppel is the operation of acquiescence: where the owner allows a person to spend money on the basis of a mistake. There is no equivalent of this in constructive trusts.

This is not to say that a combined doctrine could never embody all these points. Rather, it is not feasible to think about the simple elimination of one of the doctrines: each has its special rules and uses. What might be expected is that, where they overlap, their rules may converge so that each principle produces the same answer. Thus, *Yaxley v Gotts*[27] (Extract 5.2.11) (a case on the overlap in the context of contracts to sell land) regarded the doctrines as 'closely akin to, if not indistinguishable'. It would be most unfortunate if we were to say that a person loses because they have relied on, say, estoppel when a constructive trust would have brought success.

We now turn to the principal areas in which comparisons can be made.

Common intention compared with assumptions and expectations

Is the common intention of the constructive trust different from the assumption or expectation of estoppel? It might be possible to argue that common intention is a form of agreement between the parties – rather like contract. On the other hand, estoppel is more unilateral in nature. Some cases involve representations, most obviously in the

[26] [1986] Ch 638.
[27] [2000] Ch 162.

informal gifts cases (for example ***Dillwyn* v *Llewelyn***[28] (Extract 7.2.1), in which the father orally gave land to a son), whereas others involve mistakes and acquiescence.

Differences between the operation of the doctrines might be justified if they do in fact deal with different sorts of factual situations. Yet it is not clear that factual situations can be neatly distinguished in this manner. *Dillwyn* is a good example of a representation, but many other leading estoppel cases seem more contractual in nature. For example, some of the ***Jennings* v *Rice***[29] (Extract 7.2.5) line of cases can be seen as being close to contract: the owner agrees to leave property by will to the claimant, in return for care services. This is emphasised by the distinction drawn by Robert Walker LJ between two types of estoppel cases: those which have a 'a consensual character falling not far short of an enforceable contract' and others in which there are uncertain expectations.

Some commentators have argued that estoppel may provide greater flexibility: there is less need for certainty as to the property right involved. Yet both principles are based on unconscionability and it would be surprising if great precision were required by either. We saw in Chapter 8 that ***Cobbe* v *Yeoman's Row Management Ltd***[30] (Extract 7.1.4) and ***Thorner* v *Major***[31] (Extract 7.1.5) contain differing views on the role of certainty in estoppel.

Detrimental reliance

This area was discussed by Sir Nicolas Browne-Wilkinson V-C in the common intention case of ***Grant* v *Edwards***[32] (Extract 8.6.1). Most discussion of detrimental reliance is found in estoppel cases and Browne-Wilkinson V-C considered that the common intention principles should be influenced by those cases.

Is it necessary to prove that the detriment was incurred because of the common intention? Many family activities might be undertaken anyway because of the family relationship, regardless of whether there is a common intention as to property rights. In the estoppel setting,[33] we saw that the courts presume the detriment to be incurred because of the assumption or expectation: a principle which is very favourable to claimants. ***Grant* v *Edwards*** supports the application of the same principle to the constructive trust.

Remedies

It has been seen that the courts have a distinct discretion as regards the remedy in estoppel. Constructive trusts, by contrast, place less stress on discretionary remedies. For a time it looked as if this would change: in ***Oxley* v *Hiscock*** (Extract 8.4.14) Chadwick LJ relied on the estoppel cases for his conclusion that the courts would award a fair share to each party. We have seen that the result of *Stack* and *Jones* is that imputed intentions (which can be seen as much the same as fair shares) operate, but only if there is no actual or

[28] (1862) 4 De GF&J 517 (45 ER 1285).
[29] [2003] 1 P&CR 100.
[30] [2008] 1 WLR 1752.
[31] [2009] 1 WLR 776; see above (p. 83).
[32] [1986] Ch 638.
[33] See p. 85, above.

inferred common intention. However, where an intention is inferred the criteria employed look very different from the discretion in estoppel.

The relationship between estoppel and constructive trust is further developed by Lord Walker in *Stack*. He stresses that constructive trusts are used to determine the shares of the parties, whereas an estoppel simply provides jurisdiction to award a remedy, which is designed to be the minimum to do justice and may be a monetary award. He observed that his own dicta in *Yaxley* promoted the linking of estoppel and constructive trust. Plainly, *Stack* displays second thoughts and he is now 'rather less enthusiastic' about any complete assimilation of the concepts. It does not seem that this is materially affected by the developments in *Jones*.

Should the law rationally treat constructive trusts and estoppel as different regarding remedies? One might argue that where the parties are acting together (common intention constructive trust) then it makes sense to award what they have agreed. Where there is a simple representation or acquiescence (estoppel), then awarding the expectation is more likely to be disproportionate. This is seen in the willingness of Robert Walker LJ in *Jennings* to award the expectation in those estoppel cases which are based on consensual agreements. Whether this analysis justifies the distinction drawn in the cases is more arguable.

Proprietary status

Despite some earlier doubts regarding estoppel, it appears today that both estoppel and constructive trust give rise to proprietary rights capable of binding purchasers. One problem will be discussed: the application of trusts of land on the acquisition of a family home.

When a constructive trust analysis is used, there will be a **trust of land** giving effect to the appropriate shares. As is seen in more detail in Chapter 12, the land can be sold or mortgaged by two trustees. The beneficiaries will then have no claim against the purchaser or mortgagee: their interests are said to be overreached and take effect against the purchase/mortgage money. Suppose, however, that the claimants rely on estoppel rather than a constructive trust. Can they then argue that **overreaching** does not apply to estoppels so that the estoppel binds (for example) a mortgagee? This argument was raised in *Birmingham Midshires Mortgage Services Ltd v Sabherwal*[34] (Extract 8.6.4). Fortunately, the Court of Appeal held that overreaching applies to both estoppel and constructive trusts in the family setting. This seems desirable, as it would be most unfortunate if different results ensued according to which analysis the claimant argued. It means, of course, that we need to distinguish these family cases from other examples of proprietary estoppels in which overreaching would not apply. For example, overreaching would be quite inappropriate for the right to an easement in *Crabb v Arun District Council*[35] (Extract 7.2.2), a right of way cannot be exercised over the proceeds of sale. Whether it apples to a claim to the fee simple (as in *Dillwyn v Llewelyn*) remains to be seen.

---

[34] (1999) 80 P&CR 256.
[35] [1976] Ch 179.

Assessing the comparison

For most of the past 20 years, the two doctrines have been drawing steadily closer. Although no attempt has been made to merge them, the courts have been increasingly concerned to ensure the compatibility of their rules. Examples are seen in *Grant v Edwards* on detrimental reliance and *Yaxley v Gotts*[36] (Extract 5.2.11) on contracts for the sale of land.

Some commentators have argued that the doctrines have different bases and that much would be lost if they were to be integrated. This gains some support from the dicta of Lord Walker in *Stack*, discussed above. If this represents general judicial thinking, then the doctrines will retain separate identities with some different rules. However, it is important to remember that it is 'complete assimilation' which is questioned by Lord Walker. This does not mean that the two areas cannot learn from other, nor that the movement towards minimising the differences will be reversed. It may still be predicted that the two will enjoy near identical rules in some respects of their operation. Even if the courts were to be more enthusiastic about assimilation, that does not mean we are likely to end up with a single principle. As has been explained, each contains special features as regards their sphere of operation. Thus estoppel would remain useful to explain acquiescence and constructive trusts useful to explain inferred common intentions.

[36] [2000] Ch 162; see above (p. 110).

CRITICAL ISSUE

Questions to consider

1. What is the difference between a resulting trust and a constructive trust in the family home context?

2. If a house is put into joint names, what is the consequence as regards the beneficial interests? Is the result immutable?

3. What is meant by inferred intention? Does it differ from imputed intention?

4. When, in a single name transfer, will a common intention to share the property be found?

5. What developments in single name transfers are likely to result from *Stack* and *Jones*?

Further reading

Douglas, G, Pearce, J and Woodward, H (2009) 72 MLR 24: 'Cohabitants, property and the law: a study of injustice'.

Etherton, Sir Terence [2008] CLJ 265: Constructive trusts: a new model for equity and unjust enrichment.

Ferguson, P (1993) 109 LQR 114: 'Constructive trusts – a note of caution'.

Gardner, S (2008) 124 LQR 422: Family property today

Hughes, D, Davis, M and Jacklin, L [2008] Conv 197: 'Come live with me and be my love': a consideration of the 2007 Law Commission proposals on cohabitation breakdown.

Piska, N (2009) 'Constructive trusts and constructing intention', in Martin Dixon (ed.) *Modern Studies in Property Law*, Vol 5, Chapter 9. Oxford: Hart.

Rotherham, C [2004] Conv 268: The property rights of unmarried cohabitees: the case for reform.

10 Priorities and registration

Nature and importance

The nature of property rights is that they bind purchasers.

> A very simple approach to priorities is to say that if Andy has a proprietary interest in Brian's land, then this will bind Carla if she purchases from Brian. In the language of this chapter's title, Andy's interest has priority over Carla. First in time priority lies at the heart of many of the priority rules relating to competing interest holders. It is shown in the Latin saying *nemo dat quod non habet* (nobody can give what they do not have). Brian himself holds the land subject to Andy's interest and cannot give Carla any better right than he possesses.

However, priority rules are more complex than simply favouring the first in time. English land law has been dominated by equitable analyses for many centuries. The courts of equity would allow equitable claims to affect only those purchasers whose consciences were affected. This grew into the doctrine whereby purchasers are bound by equitable interests only if the purchaser has notice of that interest. In the modern law, the old principles, whether based on *nemo dat* or the **doctrine of notice**, have lost most of their significance. Instead, we apply statutory **registered land** rules to resolve disputes – many interests will not bind a purchaser unless they have been registered. Close to 95 per cent of titles to land are today registered, so we will concentrate on registered land. Nevertheless, we also need to look at the earlier principles. As well as still being relevant for **unregistered land**, they have provided the basis of priorities thinking for centuries and continue to be influential today.

Priority rules are crucially important. Even if Andy has a proprietary interest in Brian's land, it may be worthless if he fails to register it before Carla's purchase. A rather different point is that priority principles establish what purchasers of land should do and how claimants should protect themselves: we move into the procedures involved in land transactions. Though this is important, especially as regards land registration, we will concentrate on working out the priority of competing interests.

Legal and equitable priority rules

Although our main concern is with registered land, we will consider here the old rules relating to unregistered land.

First in time

The time order of interests plays a significant role. As between two legal interests or two equitable interests, the first in time will generally have priority: this may be seen as the default position. Even in these cases, however, it is not an immutable rule. If the first interest holder does something that creates a trap for purchasers, then the first interest may be postponed. A good example is found in the law of mortgages. The first lender invariably takes possession of the **title deeds**. This is very important because any purchaser expects the seller to possess the title deeds: their absence is a very strong indication that there has been a mortgage. Conversely, that the seller has the title deeds indicates that there is no mortgage. It is unsurprising that a lender who fails to obtain the title deeds will be postponed to a later purchaser who is unaware of the mortgage.[1]

The doctrine of notice

The Court of Chancery developed the doctrine of notice in order to avoid unconscionable conduct on the part of purchasers. A purchaser from a trustee would be bound by the trust if, but only if, his or her conscience is affected. Over the centuries, this flexible approach hardened into the doctrine of notice: a purchaser in good faith of a legal estate for value and without notice of the trusts will not be affected by the trusts. Notice may be actual or constructive. There will be **constructive notice** if a reasonable purchaser would have discovered the existence of the trust, whether by careful reading of the title deeds or by inspecting the land.

The inspection of title deeds is the purchaser's central task. The purchaser has to establish that the seller does indeed own the land and that there are no existing interests (such as leases and easements) that may be binding on purchasers. To enable this, the seller has to provide the purchaser with the title deeds (principally, transfers of the land from one person to another) for a set period. That period has been substantially reduced over the years. Since 1969,[2] the seller has to produce the first document older than 15 years and all the more recent ones. The choice of a relatively short period is assisted because adverse possession for 12 years will cure many defects in titles. A century ago, inspecting title was a long and difficult task. The period was much longer (40 years) and conveyances were frequently lengthy and complex. Today, there are likely to be two or three quite short and simple documents. Those documents have to be read very carefully. As well as being the best way of discovering legal interests (these bind the purchaser automatically), they will give the purchaser notice of equitable interests revealed by them.

---

[1] *Jones v Rhind* (1869) 17 WR 1091; *Walker v Linom* [1907] 2 Ch 104.
[2] Law of Property Act 1969, s 23, amending Law of Property Act 1925 (hereafter LPA), s 44 (Extract 9.1.1).

In addition, the purchaser must inspect the land: this guards against notice of the rights of occupiers. Usually, of course, the seller will be the occupier. But if somebody different is there (possibly a tenant under an equitable lease) or another person shares occupation with the seller (most likely a partner of the seller, sharing ownership under a trust), then the purchaser must make enquiries of them in order to be safe.

Although these duties might seem reasonable, by the end of the nineteenth century it was generally agreed that purchasers faced great burdens. This meant that purchasing land was a time-consuming and costly exercise, with no certainty that all adverse interests would be discovered.

History tells us why notice rules were applied to equitable interests, rather than the normal first in time principle. Can we justify the different rules in terms of their modern operation? The only convincing response is that legal interests tend to be the older and most important rights, thereby deserving greater protection against purchasers. In addition, equitable interests are less likely to appear from the deeds or occupation and so present more of a trap for purchasers. Giving purchasers some greater protection against equitable interests can be justified, though it is difficult to rationalise all the rules.

Exceptional cases

Dealings with equitable interests

Such dealings are illustrated by this example.

> Gordon holds land on trust for Harriet. Harriet transfers her interest first to Imelda and then (inconsistent with that) to Janet. Who of Imelda and Janet succeeds? The priority rule is that the first to give notice to the trustee has priority.[3]

The logic of requiring notice is that the trustee needs to know to whom the trust obligations are owed.

Equities

Some rights, generally those based on the exercise of an equitable remedy such as rescission or **rectification**, are accorded the status of equities. Equities are weaker than equitable interests in two respects. The first relates to the holder of an equity who is in occupation. Contrary to the normal rule for equitable interests, occupation does not provide notice. This is because occupation may not indicate anything out of the ordinary. If a tenant has a right to rectify the lease (perhaps to reduce the rent), then the occupation of the tenant provides no warning as to the right to rectify – one expects any tenant to occupy. The second concerns the type of purchaser who can defeat an equity. A bona fide purchaser without notice of an *equitable* estate will not defeat a prior equitable interest (a legal estate is required), but will defeat an equity.

---

[3] *Dearle* v *Hall* (1828) 3 Russ 1 (38 ER 475). This rule applies to all assignments (e.g., of contractual rights), though not to transfers of equitable interests in land other than those under trusts: LPA, s 137(10).

The need for reform

Criticism of these old rules concentrates on two points. First, selling and buying land is complex and expensive. In particular, each purchaser has to look carefully at all the old deeds. This involves repetition, as well as the danger of misreading deeds. Next, there will always be uncertainty. If there is an earlier legal interest or the purchaser is held to have notice of an equitable interest, then the title may be badly affected and, in the worst cases, the purchase money thrown away. Meanwhile, the holder of an equitable interest is also at risk: it may be lost if somebody purchases the land without notice.

It has been apparent for centuries that registration is the best way to deal with these issues. Purchasers can discover registered rights by the simple act of looking at the register.

Suppose Carla contracts to sell her land to Davina. Carla subsequently transfers the land to Edwina. If Davina registers her interest (an **estate contract**), Edwina can readily discover it. She will be bound by it, whether or not she checks the register. Most registration systems protect purchasers (such as Edwina) against unregistered interests.

In England, there have been three forms of registration. Registration of deeds is the oldest. It identifies the sort of document that must be registered. Despite being the oldest, it was never widely applied and has been dropped. Next there is registration of **land charges**. This is designed to replace the doctrine of notice: there is a list of interests (mainly equitable interests, such as Davina's estate contract) that have to be registered. Finally, there is registration of title. This requires ownership to be registered, with adverse rights (such as estate contracts) also requiring entry on the register. It is often called land registration and, once registered, land within the scheme is called **registered land**. This is the most ambitious form of registration. Introduced in the 1860s, it has been slowly expanded so that close to 95 per cent of titles are today registered. We should approach 100 per cent registration within the next decade. Where title is registered, neither the doctrine of notice nor land charges applies. Though notice and land charges both still apply to the remaining 5 per cent of titles, they are obsolescent and not worthy of prolonged analysis.

Land charges

The system of land charges is governed today by the Land Charges Act 1972 (Extract 9.6.3), though it has been little changed since 1925. It is a limited system, focused on registering equitable interests. In particular, legal fees simple and leases cannot be registered. It follows that registration is a warning of the existence of equitable rights, but it does not prove ownership of estates; it cannot begin to take the place of the title deeds. The purchase of land is made no easier, though priority over earlier interests is made more certain.

What rights can be registered? The wording 'land charges' conjures up mortgages, but the list of registrable interests is much wider than that. In particular, second mortgages,[4] estate contracts and restrictive covenants are included. Interests under trusts of land are deliberately omitted. Two trustees can overreach these interests on a sale or mortgage, so that the interests take effect against the money proceeds of the transaction rather than against the land.[5] Because interests under trusts will not normally bind purchasers, there is no reason to bring them within the registration system. In addition, not all equitable interests are listed; non-listed interests remain subject to the doctrine of notice. Equitable proprietary **estoppel** provides one example.

How does the system work? As there is no register of ownership, we cannot use a register relating to the land. The solution is to register against the name of the legal owner at the time the interest is created. When the land is later sold, the purchaser will request a search against the names of the owners over the years. The land registry conducts the search and gives the purchaser a search certificate containing the results. If an interest is registered, it automatically binds purchasers. If a registrable interest has not been registered, then it will fail against a purchaser. Indeed, a purchaser who obtains a clear search certificate (one not identifying a registration) will be protected even if an interest has been entered on the register.[6] This system of registering and searching is administratively simple and has long been computerised.

Unfortunately, the system is fundamentally flawed, even leaving aside the limited range of interests covered. The cases show that it is common to get the name wrong. This may be simply a typing error, but more problematic are cases where an individual's name may not be known accurately by the parties. Is Andy Smith really Andy Smith, or is it Andrew Smith? Problems often occur because the full names of the individual are not always used. Thus in *Diligent Finance Ltd v Alleyne*[7] a wife registered a claim against her husband as Erskine Alleyne, unaware that his full name was Erskine Owen Alleyne. A search by a mortgagee against the full name failed to identify the registration against the shorter version. Because the holder of a clear search certificate is protected, the mortgage defeated her claim. Even worse problems were feared because purchasers may not be aware of the names of owners of the land prior to the 15-year title period. It is not feasible to update registrations when land is sold: neither the interest holder nor the registry may be aware of the sale. In practice, this unknown names problem has not proved serious so far, though the land registry pays compensation to purchasers who are bound by undiscoverable land charges.[8]

---

[4] More technically, mortgages (legal or equitable) not protected by the deposit of title deeds have to be registered. The deposit of deeds provides its own warning to purchasers.
[5] For overreaching, see above (p. 17), and below (pp. 182–4).
[6] Land Charges Act 1972, s 10(4).
[7] (1972) 23 P&CR 346.
[8] Law of Property Act 1969, s 25 (Extract 9.6.6).

Land registration

Introduction

Land registration sets out to record both ownership and other interests (legal and equitable) in the land. There is a map from which the relevant registers can be identified. It is far more ambitious than the land charges scheme. The task facing the purchaser of registered land is quite straightforward. Instead of going through lengthy and possibly opaque deeds, the purchaser discovers from the register who owns the land and what adverse rights there are affecting it. Significantly, this information is guaranteed to be accurate.

That is the aspiration, though the reality is a little different. For a start, purchasers are concerned about more than the state of title, so registration doesn't answer all a purchaser's questions. For example, purchasers will be interested in the physical state of the premises (this requires a survey), and whether there is **planning permission** for the intended use. These issues lie entirely outside the registration system. Even as regards interests in land, we shall see that some enjoy overriding interest status; these bind purchasers despite not being entered on the register.

Registration of title involves a complex statutory scheme. It was updated by the Land Registration Act 2002 (LRA or 2002 Act), which introduced significant changes. Though most of the basic ideas pre-date the 2002 Act, the earlier cases have to be viewed with caution. The present survey can do no more than sketch the principal attributes of the system: no attempt is made to deal with all the details and statutory provisions. We should also remember that the system is as much about the procedures involved in purchases and other dealings with land as it is with priorities. We are not especially interested in that element of it, though in Chapter 7 we investigated the future significance of e-conveyancing.

The development of registration of title

Although land registration dates back to 1862, it was little used until compulsory registration was introduced in London in 1897. Compulsory registration then, as now, means compulsory registration on sale or other triggering events. Over a century later, there is still some unregistered land in London. Compulsory registration gradually expanded beyond London, until all of England and Wales became covered in 1990. The 'triggers' for first registration have been expanded over the decades, so that any transfer of the legal title (including gifts and on death) has to be registered. The outcome is that close to 95 per cent of titles are registered, that percentage increasing by around 0.5 per cent each year. However, only about 79 per cent of the land area was registered by 2012. This is because, until 1990, compulsory registration concentrated on urban areas where plots were smaller and more easily mapped. The land registry is now attempting (with some success) to encourage large landowners to register their titles on a voluntary basis. The 79 per cent figure has grown quite fast over the past decade.

Categories of interest

There are three categories of interest, around which the priority rules are constructed. They are: registered interests, protected interests (we will call them 'minor interests', as did the 1925 legislation) and overriding interests. Overriding interests are especially significant and controversial: they are effective without any entry on the register.

Both registered and minor interests should be entered on the register. We refer to *registering* registrable interests and *protecting* minor interests. As will be seen in more detail later, the provisions relating to registering and protecting are different. The most important difference is that the system guarantees that registered interests exist, whereas there is no such guarantee for minor interests.

> A house belongs to Sheila, but Timothy (unaware of this) is registered as **proprietor**. Timothy's registration is guaranteed and will, subject to any overriding interest, defeat Sheila's original ownership, though we shall see later that she may well be able to claim compensation from the land registry ('indemnity' in the language of the legislation).

This is to be contrasted with protecting minor interests.

> Suppose that Ursula, the registered proprietor, has contracted to sell the land to Vanya, but the contract is void because it does not satisfy writing requirements. Vanya's protecting this claim on the register (as a minor interest) attracts no guarantee: it has no effect on Ursula's right to deny its invalidity. The only effect of protection is that future dealings with the land are bound by the estate contract, if it is valid.

Accordingly, we can say that both registered interests and protected minor interests give protection as regards future dealings, but only registered interests confer protection as regards past defects (such as Timothy's not owning the land before he was registered).

Registered interests

Land registration is a misleading term. What is registered is a freehold or leasehold estate, not the land itself as a geographical area. This is why 'title registration' is a more accurate term than 'land registration'. It follows that there can be two or more registered titles in relation to the same plot of land: a freehold title and a leasehold title. There can be good sense in this: freehold and leasehold titles may be separately sold and mortgaged. It also aided the growth of registration by permitting the registration of long leases, despite the freehold not being registered.

The upshot is that both legal fees simple absolute in possession and legal leases over seven years can be registered. Indeed, they must be registered when they are created or transferred – whether or not the relevant freehold was previously registered. If the freehold is already registered, then the purchaser or tenant will obtain a legal estate only on the registration of the transfer or lease.[9] If the freehold is not registered, then the 'first

[9] LRA, s 27.

registration' rules apply. The new fee simple owner or tenant has two months in which to register. There is a normal sale or lease under unregistered land procedures (there is no registered title to consult); registration is required only after the freehold or lease has been acquired.

Registration of leases deserves a little more attention. The seven-year requirement (reduced from 21 years by the 2002 Act) has been chosen to distinguish between two categories of leases. Short leases are likely to be created informally and without legal advice: requiring registration would be unrealistic and unduly burdensome. As well as being more formal, longer leases are more likely to be assigned or charged, for which the benefits of registration are most significant. The choice of the seven-year period is necessarily somewhat arbitrary; the reduction to seven years by the 2002 Act was one of the more controversial aspects of the reforms. It is anticipated that when electronic conveyancing is fully in force, the period will be further reduced to three years.[10] The thinking behind this is that leases over three years already require a deed; lawyers are normally involved and electronic registration will be no more burdensome.

Exceptionally, two types of shorter lease must be registered. These are **discontinuous leases** (such as a lease for the first week in May for the next four years) and leases taking effect in more than three months' time (**future leases**). They require registration because otherwise they are likely to be undiscoverable by purchasers.[11]

When land is registered, a somewhat confusing complication is that there are three alternative forms of title. Virtually always, there will be absolute title. The effect of this is that there is the normal full guarantee of the new title on first registration – subject only to entries on the register and overriding interests. Occasionally, some or all of the deeds relating to the property are missing on first registration, so that nobody knows what adverse claims might exist; the land registry will not permit absolute title in such cases. However, the land registry may give either qualified title (no guarantee as regards an identified defect, such as a missing deed) or possessory title (no guarantee – designed for titles based on adverse possession).

Leases can have the same three titles, but there is also good leasehold title. This is designed for cases where the landlord's title is unregistered and accordingly unknown to the register. The lease is guaranteed, but not as regards any problems with the landlord's title. Good leasehold title is becoming redundant now that nearly all landlords are registered. Qualified, possessory and good leasehold titles are all designed to be interim; they may be converted to absolute titles later.

Freehold and the leasehold estates are registered with their own titles (or files). Other interests can also be registered, though only as part of an existing freehold or leasehold title. They are listed by LRA section 27 (Extract 10.2.4). In addition to transfers and leases, section 27 includes other legal interests in land. The most important examples are legal charges and express legal easements. It is striking that we continue to distinguish legal and equitable interests within the registration system, though their old priority rules cease to apply.

---

[10] This is authorised by LRA, s 118.

[11] LRA, s 27(2)(b)(ii) and (iii). There is no compulsory first registration (i.e., where the landlord is not registered) of discontinuous leases: s 4.

What is the effect of making an interest registrable? First, it must comply with registration requirements before it can take effect as a legal interest.[12] This means that an entry must be placed on the title of the land affected. Where other land is benefited, a further entry may be required on that land's title. Thus an easement requires an entry on the title of both the burdened and (if registered) the benefited land. Next a registered interest is guaranteed and so enjoys enhanced priority status (as mentioned above). This guarantee is most important for transfers, leases and charges. These are common and important transactions in which the assurance of getting a good title is vital. It is less clear that the other registrable interests deserve that status.

Minor interests

All other interests should be protected by way of a *notice* or *restriction* on the relevant registered title. Without such an entry, the interest will fail against a later registered disposition (unless it constitutes an overriding interest). The notice is the normal method of protection. It ensures that the protected interest binds a purchaser, though we have seen that it carries no guarantee that the interest exists. Any interest in land can be protected by notice, subject to three main exceptions[13] (Extract 10.2.7). First, interests under trusts cannot be so protected. This is because a restriction is the more appropriate entry, as discussed below. Second, leases not exceeding three years cannot usually be protected. There are good reasons for not requiring entry of short leases, given that they are often entered into informally and will be pretty obvious to purchasers. However, it is puzzling that entry is prohibited. Third, a more technical exclusion is that of restrictive covenants in leases, limiting what can be done on the premises. Nearly every lease contains such covenants. To require their protection would have the onerous effect of requiring an entry in respect of every lease. No harm is done by the exclusion, as anybody dealing with the lease will read it and be aware of the covenant.

The restriction has a more specific function. It is an instruction to the land registry not to register a disposition unless some procedure is followed. It is designed to operate before purchase by telling the purchaser what to do in order to avoid problems later when applying for registration. The best example of the use of restrictions is where there is a trust of land. It will be seen in Chapter 12 that the trustees have power to dispose of land, but only if two trustees receive the purchase money. For the protection of beneficiaries and purchasers, it is important to ensure that the two-trustees requirement is known about and complied with. This is achieved by a restriction requiring there to be two trustees before a transfer is registered. This gives the beneficiaries the protection they need, while at the same time telling the purchaser what needs to be done. We do not set out to bind purchasers (as with the notice), but rather to ensure that the purchase money is paid to two trustees and that the purchaser gets a good title. The restriction is so suitable for trusts that protection by notice is prohibited.

One further aspect of the restriction deserves mention. Because of its focus on procedures, it can be used even where there is no interest in land. A trust of land may require

---

[12] When e-conveyancing is compulsory, it will have no effect at all without registration.
[13] LRA, s 33.

a person's consent before the trustees sell the land. A restriction can be used to ensure that no registration can take place without that consent. That consent requirement is recognised statute. However, the parties can, in principle, select any condition (not limited to consent) for use in a restriction. This means that restrictions have the potential for use in a capricious manner, which could cause uncertainty. An example might be that a transfer should not be registered unless a building is in good repair: not something the land registry can be expected to adjudicate upon. As a result, the land registry has to approve any non-standard restriction.

Overriding interests

Overriding interests are important and controversial because they form an exception to the normal protection of purchasers: they bind purchasers despite not being entered on the register. Why are they allowed? The Law Commission[14] has explained that 'interests should be overriding where protection against purchasers is needed, yet it is either not reasonable to expect or not sensible to require any entry on the register'. Yet this by itself concentrates on the holder of the interest and overlooks another vitally important factor: can we expect purchasers to discover the interest? Any legal system requires a balance to be established between the needs of interest holders and the needs of purchasers. The registration system firmly shifts that balance in favour of purchasers, but overriding interests provide the principal guard against going too far. They form a safety valve against excessive rigidity within the registration system. Too rigid a system may induce the courts to find exceptions in order to avoid what are perceived as unjust outcomes. Such exceptions may be more uncertain and capricious than a well-thought-out category of overriding interests.

Schedule 3 of the 2002 Act lists a large number of overriding interests. Many of them are esoteric and archaic, but several of those are abolished in 2013 (human rights considerations required time to be allowed for entering them on the register). This was part of a concerted effort in 2002 to limit overriding interests as far as possible. This is reflected in the new rule that, once an overriding interest is protected on the register, it loses for ever its status as an overriding interest.

We will consider three forms of overriding interest, all of them mainstream property interests. Paragraph 2, which covers interests of those in actual occupation, is the most controversial and is discussed as a Critical Issue.

Leases

Paragraph 1 covers leases not exceeding seven years. We have already seen that there are good reasons for not making short leases registrable. Many of the same reasons explain why it shouldn't be necessary to protect them on the register and, as a consequence, why they should be overriding interests. There is, perhaps, a stronger case for requiring leases over three years (those which require a deed) to be protected by way of notice, but a reduction from 21 years to seven years in 2002 was probably as large a change as could be made at one go. In any event, we have seen that it is expected that the law will

---

[14] Law Com No 158, para 2.6.

change in the coming years so that leases over three years will have to be registered. Looking at the position from the perspective of the purchaser, two points justify overriding interest status. The first is that the presence of a lease is likely to be obvious from the occupation of the land, either by the tenant personally or a sub-tenant. The second is that a rent will normally be payable, so that the financial impact on the purchaser is not too serious.

Only legal leases fall within paragraph 1.[15] Many leases (including all those over three years) have to be created by deed. Failure to use a deed means that the lease can, at best, be an equitable lease. It therefore cannot fall within paragraph 1, even if it is for seven years or less. However, it will fall within paragraph 2 if the tenant is in actual occupation.

We have already seen that future leases and discontinuous leases have to be registered, regardless of their length. It comes as no surprise that they cannot be overriding interests within paragraph 1.

Actual occupation

The interest of a person in actual occupation falls within paragraph 2. This provision, which long pre-dated the 2002 Act, received almost no attention until the 1950s. Since then, it has become the most litigated and disputed aspect of registered land.

We first consider the scope of the overriding interest and then assess its role within land registration.

The interest

Actual occupation is not itself an overriding interest. Instead, it is the interest of the occupier which binds a purchaser. It follows that we always have to ask two questions: is there actual occupation, and does the occupier have an interest?[16] The interests that count are those which are generally recognised as binding purchasers. To take one example, it is generally thought that contractual licences (permissions to enter land) are not proprietary interests and do not bind purchasers (see Chapter 15). It is irrelevant that the licensee is in actual occupation of the land – the licence still will not bind purchasers.

It has been argued[17] that all claims of occupiers should bind purchasers. This would be a radical change and there is no sign of its gaining acceptance. The present law seems well justified: to recognise all claims would lead to too much uncertainty as to what to look for when buying land, as well as the danger of over-burdening purchasers. That said, there may be scope for more cautious developments of the range of interests recognised as proprietary; this is seen in provisions in the 2002 Act relating to estoppels, equities and pre-emptions.[18] One of the reasons for restricting the range of property interests lies in the difficulty in discovering them. This may not be such a problem where there is actual occupation and inquiry is made of the occupier.

---

[15] *City Permanent BS v Miller* [1952] Ch 840.
[16] *National Provincial Bank Ltd v Ainsworth* [1965] AC 1175 (Extract 10.2.20).
[17] Tee [1998] CLJ 328.
[18] LRA, ss 115, 116 (Extract 10.3.4).

CRITICAL ISSUE

Actual occupation: its meaning and application

First, we need to consider why we protect actual occupation and whether this can be justified today: the answers influence the interpretation of actual occupation. Some have said that the register is designed to replace the title deeds of unregistered land. Just as a purchaser of unregistered land had to inspect deeds and the land, so also should a purchaser of registered land inspect the register and the land. Many lawyers have observed similarities between constructive notice from occupation and paragraph 2 (actual occupation). The doctrine of notice may be obsolete in registered land, but its influence survives in paragraph 2.

These comparisons with unregistered land provide a short-sighted view of what our registration system should aspire to in the twenty-first century. Today, we invest the register with greater significance than simply replacing title deeds. More important is the justification of overriding interests as those which it is not reasonable to require to be protected on the register. Many of the cases involve resulting or constructive trusts of the family home.

> A typical case would be where Robert and Susan buy a home together, but the legal title is put into Robert's name only. They both pay the mortgage instalments, which will almost certainly lead to a constructive trust whereby Robert holds on trust for himself and Susan. Robert later borrows money from Terrific Bank to cover his gambling debts and charges the land to secure the debt; the **charge** is registered. To expect Susan to protect her interest is plainly unrealistic. On the other hand, it is realistic to expect purchasers and chargees to inspect the land.

Discussion of what suffices as actual occupation is split into two parts: the nature of the test and how it is applied to individual cases. Especially when looking at the older cases, we need to bear in mind a new provision in the 2002 Act: purchasers are not bound if the 'occupation would not have been obvious on a reasonably careful inspection of the land' (assuming no knowledge of the occupier's interest).

The nature of the test

Sometimes there is an innocent explanation for actual occupation. Is this relevant? Taking Robert and Susan, it is not as if Susan's occupation looks inconsistent with Robert's ownership. We expect Robert's wife/girlfriend to be living with him. This issue arose in the leading case on the area: ***Williams & Glyn's Bank Ltd v Boland***[19] (Extract 10.2.19). The facts were very similar to our example: the occupying co-owner was the wife of the proprietor and the registered charge secured a loan to the husband's business. The House of Lords expressed no hesitation in holding that the words of the legislation mean what they say. If we can describe the wife as being in actual occupation, then paragraph 2 applies. Given that the land was the wife's home, the only conceivable answer was that she was in actual occupation.

[19] [1981] AC 487.

Should actual occupation be influenced by the doctrine of notice as it applies to occupation? This question was also raised in *Boland*. Lord Wilberforce, delivering the principal judgment, was clear: 'the law as to notice as it may affect purchasers of unregistered land . . . has no application even by analogy to registered land'. Even though actual occupation may be historically based on the doctrine of notice, it provides a new and independent test. We should remember that the uncertainties of notice caused real problems for unregistered land. Actual occupation may not always be easy to apply, but it is based on physical acts rather than what people should do; its operation is more predictable.

It is surprising that, a few years later, the Court of Appeal in *Lloyds Bank plc v Rosset*[20] (Extract 10.2.28) stated that, in addition to actual occupation, the test was whether 'appropriate inquiries made by the bank [would] have elicited the fact of her interest'. Though this seems to fly in the face of *Boland*, the clash is not as significant as it might seem. In *Boland*, it was plain that the wife was in actual occupation. If the claimant is not living in the house, matters are by no means as settled. Thus in *Rosset* the wife was supervising building work on a semi-derelict house. It is not obvious that this counts as actual occupation. When actual occupation is not clear-cut, it seems quite appropriate to consider how obvious the occupation is to a purchaser. On the facts, the Court of Appeal split 2:1 in holding that there was actual occupation.

Since the 2002 Act, purchasers have been protected if the occupation is not obvious. This protection is likely to take the heat out of the older clash between the pre-2002 cases, though one may doubt whether many (or even any) of them would be differently decided under the 2002 Act. The Law Commission is emphatic that the new law does not embody the doctrine of notice: it is the *occupation* that has to be obvious rather than that there be notice of the *interest*. Even so, it is designed to deal with the genuine concern that purchasers should not be bound unless they can be expected to discover the interest. The modern stress is on balancing the protection of the occupier against the need to protect purchasers against hidden interests. This balancing, of course, applies to all overriding interests.

The application of the test

Living in a house is actual occupation, but what else suffices? The nature of the premises is important. In *Rosset*, it was easier to find actual occupation because the house was semi-derelict. It would be similar if the couple had been building a house on a vacant plot. In a subsequent case on derelict land, it was held that minor acts of storage and fencing sufficed.[21] Parking of cars has come up in two cases. In *Epps v Esso Petroleum Co Ltd*[22] (Extract 10.2.35), the claimant parked a car on a strip of land that looked as though it belonged to his neighbour. It was held that this sort of conduct was insufficient. By contrast, in *Kling v Keston Properties Ltd*[23] the claimant parked his car in a garage. This

---

[20] [1989] Ch 350 (in the House of Lords [1991] AC 107 it was held that the wife in fact had no beneficial interest in the first place).
[21] *Malory Enterprises Ltd v Cheshire Homes (UK) Ltd* [2002] Ch 216 at [82] (Extract 10.2.34).
[22] [1973] 1 WLR 1071.
[23] (1984) 49 P&CR 212.

was held to be actual occupation. One can see a real distinction between the cases. People do commonly park on vacant pieces of land – there isn't anything in this conduct that looks as though any sort of interest is being claimed. On the other hand, people do not normally park in others' garages – this is more properly to be considered as occupation.

Parking of cars prompts the question whether the exercise of easements can amount to actual occupation. For rights of access, it was confirmed recently by **Chaudhary v Yavuz** that there is no actual occupation.[24] The case is interesting because the existence of the access route was obvious from looking at the land. That however, is not the essence of the overriding interest – there has to be some activity that can count as occupation. But it may be wrong to assume that no easement could ever qualify – exercise of an easement of storage (or parking) might have a better chance of constituting occupation.

Occupation of houses (even if not semi-derelict, as in **Rosset**) sometimes poses problems. One of the most difficult pre-2002 cases is **Kingsnorth Finance Co Ltd v Tizard**[25] (Extract 10.2.32). A wife had left the family home, but returned most days to help look after the children. She kept clothes at the house and occasionally slept there if her estranged husband was away. The trial judge held that this counted as actual occupation. One has the feeling that the purchaser is being expected to play the role of a private detective in discovering such occupation. It would not be surprising if a court were to say that, under the 2002 Act, her occupation was not obvious on a reasonably careful inspection.

A related point is that it does not suffice simply to have furniture and other things on the premises. In **Strand Securities Ltd v Caswell**[26] (Extract 10.2.31), a claimant allowed his stepdaughter to occupy a flat rent-free. That his furniture was there was not enough to protect him. The court in **Caswell** accepted that one can occupy through another person such as a caretaker (or a builder, as in **Rosset**). However, it wasn't enough just to give a licence to the stepdaughter: she was not occupying on the claimant's behalf.

A quite different question is when actual occupation starts on house purchase. It is moderately common for purchasers to be allowed to move belongings into a house shortly before completion of the purchase (the date of the transfer). Is there actual occupation before the transfer? Normally, overriding interests have to exist at the time of registration (some weeks after the transfer), but for actual occupation paragraph 2 specifies the time of the transfer. It would be unfortunate if minor acts before completion or moving in a couple of minutes early were to have significant legal effects: this would leave too much to chance. In **Abbey National BS v Cann**[27] (Extract 10.2.36), the House of Lords held that moving furniture 35 minutes in advance of completion clearly did not count. A frequently quoted statement of Lord Oliver is that there must be 'some degree of permanence and continuity which would rule out mere fleeting presence'. **Rosset** raises a similar point in that the purchaser had been allowed to undertake work on the land before completion. However, the extent of the work and the lengthy period involved (around six weeks) each justify the court's finding of actual occupation.

---

[24] [2012] 3 WLR 987. Access was by a metal 'balcony' built on to the servient land by the dominant owner. The balcony itself could not be the occupation, as it had become part of the servient land.

[25] [1986] 1 WLR 783.

[26] [1965] Ch 958.

[27] [1991] 1 AC 56.

When does actual occupation end?

Once actual occupation has started, actual physical presence is not always required to prove an overriding interest. The striking facts of *Chhokar* v *Chhokar*[28] provide a good example. While his wife was in hospital having a baby, the proprietor (husband) transferred the land to a purchaser. By the time the wife returned home, she found the locks had been changed. It is not surprising that Ewbank J held that she was in actual occupation.

Varying the facts of *Chhokar* provides instructive examples.

> Suppose the husband had removed all his wife's belongings before selling the house. Whether or not she was still in actual occupation, we can say that it is not obvious on a reasonably careful inspection. A second problem would be if the husband had brought a new girlfriend into the house. The purchaser is told that the wife's clothes and belongings are those of the girlfriend. This may seem entirely plausible to a purchaser – presuming any photographs of the wife are hidden! This is a really difficult case, one in which the outcome cannot be confidently predicted. Occupation by somebody is obvious, but how relevant is the purchaser's reasonable mistake as to whose occupation it is?

A rather different sort of case is where the occupier is away for a longer period. Two quite recent cases illustrate the approach of the courts. In *Thompson* v *Foy*[29] (Extract 10.2.37), the claimant was in the process of moving out. She had taken personal belongings away and for just four days had ceased living there, though furniture and bedding were still in the house. *Caswell* (furniture not enough) could be distinguished, as nobody else had moved in. It was held by Lewison J that her actual occupation had come to an end, much stress being placed on the fact that she did not intend to return. In *Link Lending Ltd* v *Bustard*[30] (Extract 10.2.33), the claimant had been in a residential care institution for over a year. She wished to return to the house, though it was unclear whether her health would ever permit that. Though *Foy* was approved, the Court of Appeal held that there was actual occupation – based on the fact that she did wish to return and had no other home of her own. The length of the time away was obviously a factor making it a difficult case.

A feature of both cases is the stress on intention of the occupier. We tend to think of actual occupation as highly objective, so this is somewhat surprising. However, it may be seen as limiting actual occupation rather than extending it – in each case, the claimant's belongings were on the land. In any event, the protection against non-obvious occupation should be remembered, though it applied on the facts of neither *Foy* nor *Bustard*.

Protecting the purchaser

Paragraph 2 contains several limits on the actual occupation overriding interest. We have already seen the protection as regards non-obvious occupation. A further provision

[28] [1984] FLR 313.
[29] [2010] 1 P&CR 308.
[30] [2010] 2 EGLR 55.

protects purchasers if they make inquiries of the occupier and the interest is not disclosed, when disclosure might reasonably have been expected.

This establishes a standard procedure for purchasers to follow: they should discover occupiers and then ask them what rights they have. It is not enough to do what purchasers are often tempted to do – to ask the *seller* why the occupier is there. This is well illustrated by *Hodgson v Marks*,[31] in which the seller described the occupier as a lodger. The occupier was in fact the **beneficial owner** of the land and her rights bound the purchaser. The inquiry must also be carefully framed.

> The owner of land, Kerry, leases it to Laura for five years. A year later, she contracts to sell it to her. Kerry then mortgages the land to Mindy, who asks Laura 'Why are you there?' Laura replies that she is a tenant. Because the inquiry did not require mention of the contract, Mindy will be bound not only by the lease (paragraph 1), but also by the contract to buy the freehold. This example shows that the purchaser must ask the occupier what rights are claimed.

The reference to the reasonableness of disclosure is new in the 2002 Act. In theory, it might have a wide effect, with all sorts of excuses being made for not disclosing the interest. There are no cases so far, but the new provision seems unlikely to provide a defence if an appropriate inquiry has been made. One further point may be noted. It cannot be expected that the occupier will identify their precise interest: occupiers will be unaware of the niceties of categories of interests in land. The most that can be expected is a general statement of a claim to the land. A statement such as 'I have a right to live here' should suffice even though it reveals no specific land law interest. The onus is then on the purchaser to dig deeper.

Even where there is no inquiry, the conduct of an occupier may defeat their interest. This is best explained by the following example.

> Sheila is the registered proprietor of a house. She holds it on trust for herself and her partner Tim. They plan an extension to the house, to provide more room for their children. Like most young couples, they have virtually no savings and Sheila obtains a loan of £80,000 from a bank to cover the costs of the building work; the bank is protected by a registered charge. Can Tim (very clearly in actual occupation) claim that his beneficial interest defeats the charge? Success would mean that Tim would get his share of the proceeds of any sale before the bank could claim its £80,000.
>
> The courts have held that occupiers such as Tim, for whose benefit the loan has been obtained, must be taken to have approved the loan.[32] It would be plainly wrong to say that Sheila was acting improperly in charging the land. How else could Tim believe that the money could be found? Even if he took no part in the financial planning (fairly improbable) he must implicitly be permitting Sheila to raise the necessary funds by way of a charge. Very

---

[31] [1971] Ch 892.
[32] *Bristol & West BS v Henning* [1985] 1 WLR 778 (Extract 10.2.23); *Paddington BS v Mendelsohn* (1985) 50 P&CR 244 (Extract 10.2.24).

generously to banks, the courts have held that once approval is given, it extends to the full sum in fact borrowed.[33] Suppose Sheila had actually borrowed £150,000 and gambled away the excess £70,000. The bank would have priority as regards the full £150,000 borrowed. It is difficult to see any justification for this.

How far does the principle in the above example extend? In *Boland*, the loan was for the proprietor's business. Both he and Mrs Boland (by a higher standard of living) would benefit if the business prospered. These facts came nowhere near to approval of the mortgage. Tim, by contrast, obtains a direct benefit: a share in a more valuable house. Furthermore, it is a benefit he actively wants to obtain. It might have been different if Sheila had misled Tim into thinking that she had substantial savings which she could use for the building work – then it might not be appropriate to infer approval of the charge. Another difficult case would be one like *Boland*, except that the proprietor tells the claimant that he is planning to charge the land because the company needs the money. As in *Boland*, the claimant obtains no direct benefit. If she expressly agrees that the house should be charged then the proprietor can be regarded as her agent in charging the land. If she is told of the impending charge but fails to say anything positive or negative, that looks very borderline.

Assessing the actual occupation overriding interest

As has been repeatedly stressed, registered land has to balance the needs of interest holders (those in actual occupation) and purchasers. Both are usually innocent parties. If we always protect purchasers, occupiers will be thrown out of their homes when we cannot reasonably expect them to place an entry on the register. If we always protect occupiers, we run the risk of making the purchase (or mortgage) of land an unduly complex and risky affair. A large part of the problem is that few members of the public are aware of property rights or of registration requirements. A massive public education exercise seems both unlikely and doomed to failure. Protecting occupiers has the advantage of taking a 'let sleeping dogs lie' approach: it means that occupation is allowed to continue. It would be more palatable if the wholly innocent purchaser were compensated, but we will see that this is not permitted.

Against that background, it is entirely reasonable to protect occupiers if (1) the occupation is obvious and (2) no inquiry has been made (also that the transaction has not been authorised). Necessarily, care has to be taken not to expand actual occupation to an extent which interferes too much with the process of buying land. The objective of simple, fast and inexpensive land transfer is an important one. The nineteenth-century doctrine of notice appeared to assume that unlimited time and money could be expended on land purchase. We must be vigilant as regards the risks of slipping back to that position. Yet it also has to be remembered that purchasers, unlike the typical occupier, almost invariably employ

[33] *Abbey National BS* v *Cann* [1991] AC 56 at p. 94 (Extract 10.2.29).

lawyers. It may be reasonable to place demands on purchasers: we can rely on their lawyers complying with them. That is no excuse for burdensome requirements, but an obligation to make inquiries of obvious occupiers seems appropriate.

Are all occupiers deserving of protection? The cases mostly involve resulting or constructive trusts of the family home: these occupiers seem thoroughly deserving. Yet any occupier can claim the benefit of actual occupation. This includes people who could reasonably be expected to protect their interests. An example is a person in actual occupation who has contracted to lease or buy land, employing a lawyer for this purpose. That person has little excuse for not protecting the contract on the register,

E-conveyancing, if and when made compulsory, is likely to provide an answer to that problem. Without electronic registration or protection, there will be no interest. If there is no interest because there is no electronic entry, there can be no overriding interest. The example of contracts to buy or lease land will disappear: without electronic entry, there will simply be no contract at all. However, it is expected that trusts will be exempted from compulsory electronic registration and accordingly beneficial interest under trusts will continue to fall within paragraph 2. It follows that the e-conveyancing rules will operate to distinguish which interests are deserving of protection under paragraph 2, though this lies quite some time in the future.

Easements

The third overriding interest is a legal easement (or profit): paragraph 3. The position of easements in registered land is quite complex. Express easements are registrable dispositions, as discussed above. It follows that if they are not registered then they cannot be legal. This means that an unregistered express easement cannot fall within paragraph 3, which is explicitly limited to legal easements. However, when we study easements we will see that they can be created in a variety of ways. They can be implied, whether by common law rules or statute, and they can arise by reason of long use (**prescription**). Because there is no express creation of these easements, the chances of registration are minimal. Unless they were to be accepted as overriding interests, these easements would rarely affect purchasers. They are therefore exempted from the normal registration requirements and fall within paragraph 3. The result can also be supported as easements are frequently necessary to enable efficient land use, with relatively little effect on the burdened land.

Does this mean that purchasers may be bound by easements that are virtually impossible to discover? Paragraph 3 provides some protection against this. The protection is well intentioned, but very limited in scope. The purchaser is protected if the easement is not 'obvious on a reasonably careful inspection of the land'. This looks promising, but it does not apply in three cases. The first is where the purchaser is aware of it – fair enough. More serious is that it is inapplicable if the right has been exercised in the past year. It is difficult to comprehend how a purchaser should be aware of a right that was last exercised 11 months ago! However, it is a warning to holders of non-exercised easements that it would be wise to register them. Even more telling is a separate provision[34] that pre-2002

---

[34] LRA, Sched 12, para 9.

easements remain overriding interests, free of the more restrictive rules in the 2002 Act. The huge majority of non-exercised easements are likely to be older ones and this means that the protection for purchasers will have little practical effect for many years in the future.

Priority rules

General principles

Having considered the various types of interest, we can now investigate in more detail the application of priority rules to them.

What happens if Andrew contracts to sell to Brian (who places no entry on the register), but then contracts to sell to Caroline (who protects her estate contract by entering a notice) and then leases the land to Davina for ten years (Davina registers her lease). These transactions are inconsistent with each other and we need some way to decide who wins.

Let us start with Davina's registered lease. The protection of registered dispositions is established by LRA section 29. This enacts that a registered interest defeats any prior claim unless it is 'protected'. Claims are protected for the purposes of section 29 if they are protected by notice or are overriding interests. This means that Davina is bound by Caroline's contract, but not by Brian's unprotected contract. Section 29 establishes that, leaving aside overriding interests, Davina can rely upon the register being conclusive.

We should note a few points. Only those giving consideration are protected. If there were a gift of a lease to Davina, she would have been bound by Brian's contract. The registration system exists to benefit purchasers rather than donees (who pay a much reduced fee for registration). Next, and vitally important, it is only registered dispositions – legal interests listed in section 27 – that are protected by section 29 (Extracts 10.2.4, 10.2.5). Caroline, despite protecting her interest by notice, does not hold a registered disposition: estate contracts are not registrable dispositions. Accordingly, Caroline receives no priority over Brian's contract. This is the reason why we have to be so careful in distinguishing registered interests from protected minor interests. A third point is that interests protected by restriction are not 'protected' for the purposes of section 29. In the rare event that the restriction is not complied with by the land registry, then the interest will not bind a purchaser.

Forgeries

How does the system deal with forgeries? Two situations are clear.

If Francis forges a transfer of Graham's registered land to himself and is registered, nobody supposes that Francis can rely on his own fraudulent act to assert a good title. The second situation is where Francis forges a transfer of Graham's land to Henrietta, who is entirely innocent and is registered as proprietor. Henrietta later transfers the land to Ivy (again innocent and registered). This time it is clear that Ivy wins. Any claim that Graham might have against Henrietta falls within section 29: at the time of Ivy's purchase it is a prior unprotected claim, which is defeated by her registered disposition (always assuming that Graham cannot claim an overriding interest).

The final forgery situation is the problematic one.

> In the Francis, Graham and Henrietta example, assume that Henrietta is still the registered proprietor. Can she, innocent of any wrongdoing, claim a good title? Unlike Ivy, Henrietta has not relied upon the register – rather, she believes she is dealing with Graham when in fact she has been dealing with the fraudulent Francis. The register is perfectly accurate when she purchases: Graham is the proprietor. It is not an easy question to decide whether we should protect the current registered proprietor who has paid for the benefits of registration or whether we should take the approach that the system is not to blame for her being taken in.

Registration systems in other countries tend to protect the purchaser where there has been such a forgery,[35] but in England the position has received little attention. It is not easy, however, to spell out any protection from the wording of section 29 and one case[36] on the pre-2002 law held there to be no protection. Some prominent lawyers[37] have, nevertheless, argued that the purchaser is protected; we need a further case to settle the question. It might be added that the losing party is likely to receive compensation from the land registry under the statutory indemnity scheme (discussed below).

Purchasers with actual notice

Registered dispositions defeat earlier unprotected interests. Does this still apply if the purchaser is fraudulent or in bad faith, or knows about the unprotected interest? Another question is whether personal obligations affect purchasers. Personal obligations are explained below, but one simple example is where the purchaser is in breach of a contractual duty. Their significance is that they can apply in many cases of undeserving purchasers – utilising non-proprietary analyses to attack those purchasers.

Actual knowledge and lack of good faith

The role of actual knowledge and lack of good faith has provoked much debate. Different countries adopt differing approaches, showing that the arguments are not completely one-sided. It is tempting to argue that registration should replace only constructive notice, there being no good reason to protect those who are actually aware of unprotected interests. A purchaser can scarcely be said to have been misled by the register when he knows about an unprotected interest. Yet it is clear that actual knowledge is not cut and dried: it cannot easily be separated from constructive notice. Is it enough that the purchaser has overheard a rumour? Or that they are aware of a claim that is hotly denied by the seller? Or that they are aware of a claim but believe it to be unfounded and certain to be rejected by the seller as baseless? An actual knowledge test looks likely to cause more problems than it solves!

[35] *Frazer v Walker* [1967] 1 AC 569 (New Zealand, which employs the Torrens registration system encountered in several Commonwealth countries).
[36] *Malory Enterprises Ltd v Cheshire Homes (UK) Ltd* [2002] Ch 216 at [65] (Extract 10.2.34).
[37] Notably Harpum in Getzler (ed.), *Rationalizing Property, Equity and Trusts*, pp. 197–202 and Cooke [2004] Conv 482 at pp. 485–6. More recently (and fully), see Hill-Smith [2009] Conv 127.

A stronger argument is that good faith should be required. Actual knowledge would point against good faith, though good faith might still be found in the examples in the previous paragraph. Before the 2002 Act, at least one controversial case[38] held that good faith was required. Perhaps the major problem with good faith lies in knowing what it means. Good faith is very malleable and may be thought inappropriate for an area in which a lawyer needs to be able to give unambiguous advice to a potential purchaser. The problems were the greater because the old legislation was explicit that purchasers were not affected by actual knowledge of unprotected claims – not easily reconciled with requiring good faith. Nevertheless, most commentators favoured a requirement that the purchaser be in good faith.

The Law Commission[39] considered the question and came down very firmly in favour of protecting the purchaser, regardless of knowledge or the absence of good faith. The good point was made that the issue had given rise to very few cases and so could not be seen as very serious. The Law Commission's policy is to enable purchasers to rely on the register, whereas interest holders who fail to place an entry on the register have only themselves to blame. This chimes with the view of the House of Lords in a land charges case[40] that requiring good faith would be undesirable as it 'would bring with it the necessity of inquiring into the purchaser's motives and state of mind'. It may be added that the problem will be much reduced if and when electronic conveyancing becomes compulsory. At that time, many unregistered interests will simply not exist – there will be nothing that could bind the registered purchaser.

How are the views of the Law Commission reflected in the 2002 Act? It is a little disappointing that the Act is silent on the question. However, nothing in the drafting of the legislation (which is materially different from the 1925 Act) suggests that actual notice or bad faith could be relevant. That, combined with the very clear views of the Law Commission, should be conclusive: there is no good faith requirement.

Fraud

Is it different if there is fraud? The line between fraud and absence of good faith may be difficult to draw, but it is unattractive to argue that a fraudulent purchaser should be able to rely on the register. In other contexts, statutory provisions have been held inapplicable in the face of fraud. It is frequently said that 'fraud unravels all'. More specifically, fraud was held to affect a purchaser of registered land in *Lyus v Prowsa Developments Ltd*[41] (Extract 10.2.16). Registration systems in other countries place much emphasis on fraud. Though Torrens[42] registration systems in the Commonwealth generally go much further than we do in protecting purchasers, they make an explicit exception for fraud.

Personal obligations

Any difficulty over fraud may be sidestepped by arguing that fraud gives rise to a personal obligation affecting the purchaser, the topic to which we now turn. The basic idea is that

---

[38] *Peffer v Rigg* [1977] 1 WLR 285.
[39] Law Com No 254, paras 3.44–6.
[40] *Midland Bank Trust Co Ltd v Green* [1981] AC 513 at p. 530 (Extract 10.2.11).
[41] [1982] 1 WLR 1044.
[42] The name comes from the Premier of South Australia who first introduced land registration.

a registered disposition defeats unprotected property rights, but has no effect on other, personal obligations. Take this simple example.

> Ursula contracts to sell registered land to Vernon. Vernon in turn contracts to sell to Walter. At that stage, the title is transferred to Vernon, who is registered. Can Vernon argue that Walter's estate contract is defeated because it is not entered on the register? It would be monstrous if Vernon could get out of his own contract this way and it seems almost certain that he cannot. This may be explained in two ways. First, Walter is relying on a contract rather than any form of property – he is suing on an obligation entered into by Vernon. More technically, LRA section 29 (Extract 10.2.5) protects purchasers against 'any interest affecting the estate immediately before the disposition'. Walter's contract affects Vernon, rather than Ursula's pre-disposition registered estate.

Personal obligations have been discussed in Torrens cases and periodical literature, but they have been conspicuous by their absence from English registration cases. Fortunately, they are recognised and approved by the Law Commission.[43] However, what counts as a personal obligation is a difficult question. Obligations willingly accepted by the purchaser (as with Vernon's promise) cause no difficulty, but what about other forms of liability? We will take two examples.

> In the first, Rosalind contracts to sell to Sara, who does not protect her interest. Rosalind then transfers the land to Tamara, who is aware of that contract. Tamara registers the transfer. LRA section 29 tells us that Tamara defeats Sara's unprotected estate contract. Yet Tamara may be liable to Sara under the tort of inducing breach of contract. The second example involves Rosalind holding on trust for Sara, who again fails to place an entry on the register. Rosalind then sells the land to Tamara, who is aware of the trust; Tamara registers her transfer. Section 29 again defeats Sara, but this time she may argue that Tamara is subject to a constructive trust based on unconscionable receipt.[44]

The result in each of these examples has the effect of reversing the section 29 protection. The source of the liability is personal rather than proprietary, but this is unlikely to impress the purchaser! It seems strange for the Law Commission to place so much stress on the need to protect purchasers regardless of knowledge or bad faith and then to accept that a personal obligation reverses that protection. Some will think that the section 29 protection is too wide and therefore welcome this personal liability. However, there is always the risk that these forms of liability may be extended. It should provide pause for thought that the origins of the doctrine of notice lay in a concept of personal liability for unconscionable conduct. Few would wish to resurrect notice in the guise of personal liability! It is revealing that Australian courts[45] have declined to apply personal liability

---

[43] Law Com No 254, paras 3.48–49 (less directly addressed by Law Com No 271, but see paras 4.11 and 7.7, n 31).
[44] The test recognised in *BCCI (Overseas) Ltd* v *Akindele* [2001] Ch 437 at p. 455.
[45] *Farah Constructions Pty Ltd* v *Say-Dee Pty Ltd* (2007) 230 CLR 89 (High Court of Australia) (Extract 10.2.15).

when the purchaser is not the primary wrongdoer. Recognising the potential for proprietary and personal liability principles to clash, they strive to provide a reasoned solution.

When we describe liability as personal, what exactly does this mean? So far, we have
concentrated on the source of the liability. Personal liability is imposed by virtue of the
undertaking or conduct of the purchaser, rather than because there is an interest in land
coupled with a notice on the register or actual occupation. However, liability may also
be personal in the sense that, though Tamara is affected, a future purchaser from Tamara
would not be. This is the approach taken by the Law Commission and it receives some
support from the cases.[46] Yet there is an argument that some personal obligations may
give rise to a proprietary interest. If there is a contract to sell land (as in the example
involving Vernon and Walter, then it would be natural for this to be a property right
(estate contract). On the other hand, tort liability for inducing breach of contract looks
purely personal.

We should not leave this area without stressing that there are very few English cases
directly on the personal obligations. It is as uncertain as it is controversial. Clearly, we
cannot assume that the priorities rule in section 29 is the last word on the matter.

Non-registered dispositions

So far we have dealt with the priority rules for registered dispositions. Priority disputes
between other interests (two minor interests, for example) are dealt with by a simple first
in time rule: LRA, section 28 (Extract 10.2.10). It should be noted that the combination of
sections 28 and 29 leaves no scope for the old priority rules.

Earlier we considered an example where Andrew contracted to sell to Brian and then
(inconsistent with that) to Caroline. Caroline, but not Brian, has entered a notice on the
register. Section 28 establishes that Brian has priority over Caroline, despite her having
protected her estate contract. Caroline may feel that she is short-changed by the system.
That she checks the register, discovers no entry by Brian and places an entry on the register
counts for nothing. There is a strong argument that people such as Caroline deserve greater
protection, even if that would blur the distinction between registrable and minor interests. However, the position will change when e-conveyancing (discussed in Chapter 7)
becomes compulsory. There will then usually be no interest without an entry on the
register. It will follow that Brian will have no interest (or even contract). Because
Caroline is the first to protect her interest, it will also be the first to exist. Even if Brian
later protects his contract, it will not be first in time.

Establishing the time order

Sometimes, two interests may arise at what seems the same time. For all priority rules,
it is important to establish which comes first. The problem usually involves the priority
of a charge, when the money lent is necessary for the land to be bought (often called an
acquisition mortgage). The following example is based on the facts of *Abbey National BS
v Cann*[47] (Extract 10.2.36).

---

[46] See *Halifax plc* v *Curry Popeck* [2008] EWHC 1692 (Ch) at [51].
[47] [1991] 1 AC 56.

George owns a house on trust for himself and Daisy (his mother). They sell that house and buy a cheaper one. The new house is registered in George's name, financed by a small mortgage loan (less than the loan on the old house). Later, George becomes bankrupt and there is a dispute between the mortgage bank and Daisy when the bank seeks to sell the house. Daisy claims an overriding interest based on actual occupation. There are several reasons why her claim will run into difficulty,[48] but what is the time order between her beneficial interest and the bank's charge? It looks as though they arise at the same time: when the new house is bought. The House of Lords held that an acquisition mortgage always comes first – ahead of other interests (such as that of Daisy) arising on purchase. This makes sense in a typical case where the borrowed money accounts for nearly all the purchase price, but it looks overly favourable towards the bank on the facts of **Cann**. After all, the house could not have been bought without Daisy putting in her share of the proceeds from the sale of the old house; this was just as important as the bank's contribution.

When things go wrong: alteration and indemnity

In any bureaucratic system, things sometimes go wrong. Alteration of the register, governed by LRA, Schedule 4, copes with these problems. There are two forms of alteration. The first, which we will call 'simple alteration', is where the register fails to reflect legal rights.

Kathleen is registered as proprietor of land that really belongs to Liam. Liam is in actual occupation, so his ownership rights bind Kathleen by virtue of an overriding interest. Liam may have the register altered to enter him as the proprietor: this recognises his existing rights.

The second form of alteration is much more interesting: an alteration that changes current rights. The 2002 Act calls this **rectification** (before 2002, all forms of alteration were called rectification). When is rectification allowed? The 2002 Act provides the test of a 'mistake'. What is a mistake? The Law Commission's proposals provide almost no examples.

The most likely example is where the wrong person is registered as proprietor on first registration. There may then be rectification to restore the rightful owner as proprietor. Another example is where an adverse possessor has been registered as proprietor. If there was in fact no adverse possession for the required period, then the title can be rectified in favour of the original proprietor, even though the registry has complied with the procedures laid down in the legislation regarding adverse possession.[49] It is clear that there is no requirement that the registry has done something wrong before there can be a mistake.

What about mistake in the context of a forgery? Suppose Sara is the registered proprietor. Tamara forges her signature on a transfer of the property to Una. Una, now registered as

---

[48] Especially that she has consented to the charge and that she may not be in actual occupation at the time of purchase.

[49] *Baxter* v *Mannion* [2011] 1 WLR 1594; for adverse possession in registered land, see above (p. 43).

proprietor, is quite unaware of the forgery. We have seen that it is dubious whether Una is protected by the 2002 Act. If she is, then this seems an example of a mistake, otherwise it will be simple alteration. Could there be rectification against Valerie, who has purchased from Una and is now the registered proprietor? It is clear Valerie is protected against Sara, so any alteration would amount to rectification. But is there a mistake? Until recently, it seemed not: the mistake has to be in the immediate registration of the proprietor against whom rectification is sought (Una, in our example).[50] However, doubts have begun to creep in[51] and the contrary may be regarded as arguable.

Even where there has been a mistake, the proprietor in possession receives protection. There will be no rectification unless the proprietor has been careless or it would be 'unjust' not to rectify.[52] It might be added that the meaning of 'possession' is extended by LRA section 131, so that, for example, a landlord is treated as being in possession if a tenant is there and a trustee is treated as being in possession if a beneficiary is there.

Rectification is an important topic because, like overriding interests, it qualifies the guarantee given to the registered proprietor: the register is that much less reliable. However, it seems that the modern scope of mistake and rectification is quite limited apart from first registration of land. In any event, a proprietor who loses because of rectification may receive an **indemnity**.

We can now turn to indemnity: compensation paid by the land registry under LRA, Schedule 8 (Extract 10.4.1). Errors are inevitably made and around 1,000 payments are made annually (relating to around 4 million dealings and registrations). Often, these errors cause no loss to anybody, but take time to sort out. Compensation is payable for expenses in such cases. More interesting are claims for losses caused by mistakes (the basis for rectification) or rectification. The following example illustrates how the principles operate.

Samantha is by mistake registered as the first proprietor of land belonging to Tabitha. The land now belongs to Samantha, but we have seen that Tabitha may have a claim for rectification. If rectification is ordered then Samantha will be compensated. However, if the rectification claim fails (perhaps because Samantha is in possession) then Tabitha will be compensated. It follows that whoever loses will receive financial compensation, though any lack of care may exclude or reduce the compensation payable.

Indemnity is a great benefit of registered land. It avoids the all-or-nothing approach that is usually encountered in disputes over rights to land. However, it is limited to rectification and mistakes giving rights to rectification. The most important result of this is that a proprietor bound by an overriding interest gets nothing. Such cases will give rise to simple alteration, not rectification: that proprietor is already bound before the alteration. In the 1980s, it was proposed that compensation should be payable when a purchaser is bound by an undiscovered overriding interest: a significant increase in the protection

---

[50] *Barclays Bank plc* v *Guy* [2008] 2 EGLR 74. The Court of Appeal had adopted this approach before the 2002 Act: *Norwich & Peterborough BS* v *Steed* [1993] Ch 116.
[51] See the subsequent proceedings in *Barclays Bank plc* v *Guy* [2011] 1 WLR 681 at [35] (Lord Neuberger MR).
[52] LRA, Sched 3, para 3.

of purchasers. Perhaps unfortunately, the open-ended nature of such payments caused strong land registry objections and the proposal was dropped. The current level of indemnity payments is around £10 million annually, less than 3 per cent of land registry income. It has increased sharply to this level over the past decade, largely a result of large frauds (covering more than half the cost). Overall, the figures show both that relatively few errors are made and that the requirements to qualify for indemnity are quite strict.

Questions to consider

1. What is the difference between land charges and land registration?

2. What differences are there between registering interests and protecting interests on the register?

3. Why do we have overriding interests? Does the modern law keep them to the minimum?

4. Does a careful purchaser have anything to fear from overriding interests?

5. If an interest (not being overriding) is not protected on the register, are there any circumstances in which a purchaser may be affected by it?

6. What is meant by alteration and rectification? Are they consistent with guaranteeing the title of the registered transferee?

Further reading

Bogusz, B [2011] Conv 268: Defining the scope of actual occupation under the Land Registration Act 2002: some recent judicial clarification.

Cooke, E J and O'Connor, P A (2004) 120 LQR 640: Purchaser liability to third parties in the English registration system: a comparative perspective.

Harpum, C (2003) 'Registered land: a law unto itself?', in *Rationalizing Property, Equity and Trusts*, ed. J Getzler, Chapter 9.

Hill-Smith, A [2009] Conv 127: Forgery and land registration: the decision in *Malory Investments v Cheshire Homes*.

Jackson, N (2003) 119 LQR 660: Title by registration and concealed overriding interests: the cause and effect of antipathy to documentary proof.

O'Connor, P A (2005) 'Registration of invalid dispositions: who gets the property?', in *Modern Studies in Property Law*, Vol 3, ed. E J Cooke, Chapter 3.

Pottage, A [1995] 15 OxJLS 371: The originality of registration.

Thompson, M P [1985] CLJ 280: Registration, fraud and notice.

Visit **www.mylawchamber.co.uk** to access tools to help you
develop and test your knowledge of land law, including
interactive multiple choice questions, practice exam questions
with guidance, weblinks, glossary flashcards, legal newsfeed
and legal updates.

Use **Case Navigator** to read in full some of the key cases referenced in
this chapter with commentary and questions:

Abbey National Building Society v *Cann* [1990] 1 All ER 1085

Williams & Glyn's Bank v *Boland* [1980] 2 All ER 408

Part 3

Rights to enjoy land

11 Successive and concurrent ownership

Nature and importance

Land will often be owned by just one person. In more technical terms, we would say that Andrew holds the fee simple absolute in possession. However, it is possible for ownership of land to be split between two or more people, something which is made easier by the doctrine of estates. Thus Brian might have a life interest (a right to enjoy the land for life) and Carla a fee simple thereafter; this is an example of successive interests. More frequently, two people may own land together, as where a couple buy a home. We describe these as concurrent interests (or co-ownership). All these rights may be created as regards either freehold or leasehold land. For example, a couple may be co-owners of a lease. It is not unusual for successive and concurrent interests to be combined.

A man might leave the family home by will 'to my widow Audrey for life, remainder to my children Brenda and Carolyn'. Here Brenda and Carolyn are co-owners of the fee simple. Because their interest is effective ('in possession') only on Audrey's death, until then it is described as being in remainder.

This chapter considers the forms of successive and concurrent ownership. We also give some consideration to their creation. Concurrent interests are usually created expressly or by implication on the purchase of the family home; nothing further needs to be said about that. However, there is a choice between two forms of concurrent interests (joint tenancy and tenancy in common) and we investigate which is created.

An important issue concerns the operation and regulation of successive and concurrent interests. What happens if the parties cannot agree as to whether the property should be sold or who should occupy it? Whenever there are successive or concurrent interests, a trust is imposed. This trust is regulated by legislation, which confers on the court a broad discretion to resolve disputes. The imposition of the trust and its operation form the subject matter of Chapter 12.

How important are successive and concurrent interests? Prior to the First World War, a large proportion of the land in the country was held by wealthy families. Complex trusts conferred successive interests on generations of the family. This was, indeed, the heart of nineteenth-century land law. The decline in this role of those wealthy families, coupled with the ever increasing economic importance of property other than land, means that successive interests have lost their central role of a century or two ago. The twentieth century witnessed a huge expansion of owner-occupation of the family home, covering over 70 per cent of homes today. Especially since the Second World War, a large proportion of these homes have been co-owned. In part, this results from both partners in a relationship being employed and so able to contribute to mortgage costs. Concurrent interests, dealing with such a large number of homes, are clearly of huge importance.

Successive interests

What interests are recognised?

Today, the two freehold estates are the life interest and the fee simple. Most **settlements** (the term usually used for successive interests) involve some combination of these interests. The picture is more complex if an interest is made contingent on satisfying some requirement (to Jane at the age of 21) or terminable on some event occurring (to Mark until he takes up smoking).

In the past, many settlements included an *entail*. An entail (or fee tail) would last as long as the initial holder had descendants, descent being to the eldest male child (the traditional descent rule).

A settlement gives Andrew an entail, with Biruntha holding the fee simple in remainder. Andrew dies, leaving a daughter and a son who themselves never have children. The entail passes to Andrew's son, even if younger than his sister. When he dies, the entail goes to the daughter. When she dies, there are no longer any descendants of Andrew and the entail terminates; the land goes to Biruntha.

Surprisingly, an entail could sometimes be converted into a fee simple ('barring' the entail) and thereby last forever. Entails became increasingly rare and the Trusts of Land and Appointment of Trustees Act 1996 prohibited new entails. This may be welcomed: the entail was highly complex and the descent rules failed to match the wishes of most modern settlors.

Terminable interests merit further discussion. There are two different forms: the conditional interest and the determinable interest. The conditional interest involves a condition subsequent; this is to be contrasted with a condition precedent, which creates a contingent interest. An example of a conditional interest (condition subsequent) would be 'to Sarah, on condition that she does not take up smoking'. The idea is that the grantor gives the full interest and then seeks to cut it short on a specified event. By contrast, in a determinable interest the grantor defines from the start what the grantee is to take: 'to Tamara until she takes up smoking'. This could well be seen as a distinction without a difference – the substance of the two gifts looks identical.

Having these two very similar forms of interest might not matter too much if they were governed by the same rules. To the law's discredit, some of the events permitted for determinable fees are not allowed for conditional fees. The reason for this is that the law disapproves of the idea of **forfeiture** involved in conditional fees. For example, a gift to Andy on condition that he does not marry is void, whereas a gift to Belinda until she marries is valid. Another distinction is that greater certainty is required for conditional fees. Finally, failure of a condition leads to the grantee obtaining the interest granted whereas a failed determinable interest is wholly ineffective. The following examples are based on the proposition that encouraging prostitution is contrary to public policy and will cause failure.

> A gift to Carla until she gives up prostitution (determinable fee) is wholly void: Carla gets nothing. A gift to Carla on condition that she does not give up prostitution (conditional fee) leaves Carla with the fee simple absolute.

None of these distinctions between conditional and determinable interests seems to make any practical sense. The law regarding determinable and conditional fees is all too easy to mock. The examples show how a well-advised grantor can choose which to employ. There is no point in the law striking down gifts which can be validly made by a slight change of wording. It is unsurprising that the area has been judicially described as 'little short of disgraceful to our jurisprudence'.[1]

Creation of successive interests

Virtually nothing needs to be said. The normal formalities for setting up trusts of land apply: a deed for transfer of the legal estate and writing for creating beneficial interests. In the past, particular words (called *words of limitation*) had to be used to create the various estates. These rules no longer operate and today it is simply a matter of construction of the document.

Vesting and perpetuity rules

The law has long prevented landowners from controlling who gets the land many years in the future. The 'dead hand' of the settlor should not be allowed to determine entitlement after several generations. The rules depend upon the time of vesting. An interest is 'vested in possession' when it is currently being enjoyed: the holder is in physical possession or receives rent. It is said to be 'vested in interest' when the future holder is identified, no condition has to be fulfilled, but a prior interest stops it from being currently enjoyed.

[1] Porter MR in *Re King's Trusts* (1892) 29 LR Ir 401 at p. 410.

A will leaves property 'to my widow Mary for life, remainder to my eldest son John provided that he qualifies as a doctor'. John is aged six. Though we know who John is, his interest cannot be vested as he has yet to qualify as a doctor: he is said to have a contingent (or executory) interest. Suppose John qualifies as a doctor at the age of 24, Mary still being alive. His remainder then vests in interest. It is only when Mary dies that his interest can be said to vest in possession.

The perpetuity rules (which apply to all property) depend on the date of vesting in interest. They are too detailed for treatment in an introductory text, but their essence was that vesting could be postponed for one generation plus 21 years. Accordingly, a gift to Fred's children at 21 was valid, whereas a gift to Harriet's grandchildren was void.[2] Statute relaxed the common law, so Harriet's grandchildren could take if they were born within 21 years of her death. The Perpetuities and Accumulations Act 2009[3] swept away the old rules, replacing them with the far simpler rule that vesting must occur within 125 years. If necessary, we can wait to see whether vesting in fact occurs within that period. In any event, relatively few modern settlors want to tie up land for many generations in the future.

The operation of the interests

This area is today the province of trusts of land. One point, however, concerns the rights and duties of the holder of a life interest. The rules governing *waste* established their rights and obligations. In broad terms, there was no positive obligation to repair (permissive waste), though there was liability for not taking proper care of the land (voluntary waste). Today, land is managed by trustees and their obligations are determined by the law of trusts. Some of the old waste rules remain significant because they determine some of the rights of the holder of the life interest. Thus there are rules relating to entitlement to timber and mines, though we need not go into the details.

Concurrent interests

Co-ownership is not as simple as two or more people sharing ownership. English law recognises two forms of co-ownership: **joint tenancy** and **tenancy in common**.

Joint tenancy possesses the peculiar feature that, when one of the holders dies, the surviving joint tenants are entitled to the entire property. Indeed the basic concept is that each joint tenant owns the whole; when one dies, there is simply one fewer person to share it. This right of **survivorship** is useful in a number of situations. When a couple buy a family home together, it is very likely that they will choose a joint tenancy – they will intend the survivor to have the home. They are unlikely to want the survivor to share the

---

[2] Assuming Harriet is alive.
[3] Based on Law Com No 251.

home with whoever is entitled under the deceased's will. The joint tenancy is also the ideal way for trustees to hold property: the survivors are the most appropriate trustees after one has died.

It will be obvious that the joint tenancy is not suitable for all co-owners. Two friends buying a flat together would find it odd, as would businessmen purchasing land for their business. The tenancy in common is available for such cases: the share of a deceased tenant in common passes by will. A tenancy in common can be created either from the start or at any time before the death of a joint tenant. Changing an existing joint tenancy into a tenancy in common is termed **severance**.

Joint tenancy or tenancy in common?

We will now consider which form of co-ownership is created. The following chapter will explain that, since 1925, a tenancy in common cannot exist as a legal estate. All co-ownership operates under a trust of land; the choice is between equitable joint tenancy and equitable tenancy in common.

There cannot be a joint tenancy without the **four unities** being present. The very essence of joint tenancy is that each owns the whole and the four unities spell this out in more detail. The four unities are unity of possession, unity of interest, unity of title and unity of time.

Unity of possession is central to any form of co-ownership; it is the only unity required for tenancies in common.

> Two fields (of identical size) are owned by Emily and Fiona. If they are entitled to one field each, there is no unity of possession and no co-ownership. Alternatively, they might each be entitled to possession of both fields, in which case there would be unity of possession. One point to note is that unity of possession relates to entitlement rather than physical occupation. Should Emily and Fiona lease the fields to George, that has no impact on unity of possession. Alternatively, Emily might use both fields; Fiona lives a long distance away and never uses them. Again, this is entirely compatible with unity of possession.

It might be added that occupation rights are now governed by legislation (dealt with in Chapter 12).

The other unities are important in distinguishing joint tenancies from tenancies in common.

Unity of interest is the most important. It means that the interest held by the co-owners must be of the same type and the same size. A life interest holder and the holder of a fee simple cannot be joint tenants (how would survivorship work when their interests are different?) and, more important in practice, one joint tenant cannot have a one-third share and the other a two-thirds share. Though this rule on the size of shares is very clear, it may be doubted whether it should exist. It is not inconsistent for parties to desire survivorship, but to have different size shares. This might be important for taxation reasons and also as regards shares on severance. Nevertheless, the present law is clear that joint tenants automatically take equal shares on severance.[4]

Unity of title requires that the parties derive title from the same immediate document. This is rarely a problem when co-ownership is set up. More frequently, it explains severance.

Sara and Theresa are joint tenants under a will; Sara sells her interest to Ursula. Theresa's immediate title is the will, whereas Ursula's title is the sale by Sara. There is no unity of interest between Theresa and Ursula and accordingly they are tenants in common.

Unity of time means that the interests must vest at the same time. There are several situations in which this unity is not required: its significance is minimal.

There cannot be a joint tenancy without all four unities. However, the presence of all four is not conclusive: a tenancy in common will exist if intended by the settlor (or purchasers, if co-ownership arises on property purchase). This intention may be shown by an express reference to a tenancy in common. It also suffices for the parties to use language indicative of their having separate shares. The nature of a tenancy in common is that the parties are regarded as having separate shares rather than jointly owning the whole. The term 'undivided shares', an alternative name for the tenancy in common, captures this well. Thus, a reference to 'equally', 'in equal shares', 'amongst', 'divided' or 'participate' will result in a tenancy in common. It may be thought that the courts are leaning over backwards to find a tenancy in common; laymen are likely to use these words (often called 'words of severance') in a wholly haphazard manner.

There is a presumption of a joint tenancy once all the unities are present and there are no words of severance. However, there are several types of situation in which courts of equity have found the presumption rebutted. This illustrates the suspicion with which they viewed the joint tenancy, going so far as to describe it as 'odious'.[5]

The first example of such an equitable presumption is where the parties contribute differing amounts to a purchase: a tenancy in common is necessary for them to hold in unequal shares. Also important is the presumption that business partners desire a tenancy in common. Even if their contributions are equal, it is very unlikely that they will want survivorship to operate. This presumption is applied in a realistic manner. Thus businessmen who acquire property for their separate businesses will be within the rule, even though there is no joint business enterprise.[6] Conversely, if the business partners happen to be a couple who desire survivorship, then a joint tenancy will result. A final example of a presumed tenancy in common relates to joint mortgagees. Two people lending money are similar to partners and, for similar reasons, survivorship is inappropriate.

---

[4] *Goodman v Gallant* [1986] Fam 106 (Extract 8.1.1).
[5] *York v Stone* (1709) 1 Salk 158 (91 ER 146).
[6] *Malayan Credit Ltd v Jack Chia-MPH Ltd* [1986] AC 549 (Extract 11.2.2).

Although the preference for the joint tenancy may seem odd, the scope for finding a contrary intention is very wide. We will consider three types of case in evaluating these rules in the modern world. The first concerns the purchase of land in joint names. We saw above (Chapter 9) that a joint tenancy is presumed in family home purchases in joint names, regardless of unequal contributions. Modern land registry forms require the transferees to state the nature of their equitable interest: there is an explicit choice between joint tenancy and tenancy in common. As a statement of beneficial interests is generally conclusive,[7] this means that problems are unlikely to arise in recent purchases.

Next is the situation where land is purchased by one person, but a constructive trust means that there is co-ownership in equity. This will usually be where a couple (whether or not married) share ownership of property under the *Gissing v Gissing*[8] (Extract 8.3.1) and *Stack v Dowden*[9](Extracts 8.4.4, 8.4.15) principles. The transfer form does not cover such cases, as no co-ownership is apparent on the face of the transfer. If the shares are unequal, there can be only a tenancy in common (no unity of interest), but what if they both have a 50 per cent share so that the four unities are present?

The cases, perhaps surprisingly, provide no clear answer. A joint tenancy might seem appropriate because most couples opt for a joint tenancy when interests are created expressly. It would make sense to replicate this where they have not expressed their beneficial interests. However, in *Stack* Baroness Hale observed that the cases lend no support to there being a joint tenancy. In many constructive trust cases the shares are not equal, so there can only be a tenancy in common. It may be appropriate to have the same outcome where the shares happen to be equal.

The third situation in which co-ownership arises is where there is a settlement or will. It is in this setting that words of severance are most likely to be relevant. The starting point is likely to be a joint tenancy, as the equitable presumptions are not designed for this sort of case. Is the joint tenancy appropriate? Most commonly, settlements and legacies are in favour of close family members, when survivorship may be appropriate. Even so, the arguments in favour of the joint tenancy are not overwhelming. If a beneficiary dies, would not the grantor intend that that beneficiary's family (especially if there are children) should benefit from that share, rather than the other co-owners? The arguments are finely balanced, though very few cases have arisen in this context in recent decades. It is scarcely a matter of pressing concern!

After looking at these examples of concurrent interests, it may be concluded that joint tenancies will rarely be found contrary to the true intentions of the parties. There is some attraction in the rule applied in some countries that a tenancy in common is the presumed form of co-ownership. However, its practical effects would be few, at least outside settlements and wills.

It is more likely that intentions will be thwarted where survivorship is intended, but a joint tenancy cannot exist because the four unities are lacking. Arguably, the law

---

[7] *Goodman v Gallant* [1986] Fam 106 (Extract 8.1.1). The forms do not guarantee the absence of problems: *Stack v Dowden* [2007] 2 AC 432 at [52].

[8] [1971] AC 886.

[9] [2007] 2 AC 432.

should take the pragmatic approach that a joint tenancy should exist whenever it is intended by the parties and is workable. This requires the unity of possession (necessary for all forms of co-ownership) and probably that the parties possess the same type of jointly owned interest (fee simple or lease, for example). The remaining aspects of unity of interest (shares must be the same) and the unities of title and time are more difficult to justify. Their absence might indeed be a pointer against a joint tenancy, but their absence should not be conclusive. Whereas it is true that the four unities fill out the idea of each joint tenant owning the whole, a pragmatic modern response is that the joint tenancy should be important only for the application of survivorship.

Severance of joint tenancies

Joint tenants may wish to prevent survivorship. The most common example is that survivorship will be inappropriate when a couple buy their family home as joint tenants but then break up. Survivorship is the last thing they now desire! Virtually all the modern cases arise from this setting.

Conversion into a tenancy in common – severance – has always been allowed. One long-standing example is that sale by one joint tenant of his or her share severs that share. As has been seen, the transferee does not have unity of title: this means that there can no longer be a joint tenancy. The law might have said that a joint tenant has no 'share' capable of transfer, simply being entitled to the whole together with the others. No such argument has been seriously put forward in recent centuries.

Today, severance is governed by the Law of Property Act 1925 (hereafter LPA), section 36(2) (Extract 11.3.1). As a tenancy in common can never exist as a legal interest, it is never possible to sever a legal joint tenancy. This is explicitly stated by section 36(2).

Section 36(2) provides two routes to sever an equitable joint tenancy. The first is a new form of severance: notice in writing. This is designed to be a simple method for one joint tenant to sever the joint tenancy unilaterally. Previously that was possible only by the artificial route of transferring one's share. It should be noted that section 36(2) requires a notice in writing to be sent to the other joint tenants; it cannot be secret. A fairly recent decision has confirmed the statutory rule that notices are effective on delivery, even if never received by the intended recipient.[10]

The notice in writing provides an easy route to severance. Explicit words, like 'I sever our joint tenancy', are clearly effective. Often, however, letters will be sent without any mention of severance and without the sender being aware of the severance rules. A layman is more likely to say something like 'I want the property sold'. Even lawyers may write letters without thinking about severance. Though nobody would wish to see notices of severance limited to formal legal documents, there is a real danger of having to sift through correspondence on the off-chance that there is some reference to 'shares' or other language indicative of a joint tenancy.

---

[10] *Kinch v Bullard* [1999] 1 WLR 423, applying LPA, s 196(3) (Extract 11.3.7). On the facts, the giver of the notice had got hold of it and destroyed it; the intended recipient could still claim severance.

So far the courts have taken a fairly narrow view of what suffices. Several cases have involved the wording of court applications. Although **Re Draper's Conveyance**[11] held a request for sale and division of the proceeds to be effective, more recent cases (notably **Harris v Goddard**)[12] (Extract 11.3.5) have stressed the need for the notice to have immediate effect and to refer fairly explicitly to severance: a request for the court to exercise its discretion will not suffice.

Before leaving written notices, two limitations must be mentioned. First, they are effective only for land. Next, the wording of section 36(2) (Extract 11.3.1) ('where a legal estate . . . is vested in joint tenants beneficially') seems to require that the same persons be both trustees and beneficiaries. If Rosalind and Sam hold on trust for themselves as beneficial joint tenants then either can give written notice. However, if Andrew and Brenda hold on trust for Catriona and Davina then this is outside the written notice provisions. These limitations are almost impossible to justify, though it would be appropriate to require notice to be given to all trustees and beneficiaries.

The second route to severance is provided by the old equitable severance rules, which section 36(2) keeps in operation. These rules are articulated in the 1861 decision in **Williams v Hensman**[13] (Extract 11.3.2), still routinely cited:

> A joint tenancy may be severed in three ways: in the first place, an act of any one of the persons interested operating upon his own share may create a severance as to that share . . . Each one is at liberty to dispose of his own interest in such manner as to sever it from the joint fund – losing, of course, at the same time, his own right of survivorship. Secondly, a joint tenancy may be severed by mutual agreement. And, in the third place, there may be a severance by any course of dealing sufficient to intimate that the interests of all were mutually treated as constituting a tenancy in common. When the severance depends on an inference of this kind without any express act of severance, it will not suffice to rely on an intention, with respect to the particular share, declared only behind the backs of the other persons interested. You must find, in this class of cases, a course of dealing by which the shares of all the parties to the contest have been affected . . .

Of the three heads of severance identified, the second and third cause the greatest difficulty. They will be considered as a Critical Issue. The first head covers the transfer of a beneficial interest in a joint tenancy; this has already been mentioned. Several points about its application may be noted. Most straightforward is that a contract to sell the interest will be as effective as an immediate transfer. This is because equity enforces contracts relating to land and treats the purchaser as having an immediate equitable interest. However, it must be remembered that contracts relating to land have to be in writing;[14] without writing, the first head will not apply.

More difficult is the effect of transactions short of outright transfer. The effect of leases and charges (mortgages) has given rise to debate, though there is a dearth of recent English authority. It seems most likely that leases effect a severance for at least the duration of the lease, while most authorities assume that charges cause severance. Less

[11] [1969] 1 Ch 486.
[12] [1983] 1 WLR 1203.
[13] 1 J&H 546 at pp. 557–8 (70 ER 862 at p. 867).
[14] Law of Property (Miscellaneous Provisions) Act 1989, s 2 (Extract 5.2.3).

problematic is bankruptcy. The bankrupt's assets vest in the **trustee in bankruptcy** and this is considered to effect severance.

The first head permits unilateral severance: there is no need for notice to the other joint tenants. This is well settled: severance follows as a logical and inevitable consequence of the shattering of unity of title. However, is it justified as a matter of policy, especially where (as the law permits) there is a transfer to oneself? The problem is that the other joint tenants may believe – wrongly – that survivorship will operate. Another danger[15] is that the severing joint tenant may be tempted to suppress the severance if the others die first – a situation in which the severing joint tenant would benefit from survivorship.

What is the effect of severance?

Martina and Olivia are joint tenants; Martina sells her interest to Paula. The effect is clear: Olivia and Paula are tenants in common. More complex is the position where there are three or more joint tenants. An example would be Martina, Olivia and Xavier, with Martina again selling her interest to Paula. This doubtless severs Martina's share, but what effect does it have on Olivia and Xavier? The answer is that they remain joint tenants as between themselves: it is only Martina's share that has been severed. If Paula dies, then her purchased share passes under her will. If Olivia dies, however, her share passes by survivorship to Xavier, who will then have a two-thirds share.

Does it make any difference if Martina transfers her interest to Olivia, already one of the joint tenants? The answer is not – though this effects severance, again Olivia and Xavier remain as joint tenants.[16] This is shown in Figure 11.1. We may ask how a joint tenancy can exist if Olivia has two shares. The answer is that the joint tenancy is over the two-thirds share, not the property as a whole. Olivia has two separate interests: a severed one-third share under a tenancy in common and a joint tenancy in the other two-thirds. If Olivia were to be the first to die, her estate would take the severed one-third share. The other two-thirds would be held outright (through survivorship) by Xavier.

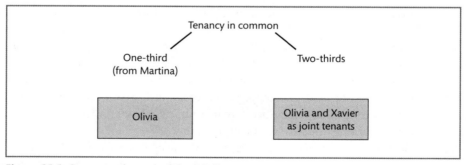

Figure 11.1 Severance by one of three joint tenants

[15] Crown (2001) 117 LQR 477 at p. 491 (in the context of declarations of trust as severing acts).
[16] Co Litt 193a.

These examples on multiple joint tenants inevitably involve considerable complexity. Multiple joint tenants can also pose problems for severance by notice.

> Alice, Beatrice and Charlie are joint tenants. Alice gives notice to Beatrice and Charlie: does this sever just Alice's share or the entire joint tenancy? The cases provide no answer. Severance of just Alice's share would seem most appropriate, whatever the wording of the notice: it limits the impact on Beatrice and Charlie as between themselves.

Very different is the principle that survivorship does not apply if one joint tenant murders another. Clearly, the murderer cannot be permitted to benefit from the crime and the courts apply public policy to say that there has been severance.[17]

Severance by mutual agreement and course of conduct

These two heads of severance, unlike transfer of interests, are unrelated to the four unities. Instead, they are based upon the intention of the joint tenants. They were developed by equity, which was always distrustful of the joint tenancy and concerned to give effect to intentions. Virtually all the modern cases involve a couple's family home. Does the joint tenancy continue after their relationship has broken down? It would be very unusual for them still to want survivorship: each party will wish to determine the destination of their shares in the future. Accordingly, one might expect the courts to apply severance as broadly as possible. It must be remembered that refusal to sever cannot be employed as a bargaining ploy: unilateral severance by written notice or transfer is always possible.

The most controversial issue is whether these two heads require both parties to intend to sever, or whether it suffices that one party has made clear their intention to sever. Two cases decided within a year of each other in the 1970s are central to this. *Nielson-Jones v Fedden*[18] (Extract 11.3.3) involved the parties negotiating as to the future of the family home, following the breakdown of their marriage. Walton J was clear that a unilateral declaration by one joint tenant did not sever: the older cases demonstrated that a notice in writing or a transfer were the appropriate methods for one joint tenant to sever. Though two more recent cases[19] had pointed in favour of unilateral severance, Walton J laid bare the woeful inadequacy of their reasoning. In *Nielson-Jones*, the parties had agreed that the family home should be sold to provide funds for a house for the husband. It was clear that the parties did not intend that the new house would belong to the husband. Walton J made the telling point that negotiations and agreement as to sale of the property are neutral as to severance. The proceeds of sale (or a house purchased with those proceeds) could well be subject to a joint tenancy. On the other hand, it is difficult to believe that the parties really thought that a joint tenancy should be any part of the eventual

---

[17] *Re K* [1985] Ch 85 at p. 100 (Extract 11.3.8).
[18] [1975] Ch 222.
[19] *Hawkesley v May* [1956] 1 QB 304 (incomprehensible reliance on the first head), followed in *Re Draper's Conveyance* [1969] 1 Ch 486.

outcome: the result has an air of unreality about it. Despite *Nielson-Jones*, it should be easier to show an intention to sever if the parties agree to split the proceeds between them (not the situation in *Nielson-Jones*). This is indicative of a tenancy in common, as it emphasises the parties having shares rather than owning the whole.[20]

Burgess v Rawnsley[21] (Extract 11.3.4) was a somewhat unusual case in that it involved a more elderly couple, whose relationship never fully blossomed. They purchased a house, on the initial understanding that each would have a separate flat. When the man realised that marriage was not going to happen, he orally agreed to purchase the woman's share. If there had been writing, this would have been a clear case of first-head severance. The Court of Appeal accepted that the unenforceable agreement to sell could be treated as an implicit agreement to sever – it was clear that a joint tenancy was not intended to continue. That implicit agreement clearly fell within the second head of severance in *Williams v Hensman*.

The facts of *Burgess* raise the question whether an agreement to sever itself has to be in writing. Given the general insistence on writing for agreements and transactions relating to land, one can see policy arguments in favour of requiring writing. Furthermore, Australian views tend in that direction. On the other hand, it is not apparent that an agreement to sever is either a 'contract for the sale or other disposition of an interest in land' (Law of Property (Miscellaneous Provisions) Act 1989) or a creation or disposal of an interest in land (LPA, section 53(1)(a)). Furthermore a course of dealing (third head) can scarcely be in writing; it would be strange if writing was required for one, but not the other, of these two heads. In any event, *Burgess* clearly states that writing is not required – even though the point is not analysed in depth.

Burgess also states that the third head is wider than an implied agreement to sever. Indeed, it might be thought that the nature of the course of dealing is that the parties assume there to be a tenancy in common, as opposed to agreeing that there should be one. This shows them to be quite different. *Nielson-Jones* (supported by some earlier cases) had adopted the opposite view. In the light of *Burgess*, should a course of dealing have been recognised in *Nielson-Jones*? In *Burgess*, Lord Denning MR seemed quite clear that the earlier decision was wrong, though Sir John Pennycuick more cautiously left the question open. In *Gore & Snell v Carpenter*[22] (Extract 11.3.6), one joint tenant died while negotiations were in progress following the breakdown of their marriage. Severance had been put forward by just one party as part of a series of proposals. This looks quite similar to *Nielson-Jones*. It was held that there was no sufficient course of dealing. The difficulty with the decision is that, whatever the outcome to the negotiations, it was certain to include severance. A more generous approach was taken more recently by the Court of Appeal in *Davis v Smith*,[23] where the joint tenants had agreed to sell the property and split the proceeds. Though the facts quite strongly supported severance, one can observe a greater willingness to find severance.

---

[20] This approach was taken for written notices in *Re Draper's Conveyance* [1969] 1 Ch 486 (p. 153, above); *Saleeba v Wilke* [2007] QSC 298.
[21] [1975] Ch 429.
[22] (1990) 60 P&CR 456 (Judge Blackett-Ord).
[23] [2012] 1 FLR 1177.

However, the most controversial aspect of *Burgess* lies in Lord Denning MR's support for unilateral severance. This would be important where a section 36(2) written notice cannot be relied upon, especially for assets other than land and where the notice is merely oral. Lord Denning MR had two arguments. The first was a technical one based on the wording of section 36(2), which could be taken to imply that severance by written notice was possible before 1925. This seems an unlikely construction of the section:[24] it would be inconsistent with the cases and an equitable rule requiring writing would be wholly exceptional. He also appears to consider that unilateral notices (written or oral) fall within *Williams* v *Hensman*. This also is difficult to accept. Page-Wood V-C referred to a course of dealing whereby the shares are 'mutually treated' as a tenancy in common and Walton J in *Nielson-Jones* had convincingly shown that the earlier cases were opposed to unilateral declarations. Lord Denning MR's analysis seems to have been rejected by Sir John Pennycuick[25] and its status is dubious. There is no authoritative decision on the points, but subsequent English dicta are hostile.[26] Perhaps more tellingly, influential Commonwealth decisions have sided with Sir John Pennycuick and Walton J.[27]

Even if the authorities persuade us to reject Lord Denning MR's attempt to recognise unilateral severance, does this represent sound policy? After all, unilateral severance is already possible by written notice or transfer. The latter does not even require notice to the other joint tenants, whereas Lord Denning MR recognises that notice is essential for unilateral declarations. At least at first sight, it seems capricious not to recognise unilateral severance.[28] The principal cause for doubt is that section 36(2) already provides a simple route involving written notice. There is a strong argument that the certainty engendered by writing is as important for severance as it is for other property transactions. Indeed, it is questionable whether we can justify the absence of writing for the second and third heads of severance.

CRITICAL ISSUE

Reform

Leaving aside the second and third heads just discussed, are reforms of other severance rules required? It has already been seen that there are limits on the scope of written notices under section 36(2) (Extract 11.3.1). These limits seem unduly technical and they demand urgent review. The status of severance by transfer has already been considered.[29] More radical is the question whether severance by will should be permitted. The principal problem is that such severance may be one-sided. If the person making the will dies then severance is effective and survivorship does not apply. If the other dies first then the maker of the will (still alive) benefits from survivorship. This problem, allied with concerns regarding hidden severances and likely problems in knowing whether the wording

---

[24] Hayton [1976] CLJ 20 at p. 24.
[25] *Burgess* at pp. 447–8; Browne LJ at p. 444 was ambivalent.
[26] E.g., *Gore and Snell* v *Carpenter* (1990) 60 P&CR 456 at p. 462.
[27] See especially *Corin* v *Patton* (1990) 169 CLR 540 at pp. 548, 584, 591 (High Court of Australia); *Re Sorensen and Sorensen* (1977) 90 DLR 3d 26.
[28] See Tooher (1998) 24 Monash ULR 422.
[29] See above (p. 153).

in a will refers to the property sufficiently clearly, has caused the idea to receive very limited support.[30]

◼ The future of the equitable joint tenancy

The existence of the two forms of co-ownership confers a useful ability to dictate how the property should pass on death. Is that benefit bought at too high a price? Virtually everybody agrees that the joint tenancy is by far the most convenient way for trustees to hold assets. Meanwhile, the tenancy in common obviously must continue as a form of beneficial ownership: it provides essential flexibility. The real question is whether the beneficial joint tenancy should be abolished.[31]

The case against the joint tenancy may be put on three grounds. Plainly, it complicates the law, resulting in inevitable extra expense. Second, it is unnecessary. If survivorship is desired, then this can be achieved by each co-owner making a will leaving their share to the other. Third, survivorship operates in many situations where it is not wanted (notably following relationship breakdown), such that joint tenancies defeat intentions as much as giving effect to them.

Taking the first point, it cannot be denied that considerable complexity is caused by recognising the two forms of co-ownership. Without them, there would be almost nothing to say on co-ownership in this chapter, save unity of possession! This would simplify life for students and, more importantly, do away with the need for advice and litigation as to what form of co-ownership has been created and whether there has been severance. Any additional choice conferred by legal structures involves added complexity: the question has to be whether the benefits outweigh the costs. On the other hand, the problems should not be exaggerated. The actual number of reported cases on these questions over the past 20 years can be counted on the fingers of one or two hands.

The second point, that the effects can be replicated by wills, is a strong one. As a matter of principle, it is difficult to challenge. On the other hand, it cannot be assumed that wills would in fact be made (this is discussed below).

The accusation that the wrong results are reached is a serious one; it requires further investigation. As explained above, the results reached on the creation of co-ownership nearly always seem appropriate. However, we might question whether the parties' statement that they hold as joint tenants always reflects their true intentions. The great majority of those buying houses together choose a joint tenancy, but almost invariably this results from the recommendation of their lawyers. How many purchasers truly understand what it is that they are agreeing to? In any event, it is understandable if they forget about it as the years go by – explanation of the forms of co-ownership will rarely seem important to most people embroiled in the stressful experience of buying a new home. Even allowing for these doubts, most couples buying a home together are likely to wish the other to have it in the event of their death. This is particularly important for

---

[30] The arguments are considered by Tee [1995] Conv 105 at pp. 111–13.
[31] The question is debated by Thompson [1987] Conv 29, 275 (for abolition) and Prichard [1987] Conv 273 (against abolition).

unmarried couples, as the survivor will be unable to take advantage of intestacy rules. Of course, a significant number of people buying a house together will wish to avoid survivorship. This would be true, for example, of friends purchasing a house and many cases where it is purchased as an investment.

It is more obvious that the wrong results are reached on breakdown of the relationship between the co-owners. The cases reveal many examples of severance not applying. Nor would it be feasible to say that relationship breakdown should effect severance: how would we define it and how would it apply to on/off/on relationships? The critics of the joint tenancy rightly point to survivorship's producing inappropriate results. These results would be avoided if the beneficial joint tenancy were to be abandoned.

These are really powerful arguments, but would a tenancy in common actually fare better? An initial uncertainty is whether co-owners would in practice make wills dealing with the property. Nearly always, problems occur when death is unexpected, especially for younger co-owners. These are exactly the people who are unlikely to make wills. For unmarried couples, the results of **intestacy** could be disastrous – quite possibly causing the survivor to face disputes with the deceased's family. This might well result in the home having to be sold. Worse still, the deceased's share might be vested in an estranged spouse, a certain recipe for disputes. This last scenario was nicely illustrated by *Delehunt v Carmody*,[32] where the unmarried couple had lived together for 30 years. We might reach the conclusion that the joint tenancy is likely to get the result wrong when the relationship fails, but the tenancy in common is just as likely to get it wrong if the relationship succeeds. The critics have a strong argument only if one takes the pessimistic approach that failure of relationships is so common as to be adopted as the norm.

A further question is as to whether a tenancy in common always produces the better result on relationship breakdown. In long-term relationships, a tenant in common's will is very likely to specify that the property is to go to their partner or spouse. What happens on relationship breakdown, followed by the death of one party? Unless their will has been amended,[33] it will produce the same result as a joint tenancy: the former partner will get the deceased's share. One may doubt whether the parties (or their lawyers) will give any more urgent thought to amending wills than they do to severing the joint tenancy. Again, we must remember that the problems usually arise on an unexpected death, when changing a will would have been given a low priority. Indeed, one might argue that the joint tenancy has a better chance of producing the right result, at least if the courts take a slightly more generous approach to finding severance from a mutual agreement or course of dealing from negotiations on relationship breakdown.

The arguments are quite finely balanced. If we were developing a legal system from scratch, probably we would recognise only the tenancy in common. However, we have a position where the great majority of co-owners opt for the joint tenancy. Even if it is sometimes the result of unthinking reliance on lawyers' advice, this practice should make us pause and think. Abolishing an option chosen by most people is a strange way of developing our legal system.

CRITICAL ISSUE

[32] (1986) 161 CLR 464.
[33] Legacies to a spouse terminate on divorce (Wills Act 1837, s 18A (Extract 5.7.1)), but problems almost always arise when a joint tenant dies before divorce.

Questions to consider

1. What differences are there between joint tenancies and tenancies in common?

2. Should the joint tenancy be abolished in a future reform of co-ownership?

3. What are the four unities? What role do they play in (i) setting up co-ownership and (ii) the operation of a joint tenancy?

4. What is meant by severance of a joint tenancy? Do we have well functioning severance rules?

Further reading

Butt, P (1982) 9 Syd LR 568: Severance of joint tenancies in matrimonial property.

Gallanis, T P [2000] CLJ 284: The rules against perpetuities and the Law Commission's flawed philosophy.

Luther, P (1995) 15 LS 219: *Williams* v *Hensman* and the uses of history.

McClean, A J (1979) 57 Can BR 1: Severance of joint tenancies.

Sparkes, P (1998) 12 *Trust Law International* 148: Perpetuities reform.

Thompson, M P [1987] Conv 29: Beneficial joint tenancies – a case for abolition? (see also the reply by Prichard, A M [1987] Conv 273 and the response at p. 275).

Visit **www.mylawchamber.co.uk** to access tools to help you develop and test your knowledge of land law, including interactive multiple choice questions, practice exam questions with guidance, weblinks, glossary flashcards, legal newsfeed and legal updates.

Use **Case Navigator** to read in full some of the key cases referenced in this chapter with commentary and questions:

Burgess v *Rawnsley* [1975] Ch 429

Nielson-Jones v *Fedden* [1975] Ch 222.

POWERED BY LexisNexis

12 Trusts of land

Nature and importance

Whenever there is concurrent or successive ownership of land, questions may arise concerning (for example) rights of occupation and sale of the land. A very simple example comes from concurrent ownership. Suppose Kathryn and Larissa are co-owners; Kathryn wants to occupy the land whereas Larissa wishes to have it sold. The law must establish procedures for resolving disputes like this. There are various ways in which this could be achieved, but since 1925 we have imposed a trust. The law establishes the powers of the trustees and controls their exercise. This means that trusts are given an extensive and vitally important role. This is a special feature of modern English land law. Today, this is the province of the Trusts of Land and Appointment of Trustees Act 1996 (TLATA) and much of this chapter is devoted to the working of the rules it establishes.

The need for regulation: successive interests

The origins of the modern law lie in nineteenth-century successive interests.

Take a simple settlement whereby land is held for Alice for life and thereafter by Brian (a fee simple in remainder). Originally, these would be legal estates and, during Alice's lifetime, the land would be managed by Alice. All would be well so long as all that needs to be done is to let the land to tenant farmers on short leases and ensure that it is properly farmed. However, problems arose as soon as anything more radical needed to be done. If part of the land needed to be sold – perhaps for housing or industrial development – then both Alice and Brian would have to be involved. This might not appear too difficult, but the various interests would frequently be far more complex and in any event Brian might be an infant or a person whose identity is unascertained. An example of the latter would be a remainder to the children of Brian: until Brian dies, we cannot be sure that we have a complete list. This made it difficult and expensive to sell or to enter into other long-term transactions, such as longer leases or mortgages.

Similar problems arose if the land needed improvement, one example being by the construction of drains. Alice may well not be willing to spend her own money, as her interest terminates on her death, whereas Brian has little immediate interest in improving land that doesn't yet provide him with any return.

The nineteenth-century response was to confer powers on the tenant for life, Alice. Alice could improve, mortgage (to borrow money) and sell the land. One very important aspect of these powers was that a sale (or other disposition) by Alice would *overreach* all the successive interests. **Overreaching** is the shifting of interests from the land to the proceeds of sale; it is studied later in this chapter. If the land is sold for £200,000, it means that Brian ceases to have an interest in the land and instead has an interest in the £200,000 (in our example, it means that he will get the money on Alice's death). A purchaser from Alice is not bound by Brian's interest whether it is legal or equitable and regardless of notice (or, today, its being an overriding interest). Accordingly, the purchaser doesn't have to deal with Brian – it is this factor that ensures that Alice can sell the land almost as easily as could an absolute owner. This settlement structure is often termed settled land; it found its final form in the Settled Land Act 1925, under which the tenant for life (Alice) is given the legal fee simple on trust.

An alternative was for the land to be vested in trustees for sale, holding on trust for Alice and Brian. Trusts for sale had long been recognised; they involve an obligation to sell the land and were originally used when long-term retention of the land was not intended. However, there would usually be a power to postpone sale and this rendered the **trust for sale** suitable for long-term landholding, despite its unpromising label. This trust was recognised by the 1925 legislation as an alternative to settled land. As one might expect, powers to deal with the land were conferred on the trustees by the Law of Property Act 1925 (LPA) and overreaching protected purchasers. One might ask why this alternative didn't take the form of a simple trust of land, rather than a trust for sale. The answer appears to be that settled land already involved the tenant for life's holding the land on trust. A contrasting form of trust (the trust for sale) was required for cases where trustees held the legal title.

Since TLATA there has been a single form of settlement: the **trust of land**. This is much more straightforward than the previous dual regimes of settled land and trusts for sale regimes, each with its own rules. The old settled land approach of conferring powers on the tenant for life was thought to be inappropriate in many cases. The tenant for life might be incompetent and, in any event, there may well be a conflict of interest between the life interest and fee simple (the tenant for life is more interested in short-term benefits). Settled land was best suited to settlements based on primogeniture (property passing to the eldest son), which is now regarded as outdated. Trusts for sale are subsumed within the new trust of land and cease to be a separately regulated landholding structure. They can still be created, but are simply one type of trust of land: one in which there is a duty to sell. They will be considered later in this chapter; suffice to say at this stage that few settlors wish to create trusts for sale today.

Extension of regulation to concurrent interests

Until 1925, concurrent interests received no equivalent attention from the legislation. However, it was perceived that some of the same problems could apply as with successive interests. The **joint tenancy** is unlikely to pose problems as it will be unusual for there to be a large number of joint tenants. Furthermore, the number will decrease as they die – survivorship (explained in Chapter 11). However, it is not such plain sailing for **tenancies in common**. The problem here is that a tenant in common can pass on his interest on death. This involves two practical points. First, it becomes necessary to trace the passing of each interest (more complex than showing a death certificate to prove survivorship). Second, the will may pass an interest to a wide class of persons.

> There are three tenants in common. One gives his share 'to my grandchildren', of whom there are ten. There are now 12 tenants in common and each grandchild has a one thirtieth share. This illustrates the potential for there to be an increasing multitude of tenants in common, which would make it difficult to get the unanimity required for dealing with the land. Even where all 12 agree, dealing with so many people and tracing the passing of interests can multiply the work (and thus time and expense) involved in buying land.

The LPA solved these problems by imposing a trust for sale in all cases of co-ownership. It enabled sale (by the trustees, usually the same persons as the co-owners) and overreaching in the same way as in successive interests. The use of a trust for sale had the strange result that a couple who had just bought their home had an obligation to sell it, though the obligation did little harm in practice. Today, there is a simple trust of land (without any need for a trust for sale) and, like successive interests, it is governed by TLATA. Trustees always hold as legal joint tenants: since 1925 it has been impossible to hold a legal tenancy in common.[1] The beneficial interest will be either a joint tenancy or tenancy in common, according to the normal rules considered in Chapter 11.

> Freda, Gerry and Harry buy land as tenants in common. The three of them will hold the legal estate as joint tenants on trust for themselves as beneficial tenants in common (there is a maximum of four trustees[2]). Should Gerry die, Freda and Harry will hold the legal estate as trustees for themselves and whoever has Gerry's share under his will. A purchaser will deal only with Freda and Harry and will not be affected by how many people Gerry leaves his share to.

Independent trustees (i.e., not the same persons as the tenants in common) are more likely where the trust is set up as part of a settlement or will.

One may doubt whether the problems caused by concurrent interests before 1925 were (or are today) anything like as great as was feared. The reforms have not been implemented in other common law jurisdictions, which do not appear to experience significant problems. Yet it would be unrealistic to abolish the compulsory trust of land. As has been observed, the trust is the key to a host of provisions regulating the rights of the co-owners and resolution of disputes. This also goes far to explain why the law imposes a trust when there is a joint tenancy, given that problems for purchasers are uncommon.

---

[1] LPA, s 1(6) (the reference to 'undivided share' is another way of describing a tenancy in common).
[2] Trustee Act 1925, s 34.

▮ A single regulatory regime for successive and concurrent interests

There is a single TLATA regime applying to both concurrent and successive interests. However, the needs of the two types of interest may well be different: one cannot assume that the rules will be applied in an identical manner. Two examples (both considered in greater detail later in this chapter) may be given. First, trustees have statutory authority to delegate their powers to a beneficiary whose interest is in possession. This is unnecessary where two co-owners are both trustees and beneficiaries: they are managing the land already. It makes much more sense when independent (i.e., non-beneficiary) trustees delegate to the holder of a life interest. Second, the courts are very willing to intervene in disputes between co-owners who are also trustees. Because trustees normally must exercise their powers unanimously, decisions cannot be taken unless they agree. If the co-owners (typically a couple) have split up and cannot agree what to do with the land, court intervention is essential to decide whether it should be sold. By contrast, the courts may display much greater reluctance to get involved if beneficiaries dispute decisions taken by independent trustees. The settlor has chosen the trustees as persons and entrusted them with decision-making. The courts retain jurisdiction to review decisions, but one may expect that it will be sparingly exercised (at least if the trustees are unanimous).

When is there a trust of land?

Unsurprisingly, there is a trust of land whenever land is held on trust. It has already been seen that the trust of land regime is intended to apply to successive and concurrent interests. In this section, the scope of trusts of land is considered in a little more detail.

▮ Successive interests

The only legal freehold estate since 1925 is the fee simple absolute in possession. This means that a life interest and an interest in remainder necessarily take effect as equitable interests, under a trust.[3] TLATA naturally applies to these successive interests.

▮ Concurrent interests

LPA section 36 (Extract 12.1.3) makes it clear that a joint tenancy must be held under a trust. This has the apparently odd result that a transfer to Ruth and Sam means that they hold the legal estate as joint tenants on trust for themselves as equitable joint tenants. It may be justified because the trust is vital for TLATA to apply, enabling effective land management and the resolution of disputes.

LPA section 1(6) prevents tenancies in common being legal estates. It follows that they must be equitable interests under a trust: a trust of land. LPA section 34(2) (Extract 12.1.4)

---

[3] LPA, s 1.

provides that a purported transfer to tenants in common takes effect as a transfer to them as joint tenants, holding on trust for themselves as beneficial tenants in common. That works well enough if there is a transfer to Richard and Susan as tenants in common. They hold the legal estate as joint tenants on trust for themselves as tenants in common.

Unfortunately, the legislation fails to cope with more complex situations. Suppose there is a transfer to Tom, when Ursula has contributed to the purchase? We saw (in Chapters 9 and 11) that the law will say that there is a constructive trust, whereby Tom holds the legal estate for himself and Ursula as tenants in common. Unfortunately, section 34(1) states that a tenancy in common shall not be capable of being created except 'as hereinafter mentioned'. The Tom and Ursula example falls outside section 34(2) as it is not a case where 'land is expressed to be conveyed to any persons' as tenants in common: this is because the tenancy in common arises from the constructive trust. This means that the situation is not 'hereinafter mentioned' as required by section 34(1) and therefore, apparently, there cannot be a tenancy in common. This would, however, be an unacceptably harsh and restrictive result: there is no policy reason why there shouldn't be a tenancy in common in such cases. Though offering no analysis, Denning LJ in *Bull v Bull*[4] (Extract 12.1.5) held that there is an equitable tenancy in common in such cases. This is the only sensible result and it has never been challenged. The consequence, of course, is a trust of land with Tom being the trustee and Tom and Ursula being beneficial tenants in common.

Other cases

A bare trust (where trustees hold on trust for one individual absolutely) is a trust of land, though without any successive or concurrent interests. This enables purchasers to be protected by overreaching when they deal with the trustees.

Some special cases are explicitly included by TLATA.[5] These include conveyances to infants (a trust is necessary to enable the land to be properly managed) and land subject to family charges. There is a family charge where a sum of money has to be paid annually to a member of the family, with the obligation charged on the land (this ensures payment). It would be difficult to sell the land subject to the charge and it is useful to be able to overreach the charge.

Might there be a trust of land in unintended circumstances? One possible example is a contract to sell land. This is an estate contract, an interest in land that can bind anyone later acquiring an interest in the land. It is often thought that the seller holds the land on trust for the purchaser, though it is a rather special form of trust. It would be very odd to apply the trust of land regime to the estate contract: this would enable the seller (trustee) to dispose of the land free of the estate contract. Estate contracts are expected to bind purchasers and cannot sensibly take effect against the proceeds of sale. We can confidently predict that the courts would find a way to conclude that there is no trust of land.

[4] [1955] 1 QB 234.
[5] TLATA, Sched 1.

Trustees' powers and their exercise

As one might expect, the trustees usually manage the land. The general philosophy is to confer almost unlimited powers on the trustees, but then to place restrictions on how they are to be exercised. It might be added that trustees of other property do not automatically have such wide powers, nor did trustees of land in past centuries.

There may be said to be four players in the operation of the trust: settlor, trustees, beneficiaries and the court. Much of the interest in the present law is as to whether each of these four is given an appropriate role by TLATA. Beneficiaries traditionally had almost no say in the running of trusts (though it was very different for Settled Land Act settlements), but we shall see that TLATA provides a number of ways in which beneficiaries' wishes are taken into account. The role of the court is vital because TLATA section 14 (Extract 12.3.5) confers jurisdiction to resolve disputes (fully discussed below).

The extent of trustees' powers

TLATA section 6 (Extract 12.3.1) confers on the trustees 'all the powers of an absolute owner'. This means that they can sell, lease or mortgage the land, as well as undertaking lesser transactions such as creating easements. This contrasts with the 1925 legislation, which conferred specific (though still wide) powers.

Section 8 (new in TLATA) allows the settlor to exclude powers; for example, the power to sell can be excluded. This is interesting because it runs counter to the policy of the past century that land must always be marketable. One reason for the change is that there are many fewer large settlements today, so that the entire issue is less significant. In any event, it can confidently be expected that few settlors will wish to limit powers: the advantages of marketability are now widely accepted.

TLATA confers other powers, going beyond land management: to acquire land (section 6(3); see also Trustee Act 2000, section 8) (Extract 12.3.1), to transfer the property to the beneficiaries (section 6(2)), to split the land among the beneficiaries (partition: section 7 (Extract 12.3.23)), to delegate powers to beneficiaries (section 9) (Extract 13.5.1) and to resolve occupation disputes (sections 12 (Extract 12.2.1) and 13 (Extract 12.2.3)). Delegation and occupation are considered later in this chapter.

Exercising the powers

A general rule of equity is that trustees must exercise their powers unanimously. This is particularly important when the beneficiaries are also the trustees, as is usual for concurrent interests. Disagreement is especially likely if the co-owners are a couple whose relationship has broken down; nothing can then be done without a court order. Although independent trustees must similarly be unanimous, in practice this gives rise to little difficulty. In addition, it must be remembered that trustees hold their powers in their capacity as trustees, not for their personal benefit. The powers must be exercised for the benefit of the beneficiaries. This is a basic trusts principle, though section 6 stresses

THE ROLE OF THE COURT

the need to have regard to beneficiaries' rights and to comply with statutory and common law (or equitable) rules.

There are a number of specific ways in which beneficiaries may be involved in management questions. Obviously, the beneficiaries may be trustees (common for concurrent interests) and we shall see later that powers may be delegated to them. Other possibilities are now considered. TLATA section 11 (Extract 12.3.3) requires trustees to consult beneficiaries when exercising their powers (when selling, for example) and to give effect to the majority view 'so far as consistent with the general interest of the trust'. This interesting provision (which can be excluded by the settlor) is less significant than one might expect. For concurrent interest trusts, the beneficiaries will typically also be trustees – nothing can be done without their active participation. Consulting themselves is an empty charade! In any event, the beneficiaries will frequently hold equal interests and there will be no majority view to resolve disagreements between them.

Section 11 may be more useful for successive interest trusts. However, it is important to note that those consulted are limited to adults holding interests in possession. A fundamental duty of trustees is to balance the interests of life tenants and holders of remainder interests. It may well be that the needs of holders of interests in remainder conflict with the interests of life tenants. Thus, a life interest holder may wish a house to be sold in order to increase income, while those with interests in remainder may regard it as the traditional home and want to live there in due course. The trustees have no absolute duty to agree with those they consult: they cannot blindly implement the wishes of the life interest holder.

A further point is that the settlor may require a beneficiary's consent before powers are exercised (section 8(2) (Extract 12.3.2)). A simple example is provided by a trust of a family home for a widower for life, remainder to children. The settlor might intend that the widower should live in the home and may therefore want the widower to have to consent before sale. Special provision is made where consent is required from an infant (parents can consent: section 10(3) (Extract 12.3.2)). There is protection for purchasers in order to avoid onerous consent requirements: if the consent of more than two persons is required then the consent of any two suffices so far as the purchaser is concerned (section 10(1) (Extract 12.3.2)).

The role of the court

The court has wide powers to settle disputes relating to the exercise of the trustees' functions. Disputes may arise because the beneficiaries disagree with what the trustees propose to do (or not do) or because the trustees disagree with each other. Virtually all the reported cases have involved concurrent interests, where the same persons are both trustees and beneficiaries. If their relationship breaks down, then they are quite likely to have differing views as to what should happen to the land, most obviously when it is occupied by one of them and the other wants it to be sold. It will take a court order to resolve these disputes.

The present jurisdiction is found in TLATA section 14, which confers wide powers on the court. Section 15 (Extract 12.3.6) lists four factors that the court must consider:

(a) the intentions of the settlor;

(b) the purpose for which the land is held;

(c) the welfare of occupying minors; and

(d) the interests of secured creditors.

In addition, the court (just like the trustees) is to consider the wishes of those with interests in possession.

The post-TLATA case law has centred on disputes involving trustees in bankruptcy or secured creditors. These disputes will be discussed as a Critical Issue. Most disputes between co-owners were decided under LPA section 30 (the precursor of TLATA sections 14 and 15); these earlier cases provide a guide to the operation of TLATA. Section 30 contained no list of considerations for the court to take into account. The courts developed an analysis whereby the land would not be sold if there was a purpose[6] underpinning the acquisition of the land (the cases invariably involved purchase rather than a settlor settling land). Once the purpose had come to an end, the land would be sold.

In the leading case of *Jones v Challenger*[7] (Extract 12.3.7), the husband and wife jointly purchased their family home. Later they divorced, seemingly because of the wife's conduct. Having left the former family home, she now sought sale. The Court of Appeal recognised that sale would not normally be ordered if the purpose was still continuing. However, on the facts, the purpose was for the occupation of both of them and that had come to an end on divorce; sale was ordered. It will be a rare case in which a couple will intend occupation by just one of them after separation.

Most cases have involved disputes between couples, whether married or not. While they are living happily together, no question of sale will arise. They may disagree whether they should move to a different house, but the chances of such a disagreement leading to litigation are almost zero. Once they split up, however, the purpose has come to an end and, in the absence of children, sale seems almost inevitable. The only realistic alternative course is for the occupier to buy out the other person's share, whereupon neither really loses out. Of course, in many cases there will simply not be the funds available for this to be practicable.

One might expect similar results under TLATA. However, two significant changes in the new legal structure can be pointed to. The first is that the old law employed a trust for sale, with the result that the fall-back position was that sale should be ordered. The present law contains no such pro-sale bias. Although this might indicate that sale is less likely today, the role of the obligation to sell in cases such as *Jones v Challenger* was already marginal. The second change is that the interests of occupying minors are clearly established as a relevant factor for the first time. The minors need not be the children of the co-owners, so the interests of grandchildren can be considered.[8]

More generally, the point can be made that section 15 is broader in its outlook. It lists criteria to be taken into account and makes it clear that other relevant factors can be

---

[6] Before TLATA, under the trust for sale the primary purpose (in the eyes of the law) was sale. This is why the earlier cases refer to *collateral* purposes.

[7] [1961] 1 QB 176.

[8] *First National Bank plc* v *Achampong* [2004] 1 FCR 18.

considered. An example might be where a house has been modified so as to provide chairlift access to an upper floor for an elderly relative: this would be a reason for not selling. The old law, it may be thought, placed rather too much stress on purposes. This can be unhelpful when purposes are not clearly articulated, especially where there are multiple purposes and one of them ceases to apply. *Bedson* v *Bedson*[9] (Extract 12.3.9) illustrates this. Property had been purchased as a home and also as a drapery shop. When the marriage broke down, it was held that the purpose of a drapery business continued so that sale should not be ordered. It is easy to see that many cases may involve multiple purposes, for example to provide a home for a couple and also their parents/children. It is as equally wrong always to insist on a sale if one of the purposes has ended as always to deny a sale unless all the purposes have ended: a balanced approach is required.

Against that background, how significant are the changes in TLATA? Apart from bankruptcy/secured creditor situations, there have been few cases. However, there is an interesting statement by Neuberger J in *Mortgage Corpn* v *Shaire*[10] (Extract 12.3.21) that the earlier cases must be treated with caution, now that the trust for sale has gone and the criteria are established by TLATA. This may well be correct as regards secured creditors (the context of *Shaire*), but it is less obviously justified in other contexts. Even though there is no longer any leaning towards sale, we have seen that this had limited significance in the older law.

How significant is the introduction of children's interests, bearing in mind that there are children in many failed relationships? Nobody doubts that parents cannot seek to evict children, at least where no other home is available – this follows from their obligations as parents. Otherwise, the courts have placed little stress on their interests, unless specific harm resulting from sale can be shown.[11] This is seen, especially, in sale applications by secured creditors. However, a more generous approach was taken by Park J in *Edwards* v *Lloyds TSB Bank plc*[12] (Extract 12.3.22). A secured creditor sought sale. Satisfactory alternative housing for the debtor's children was unlikely to be found and Park J postponed sale for five years, until the children reached 18. However, this can be explained by the circumstance that, as we will see later, the postponement did not significantly prejudice the creditor. Such lack of prejudice is uncommon: there is little evidence that the interests of children will prevent sale in more usual cases.

The question whether more weight should be accorded to children's interests is a difficult one. We must remember that parents frequently move houses, so that children have to change school and are separated from friends. It is also quite common for houses to be sold by mortgagees (exercising their powers as mortgagees, rather than applying under TLATA). In truth, children have little expectation of being able to remain in their existing homes.

One question to consider is how far the courts are likely to intervene where there are independent trustees, i.e., they are not also beneficiaries. Virtually all the cases have involved concurrent interests, with the same persons as trustees and beneficiaries. In

[9] [1965] 2 QB 666.
[10] [2001] Ch 743 at p. 761.
[11] *First National Bank plc* v *Achampong* [2004] 1 FCR 18 at [65] (Extract 12.3.22).
[12] [2005] 1 FCR 139; see below (p. 176).

these cases the trustees have been unable to exercise powers (because they disagree) and in any event they are scarcely impartial. It is unsurprising that the court feels compelled to intervene. However, if independent trustees take a decision, will the court uphold a challenge by a disappointed beneficiary? The court clearly possesses jurisdiction. Furthermore, the courts can be expected to intervene if the decision cannot rationally be defended or if the trustees have failed to comply with TLATA, perhaps by not consulting the beneficiaries. Beyond that, it is likely that the courts will be reluctant to intervene (at least if the trustees are unanimous), on the basis that the settlor has entrusted decision-making to the trustees: their decisions should be respected. However, this is unlikely to apply where a secured creditor makes a sale application – in this scenario the trustees may be viewed as being allied to the beneficiaries, who do not want a sale. One cannot reason that the settlor chose the trustees in order to hold a balance between creditors and beneficiaries!

Before moving on, it should be added that in many cases there will be separate family law jurisdiction to resolve disputes. As regards married couples and civil partners, this jurisdiction is far wider than section 14 in that it enables the court to vary the beneficial interests.[13] Further, the range of factors to be taken into consideration is wider, including the needs of the parties. The courts have held that disputes should normally be resolved under this family law jurisdiction rather than the trusts of land jurisdiction.[14] This family law jurisdiction does not apply to unmarried couples. Nevertheless, their occupation disputes may be considered under the Family Law Act 1996 (discussed below in the occupation context) (Extract 12.2.6), which employs wider criteria than found in TLATA section 15 (Extract 12.3.6). Given that questions of sale under TLATA usually relate to the issue whether one co-owner should occupy, the Family Law Act may provide the more appropriate jurisdiction for resolving disputes.

● Sale: bankruptcy and successors in title

Sale applications by a trustee in bankruptcy or a successor in title to one of the co-owners have provided the focus of most section 14 cases. Successors in title include secured creditors.

Most of the recent sale cases have arisen when one of the co-owners has become bankrupt or charged their beneficial interest. Sale is sought by the trustee in bankruptcy (the name given to the person whose job it is to sell the assets to provide funds to pay off the creditors) or secured creditor. If the land is sold, the home will be lost, but the other co-owner (not bankrupt or a party to the secured charge) will receive their share of the proceeds. The situation where all the beneficial owners jointly mortgage their interests (as where a couple buy a home with a mortgage loan) is quite different. On default, sale will follow under the normal powers of mortgagees (see Chapter 18); TLATA plays no role.

---

[13] Matrimonial Causes Act 1973, s 24; for the relevant factors, see s 25 (Extract 12.3.11).
[14] *Williams* v *Williams* [1976] Ch 278 (Extract 12.3.12); *Miller Smith* v *Miller Smith* [2010] 1 FLR 1402.

We will first consider bankruptcy. This involves special provisions, but the law on bankruptcy has been influential in the courts' thinking about secured creditors, who must seek sale under the normal provisions in TLATA sections 14 (Extract 12.3.5) and 15 (Extract 12.3.6).

Bankruptcy

The bankrupt's beneficial interest passes to the trustee in bankruptcy. The trustees of the land will be the original co-owners and it is highly unlikely that they will want the family home to be sold. In order to realise the value of that share, the trustee in bankruptcy will seek sale of the land under TLATA section 14. A special factor is that the section 15 criteria do not apply. Instead, as made clear by section 15(4), we turn to section 335A of the Insolvency Act 1986 (Extract 12.3.13).

Section 335A attempts to establish a balance between the interests of family members and those of the creditors. It draws a crucial distinction between sale applications before and after the period of one year from bankruptcy. In the first year, the provisions may be regarded as family friendly. The court has a discretion whether or not to order a sale and is to consider the needs of the children and spouse/civil partner (together with their resources and conduct regarding the bankruptcy). Few sale applications are in fact made within that one-year period. It may be anticipated that, at least where there are children, sale would rarely be ordered.

After the year, it is enacted that the interests of the creditors outweigh all other considerations 'unless the circumstances of the case are exceptional'. What is meant by exceptional? The leading case is *Re Citro*[15] (Extract 12.3.14). Though it was decided on the law before the Insolvency Act, the Court of Appeal overtly applied the same test as in section 335A. The picture that emerges from *Re Citro* is that bankruptcy inevitably involves stresses and disadvantages: homes are lost and schooling may be disrupted. This does not render the circumstances exceptional. In the words of Nourse LJ, these 'are the melancholy consequences of debt and improvidence with which every civilised society has been familiar'. Sale was ordered.

So what will count as exceptional? There was only one case cited in *Re Citro* in which sale had not been ordered: *Re Holliday*.[16] This was explained in *Re Citro* as a case in which the bankrupt (rather than the creditors) had instigated the bankruptcy. Furthermore, the bankrupt's assets covered the debts so that the creditors could be sure that their debts would be repaid. Such facts are most uncommon. Subsequent cases have held that sale should be postponed where there are severe health problems that might be exacerbated by sale (chemotherapy for cancer has provided one example). Other situations that may justify postponing sale are where premises have been specially adapted for a disabled family member, or children are taking important examinations.

Sale is clearly the normal outcome. One quite recent development emerges from a drive to enable individuals to emerge from bankruptcy relatively quickly. Family homes normally revert to the bankrupt individual (from the trustee in bankruptcy) three years

[15] [1991] Ch 142.
[16] [1981] Ch 405.

after bankruptcy.[17] It is difficult to gauge the effect of this on sale. Though the three-year period can be extended, it might be regarded as an encouragement to trustees in bankruptcy not to delay in seeking sale and as an indication that courts should avoid lengthy postponements of sale.

Equally interesting is whether the present law can be attacked on human rights grounds, placing stress on the Article 8 right to respect for home and family life. In *Barca v Mears*[18] (Extract 12.3.18), Strauss QC considered that failure to take account of moderately common consequences of losing the family home, despite their severe effects upon the parties, might be inconsistent with Article 8. This is more an attack on the interpretation of exceptional circumstances in *Re Citro* than on section 335A.

Strauss QC treats *Re Citro* as providing that 'however disastrous the consequences may be to family life, if they are of the usual *kind* then they cannot be relied on under section 335A'. Yet might not disastrous consequences render the circumstances exceptional under *Citro*? The essence of *Re Citro* is that *simply* losing one's home or having schooling interrupted is not enough. To take a specific example (not far from the facts of *Barca v Mears*), suppose a disabled child has to attend a specific school and this would not be possible if his home were sold. This would surely be exceptional, just as stress can be exceptional if linked to a dangerous medical condition.

In *Barca*, the bankrupt (separated from his son's mother) argued that the schooling of his son (who had special educational needs) would be affected by sale of the house. Strauss QC was not impressed by this argument, as the son could live with his mother (as he already did for part of the week) and remain in the same school. It was therefore unnecessary for him to decide the human rights point, as sale would be ordered in any event.

Underpinning all of this is the more fundamental question whether the law should give preference to creditors after a year. Assuming no bankruptcy, if one co-owner had sought sale, it might well have been refused on the basis that sale would be inconsistent with the purpose for which the land was bought and the needs of the children. Is there sufficient justification for putting the creditors in a better position and disapplying the section 15 criteria? It may be material that the Cork Committee,[19] whose recommendations led to the 1986 legislation, had recommended a more open-ended discretion.

The question is a difficult one. Creditors will get no benefit from the bankrupt's property unless the land is sold, while the other family members get the benefit of the entire property (not just their beneficial shares). On the other hand, as indicated above, why should those having beneficial interests be worse off because of the financial misfortune of another family member? Two factors might be added. The first is that the bankrupt may still be living in the premises. The interests of the bankrupt are (justifiably) excluded from consideration even in the initial one-year period, but this does not mean that the bankrupt may not in fact continue to enjoy the benefits of the property. The second is

[17] Insolvency Act 1986, s 283A, added by Enterprise Act 2002.
[18] [2005] 2 FLR 1.
[19] Cork Committee on Insolvency Law and Practice (1982) Cmnd 8558, especially paras 1118–1123 and 1129–1131.

that we appear to have few qualms about allowing chargees from both co-owners to sell under their powers as mortgagees. If we allow mortgagees to sell, evicting partners and children, why should we be troubled by sale to satisfy the needs of creditors on bankruptcy?

Refusal of sale looks more justifiable if the benefit to creditors from selling the family home is small. We have already seen one example of this in *Re Holliday* where (unusually) the assets exceeded the debts, so that delay in selling caused the creditors no harm. Another situation is where the bankrupt's interest in the home is worth a very small amount, usually because there are large mortgage debts charged on the land (the mortgage has to be repaid before the creditors receive anything). In this situation, the disruption to the family from sale may be thought to outweigh the very limited benefits to the creditors on sale. This is dealt with, albeit in a rather timid manner, by the Enterprise Act 2002.[20] Sale will not be ordered if the bankrupt's interest is worth less than £1,000. Some other countries give more extensive protection. Thus in New Zealand[21] there is protection where the value of the house (after deducting charges) is less than approximately £50,000.

Secured creditors

Secured creditors (those to whom a beneficial interest has been mortgaged or charged) have provided the focus of most TLATA cases. Before dealing with the cases, we should consider the role of secured debts in trusts of land. English courts generally accept that the law should provide effective ways in which secured creditors can enforce their security. If we give too much protection to the family home then the risk is that lenders will be reluctant to lend money with the home as security: loans may be more difficult to obtain and interest rates may increase to compensate for the additional risk. Either consequence might do substantial harm. This would constitute a particular problem for small businesses seeking loans, as the homes of proprietors of those businesses are often the only property on which loans can be secured.

However, it is extremely rare for there to be a **charge** explicitly over a beneficial co-ownership interest. Such charges are difficult to enforce. Sale of the equitable interest is not feasible as there is no market in equitable interests. Sale of the home would be effective, but that requires a section 14 (Extract 12.3.5) application and a sale order cannot be counted upon. It follows that virtually all lenders insist on an unincumbered legal fee simple as security; this requires a charge by all the co-owners together. Such a charge overreaches the beneficial interests and there is no need for a TLATA section 14 application. The land can be sold under the normal powers of sale conferred on mortgagees.

Charges of beneficial interests are generally found in three situations. The first is where the signature of one co-owner on the charge has been forged. Unsurprisingly, the innocent co-owner is not affected by the charge. There is, however, a charge over the forger's interest. The second situation operates as follows.

---

[20] Inserting Insolvency Act 1986, s 313A (Extract 12.3.19).
[21] Joint Family Homes Act 1964, ss 16–19.

> Allan is the legal owner of a house, holding it on a constructive trust for himself and his partner Belinda. Charles lends money to Allan and takes a charge over the house as security, believing Allan to be the sole owner and entitled to charge the house. Allan's charge to Charles is ineffective as regards Belinda, as her actual occupation gives her an overriding interest binding Charles (**Boland**). It is effective, however, as against Allan's interest.

The final situation applies whether the co-ownership is legal or merely equitable. Lenders will rarely lend money unless both co-owners join the charge. They will be identified either by being on the deeds or register (legal co-ownership) or from being in joint occupation of the land (beneficial co-ownership). When one co-owner wishes to borrow money, it happens all too frequently that the signature of the other is procured by fraud, misrepresentation or undue influence. Unless the lender has followed procedures discussed in Chapter 18, the charge will fail as against the victim of the wrongdoing. It remains effective as regards the borrower.

In all three situations, the charge is effective over the beneficial interest of the wrongdoing co-owner. However, it is important to note that this is a form of consolation prize: it isn't what the lender was setting out to achieve. Accordingly, court refusal to order sale would be most unlikely to have a marked effect on lenders. A lender who is aware of a risk of the charge not binding both co-owners is very unlikely to lend in the first place.

Secured creditors also feature in a rather different scenario: charging orders. If a person is owed money, that person can apply to court for a charge over the assets of the debtor. The creditor thereby becomes a secured creditor and can sell the assets to obtain payment of the debt. Again, it is not a case in which the creditor sets out at the time of the loan to become a secured creditor. Charging orders are designed to ensure that debts should be paid. There is very little reason why they should operate to the detriment of members of the debtor's family.

Leaving these points on one side, it will be common for the secured creditor to want to realise the value of the debtor's beneficial interest. In practical terms, this can be achieved only by selling the land. Unlike trustees in bankruptcy, secured creditors have to seek sale within the normal TLATA sections 14 (Extract 12.3.5) and 15 (Extract 12.3.6) rules. It is very significant that section 15(1)(d) identifies the interests of the secured creditors as a matter for the court to take into account.

To understand the TLATA cases, regard must be had to the way the law had previously been developing. It will be recalled that the purpose for which land was purchased was a crucial factor in deciding whether it should be sold. At first sight, the family home purpose seems to continue notwithstanding financial problems. Nevertheless, the courts adopted an approach that was extremely favourable to secured creditors. Starting in the bankruptcy context, the courts developed a distinctly artificial idea that the family home purpose was dependent upon co-owners keeping their interests in the land.[22] The passing of the interest to the trustee in bankruptcy therefore marked the termination of

---

[22] *Re Citro* [1991] Ch 142.

the purpose. Since the Insolvency Act 1986 section 335A (Extract 12.3.13) established rules for sale on bankruptcy, it has no longer been necessary to refer to purposes and to explain that they have terminated on bankruptcy. Nevertheless, the courts continued to apply the pre-1986 reasoning to secured charges: entering into the secured charge was sufficient to terminate the purpose. In addition, the courts applied the test of exceptional circumstances (similarly developed from bankruptcy) when secured creditors sought sale.

Turning to TLATA, a few initial points can be made. First, neither section 14 nor section 15 makes reference to exceptional circumstances (they are relevant only on bank-ruptcy). Next, it is crystal clear that there is no need to torture the meaning of purpose to justify sale: today, it is simply one factor for the courts to take into account. Finally, the interests of secured creditors are recognised as a relevant factor for the first time. One inference from this is that they are not a conclusive factor.

It was against this background that Neuberger J reviewed the law in *Mortgage Corpn v Shaire*[23] (Extract 12.3.21). He concluded that the old cases are no longer persuasive in the light of the new statutory structure in TLATA. This is significant, even though we may think that the older cases remain important in disputes between co-owners.[24] On that basis he decided that (unlike the pre-TLATA law) secured creditors no longer automati-cally succeed. This may be welcomed: it gives the court a wider discretion to allow co-owners to keep their homes. Nevertheless, it is just the beginning of our analysis. We shall see that the interests of secured creditors are still accorded significant weight.

In *Shaire* itself, the non-debtor co-owner ('W') had a three-quarters share in the house. If there were a sale, the remaining one-quarter share of the debtor ('M') would be available for the creditor. Neuberger J considered whether there was a way to ensure that the creditor would get its money while leaving W in possession of the house. On the facts, M's share was worth around £55,000. Though he owed far more, that was as much as the creditor could get from a sale. Neuberger J was prepared to accept a result whereby that sum was converted into a secured charge on W's land, with her being the sole owner and paying interest on £55,000. As the land was valuable, the creditor could be sure of getting £55,000 back in the future. To put it another way, the creditor was being asked to exchange a secured charge over M's share (M paying interest) for a secured charge over the entire house (W paying interest).

In reaching this conclusion, Neuberger J regarded it as important that the creditor was protected. If W was unwilling or unable to agree to the charge being transferred to the land (and to pay interest), then the house would be sold. On the facts of *Shaire*, it was feasible for W to pay interest because the case involved a relatively small sum: around £55,000. In future cases, we will need to ask whether a co-owner such as W can afford interest on both any acquisition mortgage (which binds the co-owner, of course) and the value of the debtor's share.[25] In most cases, the creditor will have a claim over a much larger share than 25 per cent and the co-owner will be unable to pay interest on its value.

---

[23] [2001] Ch 743.
[24] See p. 169, above.
[25] This assumes that the debt exceeds the value of the share. Otherwise, the debtor retains a share in the house.

Subsequent cases in the Court of Appeal have emphasised the need to provide adequate protection for the creditor. This was made particularly clear in *Bank of Ireland Home Mortgages Ltd v Bell*.[26] The co-owner had a small share and, as will be common, had no chance of paying interest on the value of the debtor's share. Sale was ordered. Although we no longer apply the pre-TLATA tests, the preference accorded to secured creditors seems little changed in practice. In balancing the section 15 criteria, the courts appear to be giving precedence to the para (d) interests of creditors.

Perhaps the only hope for the co-owner, at least where the *Shaire* solution is not feasible, is to rely on the interests of children: section 15(1)(c). *First National Bank plc v Achampong*[27] plays down this factor: the Court of Appeal readily ordered sale when there was no evidence that sale would cause specific harm to the children's welfare. On the other hand, the subsequent decision of Park J in *Edwards v Lloyds TSB Bank plc*[28] (Extract 12.3.22) provides more scope for optimism. Sale was postponed where more significant harm to the children was likely (no adequate alternative accommodation could be afforded) and the creditors were amply protected by the strength of the security. Even though sale might be postponed, the creditors could be sure of getting their money back sooner or later. It will come as no surprise that this scenario is uncommon: by the time creditors take action it is usual for the borrower to be insolvent (even allowing for the value of his share in the house).

Stepping back from these details, can we justify the fact that TLATA gives special protection to secured creditors? After all, if the debtor would have been unable to obtain sale, why should the debtor's chargee be in a better position? Yet it might be unrealistic to refuse sale. If that happens, *Alliance and Leicester plc v Slayford*[29] (Extract 21.3.6) illustrates the almost inevitable consequence that the debtor will be declared bankrupt and that sale will follow under the bankruptcy provisions discussed above. Surely it is preferable to enable the secured creditor to employ the easier, less disruptive and less expensive solution of a sale under sections 14 and 15? We might doubt whether the bankruptcy rules themselves are justifiable, but to ignore them would be short-sighted.

Other successors in title

As with secured creditors, the context is that of dealings with the beneficial interest, rather than the legal ownership of the land. The most obvious case would be a purchaser of a co-owner's share. We have seen that secured charges over beneficial interests are rarely created intentionally. For comparable reasons, sales of beneficial interests are equally rare; this explains why such sales virtually never feature in the cases. A more likely scenario is where a tenant in common dies and their **personal representatives** (or a successor in title under a will) seek sale.

[26] [2001] 2 FLR 809.
[27] [2004] 1 FCR 18.
[28] [2005] 1 FCR 139. Compare *Re Holliday* [1981] Ch 405 as regards bankruptcy: above (p. 173).
[29] [2000] 33 HLR 743.

The most useful authority is a pre-TLATA case on secured creditors: *Abbey National plc v Moss*[30] (Extract 12.3.20). The facts were unusual in that the purpose of a purchase by mother and daughter was occupation by the mother. Because the purpose was not for joint occupation, the court held that it survived a charge by the daughter. On that basis, the court held that the purpose affected the chargee and the land should not be sold. Where the purpose continues, it therefore seems that successors in title are in no better position than the original co-owner.

In the context of secured creditors, the status of *Moss* today must be doubted. Now that the interests of secured creditors are taken into account under section 15(1)(d), it is likely that the pro-sale approach in the secured creditor cases would apply even where the occupation purpose is still continuing.

For other successors in title (purchasers, for example), the position is less clear. Their interests are not mentioned by section 15, though it must be remembered that the section 15 criteria are not exclusive: a court could still properly take their interests into account. Unlike the position at the time of *Moss*, the purpose of the co-owners' purchase is no longer such a dominant factor. A relevant factor is that, without sale, the successor will obtain no benefit from the interest, given that there will (almost certainly) be no right to occupy under TLATA section 12 (Extract 12.2.1).

A related question is how far the collateral purpose does survive dealings with the beneficial interest. This was discussed in the earlier secured charges cases, though it has now faded from the picture. Now that TLATA ensures that purposes are no longer determinative of the outcome, there is scope for recognising purposes in a broader range of circumstances. Thus in *Edwards v Lloyds TSB Bank plc*[31] Park J thought the purpose of a family home could 'in part' survive the failure of the marriage. This enabled the interests of the occupying co-owner (with those of the children) to be balanced against those of the secured creditors. If purposes can continue despite relationship breakdown, it should be far easier for purposes to survive dealings with a beneficial interest.

As we have seen, beneficial interests are most likely to pass on the death of a co-owner. Can the new holder of the interest seek sale?

Frances and Gerry are tenants in common, living together. Gerry dies without making a will. His property goes to his mother Henrietta, who disapproves of Frances. Can Henrietta force a sale? The answer is likely to turn on whether we see the purpose as being for the occupation for the co-owners and whoever is the survivor, or just for their joint occupation. The cases give no clear answer, though **Shaire** leans against the purpose continuing after death. It may be thought that this is an unrealistically narrow interpretation of the intentions of a couple buying a family home. The more flexible approach of Park J in **Edwards** (marriage failure, rather than death) seems preferable. It does not mean that a house cannot be sold, rather that providing a home for the survivor is one relevant consideration. The fact that the successor in title has not paid for their interest reduces the weight of the argument that sale is the only way in which they can benefit from their interest.

---

[30] [1994] 1 FLR 307.
[31] [2005] 1 FCR 139 at [29].

Conclusions

These categories of bankruptcy, secured creditors and successors in title all provide difficult questions. For the first two categories, the statutory provisions and cases support sale in most situations. Although it is not clear that such a blanket approach is justified, the social and economic considerations are so complex that the balance between creditors and co-owners is bound to be difficult to draw. The most that can be said is that we cannot justify a simple rule that either creditor or co-owner should always succeed.

Delegation

TLATA section 9 (Extract 13.5.1) permits trustees to delegate their powers to a beneficiary with an interest in possession. This might be useful where independent trustees hold for beneficial co-owners, but delegation to a life tenant in a successive interest trust is far more likely. The life tenant may be the best person to manage the land, being a senior member of the family benefited by the trust and the person with the closest association with the land. One simple example is where a house is left to a widow or widower for life, with remainder to their children. It may be thought natural that the widow or widower should manage the land, deciding whether it should be sold if a smaller and more easily maintained home is required.

The trustees can always revoke a delegation. They must take care both in deciding whether to delegate and in deciding whether to revoke.[32] An obvious danger is that a beneficiary may be incompetent in managing the land. Occasionally the beneficiary may act fraudulently, for instance by leasing the land to a friend for a rent less than it is worth.

Occupation

Two rather different, but related, issues are considered. The first concerns rights to occupy. The second is whether the non-occupier has a right to be compensated for the other's occupation. Most of the issues discussed below apply primarily to co-owners (rather than successive interests).

■ Rights to occupy

The original common law rule was that any co-owner was entitled to possession of all the property; this was part of the unity of possession.[33] However, this right to occupy became less clear after the 1925 legislation introduced trusts into co-ownership: beneficiaries under express pre-1925 trusts were thought not to be entitled to occupy.

---

[32] TLATA, s 9A (Extract 13.5.1).
[33] This was discussed above (p. 149).

Any universal right to occupy was seen to cause difficulty. If one co-owner sold their interest in the family home, could the purchaser insist on going into occupation with the other family members? The courts preferred to take a more limited approach. They recognised rights to occupy, but limited them to the purpose for which the property was purchased.

> Fiona and George buy a house as a family home. Obviously, they intend to occupy it and they would each have a legal right to do so. Should Fiona sell her interest to her friend Hayley, then Hayley would be outside that purpose and have no right to occupy. If Fiona and George had purchased the house as an investment, then there would be no occupation purpose at all.

TLATA now makes fresh provision, which is thought to replace the old law. Section 12 (Extract 12.2.1) recognises rights to occupy where the purposes of the trust include occupation (this replicates the position with Fiona and George) or the trustees hold the land for occupation. The explanation of the latter provision is that trustees may choose to make land available for occupation for a beneficiary. This is most likely to be important in successive interest trusts, when it would be entirely appropriate to allow the life tenant to live in a house owned by the trust. It would be more difficult to apply in favour of one of several concurrent interest holders.

> Andrew, Belinda, Clare and Davina (siblings) are co-owners of a life interest under a trust. It would be difficult to justify making land available for, say, Clare's occupation. This would favour Clare above the others.

Section 12 requires that the land must be available (it might be let to a third party) and must not be unsuitable. *Chan v Leung*[34] (Extract 12.2.2) involved a couple's home. Most unusually, they also intended that the woman could live in it alone, for the duration of her university course, if the relationship failed. The court rejected an argument that the house was too large to be suitable for her needs – such an argument was inconsistent with the purpose that she could occupy. On the facts, there was only a year until her course ended. The court allowed her to occupy for that period.

Does suitability have to be satisfied only at the time occupation is first taken, or must it continue thereafter? An interesting case might be where occupation by a beneficiary, Sarah, is intended, but by reason of her increasing age and declining physical powers the house becomes unsuitable (indeed dangerous) for her continued occupation. The trustees may want Sarah to move to another, more suitable, home, but this is resisted by Sarah. It is unclear whether they can say that the land is no longer suitable and so force her out. It seems probable that they can (implicitly supported by *Chan*), though there is no direct authority on the question.

In many cases two or more beneficiaries will be entitled to occupy. The most obvious example is a couple buying a house together for joint occupation, but another is siblings

[34] [2003] 1 FLR 23 at [102].

as beneficiaries under a family trust. Quite often, the house may become unsuitable for occupation by all of them. This would happen if the partners split up, or one of the siblings marries. Section 13 (Extract 12.2.3) allows the trustees to decide who should occupy. Their preference for one over the other can be balanced by requiring compensation payments to be made to the non-occupier. This provides an alternative to selling the land, which otherwise would seem the obvious outcome.

It should be noted that the trustees cannot say that none can occupy, though they can decide that one shall occupy part and that the other shall occupy the remainder. An example of this is provided by *Rodway v Landy*[35] (Extract 12.2.4), involving a building used as a doctor's surgery by the co-owners. The court ordered that the building should be split so as to provide separate surgeries for each of them. Unsurprisingly, the trustees are required to exercise their powers reasonably. More interestingly, they cannot (without court approval) evict a present occupier to permit occupation by another beneficiary. This recognises the interests of occupiers in retaining occupation, especially important as regards homes.

These section 13 powers apply only where there are two or more beneficiaries entitled to occupy. They would not apply, for example, to a single life interest holder in occupation. However, in all cases the trustees can impose 'reasonable conditions' on occupiers. They might, for example, require the property to be kept properly decorated. However, powers cannot be exercised in such a way as to force the occupier to leave the property. For an impecunious occupier, this may lead to a clash with the trustees' belief that fairness to the other beneficiaries requires compensation payments or compliance with conditions. The cases provide no help in dealing with such problems, though the court itself is not bound by the same constraints.

Most disputes are likely to arise between a couple buying a home. In this context, two points should be made. First, the trustees and beneficiaries will usually be the same persons and their disagreements are likely to render the section 13 powers incapable of exercise. The dispute can be resolved only by the court's section 14 jurisdiction. Next, most of these occupation disputes will fall within the jurisdiction conferred by the Family Law Act 1996, most especially section 33 (Extract 12.2.6). Given that this jurisdiction – not limited to spouses – recognises a wider range of criteria than TLATA, it seems probable that it should be exercised in place of TLATA.

A final question is whether a right to occupy can be defeated by sale. Remember that the section 13 powers cannot be used to evict a single occupying beneficiary; nor can they be used to exclude rights of all the beneficiaries to occupy. Can the trustees thwart the right to occupy by selling the land? To evict beneficiaries in order to sell would seem to be inconsistent with the right conferred by section 12 and almost impossible to reconcile with the rule in section 13 that the rights of all cannot be excluded. If the trustees cannot evict the beneficiaries, can the courts do so in the exercise of their section 14 powers (Extract 12.3.5)? The section 14 jurisdiction relates to the functions of the trustees. Whether the court can order something that would be a breach of trust on the part of a trustee seems uncertain: committing breaches of trust can scarcely be the

---

[35] [2001] Ch 703.

function of trustees. On the other hand, such a power in the court would seem useful, especially if unforeseen circumstances have arisen (an example could be an exceptionally high offer from a potential purchaser). Of course, there is no problem if the purpose has come to an end (as in the cases typified by *Jones* v *Challenger*), as there is then no longer any section 12 right to occupy.

Compensation for occupation: improvements

It has been seen that the trustees may require a beneficiary in occupation to pay compensation when exercising their section 13 (Extract 12.2.3) powers to exclude another beneficiary. Usually, however, a co-owner is in sole occupation when the relationship between a couple breaks down and the other has left the family home: these are not circumstances in which trustees have excluded a beneficiary. Nevertheless, it has been clear since *Stack* v *Dowden*[36] (Extract 12.2.7) that questions about payments should be resolved by the court under its section 14 jurisdiction, using the section 15 criteria.

Prior to *Stack*, there was a substantial body of authority on the payment of compensation – based upon concurrent interest principles (often referred to as 'accounting'), rather than section 14 (Extract 12.3.5). Can this now be discarded? There is no simple answer. For a start, there are indications in *Stack* (especially from Lord Neuberger, though he dissented on the facts) that the result will frequently be the same as under the previous law – at least unless the section 15 (Extract 12.3.6) criteria require a different outcome. More technically, the section 14 jurisdiction applies only when the trustees have discretion under section 13. In turn this applies only when both parties have a right to occupy. In *French* v *Barcham*[37] (Extract 12.2.9), this analysis was employed to hold that the section 15 criteria do not apply when the person seeking compensation is the trustee in bankruptcy of one of the co-owners – the trustee in bankruptcy has no right to occupy under section 12. The courts have readily held that the occupying co-owner should pay compensation to the trustee in bankruptcy.

In the light of these developments, the older law will be very briefly summarised. The traditional view was that any co-owner could occupy the land without any need to compensate the other. This was clearly established in the leading cases of *Jacobs* v *Seward*.[38] The defendant co-owner of farmland had cut grass and taken it away. The House of Lords rejected a complaint by the other co-owner. It would be otherwise if the defendant had excluded the claimant from the land. However, the modern law (especially as regards the family home) has seen two developments.

First, some cases[39] have employed the more general test that compensation is payable whenever it is necessary to do justice (or 'equity') as between the parties. In many cases it may seem unjust for one co-owner to occupy without compensating the other. In particular, this has been applied in the bankruptcy cases. The second development relates to the common circumstance that the occupier pays the mortgage instalments.

---

[36] [2007] 2 AC 432; *Murphy* v *Gooch* [2007] 2 FLR 934 (Extract 12.2.8) confirms that this applies whether the relevant period of occupation is before or after the court hearing.
[37] [2009] 1 WLR 1124.
[38] (1872) LR 5 HL 464.
[39] Especially *Re Pavlou* [1993] 1 WLR 1046; also *Re Byford* [2004] 1 P&CR 159.

The courts are inclined to hold that the payment and the benefit of occupation usually cancel each other out.[40] Save for bankruptcy, the courts do not quantify occupation value and instalments. This produces a simple rough-and-ready solution. It remains to be seen how far these principles survive *Stack*.

Turning to improvements, there is generally no right to claim the value of improvements from another co-owner. However, the opposite applies if the land is sold – at that time, the value of the improvements can be brought into account. In the context of the modern family home, two points can be made. The first is that payment of mortgage capital (not interest) will be the most common example of improvement. Next, the courts are unlikely to compensate improvements which predate the splitting up of the couple – they are not undertaken with the intention of being rewarded.[41]

Overreaching

The origins of the trusts of land regime lie in the need to ensure that the land can be readily sold (or mortgaged, etc). Legal policy is that purchasers should not have to deal with beneficiaries. Instead, we require the purchaser to deal only with the trustees; their identity is readily discoverable and their number is limited to four by the Trustee Act 1925, section 34. The purchaser can then rely on defeating the beneficial interests, which are shifted on to the proceeds of sale. This is what is called overreaching. It makes it more accurate to view a life interest, for example, as being an interest in a fund currently represented by land, rather than as a fixed interest in the land.

Does this goes too far in promoting easy dealings with land? One risk for beneficiaries is that the trustees may abscond with the purchase money. This risk is minimised by requiring[42] capital money to be paid to at least two trustees before overreaching can apply – the risk of default by a single trustee is far higher. This requirement of two trustees cannot be excluded. Fraud by two trustees is unusual, though it does happen. One example is *City of London BS v Flegg*[43] (Extract 12.4.3), in which a married couple held on trust for themselves and the wife's parents. The couple later obtained a mortgage loan for the benefit of themselves, without the parents being aware. This mortgage overreached the parents' interests. The result was that the mortgage lenders could sell the house; the parents lost their home. Their rights against the capital money received by the trustees (the money borrowed) were useless because the trustees were bankrupt.

Overreaching can apply where no capital money is received. An example is provided by *State Bank of India v Sood*,[44] in which the trustees mortgaged the land to secure an existing loan (existing loans can be secured by mortgages). This meant that the capital money (the bank loan) had been paid long before the overreaching transaction (the mortgage). In such cases there is no need for two trustees.

---

[40] *Suttill v Graham* [1977] 1 WLR 819 (Extract 12.2.10).
[41] *Wilcox v Tait* [2007] 2 FLR 871.
[42] LPA, ss 2(1)(ii) and 27(2).
[43] [1988] AC 54.
[44] [1997] Ch 276.

Leaving fraud on one side, does the trustees' power of sale, coupled with overreaching, give adequate protection to beneficiaries? Beneficiaries with interests in possession must of course be consulted, but the land can be sold despite their opposition. On the other hand, the objective of making sale straightforward may be a good enough reason for protecting purchasers in any dispute. It must also be remembered that beneficiaries who are aware of a proposed sale can apply to court for an order under TLATA section 14 to stop the sale.

It is the beneficiary in possession for whom the greatest sympathy may be felt: overreaching may cause the loss of their home. How likely is it that transactions will take place when there is an occupying beneficiary? The risks of a sale are quite low, as few purchasers would buy with a beneficiary in possession and showing no signs of moving out: no purchaser wants the hassle of evicting occupiers (let alone the risk that the occupier might have some right to remain). The risks to beneficiaries are greater with mortgages entered into by trustees. The nature of a mortgage is that the borrower remains in possession: it is more likely that a mortgage by two trustees will go ahead despite a beneficiary being in occupation. These risks led to the Law Commission's recommending in 1989[45] that overreaching should not take place without the consent of beneficiaries in actual occupation. This would not be unduly onerous, as purchasers of registered land should already make inquiries of those in actual occupation. However, this proposal was not accepted by the government. Instead, TLATA moved in the opposite direction by giving fuller powers to trustees.

Overreaching provides a crucial protection for purchasers. However, purchasers must remember that it operates only if the purchase money is paid to two trustees. Otherwise, even if the transfer (or mortgage) is registered, the co-owner in actual occupation will have an overriding interest that will bind the purchaser. The danger to the purchaser is greatest when the register (or title documents) indicates that the vendor is solely entitled to the land, yet a resulting or constructive trust has arisen in favour of the other co-owner. This was the position in *Williams & Glyn's Bank Ltd v Boland*,[46] in which a husband obtained a mortgage loan to support his business. Unknown to the lender, the husband held the house on trust for himself and his wife. The House of Lords held the mortgage took effect subject to the wife's interest: the bank could not evict her. The moral is that inquiries must be made of all occupiers in case they possess beneficial interests. In contrast, where payment is made to two trustees *Flegg* holds that any beneficial interest is defeated by overreaching. Furthermore, this operates even if the beneficiary is in actual occupation. This is because overriding interests do not protect interests against anything other than registration: the mortgagee in *Flegg* was relying on overreaching rather than its registered title.

Overreaching can operate without any statutory provision. Thus a sale of personal property under an express power will overreach (there is no statutory regulation similar to trusts of land). For land, LPA section 2 provides for overreaching in several settings; sales by mortgagees provide one example. That section applies to trusts of land, but

[45] Law Com No 188, especially paras 3.5, 4.1–4.3; criticised by Harpum [1990] CLJ 277 at pp. 328 *et seq.*
[46] [1981] AC 487.

seems to do no more than confirm the effect of the power to sell. The basis for overreaching is therefore best regarded[47] as the exercise of powers by the trustees.

As overreaching is based on the exercise of trustees' powers, does it still apply if those powers are limited or there is some breach of trust? A simple example is where a settlor removes the trustees' power to sell (permitted by TLATA section 8). In cases like this, TLATA section 16 (Extract 12.4.6) introduces a useful protection for purchasers. A purchaser is protected against any term that limits powers (or requires consents for their exercise), provided that the purchaser is unaware of the term. Similar protection is given as regards other irregularities (including failure to consult beneficiaries).

Section 16 explicitly does not apply to registered land, which today includes the vast majority of titles. This limitation on section 16 puzzled lawyers. One possible explanation is that registered purchasers are protected by land registration principles if there is no entry (restriction) on the register. However, this doesn't convince, as the beneficiary might have an overriding interest by virtue of actual occupation. Fortunately, section 26 of the Land Registration Act 2002 (Extract 12.4.8) provides that purchasers are protected as regards limitations on proprietors' powers. This is subject to any entry on the register, *but not to overriding interests*. It means that the purchaser has to take account of limitations mentioned on the register, but need not make inquiries of occupying beneficiaries.

What is the extent of the section 26 protection? It refers to 'a limitation affecting the validity of a disposition'. The Law Commission makes it clear that this protects against exclusion of powers and consent requirements. Though it is not apparent from the wording of the legislation, it does not seem to affect the requirement to pay the purchase money to two trustees. The Law Commission[48] clearly did not intend to reverse the result in *Boland*.

It may be concluded that purchasers are well protected by overreaching so long as they pay to two trustees. This, of course, is a benefit bought at a cost to beneficiaries. It remains an open question whether the law should do more to protect beneficiaries. It must, of course, be borne in mind that too heavy a burden on purchasers may render transactions with trustees less attractive. This would be detrimental to beneficiaries, as it would diminish the value of their interests. Nevertheless, we should not exaggerate that risk.

Trusts for sale

A trust for sale is a trust of land in which there is an obligation to sell. There are millions of trusts for sale in existence. The great majority of joint purchases before TLATA were expressly structured as trusts for sale, as were most successive interest settlements. Although TLATA converted statutory trusts for sale into simple trusts of land, this does not apply to express trusts for sale. We need to consider whether it is significant today that there is a trust for sale and whether there is any point in creating such a trust.

---

[47] See the full and well-regarded analysis of Harpum [1990] CLJ 277, approved by Peter Gibson LJ in *State Bank of India v Sood* [1997] Ch 276 at p. 281 (Extract 12.4.2).
[48] Law Com No 271, paras 4.8–4.11.

Before TLATA, one significant consequence of a trust for sale was that the beneficial interests were treated as being in money (the proceeds of sale) and not in land, even before sale. This was the controversial doctrine of conversion, which could be pivotal if a document or legislation referred to 'interest in land'. Conversion was abolished by TLATA section 3 (Extract 12.5.2). It should be stressed that section 3 does not affect over-reaching. Overreaching converts the interests into money at the time of sale, whereas the old doctrine of conversion treated the interests as being in money from the beginning.

How far does the trust for sale ensure that the land will be sold? In principle, it means that the trustees must sell unless they exercise their power to postpone sale. The exercise of powers must be unanimous, so land should be sold if the trustees are divided. Yet this is misleading, at least for trusts of the family home. As has been seen, the courts placed much stress on the purpose for which the land had been acquired. If that purpose were still continuing, the land would not be sold. Likewise, section 15 ensures that purposes are relevant under TLATA. Accordingly, it makes little if any difference whether there is a trust for sale or a power to sell.

The one context in which there might be a difference is if there are independent trustees (not also beneficiaries) who disagree as to whether the land should be sold. It has been observed that the court may be less inclined to interfere with decisions by independent trustees, even if they are divided. Yet again, this seems unlikely to have a great impact. In practice, independent trustees normally discuss what to do and reach a consensual conclusion: it is exceptional for them to disagree.

Is there any point in choosing a trust for sale today? The above discussion indicates that there is little difference, so choosing a trust for sale seems pointless. Nevertheless, if sale really is intended, then an express trust for sale is one way of making this obvious – it makes it less likely that the courts will find a purpose that would delay sale. This reasoning cannot, of course, be applied to pre-TLATA trusts for sale, as then there was usually no other form of trust available. It might be noted that there will always be a power to postpone sale. Perhaps oddly, this is one provision that cannot be excluded from trusts of land.[49]

[49] TLATA, s 4 (12.5.1).

Questions to consider

1. Why is there a trust of land whenever there are successive or concurrent interests?

2. Is it correct to say that, whenever the relationship between two co-owners breaks down, the land will be sold?

3. How do the courts react to applications for sale by a secured creditor of one co-owner? How relevant are the bankruptcy rules in this context?

4. Why is it necessary for the law to regulate occupation where there is a trust of land? Are there significant constraints on the outcome (whether decided by the trustees or the court)?

5. What is overreaching? Does it adequately protect beneficiaries under trusts of land?

Further reading

Barnsley, D G [1998] CLJ 123: Co-owners' rights to occupy trust land.

Bright, S J [2009] Conv 378: Occupation rents and the Trusts of Land and Appointment of Trustees Act 1996: from property to welfare?

Ferris, G and Battersby, G (2003) 119 LQR 94: The general principles of overreaching and the modern legislative reforms, 1996–2002.

Fox, L (2005) 25 LS 201: Creditors and the concept of 'family home' – a functional analysis.

Harpum, C [1990] CLJ 277: Overreaching, trustees' powers and the reform of the 1925 legislation.

Watt, G [1997] Conv 263: Escaping section 8(1) provisions in 'new style' trusts of land.

Visit **www.mylawchamber.co.uk** to access tools to help you develop and test your knowledge of land law, including interactive multiple choice questions, practice exam questions with guidance, weblinks, glossary flashcards, legal newsfeed and legal updates.

Use **Case Navigator** to read in full some of the key cases referenced in this chapter with commentary and questions:

Bank of Ireland Home Mortgages Ltd v *Bell* [2001] 2 FLR 809

City of London BS v *Flegg* [1988] AC 54

Williams & Glyn's Bank Ltd v *Boland* [1980] 2 All ER 408

13 Leases: types and requirements

Nature and importance

The lease is a right to possess land for a certain maximum period of time – indeterminate periods are the preserve of freehold estates. The attraction of a lease is fairly obvious. Not everybody can afford to buy land or wishes to take on the commitment involved in ownership: the opportunity to have a right to land for a fixed period is then really important.

> Andrew is going abroad in a year's time. Until then, he is looking for somewhere to live. It makes no sense for him to purchase a house and then sell it a year later. A lease for a year is ideal. Alternatively, Brenda is setting up a business and needs office space. The business cannot afford to buy offices: a lease whereby an annual rent is payable is ideal for her. It also works well if her business expands and she needs to move to larger premises: a short-term lease involves limited commitment and can be sold, if necessary.

Chapter 14 considers many of the consequences of there being a lease: what obligations are involved, how they are enforced and against whom they can be enforced. In this chapter we consider the requirements for there to be a valid lease and the various types of leases. The most common form of lease is the 'term of years', an agreement whereby there is a lease for a specified period. Because this is by far the most common form of lease, most of this chapter is devoted to it. Mention might also be made of **periodic tenancies**. These last for a year, month or week and automatically renew themselves unless either party serves notice to terminate them.

Leases are very flexible and are useful for both residential and business purposes. Unsurprisingly, they are very common. Most shops and offices are leased rather than owner-occupied. This is particularly appropriate when there is a block of offices or a row of shops. The block or row can be developed by a person who then leases them out. The landlord can retain overall control so as to ensure that the premises remain in proper repair and, at the end of their useful life, are redeveloped in a coherent fashion. Leases of houses are also common. A hundred years ago, 90 per cent of houses were held under leases. Today, most people own their houses, but the numbers leased are still close to 30 per cent.

We have been concentrating on the attractions of leases for tenants. They are also useful for landlords, who retain ultimate ownership and can use or redevelop the land in the future. In addition, land subject to leases is easily sold. The purchaser will view it as a good investment, producing a safe income (rent). Many pension funds and insurance companies invest (as landlords) in offices, shops and factories, while many individuals buy houses as an investment to rent out.

The flexibility of leases is demonstrated by their length. They can last from a week to thousands of years: there is no minimum or maximum period. Short leases (perhaps six months to three years) are ideal where no real commitment is desired, whereas long leases (perhaps 99 years or more) become almost indistinguishable from ownership. In the middle are leases which involve some commitment, but which are quite different from ownership.

For short leases, the value of the premises is reflected in the rent paid: typically around six per cent of their value. Long leases are more likely to be granted in return for a capital sum and a small or nominal rent. However, there can be whatever mixture of capital sum and rent the parties choose.

One particular use of long leases has been for blocks of flats, where each flat depends on the remainder of the block being properly maintained. It is difficult to enforce positive obligations between adjoining freehold owners, which made it inappropriate to sell the freehold of flats. Even though the occupier would prefer the fee simple, long leases are used instead – lease rules (described in the next chapter) ensure that obligations to repair (or to contribute to repair costs) can be enforced against a purchaser of the lease. With the recent advent of **commonhold**, freehold has become a more viable alternative for flats. (Commonhold is dealt with in Chapter 3.)

A final observation is that the lease is one of two legal estates recognised by the Law of Property Act 1925 (LPA), the other being the fee simple absolute in possession. The significance of this is that the lease can bind purchasers. In this respect it is quite different to a life interest, which is **overreached** on sale of the land so that it becomes a life interest in the proceeds of sale. There are two reasons why leases should bind purchasers. The first is that leases are designed for use of the land over the specified period. It would be disastrous if a shopkeeper could be told to leave shop premises because they have been sold: that would hugely diminish the attraction of leases. The second is that the presence of leases has little effect on the willingness of people to buy the freehold: they are happy to have rental income from the land. By contrast, a life interest brings in no income to the owner of the land and is of unpredictable duration: nobody wants to buy land subject to a life interest.

Requirements of leases

Before going into the rules, it should be remembered that many leases have to be created by deed (if over three years in duration) and registered (if over seven years). These requirements are considered earlier in the text (Chapters 7 and 10). Failure to comply with them may be disastrous: at best there may be an equitable lease.

● Certainty requirements: rent, commencement and duration

That the principal terms of leases must be certain should cause little surprise: most agreements, including contracts and trusts, have to satisfy certainty rules.

Looking at rent first, an initial point is that there is no requirement that there be a rent,[1] even though rent is nearly always payable. If no real rent is intended (usually because the tenant has paid a capital sum, or premium, for the lease), it is common to provide for a nominal rent (conventionally one peppercorn).

The certainty requirement for rent is no more demanding than for consideration in any contract. A formula for the calculation of rent is acceptable, which is very important as longer leases usually provide for the rent to be reviewed, typically every three years.

Certainty of commencement is slightly more complex. It might be noted that leases can start in the future: there can be a lease to start in up to 21 years' time. This is more than an agreement for a future lease (an estate contract): it is an immediate legal lease, with possession postponed. The future lease is obviously a trap for purchasers, though it is common to have leases commencing a few months in the future. We have seen that this trap has led to registration being required for leases taking effect more than three months in the future, whatever their length. Knowing the commencement date is important because the essence of a lease is a right to the land for a specified period. We cannot work this out if we don't know when it is to start. Fortunately this is not normally a problem, as leases can be construed to take effect immediately if no date is specified.

However, certainty of duration of leases has caused the greatest difficulty. It is not surprising that the duration of the lease must be certain, as duration is a very significant aspect within any lease. However, the maximum duration of a lease must be specified in years (or other time measurement) at the beginning of the lease. The facts of *Lace* v *Chantler*[2] illustrate the point well. The parties agreed that the lease should last for the duration of the Second World War. This was struck down by the Court of Appeal because the maximum duration was not clear: nobody knew how long the war would last. It should be noted that the lease would have been valid if it had been for five years, but terminable on the ending of the war. This contrast shows that there is no problem in being able to work out the duration of the war. Rather, there is technical requirement for the maximum duration to be known at the outset.

This was confirmed 20 years ago by the House of Lords in *Prudential Assurance Co Ltd* v *London Residuary Body*[3] (Extract 14.1.5). Some cases had attempted to circumvent *Lace* by employing a periodic tenancy, but this was rejected by the House of Lords and the *Lace* rule was reinstated in its full vigour. Accordingly, a lease until land was required for road widening (which had not materialised 60 years later) was held void.

One may question whether the rule serves any useful purpose. In *Prudential*, Lord Browne-Wilkinson scathingly observed: 'No one has produced any satisfactory rationale for the genesis of this rule. No one has been able to point to any useful purpose that it serves at the present day.' The only explanation that seems at all convincing is that an

[1] LPA, s 205(1) (xxvii).
[2] [1944] KB 368.
[3] [1992] 2 AC 386.

interest of uncertain duration looks like a freehold rather than a leasehold. The very essence of a lease is a specified amount of time: *Lace* and *Prudential* fail that test. Yet the agreements in these cases do not look like freehold estates. Indeed, in *Lace* a determinable life interest was specifically rejected. The fact that the grantee is paying rent makes it look like a lease and nothing else. We may have discovered why the rule exists, but it is difficult to believe that it is essential for telling the difference between leasehold and freehold estates.

It was against this background that the issue went to the Supreme Court in *Mexfield Housing Co-operative Ltd* v *Berrisford*.[4] The landlord had promised not to terminate a periodic tenancy whilst the tenant complied with the terms of the lease. Though many lawyers hoped that the opportunity would be taken to reject the *Lace* principle, the Supreme Court instead found an ingenious way to circumvent it. Authority (seemingly forgotten earlier) recognised that a uncertain lease takes effect as a lease for life, terminable on the uncertain event. We shall see later[5] that a lease for life is recognised by the 1925 legislation as a legal lease. This solved the problem in *Berrisford*, but it was recognised by the Supreme Court that it cannot apply to leases to companies – there is no 'life' that can be employed. A separate point in favour of the tenant (though the Supreme Court did not express a final view) was that the promise could operate as a contract between the parties, though this would not affect anybody other than the original parties.

Exclusive possession

A principal hallmark of any lease or tenancy is that the grantee obtains exclusive possession. A lease is often regarded as involving temporary property ownership (though leases usually restrict the manner in which the land can be used) and it is exclusive possession that lies at the heart of this.

An example where there is no exclusive possession is staying in a hotel overnight. The visitor may be entitled to stay until, say, 11 a.m., but this does not mean that there is a lease over the hotel room. The visitor is a licensee rather than a tenant: simply somebody who is permitted to be there. It might be objected that the hotel could not put another guest in the same room, so that there appears to be exclusive possession. The answer to this is that the law distinguishes between exclusive possession and exclusive occupation. The visitor may well enjoy exclusive occupation. However, the right of the hotel to enter the room to clean and service it (and generally control its use) means that there is no exclusive possession.

One commonly quoted case is *Clore* v *Theatrical Properties Ltd*,[6] in which the purported lessee had 'front of the house' rights at a theatre. These are rights to sell refreshments and programmes and to manage cloakrooms. The owner of the theatre still

---

[4] [2012] 1 AC 955.
[5] (See p 206.) Technically, it takes effect as a lease for 90 years terminable on notice after death (and on the uncertain event).
[6] [1936] 3 All ER 483.

enjoyed rights and duties over the relevant area, including performing acts of maintenance such as fixing problems with the lights. The Court of Appeal held that the purported lessee did not have exclusive possession and therefore could not have a lease.

Whilst the need for exclusive possession has never been doubted, there are many borderline decisions working out how it applies. However, the question that has been most troublesome is whether the presence of exclusive possession (at least if combined with a certain duration) is conclusive that there is a lease. This is so large a topic that it is now considered under a separate heading.

Is exclusive possession conclusive?

Exclusive possession is, of course, always required for a lease, but it need not follow that it always results in a lease. This has given rise to a mountain of litigation over the past few decades.

Importance and early history

A century ago, the lease was used to explain many examples of exclusive possession, some of which don't look like leases to a lawyer today. The practical effects of there being a lease were limited: the landlord was rarely worse off.

From the early years of the twentieth century onwards, there has been increasing legal regulation of the relationship between landlord and tenant. There have, at various times, been controls over rent levels, the right to terminate leases (even after the term has come to an end) and duties to repair. These controls have been most marked in the context of housing, given the natural desire to protect people in their homes coupled with the weak bargaining position of the residential tenant.

By the 1970s, the effect of these controls was to make it financially disastrous to create leases of houses: a short lease could reduce the house value by half. It is unsurprising that landlords sought to create a licence, simple permission to use land, rather than a lease. Part of the background is that licences had always played a role as regards lodging agreements (generally over a room rather than a house). This was because a lodger does not enjoy exclusive possession: the owner provides services and has a right to enter the room.

From around 1950 the courts began to expand the role of licences, despite exclusive possession, where they thought a lease would be inappropriate. One well-known example is *Marcroft Wagons Ltd* v *Smith*,[7] in which a landlord allowed a tenant's daughter to remain temporarily after the tenant's death. The landlord needed the land and refused the daughter a new tenancy, but no immediate steps were taken to evict her and she paid the same rent as her mother. The daughter claimed to be a tenant so that she could not be evicted. The court considered that it would be wrong to treat the daughter as a tenant: this would be to tell landlords that they ought immediately to evict occupiers following the death of a tenant. There was held to be a licence.

[7] [1951] 2 KB 496.

The analysis in *Marcroft* and other cases in the decades following the Second World War was that exclusive possession is not conclusive. At the same time, the court was insistent that the parties could not simply say that they didn't want a lease: that would allow them to exclude the legislation protecting tenants. Initially, landlords attempted to insert terms whereby tenants appeared not to have exclusive possession. The courts saw through most of these devices.

By the 1970s, this approach was shifting towards a bolder recognition of licences where the landlord simply made it clear that a lease is not intended. This led to the decision of the House of Lords in *Street v Mountford*[8] (Extract 14.1.8), still the leading authority in the area.

Street v Mountford

The agreement in *Street* unambiguously made it clear that there was not to be a lease. No attempt was made to deny exclusive possession: there were no technical terms and no hiding of the reality from the occupier. Nevertheless, Lord Templeman was emphatic that exclusive possession is conclusive that there is a lease, with only very limited exceptions. At the same time, he adopted a sham analysis to strike down artificial terms in agreements that purport to show that there is no right to exclusive possession (this is dealt with in the following section).

Earlier cases support Lord Templeman's assertion that exclusive possession is the touchstone of a lease. Yet in these cases the parties were usually indifferent as to whether or not they were creating leases. It is only in recent decades that the parties have attempted to create licences. Lord Templeman reasoned that: 'If exclusive possession at a rent for a term does not constitute a tenancy then the distinction between a contractual tenancy and a contractual licence of land becomes wholly unidentifiable.' He also used a spades and forks analogy: 'The manufacture of a five-pronged implement for manual digging results in a fork even if the manufacturer, unfamiliar with the English language, insists that he intended to make and has made a spade.'

How convincing is this? Legal categories cannot be used unless their requirements are met. There cannot be a contract without consideration, whatever the parties may say. Thus there clearly cannot be a lease without exclusive possession. However, it is unusual for the law to reconstruct a transaction so as foist a legal category upon the parties against their wishes. This is true for contracts and trusts. Interestingly, a few years after *Street* the Court of Appeal held that there would not be an easement if the parties made it clear that none was intended. This makes a nonsense of Lord Templeman's assertion that the distinction would be 'unidentifiable' without an immutable test: no such problem is encountered in non-lease contexts. Though it is easy to accept that there will prima facie be a lease (or easement) if the requirements are satisfied, this need not mean that a clear contrary intention should be ignored.

What about the spades and forks example? It is facile to think that legal and physical categories must attract the same rules. Furthermore, spades and forks are mutually exclusive. It is different for leases and licences: a lease may be viewed as a subset of licences.

---

[8] [1985] AC 809.

The licence can be seen as a more generalised 'digging tool', entirely appropriate whether one is looking at a spade or a fork.

The reason for Lord Templeman's approach is not hard to find. Despite protestations to the contrary, he is influenced by the need to stop the parties contracting out of the statutory protections for tenants. He made this clear a few years later when confirming the *Street* approach in **AG Securities v Vaughan**.[9] (Extracts 14.1.10, 14.1.22) The reality is that the landlord is in a position to determine the structure of the agreement. The tenant goes along with it only because that is the only way to get accommodation. This does seem a good reason for holding that there is a lease.

Nevertheless, it remains the position that *Street* is doctrinally (rather than policy) based: exclusive possession is normally conclusive that there is a lease. This is particularly important in the context of business leases. Exclusive possession has been held to be conclusive in the business context, despite there being no strong policy justification for insisting on a lease.

In the residential setting, the role of intention seems minimal. The result of *Street*, as Lord Templeman asserts, is that the normal choice is as between a single occupier being a lodger (no exclusive possession) or a tenant. However, in business settings the courts tend to place more stress on the intention of the parties. They can do this because commercial arrangements vary so much that it is often unclear whether there is exclusive possession. An intention to have a licence may be relevant in showing that there is no exclusive possession. Examples are found with rights to operate car parks and filling stations.

Where does *Street* leave the earlier cases such as *Marcroft Wagons*? Lord Templeman rejected their analysis that exclusive possession is not conclusive. However, most of them (including *Marcroft Wagons*) were explained as not creating leases because there was no contract; only three decisions of the Court of Appeal were overruled. This is important for the credibility of *Street*: overruling a large number of Court of Appeal decisions would have reduced the standing of Lord Templeman's analysis.

Shams and lodgers

Shams and lodgers are often intertwined in the cases, though they involve two separate legal issues. The essence of a sham is a term that deliberately misleads the reader as to the true agreement. A good example (not involving lodgers) is found in **Antoniades v Villiers**.[10] There was a lease to a couple of a one-bedroom flat, one term of which entitled the owner to introduce other licensees or live there himself. The House of Lords struck this term down as a sham or pretence. The flat was not suitable for occupation by more than the couple: there was just a small living room and a bedroom. The term had been introduced to make it look as if there was no exclusive possession. It was not intended to be acted upon and was accordingly to be ignored.

What is a sham? The classic definition by Diplock LJ (not in the lease context) is a term 'intended by [the parties] to give to third parties or to the court the appearance of creating between the parties legal rights and obligations different from the actual legal

[9] [1990] 1 AC 417, considered below in the context of joint occupation.
[10] [1990] 1 AC 417.

rights and obligations (if any) which the parties intend to create'.[11] In the leases context, it is a term that neither party intends to be a true term of the arrangement: nobody intended in *Antoniades* that others would live in the flat.

In *Antoniades*, Lord Templeman said that he preferred the term 'pretence'. It has never been clear how pretences might be different from shams. At one stage it was thought that the reference to pretence might lead to a much wider scope for shams, but the cases lend little support for this. One point worth making is that the analysis of Diplock L J stresses the intention of both parties. In the leases context, the landlord's intention is all important in causing the term to be struck down: it does not matter that there is no true joint intention to deceive.

Since *Street*, the easiest way to avoid a lease is to make the occupier a lodger. A lodger typically has a room in a house, with cleaning and other services being provided by the owner. The lodger may enjoy exclusive occupation, in the sense that nobody else can be allowed to live in the room, but the owner's rights are so extensive as to preclude exclusive possession. It might be viewed as analogous to a hotel guest.

Before looking at the lodgers cases, two warnings should be added. Even with a lease, the landlord may be entitled to enter. Often, the landlord will be under a duty to repair and will have a right to enter both to repair and to check whether repair is needed. Accordingly, it is incorrect to say that any right to enter is inconsistent with exclusive possession. The second warning is that the courts do not always distinguish between exclusive occupation and exclusive possession. This means that one must not read too much into whether a court refers to one or the other.

There is an obvious temptation for landlords to use lodging agreements without taking on the obligations (cleaning, etc) that it normally involves. There is nothing wrong in making an occupier a lodger in order to avoid the protection of tenants: that is a perfectly valid choice among available legal routes. What is not permitted is to insert terms that are designed to mislead the courts.

In *Aslan v Murphy*[12] (Extract 14.1.11), the agreement provided that the occupier should leave the premises for 90 minutes each day; the owner was to retain a key and provide cleaning services. The 90-minute provision was rejected as a sham. Nobody seriously intended that the occupier should have to leave every day. Furthermore, the key was not inconsistent with a lease – it all depended on what the key would be used for. On the facts, the services were thought to be minimal: there was a lease.

It remains unclear just how extensive the services must be. Some cases stress the need for a right to unrestricted access. Yet in *Huwyler v Ruddy*[13] (Extract 14.1.13) the Court of Appeal held that cleaning services taking 20 minutes a week were sufficient. This looks generous to the landlord. Landlords in cases such as *Aslan* may have failed because they had inserted sham terms, making the courts suspicious about the agreement as a whole.

A rather different point is whether the services have to be carried out. In *Antoniades*, there are dicta of Lord Templeman suggesting that it is the actual situation that the courts will take account of, rather than rights under the agreement. However, terms may

---

[11] *Snook v London & West Riding Investments Ltd* [1967] 2 QB 786 at p. 802.
[12] [1990] 1 WLR 766.
[13] (1995) 28 HLR 550.

be intended even if they are not presently being invoked. This is given some support by *Huwyler*. Some years after the occupation started, the parties agreed that the services need not be provided for the time being (the occupier valued privacy more than the services). The court held that it remained a lodging agreement so long as the occupier could insist on the services starting again. Perhaps the same would have resulted if the parties had reached this agreement at the very beginning, so that the services had never been provided.

One problem in applying the sham analysis is that rights may be genuinely intended, but without any likelihood of their being exercised.

> Fred allows George into occupation of a flat, retaining a right to live there. Fred has his own house nearby and has no need to live in the flat. However, Fred is contemplating a possible sale of his house, when the right might be useful if there is a delay before a replacement house is acquired. This right is easily struck out if, as in **Antoniades**, it is impracticable for both of them to live there. However, suppose that there is a spare room that Fred could occupy. Fred has little intention of ever living there (he expects to have somewhere nicer to live), but he does intend to exercise the right should the need arise. Is this a sham? Lord Templeman might require him to exercise the right, but we have seen that this probably requires too much. The better view is that the right is valid so long as it is intended that there be a right to enforce it, should the question arise. If it were discussed with George, one would expect Fred to say something like: 'I don't expect I will be using the right, but you must understand that circumstances might arise in which I may wish to live in the flat.'

So far we have been looking at typical lodging agreements. **Westminster City Council v Clarke**[14] (Extract 14.1.14) involved a public sector owner and a rather different sort of arrangement. The claimants ran a hostel for single homeless men. It was not a conventional lodging arrangement as no services were provided, but the owners employed a warden and reserved the right to move occupiers as necessary; social workers assisted the occupiers as necessary. The House of Lords regarded this as a necessary way of carrying out statutory duties to assist the homeless. The provisions about moving occupiers were sufficient to show that there was no right to exclusive possession. It was, however, stressed that a private landlord could not hope to avoid a lease by inserting similar terms.

A quite different attempt to avoid statutory protection of tenants is based upon leases to companies, which lie outside that protection. This does not involve any sham as described above, but does raise the question whether the courts will permit a highly technical analysis to outflank the protection. **Hilton v Plustitle Ltd**[15] (Extract 14.1.17) provides the leading example. When an actress wanted to lease a house, the landlord insisted on a company let. A company was set up by the actress (she controlled it) and the lease was to that company. The actual occupier, of course, was the actress.

It was not suggested in **Hilton** that there was a licence, rather the question was whether there was a direct lease to the actress. She argued that this was the substance of

[14] [1992] 2 AC 288.
[15] [1989] 1 WLR 149.

what was intended and that the introduction of the company was a mere technicality designed to hide the real substance of the agreement. This argument was rejected by the Court of Appeal. The company was not a sham in the sense established by Diplock LJ: it was intended that there be a company as tenant. The courts stressed that many legal transactions involve some element of technicality and they were not prepared to take a bold 'substance over form' approach. The result in *Hilton* seems inevitable; it reveals limits to the sham analysis.

Exceptional cases

In *Street*, Lord Templeman recognised that occasionally there can be exclusive possession without a lease. The absence of any intention for legal relations has already been seen as one example. It has not proved a viable way for landlords to avoid leases, save in exceptional cases like *Marcroft Wagons*. None of the other examples has been significant post-*Street*.

(i)   Owners, mortgagees and trespassers are all categories where there is exclusive possession, but its source is quite different from a lease. Lord Templeman identified these categories, but there may be others. One example would be beneficiaries under a trust who are allowed to occupy.

(ii)   Purchasers allowed to possess prior to completion of the purchase have been treated as licensees, though originally they would have been viewed as tenants at will. The current position appears to be that they be tenants at will before a binding contract is entered into and licensees thereafter. This switch in status from tenant to licensee is somewhat puzzling.

(iii) Service occupiers are employees who are required to occupy as part of their job. Thus a caretaker has never been viewed as a tenant. However, simply providing an employee with accommodation creates a lease. Licences will be recognised only where the occupation is necessary for the performance of the duties of the employee (as with a caretaker) or the occupation is for the better performance of duties. An illustration of the latter would be where farm workers are provided with accommodation so that they can (for example) attend to farm animals quickly at all times.

Joint occupiers

In *Street*, Lord Templeman thought that, the exceptional cases aside, the only question for housing would be whether the residential occupier is a tenant or a lodger. This has proved wildly optimistic in the context of joint occupiers. However, two cases provide quite simple examples of leases. If there is an agreement for two people to take exclusive possession together, then there will be a lease to the two of them. The second is where Andy, Brenda, Clara and Davina, four students, each have rooms in a house. There may be separate leases of the individual rooms, with rights to use common facilities such as kitchen and bathroom.

Antoniades and *AG Securities*: the House of Lords analysis

These two cases, decided together by the House of Lords, illustrate the problems. In *Antoniades* v *Villiers*,[16] a couple took a flat together. It has already been seen that a term permitting the owner (or others) to share the flat was rejected as a sham. The joint occupier issue arose because the flat was not let to the couple by a single joint agreement. Instead, there were separate agreements, purporting to be licences, with each of them. It was held that this made no difference. In reality it was an agreement with both of them and they jointly held a lease. It was a failed attempt to mask joint exclusive possession. This was not a case where two people took separate (and therefore non-exclusive) rights to possess: the couple were overtly taking the flat together and the agreements between them could only be viewed as interdependent.

AG Securities v *Vaughan* had very different facts. By separate agreements, four individuals each had rights to a room in a flat. The agreements did not give any right to a specific room, so they could not be treated as tenants of their own rooms. Instead, their rights to the flat as a whole had to be assessed. Each agreement was for six months, though they started at differing times. Looking at it from the position of each individual, there was no exclusive possession: three others shared the flat as a whole.

Could they be said to enjoy joint exclusive possession? Plainly, the agreements were not interdependent as in *Antoniades*. This seems to have been the principal factor in deciding that there was a licence. It will be recalled that the **four unities** are required for there to be a **joint tenancy**.[17] The House of Lords in *AG Securities* employed the four unities to say that there was no joint tenancy and that therefore a licence was created. On the facts, there was no unity of interest (the agreements were separate and involved different rents), no unity of time (the leases started at different times) and no unity of title (there were separate agreements). Whatever the analysis, the simple choice between tenant and lodger, as articulated in *Street*, has evaporated.

Where exactly is the line drawn?

Antoniades and *AG Securities* involve facts at different ends of the factual spectrum. We now consider three less clear situations. *Stribling* v *Wickham*[18] (Extract 14.1.24), the first, is relatively straightforward. The facts were similar to *AG Securities*, save that the initial occupiers deliberately took their rooms together and their agreements started at the same time. The Court of Appeal held there to be licences. The similarity to *AG Securities* was made clearer because two of the original three occupiers had left and been replaced by individuals approved by the landlord. The initial semi-joint arrangement was simply the way in which many separate licences start.

More difficult is *Mikeover Ltd* v *Brady*[19] (Extract 14.1.23). A couple had separate agreements for a small flat, each being liable for half the rent. However, the facts showed that this rent provision was not a sham. When the woman left, the owner (far from asking for the full rent) refused an offer by the man to pay the entire rent. Following his subsequent

[16] [1990] 1 AC 417.
[17] See above (p. 149).
[18] [1989] 2 EGLR 35.
[19] [1989] 3 All ER 618.

failure to pay even half, the owner terminated the agreement and sought possession. The man now argued that there was a lease, which would restrict the owner's right to evict him.

The situation looks very similar to *Antoniades*. By itself, the woman's leaving in *Mikeover* could not change the nature of the agreement. However, the Court of Appeal held that there could not be a joint tenancy as the four unities were not present. The need for the four unities originates, of course, in *AG Securities*. The specific problem in *Mikeover* was that unity of interest requires each to be liable for the entire rent; on the facts, each was genuinely liable for part only of the rent. It is puzzling that this was not thought to be an issue in *Antoniades*. There, the House of Lords treated the arrangement as a joint one whereby each was liable for the entire rent (even though the agreements stated otherwise). It might be thought that the approach of the House of Lords in *Antoniades* was rather cavalier in imposing obligations that had not been undertaken, whereas *Mikeover* represents a cavalier treatment of binding House of Lords authority.

On their facts, both *Antoniades* and *Mikeover* involved interdependent agreements, indicating a joint lease. The problem lies in the four unities. Because this area is so technical, the opportunity arises for the landlord to manipulate the outcome, thereby making joint occupiers licensees. Even if both occupiers were to be liable for rent, the agreements could be made to start a couple of days apart (the owner being careful to ensure that the couple do not move in at the same time). This too would destroy the unity of interest.

The third difficult situation is illustrated as follows.

Richard has a two-bedroom flat, which he advertises for separate licences by two persons. If the rooms are taken by unconnected persons, this would replicate **AG Securities**. Sarah and Timothy, a couple, see the rooms and decide to take the entire flat together. They plan to use one room as a bedroom and the other as a living room. Richard is aware of this, but Sarah and Timothy enter into separate licences with him in the same way as if they were unconnected persons. Looking at their relationship, the agreements seem interdependent in the same way as in **Antoniades**. On the other hand, the premises are appropriate for separate licences: if Sarah moved out then Richard could live in one room with a new licensee in the other. In **Stribling**, the original three licensees included a couple who shared a bedroom. When the woman left, a new licensee moved into what had previously been a dining room.

Although Sarah and Timothy may regard the agreements as being interdependent, this seems no more relevant than the similar views of the friends in **Stribling**. What is more important is that the licence analysis can work effectively if the relationship breaks down and Sarah leaves. It seems more realistic to argue that Richard can put a new person into occupation (licence) than to argue that Timothy is liable for the entire rent (lease).

Hadjiloucas v Crean,[20] decided before *Antoniades*, raises rather similar issues. Two ladies took separate licences of a flat. They had separate bedrooms. One subsequently left and introduced her replacement to the landlord. The Court of Appeal considered that the ladies could be licensees, but thought that more information was needed to

[20] [1988] 1 WLR 1006.

determine whether there was a joint agreement with the two of them. However, in *Antoniades* Lord Templeman expressed the opinion that there was a lease on the basis that the right in each licence to put a second person in was a sham.

Lord Templeman's reasoning is somewhat difficult to comprehend. The premises were suitable for occupation by unrelated persons: there were separate bedrooms. Indeed, when one left, another occupant was found. This type of movement is exactly what is expected in flat-sharing agreements and looks similar to *AG Securities* and *Stribling*. One factor, nevertheless, does point towards a lease. The two ladies each agreed to be liable for the entire rent. This indicates a joint agreement with the two of them as joint tenants. Leaving that special element apart, a licence does seem the most appropriate result in *Hadjiloucas*.

Challenging orthodoxy

Before leaving joint occupiers, we should reconsider the four unities. It will be recalled that they must all be satisfied before a joint tenancy can exist, though only the unity of possession is required for a tenancy in common. The situation in cases such as *AG Securities* does appear to involve unity of possession, on the basis that each is not specifically entitled to 'their' room. As we have seen, the other unities are more difficult to satisfy.

The really difficult question is why we say there is a licence if the four unities do not apply. Normally, the consequence is a **tenancy in common**. Why do we not say that here? Just as a fee simple can be held concurrently, so can leases. The argument for a tenancy in common is enhanced by the fact that the estates of tenants in common need not be the same: a life interest and a fee simple can be held concurrently, creating a tenancy in common. If that is possible, why not also two leases?

An immediate response might be that without the four unities there is no exclusive possession. Either there is a joint interdependent arrangement, as in *Antoniades*, or else an absence of both unities and of exclusive possession. Yet *Mikeover* does not fit this analysis at all well – there really did seem to be a joint interdependent arrangement.

More generally, we need to question the meaning of exclusive possession. For several decades, it has been assumed that there cannot be a lease if others also have a right to occupy. This is demonstrated by landlords inserting terms attempting to deny exclusive possession in cases such as *Antoniades*. However, the somewhat heretical suggestion may be made that exclusive possession is not concerned with the question whether anybody else can use the land. Rather, exclusive possession may be concerned with the nature of the occupier's rights relative to the owner. This is best shown with the lodger. The reason why there is no exclusive possession and no lease is that the owner has an unrestricted right of access. When the earlier cases are studied, this is the context in which exclusive possession is discussed.

None of these problems is discussed by the cases on leases and licences, so we can but speculate on the courts' unspoken reasoning. One complication is that since 1925, there cannot be a *legal* tenancy in common: there must be a trust under which an equitable tenancy in common operates. With the fee simple, it is easy to say that co-owners hold the fee simple as joint tenants on trust for themselves as tenants in common in equity.

However, suppose that Corin and Dora take separate leases. Where is the trust? It is difficult to see what joint interest they hold on trust. Conceivably the owner could hold on trust for the tenants in common, but this produces the impossibly strange result that the owner could use his powers as trustee to defeat the lease by selling the land and overreaching the leases: this is an impermissible confusion of the ideas underpinning leases and trusts of land. We may have to face the stark proposition that the trusts of land regime (based on the 1925 legislation) makes it difficult to create a beneficial tenancy in common.

Let us return to the four unities and, in particular, the unity of interest. Why should it be necessary, as *Mikeover* asserts, for joint tenants to be liable to pay the entire rent? Unity of interest demands that the interest must be the same: for example, one cannot have a lease and the other a fee simple. However, it is far from clear that obligations have to be the same. *Mikeover* has the significant support of Lord Oliver in *Antoniades* on this point, but otherwise the proposition is far from clear from the cases.

The state of the law today

Street established that exclusive possession is normally conclusive that there is a lease. It may be seen as an important pro-tenant case, in that it widens the circumstances in which statutory protections of tenants operate. In the context of the single tenant, it can be seen to work well – the only significant litigation has related to lodgers. There, a robust approach to shams has ensured that appropriate results are reached.

The conceptual grounding of *Street* can be called into question in that it limits the freedom of the parties to determine what sort of legal relationship they are entering into. However, the need to protect vulnerable tenants can be used to justify the result (if not the reasoning), at least in the housing context.

It is a paradox of the timing of *Street* (1985) that the dismantling of the statutory protections for residential tenants began in the late 1980s. The details lie outside the scope of this text, but it was realised that there would be virtually no new private tenancies if disincentives to lease houses were too great. This would be disastrous for tenants, who would face the choice of local authority accommodation (often in short supply) or profiteering and unscrupulous private landlords (if any could be found).

Statutory protection of tenants has not completely disappeared, but today landlords are not afraid of creating leases. At least before the credit problems and housing market collapse starting in 2007, a thriving 'buy to let' market developed. More recently, many people have let their houses, rather than sell at very low valuations. For tenants, the loss of rights to remain in rented accommodation is offset by a greater choice of homes to rent. One result is that landlords no longer seek to use licences: the flow of cases in which private landlords seek to avoid leases has dried up. More recent cases have involved public sector landlords, who often argue for a licence in order to avoid repairing obligations implied into leases.

The tentative conclusion may be that *Street* works well enough in practice for single occupiers, but that it is much less important than at the time it was decided. For business leases, however, it is difficult to justify the courts' interventionalist approach. There, the courts attempt whenever possible to give effect to an intention to create a licence.

Turning to joint occupiers, criticism of the law is well justified. For a start, it appears to be in a mess: complex, inconsistent and unclear. The clarity brought by *Street* to single occupiers has been lost. It may be thought unacceptable that landlords (whose hands are tied by *Street* for single occupiers) can so readily create licences by the use of technical devices.

Nor is it clear that the resulting distinctions make much social sense. It may be argued that the shifting population in flats does not need or deserve statutory protection, justifying *AG Securities*. There is a point here, but some occupiers of flats stay for many years (as was the situation in *AG Securities* itself). More clearly, the occupiers in *Mikeover* surely deserved protection. Nor is it comprehensible that the repairing obligations of landlords (discussed in Chapter 14) should not apply to the four licensees in *AG Securities*. Neither in terms of principle nor policy have the courts adopted entirely rational distinctions.

Types of lease

As mentioned, the most obvious and common form of lease is the term of years absolute for a fixed period. This can be a legal estate, even if it takes effect in the future and even though it may be cut short according to its terms. An example of the latter would be a lease for five years that can be forfeited if the tenant breaches the covenants. The legislation provides that the lease is still 'absolute'.

Periodic tenancies

I agree with Mia that she shall possess a garage (for parking her car) on a weekly basis. This is a periodic tenancy; it will continue until either of us gives notice to terminate it. This periodic tenancy is very flexible. It commits us for no more than a week, while establishing a basis upon which Mia could use the garage for decades – if that continues to suit both of us. It is not regarded as a series of separate tenancies each a week long, but as one single tenancy. Mia has a weekly tenancy, but there can just as easily be monthly or yearly tenancies.

Periodic tenancies have been very common in past centuries, both for agricultural land (where a yearly tenancy was used to fit in with the growing season) and housing. Their use has diminished over the past century, largely because they offer insufficient protection to tenants. Today, leases are more likely to be for a specific period, which the parties can later choose to extend.

Basic principles

Periodic tenancies are subject to the same requirements as terms of years absolute. How do they satisfy certain maximum duration? The answer is that at any one time there is a maximum duration: one week, month or year. We do not bother that they may go on for a further week, etc if there is no notice to terminate them. However, we have seen that *Prudential* held that one cannot disguise a lease of uncertain duration simply by clothing it with a periodic tenancy. Thus a provision that the landlord shall not terminate a yearly periodic tenancy in the first five years would be valid (there is a certain period), whereas saying that it cannot be terminated until the landlord returns from abroad would be struck down.

A rather separate point is that a periodic tenancy can be legal: it fits within the LPA definition of a term of years absolute. It is effective even though there is no deed or writing, as formalities are not required for leases not exceeding three years. As seen earlier (Chapter 7), this is subject to the lease taking effect in possession at the best rent.

Creation

Periodic tenancies can be created explicitly, but in past decades they were commonly implied from the payment of rent. This enabled somebody paying rent to be recognised (albeit for a short period) as a tenant. It was especially important for tenant farmers, who would be protected during a growing season if it were a yearly tenancy. The period chosen by the courts would be that for the calculation of rent.

> Andrew agrees to pay Belinda an annual rent of £12,000, with £1,000 payable monthly. This is a yearly tenancy because we look to the calculation of the rent, not the frequency of payment.

Two particular circumstances in which periodic tenancies were implied were where the parties had failed to enter into a formal lease (whether because negotiations were incomplete or because they had not complied with the formality requirements) and where a tenant remained on the land, paying rent, after a lease had come to an end.

Today, it is far less likely that the courts will imply such periodic tenancies. Following cases such as *Javad v Aqil*[21] (Extract 14.2.2), the courts will imply a periodic tenancy only where the parties really intend a lease. This is unlikely where (as in *Javad*) the parties are still negotiating the terms of the lease. The reason for the modern approach is that statutory consequences may flow from there being a periodic tenancy: a tenancy of any description is unlikely to be intended if negotiations have not been concluded.

Terms

It has been seen that a periodic tenancy may be implied when an intended lease fails for non-compliance with formality requirements. Which terms of the ineffective lease will be implied into the periodic tenancy? It depends on the nature of the term: only those that make sense for a short lease (as a periodic tenancy potentially is) will be implied. Thus a term in the failed lease not to use the land for business purposes would readily be implied into a periodic tenancy, whereas an onerous obligation on the tenant to repair would not be.

[21] [1991] 1 WLR 1007.

Termination

Either party can terminate a periodic tenancy by giving notice that it should come to an end. The length of the notice can be expressly stipulated, but the courts have established rules as to what constitutes reasonable notice. These require six months for a yearly tenancy and the length of the period (week or month) for others.

The single real difficulty concerns joint periodic tenants (or landlords).

A couple, Liam and Michelle, are joint monthly tenants of a flat. They break up and Liam leaves the flat. Can Liam *by himself* give notice to the landlord to terminate the tenancy?

Two background points may be mentioned. First, joint holders of interests normally have to act together. Suppose there had been a three-year lease with a right for the tenants to extend it for a further two years. Liam and Michelle would have to act together in order to extend it. The second background point is that, should Liam be able to give notice to terminate the joint periodic tenancy, this would be disastrous for Michelle, who would find herself evicted from her home without having done anything wrong – even if she is offering to pay the entire rent.

The problem has been most common for joint periodic tenancies of houses owned by local authorities. The local authority may well be rehousing Liam and take the view that the house is too large for the remaining tenant (Michelle). Accordingly, they may tell Liam that he will be provided with alternative accommodation only if he gives notice. It should be noted that statutory protections prevent the local authority from terminating the periodic tenancy: an effective notice by Liam would circumvent those protections.

This issue arose in the controversial case of *Hammersmith and Fulham LBC v Monk*[22] (Extract 14.2.1). The House of Lords held that the notice by one joint tenant was effective to terminate the periodic tenancy. This may seem odd, as the notice might be seen as a positive act that should require the participation of both joint tenants. A notice to terminate, just like a notice to extend, might be thought to require joint participation. However, the House of Lords used a largely contractual analysis, supported by earlier authority. Each joint tenant has entered into a commitment for just one month. If one of them could not terminate the periodic tenancy then this would be an inexplicable extension of liability (to pay rent) beyond what has been agreed. This might be seen as part of an increasing tendency (discussed in Chapter 14) to apply contractual principles to leases.

Monk has been widely criticised because of its effect on the security of tenure of the other joint periodic tenant (Michelle). The Law Commission has recommended its reversal for residential tenancies.[23] A recent development is that tenants of local authorities can challenge the termination of the lease on human rights grounds, based on the Article 8 requirement of respect for a person's home. This follows the decision of the European Court of Human Rights in *McCann v United Kingdom*,[24] where the facts were based on a *Monk* notice, and the application of the *McCann* line of cases by the Supreme

[22] [1992] 1 AC 478.
[23] Law Com No 297, paras 2.44, 4.12.
[24] [2008] 2 FLR 899.

Court in *Manchester City Council* v *Pinnock*[25] (Extract 2.3.1). These controversial cases were discussed in the human rights context.[26] However, *Pinnock* was not a periodic tenancy case and we cannot be sure when the human rights analysis will permit a successful challenge to the termination of a lease.

Equitable leases

> Martha leases a house to Norman for four years, using a document that is signed but not witnessed. The lease requires a deed as it exceeds three years. On these facts, the document is not witnessed and so does not qualify as a deed: there cannot be a legal lease. The payment of rent may give rise to a periodic tenancy, but that may be terminated by giving notice.
>
> In these circumstances, the courts will treat the transaction as an agreement for a lease. The courts will then enforce that agreement. In particular, because **specific performance** is available, equity treats Norman as if there were a lease. It is this that enables us to say that there is an equitable lease for four years.

Before proceeding further, it should be noted that equitable leases themselves have formality requirements. Section 2 of the Law of Property (Miscellaneous Provisions) Act 1989 (Extract 5.2.3) requires any contract for an interest in land (this includes a lease) to be in writing signed by both parties. If there is such writing (as there was in the Martha and Norman example) then the equitable lease analysis will work. However, if there is simply an oral agreement or an exchange of letters then there will be no contract and no equitable lease.

The most interesting aspect of equitable leases concerns their effect. One clear point is that they can be more powerful than periodic tenancies. With a monthly tenancy, the landlord can get rid of the tenant after just a month. If there is an equitable lease, then notice to terminate cannot be given until the equitable lease has ended. Does this mean that the equitable lease is as good as a legal lease? The leading case of **Walsh v Lonsdale**[27] (Extract 14.2.7) suggests that it is, to the extent of denying that there is a periodic tenancy at all. The question in the case was whether the landlord of an equitable lease could seize the tenant's goods on the premises following non-payment of rent. Though this remedy, distress, was thought to be the preserve of legal leases, the court applied it to equitable leases.

However, it would be wrong to conclude that equitable leases are identical to legal leases. Three elements may be mentioned. The first is that the equitable lease analysis depends on the availability of specific performance. If for any reason specific performance is not available (it might be precluded by bad conduct on the part of the tenant), then the equitable lease analysis collapses.

The second point is that equitable leases are plainly less powerful when it comes to binding purchasers. Short legal leases (not exceeding seven years) bind purchasers as overriding interests.[28] This does not apply to equitable leases, though they will bind if entered on the register or combined with actual occupation.

[25] [2011] 2 AC 104.
[26] See above (p. 31).
[27] (1882) 21 Ch D 9.
[28] Land Registration Act 2002, Sched 3, para 1. This would include a periodic tenancy.

The third point is that not every rule applicable to leases will apply to equitable leases. One fairly technical example is that statute implies easements into legal leases. The legislation refers to 'conveyances', which includes leases but not contracts for leases. The statute therefore does not imply easements into equitable leases. The number of these examples is fairly small, reflecting the modern trend to minimise the differences between legal and equitable rights. Nevertheless, it is simply wrong to assume that there are no differences.

Tenancies at will

Tenancies at will are quite different from the leases described above in that there is no term: no length of time for which the tenancy lasts. Instead, either party can terminate it at any time (hence it is 'at will'). It is a relationship between the parties rather than an estate.

In recent decades, the tenancy at will has been eclipsed by the licence (permission to enter land). This is especially the case where there is a gratuitous permission to take possession. However, the courts also use the licence where there is consideration but no legal or equitable lease. This is because, as seen later (Chapter 15), the consideration may render the licence irrevocable as between the parties. By contrast, it is thought that the tenancy at will can be terminated at any time. It remains to be seen whether the *Mexfield* case[29] qualifies this, where there is a contract not to revoke.

Nevertheless, the tenancy at will is still encountered in some situations, including taking possession while a purchase is being negotiated.

Tenancy at sufferance

The tenancy at sufferance is similar to the tenancy at will in that there is no term and it can be terminated at any time. It operates in one specific context: where a tenant retains possession at the end of a lease. If the landlord consents to this, then there will be a tenancy at will or periodic tenancy. If the landlord tells the tenant to leave, then it will be a simple case of trespass. It is where the tenant remains there with nothing being said that there is a tenancy at sufferance. It seems dubious whether the category is worth retaining.

Special forms of lease

Tenancy by estoppel

It sometimes happens that the landlord does not own an estate capable of supporting a lease. Usually this is because of an innocent cause (not fraud): there may be a technical defect in the landlord's title or the landlord may be in the final stages of negotiating to buy the land.

---

[29] See above (p. 190).

In these circumstances, the law sets out to treat the position as if there were a normal lease. Obviously, if the true owner seeks to evict the tenant then there cannot be a lease and rent need not be paid. However, neither landlord nor tenant can get out of obligations in the lease by simply arguing that the land is not the landlord's to lease. If (as often happens) the landlord later acquires a legal title then the lease automatically becomes a full legal lease from that time: this is described as feeding the estoppel.

Leases for life

In the introduction to this chapter, it was noted that there is a sharp contrast between leases and life interests. The lease is a legal interest that may bind purchasers, whereas a life interest can only be equitable and will not affect purchasers (by overreaching, it takes effect as a life interest in the proceeds of sale).

Normally, these are clearly distinct categories, but the lease for life provides something of a hybrid. The payment of rent makes it look like a lease, whereas its lasting for life makes it look like a life interest. The modern law adopts a functional approach, treating the true character of the interest as turning on whether there is rent. Where there is rent, it takes effect as a lease for 90 years, terminable by notice on death.[30] This ensures that there is a legal term of years. If there is no rent, it will be an equitable life interest taking effect under a trust of land.

Perpetually renewable leases

It is fairly common to insert a provision in a lease that the tenant has an option to renew the lease. We refer to a lease as being perpetually renewable if each new lease has a term allowing renewal. If the tenant keeps on exercising the right, then the resulting leases could last for ever.

The 1925 legislation converts a perpetually renewable lease into a 2,000-year lease,[31] terminable by the tenant at any of the renewal periods.

Discontinuous leases

A typical lease gives a right to possession of the premises for a specified period, say five years. An alternative type of arrangement is to give Bertha a right to possession for (as an example) the first two weeks of May for the next ten years. This is called a discontinuous lease; it is clear that there is not a continuous ten-year right to possession. It is not an entirely different legal category of lease, but rather a specific and rather unusual example of a lease.

We have seen that all discontinuous leases, however short, have to be registered. This avoids purchasers being bound by leases that are not readily discoverable.

---

[30] LPA, s 149(6) (Extract 14.2.13). Similar rules apply to leases until marriage.
[31] LPA 1922, s 145, Sched 15.

Questions to consider

1. What are the present requirements for certainty of duration of leases? Are they necessary and do they operate in a reasonable manner?

2. Should the law conclude that there is a lease whenever there is exclusive possession?

3. Why do joint occupiers cause problems when deciding whether there is a lease?

4. What is a periodic tenancy? How does it satisfy certainty requirements? Are any problems revealed by the way it operates?

5. What is an equitable lease? Is it as good as a legal lease?

Further reading

Bright, S (1993) 13 LS 38: Uncertainty in leases: is it a vice?

Bright, S [2002] CLJ 146: Avoiding tenancy legislation: sham and contracting out revisited.

Gardner, S (1987) 7 OxJLS 60: Equity, estate contracts and the Judicature Acts: *Walsh* v *Lonsdale* revisited.

Hill, J (1996) 16 LS 200: Intention and the creation of property rights: are leases different?

McFarlane, B and Simpson, E F (2003) 'Tackling avoidance' in *Rationalizing Property, Equity and Trusts*, ed. J Getzler, OUP Oxford, Chapter 8.

Sparkes, P (1993) 109 LQR 93: Certainty of leasehold terms.

Visit **www.mylawchamber.co.uk** to access tools to help you develop and test your knowledge of land law, including interactive multiple choice questions, practice exam questions with guidance, weblinks, glossary flashcards, legal newsfeed and legal updates.

 **mylaw**chamber

Use **Case Navigator** to read in full some of the key cases referenced in this chapter with commentary and questions:

AG Securities v *Vaughan* [1990] 1 AC 417

Antoniades v *Villiers* [1990] 1 AC 417

Prudential Assurance Co Ltd v *London Residuary Body* [1992] 2 AC 386

Walsh v *Londsdale* (1882) 21 Ch D 9

 POWERED BY LexisNexis

14   Leases: obligations and remedies

Nature and importance

Leases are often medium- to long-term arrangements. It is essential that the lease makes adequate provision as to how the property is to be managed throughout its duration. In particular, obligations to repair should be specified. We look here at implied obligations, whether implied by the common law or statute.

Terms in leases are generally described as covenants. This is because leases are normally created by deeds (compulsory for leases over three years) and terms in deeds are generally described as covenants. This chapter uses the word 'covenants' to describe terms and obligations in leases, whether they are express or implied and whether or not a deed is used.

The enforcement of covenants is an obviously important topic: obligations become worthless if they can be ignored. We will study two aspects of enforcement. The first concerns remedies. Little will need to be said regarding liability for damages and specific performance: these are standard contract remedies. However, a very important remedy for landlords is that of forfeiture: terminating the lease for breach of its terms. Forfeiture destroys the lease and whatever value it has. It is not surprising that common law and statutory rules protect tenants: relief against forfeiture.

The second aspect of enforcement relates to who is liable on the covenants and who can sue on them. As between the original landlord and tenant, no problem arises. However, the landlord may sell the freehold and the tenant may sell the lease; such sales are generally described as assignments. We view the purchaser of the freehold (assignee of the reversion) as stepping into the shoes of the landlord and the purchaser of the lease (assignee of the lease) as stepping into the shoes of the tenant. In general terms, the covenants can be enforced between these two assignees. We shall see later (Chapter 17) that the burden of positive *freehold* covenants (those requiring work or expenditure) does not normally affect purchasers. No such problem exists for leases: the benefit and the burden of both positive and negative covenants passes to assignees.

A rather different and more general question has arisen in recent decades. This concerns the application of contract rules to leases. Many of the lease rules pre-date the modern law of contract; sometimes they differ from modern contract rules. Can the older lease rules be circumvented by reference to contract? This is the first issue discussed.

A feature of the modern law of leases is that much of it is heavily regulated by statute. This is especially the case for residential leases, as there is frequently inequality of bargaining power as between landlord and tenant. We consider only those areas in which common law and statutory rules intermesh, one example being duties to repair. Other statutory rules (including rights of some tenants to acquire the freehold: 'enfranchisement') are left to more specialist texts.

A final introductory comment is that most of the principal topics in this chapter possess a large number of highly detailed rules, especially where legislation is involved. The reader should be aware that much detail lies behind the surface of what follows.

Leases as contracts

It is easy to see a lease as a contract: it is an agreement between landlord and tenant whereby exclusive possession is granted in return for a rent. However, the law relating to leases has been established over many centuries and much of it pre-dates modern contractual principles. Some lease rules cannot be explained in contract terms. This is true, for example, of the rules on the running of covenants; under privity of contract, the burden of contracts cannot pass to third parties.

Though some lease rules may be amenable to a contractual analysis, many operate differently from normal contract rules. It is unlikely that a rule specific to leases can be challenged simply because it has no contract equivalent. An example of this is the requirement, considered earlier (Chapter 13), that the maximum duration of a lease must be certain. Although this has no equivalent in normal contract rules, this is not by itself a basis for challenging the requirement.

Contract rules are far more likely to be important where they offer an analysis that is absent in conventional thinking as to the operation of leases. An excellent example of this is provided by frustration. It is well known that a contract can be terminated by a frustrating event: if some unforeseen event renders the anticipated performance impossible. For many years, it was thought that no such doctrine applied to leases. Once a lease had been granted, the tenant had got what had been promised. If the land turned out to be incapable of use, that was simply a risk the tenant had to accept.

The application of frustration was reviewed by the House of Lords in *National Carriers Ltd* v *Panalpina (Northern) Ltd*[1] (Extract 15.1.2), involving a ten-year lease. The access road to the leased land was closed by the local authority for 20 months halfway through the lease. The tenant argued that this frustrated the lease. A majority of the House of Lords (Lord Russell disagreeing) held that leases could be frustrated. Two arguments were especially persuasive. First, any other result would mean that leases would be inexplicably different from comparable transactions such as licences of land or charters of ships. Second, refusal of frustration would make no sense if there were a lease of an upper-floor flat in a block that is burnt to the ground or of a cliff-edge house that collapses (with the land on which it was built) into the sea. However, all the judges agreed

[1] [1981] AC 675.

that the facts in *Panalpina* did not amount to frustration. Particularly for longer leases, it will take wholly exceptional facts before frustration will operate.

The interesting modern cases have involved the termination of leases for breach. Traditionally this was the preserve of forfeiture, which operates in a distinctly different manner to repudiatory breach in contract law. Over the past few decades, the courts have started to use repudiatory breach. In 1985, the High Court of Australia in *Progressive Mailing House Pty Ltd v Tabali Pty Ltd*[2] (Extract 15.1.3) held that a landlord could rely on repudiatory breach by the tenant. This might be thought surprising, as landlords would normally use forfeiture. However, it was used to justify recovery of lost rent *after* the tenant's breach (not permitted following forfeiture).

In England, *Hussein v Mehlman*[3] (Extract 15.1.4) allowed the tenant to rescind following repudiatory breach by the landlord, who was guilty of a serious failure to repair in a lease for three years. This is understandable, as forfeiture operates only in favour of the landlord. It is likely to be useful only in cases where the lease has no value – in other cases, the tenant would lose an asset if the lease were to be terminated.

More recently, the Court of Appeal in *Reichman v Beveridge*[4] (Extract 15.1.5) held that the authorities did not permit repudiatory breach to be used following a tenant's breach, so as to impose liability for future rent. This – in contrast with the Australian decision in *Progressive Mailing* – may be seen as a more timid approach towards the use of contractual analyses. It may be admitted that it would be very undesirable if repudiatory breach analyses were to sidestep tenants' protections against forfeiture. However, that argument was not employed in *Reichman* and the earlier cases had been alert to the danger.

Another important area concerns the use of contractual analyses to justify implying terms into leases. It will be seen that obligations to repair are not normally implied. The covenant for quiet enjoyment and the obligation that dwelling houses be fit for habitation are exceptional examples of implied terms in leases. However, the courts are beginning to rely upon contract principles to adopt a more interventionist approach. This is seen in the House of Lords' decision in *Liverpool City Council v Irwin*[5] (Extract 15.1.1), which involved a block of flats. The tenants complained about the state of the stairs and lifts, and their lighting. The tenancy agreement said nothing about the obligations of the landlord, not even to give a right of access over the stairs and lift. It was held that there was an implied easement to use these central facilities (scarcely surprising) and that there was an implied obligation to take reasonable care to maintain the facilities. It is doubtful whether this decision is significant outside the context of essential central facilities for blocks of flats. Although it shows that obligations can be implied using contractual principles, it has not heralded any real growth in obligations being implied.

The controversial decision of the House of Lords in *Bruton v London & Quadrant Housing Trust*[6] (Extract 15.1.6) raises a quite different question as to the role of contract. The defendants had a licence (a permission to use land, not amounting to a proprietary

---

[2] (1985) 157 CLR 17.
[3] [1992] 2 EGLR 87.
[4] [2007] 1 P&CR 358 at [26]–[27], [32].
[5] [1977] AC 239.
[6] [2000] 1 AC 406.

interest) over a number of houses. They gave exclusive possession to the claimant of one of the houses. The claim was for a breach of the statutory repairing duty of landlords, for which purpose the claimant had to possess a lease. It was undoubted that the claimant would have had a lease if the defendants had held either the fee simple or a lease.

The defendants argued that, because they were merely licensees, they could not grant a lease to the claimant: they could not give a property right which they did not themselves possess. To the surprise of most commentators, the House of Lords held there to be a tenancy: they stress the relationship between the parties far more than estates and property interests. Many commentators object that this confuses the contractual right between the parties with the proprietary status of a lease: how could the claimant have a lease when there is no property right? The decision seems to view leases as capable of operating on a solely contractual basis: a far more extreme contractual perspective than taken by earlier cases.

It may be conceded that the practical result that the defendant owed the normal duties of landlords was reasonable. However, there are doubts as to which lease rules apply to this contractual lease (sometimes called a 'non-estate tenancy'). One thing is quite clear: the tenant has no property right binding the licensor. As between the licensee (landlord) and tenant there may be a lease, but this does not affect the right of the licensor to gain possession on the termination of the licence.

When considering the status of the **Bruton** lease, a further point to consider is that property rights are regarded by English law as more relative than absolute. As **adverse possession** has demonstrated, it is possible to have more than one fee simple. A similar point is seen in leases with the tenancy by estoppel, where a lease is granted by a person who has no estate in the land. This relativity analysis may be the only way of justifying **Bruton** – as between the defendant and the claimant there was a lease, even if this did not affect those with a superior title (the licensor and anybody subsequently dealing with the licensor).

Implied obligations

Quiet enjoyment and related rights

Most of our attention is directed towards obligations to repair (especially duties on landlords) but, first, mention should be made of the landlord's covenant for quiet enjoyment. This covenant is implied into every lease. The language of the covenant is misleading. It is not focused on preventing noise. Rather, it is the core obligation of the landlord to ensure that the tenant can occupy the premises for the duration of the lease. Any conduct that excludes the tenant or substantially interferes with the tenant's enjoyment of it (by cutting off the water supply, for example) will constitute a breach.

Though 'quiet' cannot be equated with absence of noise, there is no reason why noise cannot activate the covenant. If the landlord makes so much noise in adjoining premises that the tenant cannot sleep, that is likely to be a breach of the covenant (as well as constituting the tort of nuisance).

A more difficult issue arose in the House of Lords in *Southwark LBC* v *Mills*[7] (Extract 15.2.1). The claimant had a lease of a flat in a block owned by the defendant landlord. The complaint was that the soundproofing between the flats was quite inadequate, rendering normal life difficult. It was not as if the neighbours were unduly noisy; rather, their everyday activities could be clearly heard. The principal difficulty was that the fault lay in the original state of the premises. Although the lack of soundproofing would contravene current building regulations, that is true for many older flats. Furthermore, inserting soundproofing would be extremely expensive.

It was held that the covenant could not be used to enlarge repairing duties imposed on landlords; we shall see that an obligation to repair does not require improvements in design. Quiet enjoyment relates to the landlord's conduct after the lease is entered into, whereas in *Mills* the problem lay in the state of the premises at the time of the lease. One concern expressed by Lord Millett was that lack of soundproofing was just one of several defects of local authority housing. To require soundproofing would drain huge resources from other and more pressing works of improvement. That might have to be accepted if there were clear legal liability, but it was a factor to consider in deciding whether to extend the landlord's liability.

Somewhat similar to the covenant for quiet enjoyment is the principle that a grantor (here the landlord) should not derogate from the grant (the lease). This principle applies to all grants (deeds) – not just to leases. For example, it explains the implication of easements into transfers of land. The idea is that the landlord should not act in a way which would deny or restrict the benefits intended to be conferred on the tenant. An excellent example is provided by *Harmer* v *Jumbil (Nigeria) Tin Areas Ltd*[8] (Extract 15.2.6). Land was leased for use as an explosives magazine, both parties being aware that explosives licences required that there should be no buildings within a certain radius. The landlord owned the adjoining land. It was held that it would be a **derogation from grant** for the landlord to build on that adjoining land – it would prevent the intended use of the leased land.

As *Mills* recognised, the covenant for quiet enjoyment and the non-derogation principle overlap. It may be that the non-derogation principle is more appropriate as regards special land uses, as in *Harmer*. On the other hand, non-derogation is not a panacea for all perceived wrongs. For example, the landlord can lawfully use nearby land to run a business which competes with the tenant's business. Competition affects the profitability of the tenant's business use, rather than the tenant's ability to use the land in the planned manner.

A problem over many years has been that some landlords use violence to evict tenants. A wide range of wrongs, including torts, come into operation here. In particular, the Protection from Eviction Act 1977 (Extract 15.2.4) makes it a crime to 'interfere with the peace or comfort' of a residential tenant or to withhold services so as to pressurise the tenant to leave.

Repair

All buildings, whether homes, factories, shops or offices, inevitably require maintenance and, from time to time, substantial repair. Who is responsible for painting the windows or replacing the roof?

[7] [2001] 1 AC 1.
[8] [1921] 1 Ch 200.

Common law obligations

The general common law approach is that it is up to the parties to establish obligations. If nothing is said in the lease (which would be quite exceptional for a properly drafted lease of commercial premises), then nobody is responsible for repairing. This might work for a medieval lease of agricultural land, but it looks wildly impractical for most modern leases.

The underlying problem in trying to establish a general repairing obligation is that leases differ so much. A solution that looks obvious for one lease might well not work for others. In a lease of a shop for two years, a repairing obligation on the tenant would be unduly onerous. The repair might involve much structural work, for example if the roof needs to be replaced. The only sensible outcome is that the landlord should repair. On the other hand, a lease for 99 years gives the tenant a substantial stake in the land, especially when the tenant has paid a large amount for it and any rent is nominal. One could not reasonably expect the landlord to undertake repair.

The case for the landlord repairing is greater where the leased premises form part of a larger building: a shop within an arcade or a floor of an office block. In these cases, significant repairs affect the building as a whole and cannot sensibly be left to individual tenants. However, it is not so clear that it is the landlord who must bear the cost. A common provision (especially in longer leases) is for the landlord to undertake the work, but then to charge the cost to the tenants.

Even where the landlord is subject to repairing obligations, it may be sensible to require the tenant to undertake minor work (decorating, for example). Indeed, the law has long required tenants to do very minor things in order to protect the property. Unblocking drains would be one obvious example.

All this demonstrates the difficulty in establishing common law obligations. The courts' failure to imply obligations works only because leases of commercial properties invariably contain express terms and, as will be seen shortly, statute has intervened as regards residential premises.

One implied obligation has long been recognised for leases of furnished residential accommodation. In 1843, *Smith v Marrable*[9] (Extract 15.3.5) held that the land must be in a 'state fit for decent and habitable occupation'. On the facts, infestation by bugs was held to justify the tenant's giving up the property. However, this obligation has been given a limited scope. Not only is it limited to furnished accommodation, but also it applies only to the state of the premises at the time of the lease. It is certainly not an obligation to repair afterwards. The idea behind it is that a tenant of furnished accommodation cannot be expected to check the state of the premises, whereas deterioration is a natural risk for any property.

Statutory obligations

Two forms of obligation apply to landlords of dwelling houses. Section 8 of the Landlord and Tenant Act 1985 (Extract 15.3.8) (replacing earlier legislation) requires the landlord to keep the property fit for human habitation throughout the lease. Unfortunately, it virtually never applies, as there is an upper annual rent limit of £52

---

[9] (1843) 11 M&W 5 (152 ER 693).

(£80 in London). These are low rental figures for weekly rents, let alone yearly rents! In practical terms, the provision is useless.

Much more important is the repair obligation in section 11 of the 1985 Act. This applies to leases of dwelling houses for less than seven years and cannot be excluded. It is, of course, tenants of shorter leases who cannot be expected to repair premises. It has recently been extended to public sector leases longer than seven years.[10] The obligation has three components:

1. to keep the structure and exterior in repair (this includes plasterwork,[11] but not interior decoration);

2. to keep in proper working order installations for the supply of water, gas, electricity and sanitation (this includes basins, baths and toilets but not other fittings; it follows that there is no statutory obligation to ensure that a cooker continues to work);

3. to keep in proper working order space and water heating installations (this will include central heating systems and, for example, immersion heaters).

This is a useful provision, though considerable difficulty has arisen in working out what 'keep in repair' means. This wording is found in the statutory provisions and also in express repairing duties. The courts have applied the same construction to both express obligations of commercial tenants and statutory obligations imposed on landlords. This may be criticised, as it is not completely clear that these obligations should be construed in an identical manner.

The major problems have arisen when a defect is in existence at the time of the lease. Can the repairing obligation require the property to be put into a better condition than it was in originally? The basic answer of the courts is to reject any such duty. Examples are where a house has been built without a damp course (so that damp rises up the walls) and where there are unacceptable condensation problems (common in much fairly recent housing).

On the other hand, this defence has its limits. If the problem causes damage to the house, then repair will be needed. Take an extreme example where the wooden surround for a window of a house is rotten when the house is let. If the window falls out then it is plain that the house is in disrepair; the landlord will have to undertake the necessary repairs. It does not matter that the tenant will be getting a better house (one with a secure window) than at the beginning of the lease.

A good example of these principles is provided by *Stent v Monmouth DC*[12] (Extract 15.3.11). A front door failed to keep water out. By itself, this was not disrepair – it simply was a house that was not as good as it should have been. However, the water damaged the door such that it needed to be replaced in 1979: the damaged door constituted disrepair. Unfortunately, the replacement door was no better than the first and water continued to enter the house and damaged the tenant's property. It was only when an aluminium sealed unit was installed four years later that the problem was solved. The Court of

---

[10] Localism Act 2011, s 166 (amending the 1985 Act).
[11] *Grand v Gill* [2011] 1 WLR 2253, rejecting earlier doubts.
[12] (1987) 54 P&CR 193.

Appeal held the landlord should, in 1979, have replaced the defective door with one that would have cured the problem. Accordingly, there was a breach of duty and there was liability for the later damage to the tenant's property. A test previously articulated was whether 'a wholly different thing' would be provided if the improvement were to be made: if so, then it could not be required. It could not be said that an effective water resistant door would be a wholly different thing to the original door.

Enforcing obligations: landlords' obligations

Damages and specific performance

These standard contractual remedies need little discussion. *Stent* demonstrates how damages can include damage to the tenant's property. The courts can also order landlords to undertake repairing obligations (specific performance). Problems of uncertainty and supervision mean that building contracts do not normally attract specific performance, but repairing covenants provide an exception.

Other remedies

When landlords fail to repair, tenants may be tempted to withhold rent. In general, this is not allowed. Covenants in leases are regarded as independent; this means that breach by one party does not free the other from their normal obligations. However, the law has recognised a right of set-off. This enables the tenant to deduct from the payment of rent such sums as are owing to him. An example would be a tenant who exercises the right to undertake the repair after the landlord has failed to do so – the expenditure can be recouped out of the rent. Even if the tenant has not undertaken the repair, liability on the landlord's part can be deducted from rent. However, in many cases this liability will be relatively small: the maximum is around £3,000 p.a. for serious breaches, assuming no specific injury or damage. This will not come close to justify withholding all the rent.

Personal injuries

A tenant who is injured as a result of a breach of covenant can generally sue for damages, but in the past other occupiers faced more difficulty. Suppose Harry is a tenant of a flat, which he lives in with his girlfriend Irene. While they are watching television, the ceiling collapses on them, injuring both of them. Harry can rely on breach of the obligation to repair, but no such duty is owed to Irene. Nor did the courts allow the tort of negligence to apply, even if there were a breach of repairing obligations.

This common law analysis has been overtaken by section 4 of the Defective Premises Act 1972 (Extract 15.3.17). A landlord is subject to a duty of care when there is a repairing obligation or merely a right to enter to repair. Liability extends to damage to property as well as to personal injuries. It should be noted that the duty is fault-based: it cannot be assumed that the landlord will be liable in every case.

A rather troublesome point regarding obligations to repair and personal injuries must be mentioned. The courts held that there is no breach of the statutory repairing obligations unless notice of the defect has been given to the landlord. This makes some sense when a tenant is aware of a defect, but has not informed the landlord. However, it was applied by the House of Lords in *O'Brien* v *Robinson*[13] (Extract 15.3.12) even though the defect was hidden (a defective ceiling) and the landlord had a right to enter the land. This defence removes any encouragement to landlords to discover potentially dangerous defects; it has been widely criticised.

Fortunately *O'Brien* is bypassed by the 1972 Act. Section 4 imposes a duty of care if either notice has been given or the landlord ought to have been aware of the defect: there is no requirement of a breach of the repairing obligation. This means that both Harry and Irene would be able to sue in the above example, provided that the landlord should have been aware of the defect.

Enforcing obligations: tenants' obligations

Damages and specific performance

These remedies have caused few problems. However, actions against tenants for failure to repair can be used oppressively. This is because disrepair often has a small effect on the value of the premises, especially if they are likely to be redeveloped at the end of the lease.

Accordingly, there are several statutory controls on such actions, often requiring court approval. The legislation also applies to forfeiture, as perhaps the major problem was that landlords used disrepair (despite its minimal financial impact) as a basis for forfeiting leases and thereby making windfall profits.

Forfeiture

In contract law, a serious breach may entitle the other party to rescind (terminate) the contract. Similarly, a breach of leasehold covenants may entitle the landlord to forfeit the lease. Although forfeiture has a functional similarity to rescission for breach, it has its own special rules. In particular, forfeiture has to be based upon an express term in the lease.

There is no equivalent right for tenants to forfeit leases for breach by the landlord. This is largely because leases almost never provide for forfeiture for breach by the landlord. This is not surprising. Leases are often valuable property assets for tenants (especially if the rent is below the current value of possession). A right for a tenant to terminate a valuable right would be a nonsense. However, not every lease is valuable and the tenant may want to leave the premises. If the landlord is in serious breach of the landlord's obligations then the contractual principle of rescission for breach may operate.[14]

---

[13] [1973] AC 912.
[14] *Hussein* v *Mehlman* [1992] 2 EGLR 87 (failure to repair).

Though forfeiture requires an express term in the lease, virtually every lease contains a forfeiture clause. One notable feature of forfeiture is that it does not matter how trivial the breach is: it is simply a question whether the forfeiture clause applies to the covenant in question (it normally will). Forfeiture can have a drastic effect. The tenant may have paid a large capital sum for a long lease, which would be worth hundreds of thousands of pounds if it were assigned. Yet a trivial breach, perhaps a failure to make a small rental payment at the right time, could see the lease wiped out.

Accordingly, it is not surprising that both the courts and Parliament have developed protections for tenants. Unfortunately, these protections are often very complex; they have given rise to much litigation. At least for houses, forfeiture almost invariably involves court proceedings. This is because it is a crime to evict a tenant of a dwelling house without court proceedings; it is also criminal to use or threaten violence to secure entry to any property. It is safe not to use court proceedings only if the tenant has already left the premises. Yet the technical position is that the forfeiture is effective when the landlord serves a notice of forfeiture on the tenant, whether or not there is a court order. After the notice, the lease operates in a limbo state: valid if the court decides that the lease should continue and invalid if the court concludes that it should end. This looks distinctly odd!

Fairly recent reform proposals[15] would change nearly all the rules discussed in this section. This is a reflection on the inadequacy of much of the present law on forfeiture.

Preconditions for forfeiture

It has been seen that forfeiture can operate even if there is a minor breach. It can also be used to threaten tenants even if it is not clear that a breach has been committed. Some of these issues are covered by new provisions in the Commonhold and Leasehold Reform Act 2002[16] (Extract 17.1.1), which applies to residential leases exceeding 21 years.

The main rules are:

1. notice of liability for rent must be given before forfeiture for non-payment, requiring payment within 30–60 days (this ensures that the tenant is made aware of the need to pay before proceedings commence);

2. for other breaches, it must be established (usually by a leasehold valuation tribunal or court) that there is a breach before the forfeiture procedure can be commenced;

3. where money is due, it must exceed £350 or have been unpaid for three years (this prevents forfeiture for trivial breaches).

A quite different point is that the common law required a 'formal demand' before forfeiture for non-payment of rent. The delightfully absurd rules required a demand on the premises before sunset on the day the sum is due. Virtually every lease excludes the need for a formal demand and statute removes any need for it if more than six months' rent is due. Formal demands should have been abolished long ago.

[15] Law Com No 303 (2006).
[16] Sections 166–171.

Waiver

The breach by itself never terminates the lease: the landlord has a choice whether or not to forfeit. The right is lost (by waiver) if the landlord chooses not to forfeit, though it revives if the breach continues (for example, where there is continuing use of the premises for a prohibited purpose) or there is a fresh breach.

None of that is surprising. Less obvious is that any conduct by the landlord which treats the lease as continuing acts as waiver. The most frequent example is where the landlord claims or accepts rent for a period after the breach. The idea is that no rent is payable after the lease ends, so acceptance of post-breach rent shows that the landlord wants the lease to continue. In practice, rent is often received because of an administrative error by the landlord's employees. There is still waiver, even if the tenant was aware that the landlord intended to forfeit. This is tough on the landlord and can be explained only on the basis that the courts are attempting to restrict an overly powerful weapon in the landlord's hands.

Relief against forfeiture: non-payment of rent

The main protection for tenants is that the courts can refuse forfeiture: relief against forfeiture. The jurisdiction is partly common law and partly statutory. Underpinning all the rules is the idea that the right to forfeit is a justifiable way of ensuring that covenants are complied with. If the tenant (albeit belatedly) puts things right, then there is no longer any justification for the lease to be brought to an end. This might be thought too generous to those tenants who constantly breach leases and remedy the breaches at the last moment: reform of forfeiture will limit relief in such cases.

An unfortunate element of the present law is that there are wholly different rules for rent breaches and other breaches; this complicates matters unnecessarily. Likewise, having different provisions for High Court and County Court proceedings (the County Court has unlimited jurisdiction in forfeiture actions) scarcely helps. We now summarise the principal provisions relating to failure to pay rent.

Two situations need to be distinguished. If the tenant pays arrears before court proceedings, then there is an absolute right to relief: the lease continues. It does not matter that the tenant has a bad payment record and pays at the very last moment. After forfeiture has taken place, then relief is still possible on a discretionary basis (partly equitable and partly statutory). Relief must be sought within six months of forfeiture, though relief will be virtually automatic within that period if arrears are paid (unless the property has been relet).

Relief against forfeiture: other breaches

For other breaches, relief is governed by the Law of Property Act 1925 (LPA), section 146 (Extract 15.4.11). The central concern is with remedying the breach. This is more complex than paying arrears of rent. Some breaches may be serious and some minor. Some may have a transitory effect (decorating a house in May, rather than April as the lease requires), while others will have permanent effects (failure to maintain fire protection systems, if the property has burnt down as a result).

Under section 146, the landlord must serve notice of the breach on the tenant. If the breach is remedied, then this bars forfeiture. If the breach has not been remedied within a reasonable time, the court has a discretion to give relief. If the court allows forfeiture, then this is conclusive. Unlike non-payment of rent, there is no scope for relief thereafter.

Before going into detail as to the operation of section 146, an initial and rather difficult question is how far it applies if there is forfeiture out of court. This is usually described as peaceable re-entry. It is quite clear that notice must be served before any sort of re-entry (peaceable or by court order) and that remedying the breach precludes re-entry. More difficult is whether the court possesses a statutory discretion to order relief after peaceable re-entry. The problem is that section 146(2) (Extract 15.4.11) confers discretion: 'Where the landlord is proceeding . . . [to enforce forfeiture]'; the use of the present tense ('is proceeding') might seem to rule out cases where forfeiture has been completed. However, the House of Lords in *Billson v Residential Apartments Ltd*[17] (Extract 15.4.1) thought it unacceptable that a landlord could be better off by employing peaceable re-entry. Such a limit on the statutory discretion would encourage direct action by landlords, which might have public order consequences. Accordingly, the section was given a bold construction so as to apply to peaceable re-entry.

The notice

The notice must specify the breach, require it to be remedied and require compensation to be paid (if the landlord wants compensation). Specifying the breach is crucial, as it is this that has to be remedied.

It is necessary to require the breach to be remedied only if remedy is possible. It is widely recognised that some types of breach are irremediable, but deciding which breaches are irremediable has caused considerable difficulty. The leading authority of *Rugby School (Governors) v Tannahill*[18] (Extract 15.4.12) involved premises used as a brothel, in breach of a common clause excluding immoral or illegal conduct. The court reasoned that the breach would cause a stigma to be attached to the premises, such that simply stopping the brothel use would not put them back into their original state. Accordingly, the breach was not capable of remedy. It might be otherwise if, as in *Glass v Kencakes Ltd*[19] (Extract 15.4.13), the prostitution use is by a subtenant (a person to whom a tenant has leased the land). This is because the tenant could rid the property of the stigma by evicting the offending subtenant; the breach would be remedied.

Rugby School is quite clear, but some have argued that no breach of any negative covenant can be remedied. This is supported by two arguments. First, one can never remove the fact that there was at one time a wrongful user. Next, the tenant might have stopped the user before the notice and how then could one talk about its being remedied? These considerations led the Court of Appeal in *Scala House & District Property Co Ltd v Forbes*[20] to hold that breach of a covenant not to sublet could not be remedied. However, that position is now thought to be far too strict, bearing in mind that some

[17] [1992] 1 AC 494.
[18] [1935] 1 KB 87.
[19] [1966] 1 QB 611.
[20] [1974] QB 575.

breaches might be both trivial and transitory. *Expert Clothing Service & Sales Ltd* v *Hillgate House Ltd*[21] (Extract 15.4.14) establishes that, in principle, the breach of both positive and negative covenants can be remedied. This does not mean that every breach can be remedied: it all depends of the facts. In *Expert Clothing*, a breach of a covenant to undertake building work could be remedied by undertaking the work late.

Consequences of the notice

A reasonable time must be allowed before taking court proceedings. What is reasonable will depend on the facts, but three months for repair is at the upper end. For irremediable breaches, something like 14 days should be allowed for the tenants to consider their position.

If the breach is remedied, then we have seen that this bars forfeiture. In other cases, section 146(2) confers discretion on the court to give relief. Where damage to the landlord is limited, it is likely that relief will be ordered. It is interesting that relief was allowed in *Scala*, even though the court considered the subletting to be irremediable. On the other hand, in the 'stigma' cases the courts have usually denied relief.

This means that holding a lease to be irremediable is of little significance: relief may still be given. The argument that it is unjustified to treat minor breaches as irremediable possesses little force. The remediable/irremediable distinction, however, retains some significance. First, the notice will be invalid if it does not require remedy of a remediable breach; secondly, remedying a remediable breach automatically debars forfeiture. It would seem preferable to drop the distinction and to rely upon court discretion in all cases. This would simplify the law, remove technical objections to notices and deal with the problem tenant who constantly and deliberately breaches covenants and then remedies the breach at the last minute.

Relief against forfeiture: subtenants and mortgagees

If a lease is forfeited, any rights created out of it are destroyed. This is disastrous for any subtenants (**subleases** are discussed below) and leasehold mortgagees (leases can be mortgaged just as can the fee simple).

In Figure 14.1 below, Len has leased land to Tara for 30 years at a rent of £10,000 p.a. Tara later subleases half of the property to Sam for three years at £15,000 p.a. (rental levels have increased sharply). Tara has also mortgaged the lease to Mary as security for a loan. If Tara fails to pay rent and the lease is forfeited, then Sam's sublease and Mary's mortgage disappear: Len can recover the land free from any rights of Tara, Sam and Mary.

There are a number of ways in which Sam and Mary may be protected. They can claim relief by paying arrears of rent or using section 146(2) for non-rent breaches. Either way, the original lease continues if relief is given.

---

[21] [1986] Ch 340 (see also *Savva* v *Hussein* (1996) 73 P&CR 150 (Extract 15.4.15) and *Akici* v *LR Butlin Ltd* [2006] 1 WLR 201).

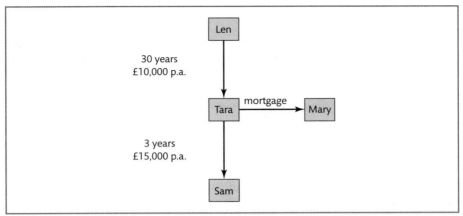

Figure 14.1 Forfeiture: effect on subtenants and mortgages

However, the most common basis for relief (whether rent or non-rent) is found in section 146(4). This is designed specifically for subtenants and mortgagees; it gives the court discretion to give relief. If relief is granted under section 146(4) (Extract 15.4.18), a new lease is granted, rather than the original lease continued. Why is this important?

Consider the example above. A result of having a new lease is that Mary and Sam have to compensate Len for the use of the land between forfeiture and the new lease. In that example, this will exceed the rent due to Len under the original lease. It also means that Tara does not retain her lease. By contrast, relief under section 146(2) means that the original lease continues. This could be problematic if Tara wants no further involvement with the land or the court considers that her conduct makes it inappropriate that she should continue to be a tenant of the property.

It is likely that Mary or Sam will be given relief under section 146(4), presuming that they have no involvement in the breach. They will have to make good any breaches by Tara in the period before relief: this fits the general principle that relief is given if the breach is remedied or the landlord compensated. If Tara has failed to pay rent then Sam will have to pay this to Len if he seeks relief. The fact that Sam has already paid his £15,000 rent to Tara does him no good: he also has to pay what Tara has failed to pay. The one crumb of comfort is that this is relevant only to the part sublet. If there is a sublease of half the premises, Sam will have to pay half the arrears.

Assuming relief, what terms will apply to the new lease ordered under section 146(4)? This is most likely to be a problem for Sam's sublease. Will he have a lease of all the premises? If a lease of the relevant half, is the rent £15,000 or £5,000 (half the rent payable to Len)? All that section 146(4) tells us is that the length cannot exceed that of the sublease (three years). Beyond that, the court has discretion. The courts seem happy to limit the new lease to part of the premises. This would be crucial if, for example, Tara had been tenant of a large office block and Sam was a subtenant of a small part. No subtenant could afford to take on a lease of the entire block. On the other hand, the choice of rent level is favourable to Len: the higher of the rent in the original lease and the sublease will be chosen.

Distress

The ancient remedy of distress enabled the landlord to seize ('distrain') the tenant's goods from the land and, if necessary, sell them. Such goods frequently sold for a tiny fraction of their initial cost: the remedy served more as a potent threat to tenants than an effective way of raising money. Distress was thought difficult to reconcile with human rights legislation and was abolished by the Tribunals, Courts and Enforcement Act 2007. A replacement commercial rent arrears recovery scheme was enacted for commercial leases. This protects tenants by requiring notice and allowing court intervention prior to seizure.

Who is liable on the covenants?

It is important that it is common for the landlord and the tenant to sell and transfer ('assign') their interests. As regards the landlord, it comes as no surprise that a valuable fee simple may be sold. Many purchasers (assignees) will not be worried that a tenant is there: the land may be viewed as an income-earning asset. Of course, with a short lease there may be both rent in the short term and possession in the medium term. There is an active market in buying property subject to leases.

Tenants may wish to assign their leases.

In Figure 14.2, Tabitha is the tenant of a shop for 15 years. After five years, her business expands such that she needs larger premises. She could agree with Larry (the landlord) to terminate the lease, but Larry might be reluctant to give up a safe source of rent for the next ten years. In any event, Tabitha might see the lease as possessing value that cannot be realised by an agreement with Larry. It will suit both Larry and Tabitha for Tabitha to assign the lease (for the ten years left) to Alison. Alison will take over the payment of rent to Larry. If the rent is below current market levels, then a capital sum may be paid by Alison to Tabitha to reflect the fact that she is getting a good bargain. Conversely, if rent levels have dropped (a good reason why Larry may want the lease to continue) then Tabitha will have to pay Alison for taking on an otherwise uneconomic burden. Figure 14.2 also shows that Larry assigns the fee simple to Arthur.

An important aspect of **assignment** (whether by Larry or Tabitha) is that the assignee takes over the rights and obligations of the original landlord or tenant. The situation after the assignments is treated as if Arthur and Alison were landlord and tenant. The terms in the lease can be enforced between them, just as between Larry and Tabitha originally.

The example in Figure 14.2 also shows a **sublease** from Alison to Steve. A sublease is a lease created by a tenant: tenants can create leases just as holders of the fee simple can. Why would Alison wish to sublet rather than assign? The answer is based on two interlocking factors. The first is that in a sublease Alison keeps a stake in the land: she remains tenant to Arthur and has a say as to how the land is used by Steve. More importantly, the terms of the lease and sublease may be very different. One obvious element of Steve's sublease is that it is for just one year, when the lease has eight years still to run. Steve is committed for only one year; thereafter, Alison can resume possession. In addition, the lease may have been at

---

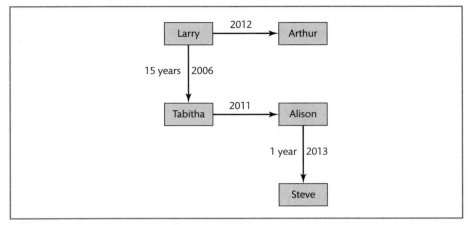

Figure 14.2 Assignments and subleases

a fixed rent of £10,000 for the duration of the lease and require Alison to repair the premises. Steve is willing to pay a rent of £15,000, but on the basis of Alison undertaking repairs.

A sublease can give full effect to these intentions. Obligations in leases bind assignees, but not (generally) subtenants. Accordingly, Steve has obligations to Alison, but not to Arthur. Assignment to Steve wouldn't work for several reasons. One cannot assign for a period shorter than the lease, the rent level cannot be different from the original lease and all the obligations (including repair) pass to the assignee. In other words, assignment and subletting form two very different ways of dealing with the land. They are as different as a freeholder either selling or leasing the land.

Assignment and subletting

In this section, we consider how to distinguish assignments from subleases and whether there are any limits on a tenant's power to assign and sublet.

Assignment or sublease?

The duration of the new agreement is crucial to whether there is an assignment or sublease. If it is for less than the original lease, then there can only be a sublease: tenants cannot assign for a limited period.

Much more problematic is the law's stance that a sublease for the entire length of the lease must be an assignment.

Brian leases land to Carla for ten years at £10,000 rent, with Carla being liable for repair. After five years, Carla purports to sublet to Derek for the remaining five years. This can operate only as an assignment, as it is for the full remainder of the lease. The problem is that the parties may have put very different terms in the sublease. Thus, Derek may have agreed to pay £15,000 rent, but on the basis that Carla is to repair.

> Because the law insists on treating Derek as an assignee, he is liable on the terms in the lease. This means that he is bound to repair. Disaster! What about rent? Brian can claim the original £10,000 rent from Derek and it is not clear what happens to the additional £5,000 Derek agreed to pay. The result is a mess. It could have been avoided by the simple expedient of subletting to Derek for the remaining period of the lease less (say) ten days. It does no credit to the law to require parties to enter such artificial terms in order to realise their objectives. If the sublease is as long as the lease, it may make sense to *presume* an assignment, but not to prohibit a sublease.

Power to assign and sublet

The first point is that the nature of a lease as a property interest entitles the tenant to assign or sublet. Even if the lease says the tenant cannot do so, an assignment (for example) is still effective. Breach of the lease may, however, involve very unpleasant consequences, including the possibility of forfeiture. This means that no sensible person would accept an assignment or sublease in the face of a prohibition in the lease.

The second point is that express terms almost always restrict the right to assign or sublet. This is natural: any landlord will be very worried by the prospect of an assignee who cannot afford the rent or seems likely to breach other obligations. The identity of subtenants is less crucial, as the original tenant remains liable. However, most landlords will be worried if a subtenant is unable to pay rent (this will affect the tenant's ability to pay the landlord) or is likely to cause a breach of other terms in the lease.

It is possible for a lease to prohibit assignment or subletting, but such an absolute prohibition greatly diminishes the value of the lease and is very unusual. However, leases almost invariably require the tenant not to assign or sublet without the consent of the landlord. If consent is not obtained, the lease is liable to forfeiture. A very important point is that section 19 of the Landlord and Tenant Act 1927 (Extract 16.2.3) requires that consent should not be unreasonably withheld in such 'qualified' prohibitions. This requirement cannot be excluded.

The giving of consents has for decades been a contentious area. In practical terms, an assignment or sublease cannot go ahead without consent. If the landlord is slow or awkward, then the proposed assignee or subtenant may well pull out of the deal. In response to these concerns, the Landlord and Tenant Act 1988 (Extract 16.2.4) requires the landlord to decide within a reasonable time and to give reasons. Importantly, the landlord has to show that there were reasonable grounds for refusing consent. The tenant can sue for losses caused by a breach of these duties and the landlord can rely on only those reasons for refusing consent that have been communicated to the tenant.

The 1927 and 1988 Acts have given rise to a lot of cases, though they mostly depend on their own special facts. However, they demonstrate that justifying refusal of consent is difficult if the assignee is able to pay the rent and likely to comply with the covenants. The landlord cannot use the need for consent to renegotiate the lease. Further, the landlord cannot rely on matters that are collateral to the premises or lease.

Frances owns a number of shops, one of which is leased to Gerry for ten years and another is leased to Helen, with six months left. Frances expects Helen to renew her lease. Gerry now proposes to assign his lease to Helen, who would no longer renew her existing lease. Frances is unhappy with this, as it will soon leave her without a tenant of Helen's present shop. This will not justify Frances refusing consent: it has nothing to do with Gerry's shop or Helen's suitability as a tenant.

Since the Landlord and Tenant (Covenants) Act 1995 (the 1995 Act), the lease can specify circumstances in which the landlord can refuse consent or impose conditions before consent is given. It is then reasonable for the landlord to refuse consent on these grounds. This provision relating to consents balances other new rules favourable to tenants. All this is discussed later in this chapter.

A final point in this area is that we are dealing with assignment by the tenant. There are no equivalent rules relating to assignment by the landlord. In practical terms, leases almost never contain limits on the ability of the landlord to assign. In part, this is because tenants have less bargaining power in settling the terms of the lease; in addition, the identity of the landlord is generally less crucial than that of the tenant.

Enforcement of covenants following assignment

Figure 14.3 provides an example which is similar to that used above.

Larry and Tabitha are the original landlord and tenant and remain such until Tabitha assigns the lease to Alison in 2011. For two years, Larry is the landlord and Alison the holder of the lease. We say that there is *privity of estate* between them. All this means is that Larry is the current landlord and Alison the current tenant. Larry and Tabitha are in privity of estate until 2011, but that is of little significance as there is (on normal contract principles) **privity of contract** as between them. From 2013, there is privity of estate as between Arthur (current landlord) and Alison (current tenant).

The basic rule is quite simple: the covenants in the lease are enforceable between the parties who are, at the relevant time, in privity of estate. If Alison fails to pay rent in 2014, it will

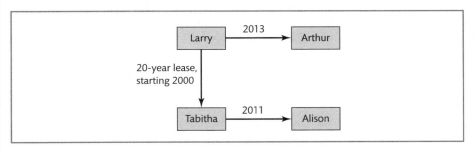

Figure 14.3 Privity of contract and privity of estate

be Arthur who is entitled to sue. Larry is out of the picture by that time. If Arthur fails to comply with a repairing covenant in 2014, it will be Alison who can sue. Tabitha is out of the picture then.

However, things are made more complex because privity of estate is not an exclusive basis for liability on covenants. We look at this in more detail below, but suppose Alison fails to pay rent in 2012. Larry may seek to sue Tabitha for this, given that Tabitha has promised to pay rent for 20 years and there is privity of contract between them.

A vitally important factor is that the Landlord and Tenant (Covenants) Act 1995 provides a comprehensive structure, with completely new rules, for the running of covenants. The 1995 Act is not retrospective, so pre-1996 leases are unaffected by it. Accordingly, there are two different sets of principles applicable to covenants, according to the date of the lease. There are many thousands of long leases which pre-date 1996 and which will continue for decades to come. Nevertheless, the proportion of 'new tenancies' (the term used in the 1995 Act, but we will call them '1995 Act leases') obviously grows as the years go by. We look at the old rules only briefly.

Which covenants run?

When we refer to covenants running, we mean that the benefit can be enforced by an assignee and that the burden is incurred by an assignee. In our example, it means that the burden of the obligation to pay rent passes to Alison and the benefit of that obligation passes to Arthur. However, not every covenant runs.

The law before the 1995 Act (still applicable to pre-1996 leases) required that a covenant should *touch and concern* the land before it would run. The traditional test is that 'the covenant must either affect the land as regards mode of occupation, or it must be such as *per se*, and not merely from collateral circumstances, affects the value of the land'. A more general and modern expression of the test is whether the covenant 'affects the landlord in his normal capacity as landlord or the tenant in his normal capacity as tenant'.

Typical covenants such as payment of rent, repair of the premises and restricting land use clearly touch and concern. An option for the tenant to purchase the freehold, however, does not touch and concern – it has insufficient effect on the lease or the land. Covenants relating to the identity of those employed on the land have caused difficulty. They only touch and concern is if the person's identity is important as regards the land (not just to the individuals who are landlord and tenant). Thus a promise not to employ persons convicted of arson in a lease of a refinery would touch and concern, whereas a covenant to employ the landlord's son as manager of a leased shop would not touch and concern. Covenants that relate to other land are unlikely to touch and concern unless there is some direct link between the plots. Accordingly, a covenant by a tenant to build a house for the landlord on adjoining land would not touch and concern, whereas a covenant by a landlord not to use adjoining land for business purposes (so as to protect the amenity value of the leased land) would touch and concern.

It is easy to grasp the basic idea that only covenants relating to the landlord and tenant relationship should run on assignments. However, the test has given rise to large numbers of cases. Romer LJ expressed his opinion trenchantly:[22] 'The established rules . . . are purely arbitrary, and the distinctions, for the most part, quite illogical.'

Fortunately, the touching and concerning requirement is removed for 1995 Act leases. For these, the simple general rule is that all covenants run with the land. This applies to 'landlord covenants' and 'tenant covenants' (those to be complied with by landlord and tenant respectively). Some covenants will patently not be entered into as landlord or tenant.

> Tabitha, the tenant, covenants to build on adjoining land (owned by her). Will this obligation run to bind an assignee of the lease? This wouldn't make sense if the assignee does not also own the adjoining land. It is probable that the courts would hold that this was not, in the language of the Act, 'a covenant falling to be complied with by the tenant of premises demised [leased] by the tenancy'. It is a covenant to be complied with by the owner of the adjoining land rather than by the tenant, though they happen to be the same person initially.

In a similar fashion, the rules on the running of covenants do not apply to those 'expressed to be personal to any person'. This seems not to require express words: the intention can be made clear from the circumstances.

These rules enable the courts to hold that patently personal obligations do not run in an obviously inappropriate manner. It would be wrong, however, to suppose that they replicate the old touching and concerning rules. Many covenants that did not touch and concern will today run in 1995 Act leases.

Privity of estate

The law here is fairly straightforward. Returning to the example above, Arthur and Alison will be able to enforce the covenants in the lease between each other. For leases after the 1995 Act, section 3 (Extract 16.3.1) makes this clear. For older leases, it is the combined result of *Spencer's Case*[23] (Extract 16.3.3) (assignment of lease) and LPA sections 141 and 142 (Extract 16.3.2) (assignment of reversion).

Just one point of detail is worth observing, relating to a covenant that affects just part of the premises.

> Tabitha takes a lease of a house and field, covenanting to keep the house in repair. Subsequently, Tabitha assigns the lease of the field (but not the house) to Alison. Section 3 makes it clear that Alison has no liability for the repair of the house, as it relates to a part of the leased land that was excluded from her assignment.

Breaches before assignment

There are two questions to consider: who can be sued and who can sue. We will take liability first.

---

[22] *Grant v Edmondson* [1931] 1 Ch 1 at p. 28.
[23] (1583) 5 Co Rep 16a (77 ER 72).

Suppose that Tabitha failed to pay rent before the assignment to Alison in 2011. Both before and after the 1995 Act, it is clear that Alison has no liability – it is not her breach. However, Tabitha's breach entitles the landlord to forfeit the lease and this would place huge pressure on Alison to pay the arrears. In practice, Alison would not purchase the lease without getting an assurance that there is no breach (nor would Tabitha consent to assignment until the arrears have been paid).

Rights to sue have proved more difficult.

If arrears are owed by Tabitha or Alison in 2013, can Larry (the landlord at the time of the breach) or Arthur (the present landlord) claim? Larry is owed a debt by Tabitha (or Alison) prior to the assignment of the reversion and it is always possible to assign the benefit of a debt. The question is whether the sale of the land also operates as an assignment of the debt. A certain and clear answer is required for Larry and Arthur to work out how much Arthur should pay. If Arthur can claim £10,000 arrears, then he will pay more for the land.

Prior to the 1995 Act, **Re King**[24] (Extract 16.3.21) held that the benefit did pass to the assignee of the reversion (Arthur). This had some merit in that the right to forfeit and the right to damages were held by the same person. However, section 23 (Extract 16.3.20) of the 1995 Act reverses this and adopts more of a 'clean break' approach: the benefit does not pass, absent any express assignment. Perhaps surprisingly, the assignee can still bring forfeiture proceedings.

Breaches after assignment

It follows from what has been said above that Alison and Arthur can sue each other. The question whether Larry and Tabitha can be made contractually liable for the wrongs of their assignees has caused controversy. It is studied under the final heading in this chapter.

Equitable leases and equitable assignments

Before the 1995 Act, most cases indicated that privity of estate requires a legal lease and a legal assignment. Accordingly, covenants would not run if there were an **equitable lease** or (the most likely problem) if there were an equitable assignment of a legal lease. None of this fits well with the idea discussed in the previous chapter that an equitable lease is as good as a legal lease.

Fortunately, the 1995 Act provides (but only for 1995 Act leases) that the new rules apply to equitable leases and equitable assignments. It is not worth discussing the very complex old rules further.

Concurrent leases

Concurrent leases are created when a landlord leases land first to one person and then to a second. It sounds as if there is a conflict between the two leases, but the law finds a

---

[24] [1963] Ch 459.

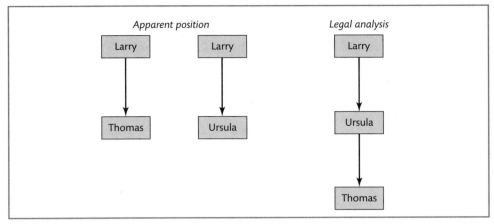

Figure 14.4 Concurrent leases

way of making good practical sense of the situation. We can start with one clear proposition: the first tenant can always claim possession. The *apparent position* in Figure 14.4 represents the position as it initially seems, with the leases apparently conflicting. The *legal analysis* shows how the law treats the relationship between the two leases.

The practical effect of the concurrent leases is to make Ursula the immediate landlord of Thomas, for so long as her lease continues. Ursula can collect and keep the rent and is able to enforce the covenants. Thomas, of course, possesses the land. However, it is not a true sublease. If it were, then Thomas's lease would fail if Ursula's lease were forfeited for breach of covenants by Ursula. That certainly does not happen here: Thomas's claim to the land is quite independent of Ursula's lease.

Subleases

The example illustrated in Figure 14.5 was used above, when we noted the main rules applicable to subleases. We have seen that Arthur and Alison are in privity of estate and can enforce the covenants against each other. Steve, the subtenant, is not in privity of estate with Arthur and is not liable to him.

However, it would be wrong to think that the contents of the head lease are of no significance to Steve. When Alison sublets to Steve, she will be aware that she remains liable for any breach of covenant. Steve's conduct is most likely to put her in breach if there is a negative obligation (not to use the land for business, for example) in the head lease. She will ensure that Steve covenants to comply with this sort of obligation. However, his obligation is owed to Alison rather than Arthur. Nor is it likely that terms of the sublease will be intended to benefit the landlord such as to enable him to sue under the Contracts (Rights of Third Parties) Act 1999.[25] (20.1.5)

What action can Arthur take if Steve acts in breach of the head lease? He can claim forfeiture of Alison's head lease. This will destroy the sublease regardless of whether it contains

---

[25] This Act is discussed in more detail in Chapter 17; see especially p. 285, below.

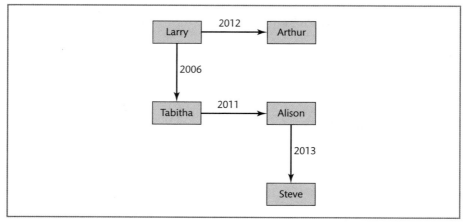

Figure 14.5 Subleases

the relevant term in the head lease. Steve must comply with the head lease if he wishes the sublease to survive.

The next possibility for Arthur turns on the law relating to restrictive covenants. As we shall see in more detail in Chapter 17, covenants restrictive of the use of land can be proprietary interests binding anyone coming into contact with the land. Suppose Tabitha covenants that the premises should not be used for business purposes. This is a restrictive covenant that will be binding on Alison (here it overlaps with privity of estate liability) and, more importantly, Steve. That Arthur can enforce the covenant against Steve is confirmed by the 1995 Act, section 3(5) (16.4.2).

Two points should be made about this restrictive covenant liability. The first is that restrictive covenants usually involve two plots of land: the benefited land and the burdened land. For Tabitha's covenant, there is only one plot: the leased land. This problem is resolved by treating the landlord's estate (the freehold) and the tenant's estate (the lease) as if they were different plots: the freehold estate is the benefited land and the lease is the burdened land. It is a somewhat generous rule but seems to work satisfactorily.

The second point is that restrictive covenants normally have to be registered in order to bind purchasers (Steve counts as a purchaser for these purposes). However, restrictive covenants in leases (if affecting the leased land, as does Tabitha's covenant) are exempted from this requirement.[26]

CRITICAL ISSUE :

Contractual liability of assignors for breaches after assignment

One factor has been added to the example we have already investigated: a further assignment of the lease to Belinda (see Figure 14.6). The question to consider is whether Tabitha is liable for failures by Alison and Belinda to pay rent. There can be equivalent

[26] Land Registration Act 2002, ss 29(2)(b), 33(c) (Extract 10.2.7).

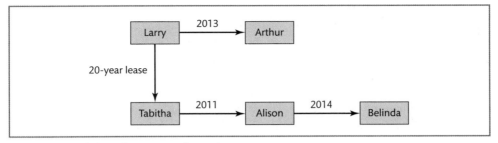

Figure 14.6 Liability of assignors after assignment

issues as to whether Larry can be made liable for Arthur's breaches (failure to repair, for example), but that question rarely arises.

Why should Tabitha be liable? The answer is based on two factors. The first is that Tabitha has promised to pay rent for 20 years. The fact that she has assigned the lease does not remove this contractual liability undertaken by her. Indeed, statute provides that the tenant covenants 'on behalf of himself his successors in title and the persons deriving title under him'.[27]

The second factor is the practical point that a tenant cannot be permitted to get out of liability by assigning the lease to a person who patently cannot afford to undertake the obligations (a man of straw). These factors together explain the very old rule of contractual liability of tenants: Tabitha remains liable throughout the lease.

The problem

A number of factors combined to bring the law into disrepute by the 1980s, whereupon it was reviewed by the Law Commission.[28] It was central to the thinking of the Law Commission that tenants regard assignment as a termination of their relationship with the land. Even though the tenants sued are almost invariably tenants of commercial premises who have legal advice, this has not stopped their being surprised when contractual liability has been asserted.

More powerful, perhaps, is the point that the danger of assignment to a man of straw is negligible today. We have seen that the landlord nearly always has to consent to an assignment. Before consenting, the landlord will seek to establish that the assignee will be able to pay the rent. Accordingly, the landlord has taken the choice of allowing the assignee to take over. If things go wrong, it is far from clear that the tenant should foot the bill.

Furthermore, the circumstances and extent of liability can be oppressive. The landlord can readily monitor the assignee's payment of rent and take steps if things look to be going wrong. In contrast, the first the original tenant (Tabitha) is likely to know of a problem is when presented with a large bill for arrears over a lengthy period. It is difficult for her to make proper provision for (or guard against) such sudden and unpredictable

---

[27] LPA, s 79; considered in more detail in Chapter 17.
[28] Law Com No 174 (1989).

liability. These problems were brought home when economic recession in the 1980s led to many assignees defaulting on rent repayments and landlords began more aggressively to pursue tenants for arrears. To the horror of tenants, they also found themselves liable for increases in rent above that in the original lease and for periods of renewal beyond the original length of the lease.

Although liability is based upon contracts freely negotiated between businessmen, the Law Commission concluded that reform was needed. This was the principal reason why the 1995 Act was enacted.

The solution: pre-1996 leases

Generally, the legislation does not apply to pre-1996 leases. However, the problems with contractual liability were thought so serious as to require some immediate changes. There are three separate protections, applying to both pre-1996 leases and 1995 Act leases.

Section 17 (Extract 16.3.15) requires the landlord to give notice to the original tenant (Tabitha) within six months of the breach. This avoids the problem of large arrears building up before Tabitha becomes aware of the problem, though by itself it doesn't enable Tabitha to do anything about it.

Section 18 (Extract 16.3.15) sets out to deal with the problem of variations of leases between the landlord and the assignee.

> Suppose a post-assignment variation makes Tabitha's liability more extensive than under the original lease. Greater liability can be imposed on Tabitha only if Larry (or whoever is the landlord at the relevant time) can refuse the variation. Thus, Tabitha will not be affected if Alison and Larry negotiate an extension to the lease. However, if Alison exercises a right to extend the lease then there would be no protection – this is a situation in which Larry has no right to object. Just before the section came into effect, the Court of Appeal in **Friends' Provident Life Office v British Railways Board**[29] (Extract 16.3.12) limited the liability of tenants in a similar fashion by interpretation of the contractual obligation. Arguably, section 18 has been proved unnecessary.

A third protection applies once arrears have been paid by the original tenant.

> Tabitha has paid the arrears; she can claim an 'overriding lease'. This is a lease from Larry for the same length as the assigned lease; it takes effect as a concurrent lease.[30] Its gives Tabitha control over Alison (and Belinda): she can take steps to ensure that they pay rent or have their lease forfeited. However, this protection applies only after Tabitha pays arrears; it does not apply when the section 17 notice is issued. By the time Tabitha is called upon to pay, it may be too late to remedy the situation.

[29] [1996] 1 All ER 336.
[30] See above (p. 228).

The solution: 1995 Act leases

Section 5 of the 1995 Act (Extract 16.3.10) starts from a very different perspective: once the lease is assigned, the original tenant has no liability.

Tabitha (assuming a lease after 1996) faces neither privity of contract nor privity of estate liability after assignment. This cannot be excluded by the parties. Tabitha will still be liable if she assigns in breach of covenant (Larry hasn't approved the assignee) or the assignment follows her bankruptcy, but these are minor exceptions.

Unfortunately for tenants, the new law does not stop there. Section 16 (Extract 16.3.14) permits the landlord to enter into an *authorised guarantee agreement* with the tenant, guaranteeing performance of the covenants by the assignee.

Larry can obtain such a guarantee from Tabitha, guaranteeing Alison's performance. There is some justification for this in that Tabitha has chosen Alison as an assignee and shares responsibility with Larry if Alison turns out not to be able to pay the rent. Nevertheless, it means there is no clean break at the time of assignment.

A very important limitation on the guarantee is that it covers only the immediate assignee.

Once Alison assigns to Belinda, Tabitha's liability ends. Section 25 (Extract 16.3.16) prohibits any attempted variation of these rules. However, it is possible for Larry to enter into a fresh authorised guarantee agreement with Alison, whereby Alison guarantees performance by Belinda. It follows that the landlord can ensure that the immediate assignor is liable as well as the current tenant.

It may be recalled that the 1995 Act permits the parties to specify when consent to assignment can be refused. This was inserted so that Larry could put a term in the lease that consent to assignment can be refused unless the assignor enters into an authorised guarantee agreement. This means that such agreements will be very common. The protection for pre-1996 tenants (notice, variation, overriding leases) applies to liability under authorised guarantee agreements.

Recovery by tenants

Suppose Tabitha has had to pay rent because of default by Alison or Belinda. Can she recover payment from anybody? The current tenant has primary liability to pay rent and must compensate Tabitha. In reality, tenants who have failed to pay their rent are unlikely to be able to pay Tabitha – at least, unless they win the lottery.

Further, a term is implied into assignments whereby the assignee accepts liability for the duration of the lease. This means that Alison is liable to Tabitha for breach by herself or Belinda. As regards Belinda, this ceases to be relevant in 1995 Act leases – Tabitha can never be liable after Alison assigns.

▉ Contractual liability of landlords

The rules so far relate to the liability of tenants. Landlords can face similar contractual liability, though this is very unusual.

The 1995 Act attempts to allow landlords to have a clean break, just like tenants. However, it is not possible to replicate the rules exactly, as tenants do not consent to assignment of the reversion. The solution is to permit the landlord to serve notice on the tenant.

> Alison was the tenant when Larry assigns in 2013. If either Alison does not object when Larry serves notice or the court declares that it is reasonable for Larry to be released from the covenant, then Larry ceases to be bound.

▉ Conclusions

We will concentrate on 1995 Act leases. It is plain that tenants are better off than before as regards contractual liability. We still have to ask ourselves how far it is justified to interfere with freedom of contract in commercial contracts. Nevertheless, experience seems to show that landlords have the stronger bargaining power and are able to dictate the terms of the lease. The protection of the original tenant is, of course, significantly qualified by the authorised guarantee agreement. For Tabitha, it is a matter of chance how her liability might develop. If Alison never assigns, then Tabitha remains liable for the duration of the lease. She may gain some protection from sections 17 to 19 (Extract 16.3.15). On the other hand, Alison might assign to Belinda after six months, in which case Tabitha's potential liability terminates. For somebody who needs to be able to assess the extent and duration of risks faced, it may be thought that the law still fails to provide Tabitha with the clean break she wants.

CRITICAL ISSUE

Questions to consider

1. Are there good reasons why some contract rules do not apply to leases?

2. Is it possible to make sense of the finding of a lease in *Bruton*?

3. Does the law adopt a sensible approach in establishing repairing duties on landlords and tenants?

4. Should forfeiture of leases be abolished? If it is retained, does it require reform?

5. Is it accurate to summarise the running covenants by the simple proposition that the current landlord and tenant, but only those persons, can sue and be sued on leasehold covenants?

6. To what extent has the law interfered with freedom of contract in establishing liability on covenants in leases? Does the present law operate fairly?

Further reading

Bridge, S [1996] CLJ 313: Former tenants, future liabilities and the privity of contract principle: the Landlord and Tenant (Covenants) Act 1995.

Elliott, D W (1964) 80 LQR 244: Non-derogation from grant.

Fancourt, T [2006] Conv 37: Licences to assign: another turn of the screw?

Lower, M [2010] Conv 38: The Bruton tenancy.

Morgan, J (2009) 'Leases: property, contract or more?', in *Modern Studies in Property Law*, Vol 5, ed. M Dixon, Chapter 17.

Reynolds, J I (1974) 37 MLR 377: Statutory covenants of fitness and repair: social legislation and the judges.

Roberts, N [2012] Conv 87: The Bruton tenancy: a matter of relativity.

Smith, P F [2003] Conv 112: Disrepair and unfitness revisited.

Tromans, S [1986] Conv 187: Forfeiture of leases: relief for underlessees and holders of other derivative interests.

Visit **www.mylawchamber.co.uk** to access tools to help you develop and test your knowledge of land law, including interactive multiple choice questions, practice exam questions with guidance, weblinks, glossary flashcards, legal newsfeed and legal updates.

Use **Case Navigator** to read in full some of the key cases referenced in this section with commentary and questions:

Billson and others v *Residential Apartments* [1992] 1 All ER 141

Bruton v *London and Quadrant Housing Trust* [1993] 3 All ER 481

Part 4

Other interests in land

15 Licences

Nature and importance

Licences constitute a rather unusual topic. Most land law involves settled principles that have been recognised for centuries. By contrast, almost all the material in this chapter dates from after the Second World War. Traditionally, licences have not been regarded as interests in land: they do not bind purchasers. It is exciting to see the law's struggle with controversial ideas that might lead to a new branch of interests in land. Because the law is still developing, it reveals many uncertainties and contradictions.

What are licences?

When we deal with interests in land such as leases and easements, we have a pretty good idea of the nature of the right we are talking about. Licences are different because they constitute a residuary group of rights relating to land. A licence is any permission to do something on land that is not a lease, easement or other property right. Licences include situations as diverse as having a ticket to see a concert or sporting event, visiting a friend for dinner, going onto a neighbour's land to find a football that has been kicked over the boundary fence, going to a club, staying in a hotel and living with a boyfriend or girlfriend. There may also be a licence to do something on one's own land (such as creating noise) which would otherwise be a nuisance.

This huge range of circumstances has made it difficult to develop legal principles governing licences – at least unless we wish simply to say that land law should ignore licences! Perhaps we should distinguish some forms of licence and treat them differently. Thus some people have argued that we should give greater recognition to licences that involve occupation of premises as a home. Such licences look similar to leases. They involve exclusive possession (perhaps jointly), but lack some vital requirement such as a fixed term. As yet, however, the cases provide little support for distinguishing between different forms of licence.

Most land law interests – all leases and easements, for example – could be classified as licences if the relevant property category were not available. However, there are interests that look quite different from licences. There are two principal examples. The first is a security interest, such as a mortgage. This enables the lender to realise the value of property in order to ensure the payment of the debt. Covenants form a second example. A restrictive covenant (such as a covenant not to build on land) involves no right to do anything on land.

Methods of protection

The normal way of dividing up licences – adopted in this chapter – is by reference to how they are created. A bare licence is no more than simple permission; there is no contract, for example. An example would be inviting somebody for a drink at your home. Bare licences can be terminated and the only question is how much time has to be allowed for the licensee (the person to whom the licence was given) to leave. For the drink invitation this would be a matter of seconds, but it would be much longer for somebody allowed to live in a house.

At the other end of the spectrum, licences can operate as part of another interest.

Sara has a right to take fish from a lake on Valerie's land (this is a proprietary interest called a profit). A moment's thought will reveal that Sara has to go on to Valerie's land in order to reach the lake and catch fish. The courts accept that this licence to enter the land should be treated as part of the profit; it binds purchasers from Valerie in the same way as the profit.

That example is straightforward. It has been extended to situations where Sara owns an object (felled timber could be an example) on Valerie's land and needs a licence to get possession of it. Much more controversial are dicta in a few cases that the licence can be connected with a merely contractual right. That would have the effect that any contractual licence would bind purchasers, which we shall see is not the law. The dicta seem to overlook the requirement that the licence must be connected with a *property* interest; they should be disregarded.

Most problems have arisen with licences protected by a contract or estoppel, or else where there is a constructive trust. The remaining sections of this chapter are devoted to these areas. We shall see that the law may be criticised as being incoherent in its treatment of licences created in different ways.

Should we be worried about licences as interests in land?

As seen in Chapter 1, the law recognises only specified interests in land. At least until recent decades, those interests have not included licences. Accordingly, licence cases are important in demonstrating what it is that makes an interest proprietary: how and why we don't recognise every right as proprietary. Licences are, at most, on the outer edge of interests recognised as proprietary.

Why should the law restrict the range of interests in land and, in particular, have difficulty with licences? Purchasers need to be able to identify clearly the burdens by which they may be affected. This ensures that land remains as useful and marketable as possible. If unlimited obligations were to bind purchasers, there is a risk not only that selling land would become more difficult, but also that economically efficient land use might be seriously impeded.

Routes to the enforcement of licences

The controversial nature of licences is such that nearly all the material could be treated as a Critical Issue. Of the categories of licences, bare licences and licences coupled with an interest have already been considered. Contractual licences will be considered first. Constructive trusts and estoppel licences will then be discussed as a Critical Issue. It is worth noting that these last two forms of protection apply to licences that start off as bare or contractual licences: the categories are not mutually exclusive.

Contractual licences: licensor and licensee

When considering licences as possible proprietary interests, it is first necessary to establish that they can be enforced as between licensor (landowner) and licensee.

> Rachel allows Sally to use her land. Suppose that the law permits Rachel to evict Sally. It is plain that any purchaser from Rachel can likewise evict Sally. That is one reason why bare licences are very clearly not proprietary: they need not be considered further. If a contract forms the basis of Sally's licence, the first question is whether Rachel can evict Sally in breach of contract.

The nineteenth-century approach was to say that the contract did not limit the rights of the landowner. The licensee (Sally) can be evicted from the land, though she may have an action in contract for damages. The twentieth-century cases gave greater effect to contractual rights. In *Hurst* v *Picture Theatres Ltd*[1] (Extracts 18.1.1, 18.1.4), the licensee had bought a cinema ticket. When the cinema manager used force to evict the licensee, this was held to constitute the tort of assault. To reach that conclusion, the court had to accept that the licensee was entitled to remain on the land. The earlier cases were explained on the basis that they were decided in courts of common law, whereas *Hurst* was based on the enforcement of a contract in equity (using equitable remedies such as injunction or specific performance). We no longer have separate courts of law and equity, so there is no longer any difficulty in applying the equitable right to remain.

This equitable right to remain deserves a little more explanation. If there is a contract for a legal interest (a fee simple, for example), then equity will treat the contract as carried out. In the eyes of equity there is already a fee simple from the date of the contract: in the words of the maxim, 'equity looks on that as done which ought to be done'. This explains the status of the estate contract as a proprietary interest; there is no need for a

---

[1] [1915] 1 KB 1.

remedy to have been sought or awarded. *Hurst* applies similar reasoning to licences. The courts will give equitable remedies such as specific performance (to enforce the contract) or injunction (to prevent revocation in breach of contract). If such a remedy had been given to Mr Hurst, it is plain that he could have stayed in the cinema and that any attempt to evict him would have constituted an assault. Of course, no such remedy had been awarded in *Hurst*, but we apply the maxim that equity treats as done that which ought to be done.

This reasoning nevertheless contained a weakness: it fails to recognise that a licence is not a legal interest like a fee simple. Nevertheless, the enforceability of licences was accepted in *Winter Garden Theatre (London) Ltd* v *Millenium Productions Ltd*[2] (Extract 18.1.5). The case involved a licence to produce plays in the licensor's theatre. The Court of Appeal held that the licensor could not terminate the licence, as there was an implied term not to revoke it. Though the House of Lords decided that no such term should be implied, the judges agreed that its effect would have been to prevent termination.

It now appears settled that contractual licences will normally be enforced as between the licensor and licensee. One memorable case is *Verrall* v *Great Yarmouth BC*,[3] in which the National Front had contracted to hold their annual conference in the defendant's Wellington Pier pavilion. When the Labour Party took control of the council, the licence was purportedly revoked. The Court of Appeal granted specific performance. The political context makes it an interesting case, though the licences aspects were by that time (1979) quite settled. In particular, any argument that specific performance would not be ordered for a short-term licence was roundly rejected.

Even so, equitable enforcement of contractual licences raises controversial issues. Is it really the case that landowners should be prevented from terminating licences? In some circumstances, most people would agree that specific performance is not practicable. A standard example is where two people share premises. If their relationship has broken down, it will often be the case that continuing to share the premises simply will not work. *Thompson* v *Park*[4] provides a good example. Two headmasters agreed to share the school of one of them. After disagreements had arisen, the licence was revoked. Undaunted, the licensee forced his way back into the school. The Court of Appeal was emphatic that the licensee had no right to return to the school once the licence had been revoked, whether lawfully or not. This is well justified by the observation that 'the court cannot specifically enforce an agreement for two people to live peaceably under the same roof'.

A more general attack has been mounted in Australia, especially in the High Court in *Cowell* v *Rosehill Racecourse Co Ltd*.[5] The Australian courts have accepted an argument that landowners should be allowed discretion as to the use of their land, which restricts the availability of equitable remedies for licensees.

Two examples may be given in support of this. In sporting or entertainment cases (the context of both *Hurst* and *Cowell*), the licensor may sometimes need to eject the

---

[2] [1946] 1 All ER 678 (Court of Appeal); [1948] AC 173 (House of Lords).
[3] [1981] QB 202.
[4] [1944] KB 408.
[5] (1937) 56 CLR 605.

licensee, whether because of misconduct or public safety considerations. Whether ejection can be justified involves a question of judgment; it may be too heavy-handed to impose liability in assault if the wrong choice is made. The second example concerns building contracts, under which the builder has a licence to enter and construct a building. If the landowner loses confidence in the builder, is it really justified to say that the builder has a right to complete the building? Both these examples may be best resolved by damages liability for loss caused by breach of contract. The Australian approach does not treat equitable remedies as impossible for licences, but it is far more cautious as to the circumstances in which they are appropriate. There is a lot to be said in its favour.

Contractual licences: licensee and purchaser

We have just seen that English law provides equitable remedies against the licensor. If the licensor sells the land, is the purchaser bound?

Suppose Jeremy is promoting a concert in his stadium. Irene buys a ticket for £40 for a date in September, three months away. In August, Jeremy sells the stadium to Kelly. Kelly has no wish for it to be used for a concert and informs Irene and other ticket holders that the concert will not take place. Until licences were regarded as giving equitable remedies against the licensor, there was no chance of their affecting purchasers such as Kelly.

The early cases after *Hurst* continued to assert that purchasers were not affected.[6] In the 1950s, the Court of Appeal in *Errington v Errington*[7] (Extract 18.1.8) surprised lawyers by holding that a successor in title was bound. A father (licensor) allowed his son and daughter-in-law to occupy land, on the basis that they would pay the mortgage instalments and have a right to the land when the mortgage was paid off. The father died and the property passed to his widow (the successor in title). When the son left the daughter-in-law, it was held that the widow could not evict her. The problem with *Errington* is that the court discusses the enforcement of contractual licences against licensors, but barely mentions the really difficult question of liability of successors in title.

Why might the contractual licence in *Errington* bind successors? One possibility is that the equitable remedy (available against the licensor) binds the successor in title. This analysis depends more on remedies rather than licences. It is an idea that has surfaced several times over the centuries in attempts to broaden categories of proprietary interests. However, it has almost always been rejected. In the licences context, the House of Lords firmly threw it out in *National Provincial Bank Ltd v Ainsworth*[8] (Extract 18.1.9) and the point now seems unarguable. It would lead to an unprincipled growth in proprietary interests.

---

[6] Two commonly cited cases are *King v David Allen & Sons, Billposting, Ltd* [1916] 2 AC 54 (right to fix advertisements to a wall) and *Clore v Theatrical Properties Ltd* [1936] 3 All ER 483 (right to use 'front of house' rights to sell refreshments, etc. in a theatre).

[7] [1952] 1 KB 290.

[8] [1965] AC 1175 (deserted wife as licensee).

A second possibility is the bold assertion that a contractual licence is a new interest in land. This seemed credible for a time after *Errington*, but it was rejected by the Court of Appeal in *Ashburn Anstalt* v *Arnold*[9] (licence to use shop premises). The court concluded that the authorities were clear that contractual licences are not interests in land. *Errington* itself was said to be explicable on estoppel grounds (discussed below). Although there may be some flaws in the *Ashburn Anstalt* decision (not all the relevant cases were cited and other aspects of the decision have been reversed), the reality is that no subsequent attempt has been made to revive the contractual licence. *Ashburn Anstalt* on licences has always been quoted with approval by other cases.

Contractual licences are therefore dead as regards proprietary status; it is clear that Irene's ticket gives her no rights against Kelly. It is virtually unthinkable that this will change in the foreseeable future. Perhaps licences to occupy homes should receive special protection, but there is no hint of this in the cases.

It is sometimes argued that new proprietary interests are made impossible by section 4 of the Law of Property Act 1925 (Extract 3.1.19): 'after the commencement of this Act . . . an equitable interest in land shall only be capable of being validly created in any case in which an equivalent equitable interest could have been created before such commencement.' Although that provision could bear that meaning, it would be odd for Parliament permanently to limit what the courts could do. It is better explained as a statement as to the effect of the 1925 legislation itself; in other words, the changes in 1925 did not create new interests.

Another weak argument is that *Ainsworth* might be subverted by a somewhat puzzling provision in the Land Registration Act 2002. Section 116 enacts that a 'mere equity' (which is how we generally describe equitable remedies) is capable of binding purchasers of registered land. If this were to apply to contractual licences, it would be a radical development. It is clear that section 116 was intended to clarify rather than change the law, as shown by its wording 'for the avoidance of doubt'. It is very unlikely to apply to licences. As intended by the Law Commission, it applies to equitable remedies giving rise to normal proprietary interests. An example is a right to rectify a transfer of land so as to correct a mistake in the area of land transferred.

Even if contractual licences (or some of them) were one day to be recognised as proprietary, land registration principles would have to be remembered. As lawyers are often not involved in creating licences, it is extremely unlikely that licences will be protected on the register. Without such protection, purchasers will not be bound unless there is actual occupation. This means that Irene's £40 ticket would still do her little good against Kelly.

If contractual licences are to have any proprietary effect, it is most likely to be in conjunction with constructive trust or estoppel analyses. These are discussed later.

Remedies available to licensees

Does a licensee have remedies against complete outsiders (neither the licensor nor a successor in title)?

---

[9] [1989] Ch 1.

> Ursula gives Vera a contractual licence to occupy land for an indefinite period. Six months later, Winona (who has no connection with either Ursula or Vera) enters the land. Does Vera possess any remedy against Winona?

It is sometimes thought that a proprietary interest is required for remedies such as trespass (most suitable for Vera) or nuisance. However, the true position is that possession (or at least exclusive possession) is sufficient. This fits with English property principles, which place more stress on possession than on ownership; generally we avoid special actions for ownership claims. It would, of course, be highly disadvantageous for Vera if only Ursula could take action to evict Winona. *Manchester Airport plc v Dutton*[10] (Extract 18.3.1) involves a somewhat controversial extension of possession-based remedies. The licensee was allowed an order to evict intruders, despite the licensee's not yet having taken possession. That this is controversial was recognised by Lord Neuberger MR in *Mayor of London v Hall*,[11] but the point was obiter and no conclusive view on *Dutton* was expressed.

Nuisance is the remedy generally employed for complaining about activities of neighbours (an example would be unacceptably noisy parties). It is quite clear that licensees, even if living on the land, cannot normally sue in nuisance: the owner (or tenant) is the most appropriate person to take action. This was authoritatively confirmed in a well-known decision of the House of Lords: *Hunter v Canary Wharf Ltd*[12] (Extract 18.3.2). Licensees living with the owner in homes near Canary Wharf Tower were unable to sue for interference with television signals caused by the Tower. However, dicta in *Hunter* indicate that licensees could sue if in exclusive possession.

These remedies demonstrate a somewhat hybrid status for licences. Although they do not enjoy the range of remedies normally available for proprietary interests, trespass and (probably) nuisance may be available in some cases. However, licences that do not confer occupation (an example would be a right to use boats on the licensor's lake) probably receive no such protection: these licensees have to look to the licensor to take action against anyone who interferes with them.

Constructive trusts

When will there be a constructive trust?

> Graham enters into a contractual licence with his friend Harry, allowing him to occupy a house as long as he wishes (the indefinite duration precludes a lease). The house is one of a group of five that Graham sells to Inga. Graham wants to ensure that Harry can continue to live there and Inga orally accepts this. The purchase price of £1.5 million for the five houses is reduced to £1.4 million in return for Inga's agreeing to allow Harry to occupy his house.

CRITICAL ISSUE

[10] [2000] QB 133 (Chadwick LJ dissenting as there was no right to exclusive possession).
[11] [2011] 1 WLR 504 at [26]–[27].
[12] [1997] AC 655 (Lord Cooke dissented).

It would look wrong for Inga to be able to reject the agreement and evict Harry. She has benefited from a reduced purchase price and made a clear promise in favour of Harry. Two analyses may be possible. The first is to apply the Contracts (Rights of Third Parties) Act 1999 (Extract 20.1.5) to allow an action in contract, despite absence of privity as between Inga and Harry. However, an oral agreement may not survive the statutory writing requirements for sales of land. The second analysis employs a constructive trust to avoid such unfair and unconscionable conduct by Inga, for which lack of writing would not matter.

In **Binions v Evans**,[13] (18.1.11) employers had given an employee's widow a contractual licence over a cottage. The purchaser bought the cottage subject to her licence, paying less as a result. Lord Denning MR held the purchaser bound by a constructive trust. **Binions** is the origin of the recent cases in this area. One important point to note is that the constructive trust is not an example of existing interest binding a purchaser; it exists because the purchaser has undertaken a new obligation. There is no reason why it cannot apply to a bare licence (a licence not linked to a contract or separate proprietary interest) just as much as to a contractual licence. An example would be if Harry (or the employee in **Binions**) had been permitted to live on the land free.

What sort of promise is required for a constructive trust?

Malcolm gives his friend Naomi a bare licence to store building materials on a vacant plot. In sudden need of money, Malcolm agrees to sell the land to his neighbour Olga. Naomi refuses to move her building materials immediately, even though she has no right to refuse. Normally a licensor such as Malcolm would evict Naomi before selling, but the tight schedule renders this impossible. The land is worth £4 million with vacant possession. If Naomi had a right to remain, the land would be worth £3 million. In negotiating the sale, both Malcolm and Olga believe that Naomi has no right, though there is a faint possibility that she might be able to assert an estoppel (discussed below). Malcolm wants to get as much money as he can, while Olga wants to pay as little as possible. They settle on a sale price of £3.5 million and Olga buys the land 'subject to' Naomi's licence.

Does this 'subject to' purchase give rise to a constructive trust? That question was raised in **Ashburn Anstalt**, where a purchaser bought subject to a licence. The Court of Appeal was clear that such wording is not by itself enough to give rise to a constructive trust: it is necessary that the purchaser should agree to give effect to the licence. It is clear that neither Malcolm nor Olga want Naomi's right to continue. Indeed, if Naomi's right were binding, £3.5 million would have been a very generous amount to pay. So why did Olga purchase subject to the licence? The reason is that Malcolm wants to protect himself against Olga making any future complaint about Naomi's occupation. Essentially, Olga is paying half a million pounds less for the land because she is taking the slender risk of there being problems in evicting Naomi. In all probability she gets a very good deal; she cannot complain in the unlikely event that those risks materialise.

[13] [1972] Ch 359.

In *Ashburn Anstalt* itself, the promise was held to be intended to protect the licensor/ seller rather than the licensee. Indeed, this is the standard construction of 'subject to' promises. Recently, the Court of Appeal in *Chaudhury v Yavuz*[14] confirmed that proof of a constructive trust is not easy: that the claim was obvious from the facts came nowhere close (despite a 'subject to' clause) to proving the necessary promise by the purchaser.

The example involving Olga shows that it is not enough to show that the purchase price is reduced: the reduction is explained by the purchaser taking a risk. No sane purchaser would pay the full price for land without obtaining vacant possession. Of course, the scale of the reduction may point to the purchaser having promised to be bound. Nor is it essential that there be any reduction in price. It is sufficient if the seller makes it clear that a sale will be agreed only if the licence is given effect to.[15]

Everything therefore depends on the facts of the individual case. Apparently powerful factors, such as buying subject to a claim and paying less for the land, can be explained away very easily. A constructive trust most obviously arises when the licensor really wants the licence to continue and makes this a condition of the sale. Such circumstances will be rare.

Even a promise to give effect to a licence is not free from difficulty. The problem arises when the licensor wants the purchaser to comply with the licence, but only to protect himself against contractual liability to the licensee. If the purchaser evicts the licensee, the licensor may be liable in damages to the licensee for breach of contract. Though the licensor couldn't care less about the licensee, the licensee benefits if the purchaser complies with the promise. In summary, the licensor does want the licence to be complied with, but not with the motive of benefiting the licensee.

This promise would not seem to give rise to liability to the licensee under the Contracts (Rights of Third Parties) Act 1999 (Extract 20.1.5). It might be regarded as odd if the constructive trust were to produce wider liability than the 1999 Act. Unconscionability may be difficult to argue when the real point behind the promise relates to the financial position of the seller: contractual damages payable by the purchaser to the seller provide an adequate remedy.

The nature of the constructive trust

Let us return to the example concerning Inga and Harry, where it was concluded that Inga held on a constructive trust to give effect to Harry's licence. Suppose that a year later (Harry still living in the house) Inga borrows money from Jeremy and mortgages the five houses to him as security. Is Jeremy bound by Harry's licence? It may be noted that Harry is in actual occupation and so Jeremy cannot rely on land registration principles to defeat his claim.

---

[14] [2012] 3 WLR 987 (the facts involved an easement which failed for absence of entry on the register).
[15] *Lyus v Prowsa Developments Ltd* [1982] 1 WLR 1044 (purchaser giving effect to estate contract, rather than licence).

This is a very uncertain area, with two alternative analyses possible. The first is that the constructive trust constitutes a normal proprietary interest, just like a constructive trust where there are contributions to a purchase of a family home. The family home trust certainly binds purchasers such as Jeremy. The second is that the constructive trust represents a purely personal obligation, incapable of binding Jeremy (unless he enters into a fresh promise to give effect to the licence, which would give rise to a second constructive trust). This would produce the same result as where Inga is contractually liable to Harry under the 1999 Act.

There is no clear authority. This sort of situation arose in *Chattey* v *Farndale Holdings Inc*,[16] where the Court of Appeal held a purchaser not to be bound. However, the beneficiary under the trust was not in actual occupation. It is unclear whether the beneficiary failed because the trust was incapable of binding a purchaser or because it was not protected on the register (and not an overriding interest).

Although we normally think of trusts as binding purchasers, it is far from clear that this is true of all constructive trusts; some can be seen more as remedies than as proprietary institutions. This is especially important when it is a licence that is protected by the trust. If a licensor (Graham) promises to give effect to a licence by contract, *Ashburn Anstalt* demonstrates that this is incapable of binding purchasers. It would be very odd if a similar promise by a purchaser (Inga) were to have a stronger effect in that it would bind future purchasers (Jeremy). It is true that only Inga's promise gives rise to a trust, but this underplays the underlying similarity between the promises.

Indeed, one may ask whether it is possible to have a trust of a proprietary nature to give effect to a non-proprietary interest such as a licence. It would indeed be strange if a licence could be elevated to the status of a right binding purchasers by the simple expedient of creating a trust.

Suppose Graham and Harry, at the time a licence is created, both want it to bind purchasers. Could they achieve that objective by the simple expedient of Graham's agreeing in writing to hold the house on trust for Harry, so as to give effect to the licence?

Every instinct is against purchasers being affected: it would make a mockery of attempts to limit the range of proprietary interests. Yet matters are not quite so simple. A trust of land to give effect to a licence may be seen as analogous to a trust of land for the purpose of (for example) educating somebody. The latter trust is recognised. Nevertheless, it may be thought that a trust to give effect to a licence goes too far in expanding proprietary interests; it should not be effective to bind purchasers.

[16] (1996) 75 P&CR 298 at pp. 313–17 (trust to give effect to an estate contract, rather than a licence).

CRITICAL ISSUE

Licences protected by estoppel

The role of the licence in estoppel claims

We saw in Chapter 8 that a claim based on estoppel may be brought where a person has relied to their detriment on a representation or assumption. Here, we will concentrate on their significance for licences.

One early case on estoppel is *Dillwyn* v *Llewelyn*[17] (Extract 7.2.1), in which there was a claim to a fee simple. A father made a gift of land to his son, but it was ineffective as there was no deed or writing. As intended, the son built a house on the land. The court found an estoppel and ordered that the fee simple should be transferred to the son. Although the son had no more than a licence before the estoppel arose, this licence seems completely irrelevant to the claim. It was a claim to a fee simple which was satisfied by a transfer of the fee simple. Suppose the son had previously been a tenant of the land. There would never have been a licence, but the estoppel claim would have operated in precisely the same way.

When do licences form a significant component of an estoppel claim? Two types of case, neither of them common, are now considered. The first is where the representation (or assumption) is of a licence. A statement that the claimant 'can stay as long they wish' or 'until they get a job' provides an example. These rights do not look like a fee simple or life interest and there is no fixed term as required for a lease.

The second type of case is where a court gives a licence as a remedy. This may apply whether or not the representation is of a licence. Perhaps the best example is provided by the analysis in *Pascoe* v *Turner*[18] (Extract 7.2.3). Following the breakdown of a relationship between the parties, the defendant was told by her former lover that a house was hers. As in *Dillwyn*, formality requirements were not complied with. She spent a significant part of her savings (not a large sum) on the house, whereupon an estoppel arose. The Court of Appeal initially inclined to the view that a licence simply allowing her to remain in the house would be the most appropriate remedy, given the relatively small expenditure. However, her lover's hostile and ruthless conduct persuaded the court that she should be awarded the fee simple. Despite the final result, the case shows how a licence might be the appropriate remedy.

Estoppel licences as proprietary interests

That licences can fit within estoppel claims is uncontroversial. More troublesome has been the question whether estoppel licences can affect purchasers, in the two types of case just identified. The licensee is usually in actual occupation, so the claim is unlikely to encounter registration problems.

---

[17] (1862) 4 De GF&J 517 (45 ER 1285).
[18] [1979] 1 WLR 431.

Prior to the Land Registration Act 2002, it was unclear whether estoppel bound purchasers; the question attracted a fair amount of attention from commentators. It was conventional to draw a distinction between the position before the remedy (often called 'inchoate equities') and after the remedy. Before the remedy, most cases seemed to recognise that purchasers could be bound, though there were few cases involving licences and the position was never firmly settled. Once a court had decided there was a licence as a remedy, then most lawyers considered that purchasers would not be bound, though there was very little authority. The thinking was that a licence ordered by the court had no better entitlement to proprietary status than a contractual licence agreed by the parties.

How could the law justify proprietary status at the inchoate stage? The only credible answer could be that estoppels protect a wide range of claims, both of a proprietary and non-proprietary nature. As illustrated by *Pascoe*, the extent of the court discretion is such that one cannot know in advance what the remedy will be. Accordingly, we cannot say that it is a licence (or fee simple or whatever else is represented) that binds a purchaser: nobody knows what remedy the court will order. Instead, we have to say that it is the estoppel claim – the right to go to court and seek a remedy – that binds the purchaser.

Yet that analysis is also open to criticism. To describe an estoppel claim as a proprietary right is rather like saying a contract is a proprietary right. The latter is patently not the case. A contract for a legal estate is proprietary (an estate contract), but not a contract for a licence. The estoppel suffers from the further problem that the uncertainty as to the remedy may be thought to make it even less suitable for proprietary status than are contracts. It is all very puzzling.

Against that background, the Law Commission set out to clarify the law. Their intention was to confirm that inchoate estoppels do bind purchasers and that this does not apply to the licence ordered as a remedy.[19] Accordingly, section 116 of the Land Registration Act 2002 declares that 'an equity by estoppel . . . has effect from the time the equity arises as an interest capable of binding successors in title'. This seems to settle the question for the future, at least for registered titles (around 95 per cent of titles).

Nevertheless, McFarlane[20] has argued that we should not distinguish between inchoate equities and those where a remedy has been granted. He argues that estoppel licences should never affect successors in title; the same would be true of other non-proprietary remedies such as payment of money. There is something to be said for this view, especially as it mirrors the approach we take for contracts. On the other hand, it fails to recognise the extent of the discretion exercised by the courts in estoppel claims. In practice, the court would be put in an almost impossibly difficult position in deciding what remedy to give. If it is thought that a purchaser deserves to be bound, how could a court fail to be influenced by the knowledge that this could be achieved only by granting a proprietary remedy? In any event, it is almost impossible to square with the wording of section 116 and flies in the face of what the section was intended to achieve.

---

[19] Law Com No 271, paras 5.4, 5.29–31.
[20] [2003] CLJ 661.

Relationship with contractual licences

We have seen that estoppel licences probably bind purchasers, though only before the court gives a remedy. How can we justify the contrast with contractual licences, which do not bind purchasers?

The question is especially difficult because the dividing line between contract and estoppel can be a very fine one. If the licensor and licensee agree that the licensee shall do something (put a house in good repair, for example), this will constitute consideration and give rise to a contractual licence. If the licensee does such acts without being asked, then there will be an estoppel licence. How can it make sense for only the second example to bind a purchaser? It should be remembered, however, that contractual consideration does not always constitute detriment for estoppel. Thus a promise to do something is consideration, but not detriment for estoppel. For estoppel, the act has actually to be done.

Probably the best way of justifying a distinction is to stress the estoppel rather than the licence. Estoppel claims include proprietary as well as non-proprietary interests; at the inchoate stage we cannot be sure what remedy may be given. This is true even where a licence is promised: the court might decide that a short lease is the most appropriate remedy. Accordingly, it is not really the case that we are enforcing estoppel licences. Rather, we are enforcing estoppels in situations in which a licence *might* be awarded. Further, it may be argued that the discretion in the remedy enhances the case for proprietary status, despite the uncertainty it involves. Where there is a contractual licence, we fear that the parties could establish novel and very varied proprietary interests over which the court has no control. This is less of a problem with estoppel licences, as the court can simply decline to give the remedy claimed. The court's control over the remedy means that there is less risk of the range of proprietary interests spiralling out of control.

A rather different point concerns the overlap between contractual and estoppel licences, an area little touched upon in the cases.

> Robin contracts with Susan that she can live in a house until she finds a job, paying £20 a week. This is a contractual licence. Susan spends £1,000 in improving the house on the basis of her being likely to live there for some time. This would seem a fairly clear case of estoppel, even though it originates out of a contractual situation. It would be important if Robin were later to mortgage the house to Tara, who claims not to be bound by the licence.
>
> Would it make any difference if the agreement between Robin and Susan specified the repairs as being the consideration (instead of paying £20 a week)? Would the carrying out of repairs convert this contractual licence into an estoppel binding on successors in title? Here the detriment is the same as the contractual consideration.

The question just raised is an important one, as many contractual licences might be made binding on this basis. An overlap seems to be accepted by the Court of Appeal in *Ashburn Anstalt*. They observed that the contractual licence in *Errington* might have been properly enforceable against the successor in title by way of estoppel.

The discretionary nature of the remedy in estoppel has a further effect. In many cases, the consideration/detriment may be of a continuing nature. Relative to the benefit received by the licensee (occupation) it will be small; no estoppel remedy will be appropriate. This payment by Susan of £20 per week might possibly be detriment, but at most it would justify one week's occupation.

We may conclude that there are ways in which the contrast in the proprietary effects of estoppel and contractual licences can be justified. However, the outcomes for the types of licences do provide some inconsistency and it may be thought that the law is unlikely to remain in its present state.

Questions to consider

1. What is a licence?

2. Why are the courts reluctant to allow a contractual licence to bind purchasers?

3. What is the role of licences in estoppel claims? Is it ever justifiable to allow an estoppel licence to bind a purchaser?

4. Is a constructive trust anything more than a method to allow a purchaser to be bound by a licence whenever a court wishes that result to follow?

Further reading

Battersby, G [1991] Conv 36: Contractual and estoppel licences as proprietary interests in land.

Baughen, S (1994) 14 LS 147: Estoppels over land and third parties: an open question?

Briggs, A [1983] Conv 285: Contractual licences: a reply.

Evershed, Sir Raymond (1954) 70 LQR 326: Reflections on the fusion of law and equity after 75 years.

McFarlane, B [2003] CLJ 661: Proprietary estoppel and third parties after the Land Registration Act 2002.

Visit **www.mylawchamber.co.uk** to access tools to help you develop and test your knowledge of land law, including interactive multiple choice questions, practice exam questions with guidance, weblinks, glossary flashcards, legal newsfeed and legal updates.

16 Easements

Nature and importance

We will now consider **easements** and **profits**. Both these interests involve limited rights over another person's land: the most obvious example is a right of way. If my land is next to a road, then access is not a problem. However, sometimes there is other land between my land and the road. A right of way is then essential – it will provide the necessary access to my land and be unaffected by sale of the land over which it is exercised. Unlike estates, easements and profits confer no general right to enjoy land – they are rights exercised over somebody else's land.

Easements can be as varied as rights of way, rights to pass water through pipes, rights to store and rights to use a garden. A particular feature of easements is that they can exist only if other land is benefited. This is obviously the case for the right of way described above – the access benefits my land. Other situations may fall foul of the requirement.

> As I want to be able to park my car near the office where I work, I agree with the owner of nearby land that I can park my car there. The right to park cars can constitute an easement. However, unless I own the office where I work, there will be no benefited land and my right can exist only as a contractual licence (not proprietary in nature).

Profits can be more invasive: they give a right to take something from the land. They cover rights as diverse as grazing rights and rights to fish. Like easements, they can exist for the benefit of other land (profits *appurtenant*). Unlike easements, however, they may also benefit a person personally (profits *in gross*). A right to fish, for example, need not involve any benefited land. It might be thought that profits in gross are much more beneficial, especially as the use is not limited to the needs of the land. However, it can be more difficult to create profits in gross and their benefit has to be transferred expressly. If the holder of a profit in gross does in fact own adjoining land and sells that land, the benefit passes to the purchaser only if the profit is expressly assigned. In contrast, profits appurtenant will pass automatically to a new owner of the benefited land.

Why do we require benefited land for easements, but not for profits? With profits, it may be said that we are dividing ownership by content (A has fishing rights, while B has the remaining general ownership rights) rather than by time. Dividing by time is the role of freehold estates and leases.

In theory, the same could be argued as regards easements. However, rights to use another's land are most commonly encountered in the context of two adjoining land-owners. Where there is no benefited land, the use right may be regarded as insufficiently important to be worth elevating to proprietary status. We have seen that English law recognises a limited range of proprietary interests. The objective is to provide a balance between the benefits of flexibility on one side and the need not to overburden land with ill-defined rights on the other. The easement and profit rules illustrate how that balance is currently worked out.

A legal system which did not recognise easements would be seriously defective. Efficient land management often requires the landowner to have rights over another person's land. Without a right of way or contractually negotiated access, land-locked plots of land would be useless unless the owner has a helicopter! Especially in a crowded urban environment, I may need to have a right to run drains under a neighbour's land to a sewer or a right to run pipes or cables across a neighbour's land. With all these examples, it would not be enough to have merely a contractual right. If the burdened land were sold, then the new owner would not be bound. Not every easement is as critical to land management, but the category clearly deserves its proprietary status. Evidence of their longstanding importance is that easements were recognised by Roman Law (called *praedial servitudes*).

Profits are, perhaps, less essential. Though some are very useful to benefited land (grazing can be very important in a rural economy), it may be thought that land management could be efficiently carried out without most profits. Nevertheless, it has been observed that they permit a useful functional division of land ownership. They are long-established rights and appear to cause relatively few problems.

This chapter concentrates upon two major areas: what can be an easement or profit and how they are created. One topic from each area is considered as a Critical Issue. The first is when easement claims fail because they are too close to a claim to possession. The second is as to when easements can be implied on the sale of land. A particular feature of easements is that the courts have developed generous implication rules. It may be added that easements were reviewed by the Law Commission in a report published in 2011.[1] Although the Law Commission reviews most of the issues considered in this chapter, the most significant reforms are likely to be in the area of creation of easements.

What can be an easement or profit?

Profits have given rise to few problems: standard examples include rights to graze animals and to fish. Easements cover a wider range of possible rights and have caused greater difficulty; the rest of this section is devoted to easements. Much of what follows makes most sense when we remember two related factors. First, we have to distinguish

[1] Law Com No 327.

rights that benefit individuals from rights that benefit land – a consequence of requiring benefited land. Second, easements are to be contrasted with ownership (or leases). If the rights in question are most accurately considered as ownership, then an easement is not appropriate. Quite different rules apply to easements and ownership. For example, easements (unlike ownership) are frequently implied.

General requirements

The requirements for easements are commonly treated as having been laid down by Evershed MR in *Re Ellenborough Park*:[2] (19.1.2)

> (1) there must be a dominant and a servient tenement: (2) an easement must 'accommodate' the dominant tenement: (3) dominant and servient owners must be different persons, and (4) a right over land cannot amount to an easement, unless it is capable of forming the subject-matter of a grant.

The first requirement establishes the need, already mentioned, for there to be benefited ('dominant') land. The second requirement stresses that there must be benefit for the dominant land, not merely a benefit for the owner of it.

> Mary owns a large open space in Manchester. Manchester United wish to purchase this as a training ground. As part of the deal, Mary negotiates for her house close to Old Trafford (the club's main ground) to have a free right of entry for two persons for every match at Old Trafford. Doubtless this would be a very valuable right: the value of the house would be increased substantially. However, it cannot be said to accommodate the house: it doesn't make it a better or more useful house. The benefit is purely for the owner of the house and it is not an easement.

Does this second requirement cause problems for rights that benefit businesses on the dominant land? No – the law has never taken such a restrictive approach. It is very clear that rights which we recognise as easements – a right of way is the best example – can operate in a business setting. Thus there can be a right of way to allow access by hotel guests. More interesting is the recognition in *Moody v Steggles*[3] (Extract 19.1.4) of a right to have an advertising sign for a public house. Unlike a right of way, the very essence of an advertisement relates to business. The public house in *Moody* was set back from the road; the sign was affixed to an adjoining house. The sign should be reasonably close to the benefited land: advertising a hotel five miles away would not suffice. *Moody* illustrates the ability of the law to develop new examples of easements, provided that they comply with underlying easement principles.

A well-known case on the other side of the line is *Hill v Tupper*[4] (Extract 19.1.3), in which the claimant owned a small area of land next to a canal. He claimed an easement to put

---

[2] [1956] Ch 131 at p. 163.
[3] (1879) 12 Ch D 261. Remember that, as with all the examples in this section, the parties must have created the easement.
[4] (1863) 2 H&C 121 (159 ER 151).

boats on the canal. In this case the putting of boats on the canal was the business; it was too commercial a claim to be recognised as an easement. By contrast, if the claimant had owned a hotel next to the canal then a right to put boats on the canal would have been beneficial to the hotel. Another aspect of the claim in *Hill v Tupper* merits attention. The claimant sought to stop others from putting boats on the canal. An easement is a right to do something, not a right to prevent exploitation of the land by others – at least where the right is compatible with use by others.

Returning to the *Re Ellenborough Park* requirements, the third requires the two plots of land to have separate owners: one cannot have an easement over one's own land. However, the requirement is not quite as strict as it might appear. A tenant can have an easement over the landlord's adjoining land, though both plots are owned by the land-lord. Separate ownership is not insisted upon so long as different persons have estates in the two plots.

What of the fourth requirement, 'capable of forming the subject-matter of a grant'? This sounds like a circular proposition: a right is an easement if it is recognised as an easement. The cases show that very many rights have been recognised – rights as varied as putting up a clothes-line, storing items, allowing projections over the burdened land and use of a toilet. Furthermore, *Moody v Steggles* illustrates that there is no rule that novel rights are not permitted. The fourth requirement was discussed in *Re Ellenborough Park* in the context of a claim to use a communal garden. It had been thought that a right to wander around another's land (the *ius spatiendi*) could not be an easement. The Court of Appeal, however, upheld the claim. Although claims to a view, to privacy and to a natural flow of air have been held too uncertain to be easements, the right to use the garden was defined with sufficient certainty. Especially significant is that houses commonly have gardens. The right provided the house, therefore, with an attribute associated with houses. This made it more than a simple claim to recreation or amusement. Could a right to use a neighbour's hot tub be an easement? This probably falls on the other side of the line – it looks more like a personal benefit.

Additional requirements

Three further requirements are commonly added to those stated by Evershed MR.

No claim to possession

If the claim is, in essence, to exclusive possession of the land, then it cannot be an easement. It is more appropriate that it should be a fee simple, life interest or lease.

The seminal case is *Copeland v Greenhalf*[5] (Extract 19.1.8). The defendant had a business as a wheelwright. He used part of the plaintiff's land (a strip 150 feet long and between 15 and 35 feet wide) to store lorries and other vehicles awaiting repair. Upjohn J held that a prescription claim must fail:

> This claim . . . really amounts to a claim to a joint user of the land by the defendant. Practically, the defendant is claiming the whole beneficial user of the strip of land on the

[5] [1952] Ch 488.

south-east side of the track there; he can leave as many or as few lorries there as he likes for as long as he likes . . . In my judgment, that is not a claim which can be established as an easement.

It is interesting that Upjohn J recognised that the adverse possession rules would have to be satisfied before the claim could be made good, showing that it was really a claim to the fee simple.

The clarity of this analysis is clouded by three factors. The first is that very many easements give use of the land to the claimant for a limited time. Even the exercise of a right of way means that the servient owner cannot use the land at the same time. Plainly, this causes us no difficulty. Other rights seem more intrusive, but still they are recognised. One example is the right to use a lavatory in an office block in *Miller v Emcer Products Ltd*[6] (Extract 19.1.9). This right involves short-term use. Other rights may involve longer, but less frequent, use. A good example is *Ward v Kirkland*.[7] (19.1.10) A cottage was built close to a boundary, so that maintenance of one wall required access from the adjoining servient land. Could there be an easement to use the servient land for such access? Ungoed-Thomas J observed that access would be no more frequent than monthly (for window-cleaning) and had no hesitation in holding that this could be an easement. Occasionally, more extensive maintenance might involve ladders or scaffolding for days or weeks.

The second factor is that rights to store have long been recognised as easements, even though the nature of a right to store appears to be little different from the right rejected in *Copeland*. This right has been recognised at least since the 1915 decision of the Privy Council in *Att-Gen of Southern Nigeria v John Holt & Co (Liverpool) Ltd*.[8] This decision was discussed in *Copeland v Greenhalf* (Extract 19.1.8) and apparently distinguished on the basis that *Copeland* was a claim to unrestricted use of the land in question.

Suppose the owner of a pub has a right to store beer barrels in an adjoining building (the servient land). A right to use a room *exclusively* for storing beer barrels might face problems in qualifying as an easement. On the other hand, the law would readily accept a right to store beer barrels in a room which the servient owner also used for other purposes.

The third factor is that some cases, including some of the most recent ones, have adopted a much more generous approach. A well-known early example is *Wright v Macadam*,[9] which recognised an easement to store coal in a coal shed. It is a difficult case for two reasons. First, it is not clear whether the coal shed was used exclusively for storage of the claimant's coal. Second, the court made no mention of exclusive possession – it seems to be treated as a straightforward case of storage. The problems are compounded because *Wright* was not cited in *Copeland*.

Of great importance is the recent House of Lords decision in *Moncrieff v Jamieson*[10] (Extract 19.1.11). This involved a right that has featured in several recent cases: a right to

---

[6] [1956] Ch 304.
[7] [1967] Ch 194.
[8] [1915] AC 599.
[9] [1949] 2 KB 744.
[10] [2007] 1 WLR 2620.

park cars. The first full analysis of parking was that of Judge Paul Baker QC in **London & Blenheim Estates Ltd v Ladbroke Retail Parks Ltd**.[11] The case involved a claim to park cars in a private car park for shops and businesses. The judge held that this could be an easement, as it could not be said to leave the servient owner without any reasonable use for the land. It might be noted that there was no right to park in a specific space: it was a right to use car parking facilities so long as there were spaces available.

The recognition of car parking on the facts of **London & Blenheim** looks entirely justifiable. There was no claim to exclusive possession over any specific area and the right looks very much like that recognised in **Att-Gen of Southern Nigeria**. The same might be true if there is a right to park in a single space if it happens to be free. What is more difficult is a claim to park in a garage or a single parking space, where this precludes the servient owner's parking there.

Moncrieff involved a non-exclusive right to park and it is not surprising that such a right was recognised as capable of being an easement. However, Lord Scott proceeded to criticise some of the earlier cases. It is difficult to assess the significance of his dicta, given that they are obiter dicta in a Scottish case. Lord Neuberger indicated general approval, but was not prepared to express a final view on an issue that had not been argued. The other judges do not address the question.

There are, perhaps, two central points in Lord Scott's analysis. First, in **London & Blenheim** Paul Baker QC argued that the contrast between **Wright** and **Copeland** turned on a matter of degree: 'A small coal shed in a large property is one thing. The exclusive use of a large part of the alleged servient tenement is another.' This argument is full of problems. In particular, what happens if a large part of the servient land (not including the area over which the right is exercised) is sold off? Does the easement suddenly cease to qualify because it is now exercised over a 'large part' of what is left? The matter of degree test is rejected by Lord Scott, who stresses that the relevant land is that over which the right is exercised (the coal shed, for example). Other recent cases adopt a similar view and Lord Scott's analysis seems well justified.

The second point is more controversial. The Court of Appeal in **Batchelor v Marlow**[12] considered the defendant's claim to park vehicles during the day on a strip of land owned by the plaintiff. The court asked the question: 'Would the plaintiff have any reasonable use of the land for parking?' and had no hesitation in rejecting the defendant's claim. Lord Scott considered this to be the wrong test. So long as the servient owner is not excluded from the land, the parties are free to create easements involving very extensive rights. Indeed, Lord Scott expressed some doubts about the result in **Copeland**, though he approved the reasoning.

One attraction of Lord Scott's analysis is that claims will be either to an estate or to an easement; there is little or no gap between them into which claims such as that in **Batchelor** might fall. Lord Scott stresses that even if the factual exercise of the right excludes the occupier, this does not matter. Thus in **Wright**, it would not matter that the coal completely filled the shed – the owner could use the shed, as and when space was

---

[11] [1992] 1 WLR 1278; not considered on appeal [1994] 1 WLR 31.
[12] [2003] 1 WLR 764. A similar test had been applied in *London & Blenheim*.

available. Nor would it matter that the right gave the sole right to store coal: the owner could use the shed for other purposes. Returning to car parking in a garage, the owner can still use the sides or roof area of the garage for his own purposes. It appears that the only type of claim which is likely to fail is where the owner is excluded – perhaps because the claimant possesses all the keys to the shed or garage (possessing the single key might not be enough to show exclusion of the owner, who might be intended to use it when unlocked).

It is not easy to know how to conclude, given that the views in *Moncrieff* are those of a single judge on an issue that was not argued. Subsequent cases[13] have held that *Batchelor* remains binding authority. However, it has been applied so as to be consistent with the more generous recognition of easements urged by Lord Scott. Thus in *Kettel* v *Bloomfold Ltd*[14] a right to use a specific car parking space was recognised – the owner could lay pipes under it, build over the top of it or use it if there weren't a car parked there at the time. All this is very sensible, but is not easy to reconcile with the facts of *Batchelor* (or, indeed, those in *Copeland*).

It is interesting that the Law Commission also advocates a wider view of easements. Although a claim to exclusive possession cannot be an easement (it looks like an estate), it recommends the abolition of the *Batchelor* requirement that the servient owner must retain reasonable use.

The right normally must confer positive rights

We regard easements as rights to do something on a neighbour's land, rather than rights to stop a neighbour from doing something. The latter type of right is recognised only as a restrictive covenant. Without this requirement, easements and restrictive covenants would overlap. The reasons for having separate categories are discussed in Chapter 17. Suffice to say now that they share the characteristic that land is benefited by a right over neighbouring land.

The leading case on the requirement is *Phipps* v *Pears*[15] (Extract 19.1.7). Two houses had been built close together, so that each sheltered the other from wind and rain penetration. The owner of one claimed a right to stop the neighbour from pulling down a wall so as to open the claimant's wall to the elements. This was held not to be an easement. Lord Denning MR explained that recognising such an easement 'would unduly restrict your neighbour in his enjoyment of his own land [and] hamper legitimate develop-ment'. A restrictive covenant might be thought to carry some of the same risks, but restrictive covenants have to be expressly created – in *Phipps*, the claim was to an implied easement.

Restrictive covenants have been recognised as proprietary interests only since the mid-nineteenth century. Before that time, some negative easements had been recognised. The right to light is phrased in positive language, but the substance of the right is to prevent a neighbour from building so as to block the light. The right to light is well

---

[13] *Polo Woods Foundation* v *Shelton-Agar* [2010] 1 All ER 539 at [121]; *Kettel v Bloomfold Ltd* [2012] L & TR 514 at [12].

[14] [2012] L & TR 514.

[15] [1965] 1 QB 76.

established, though it is somewhat anomalous and subject to the criticism that it may hamper legitimate development.

The easement of support has also been viewed as negative. It has some positive content in that the claimant's land is pressing on the burdened land. However, its essence is that it prevents a neighbour from withdrawing support, where such withdrawal would cause the collapse of the claimant's land or buildings. Its effect is to restrict excavations close to the boundary with the claimant's land.

Rights to light and support have caused difficulty for **prescription**: the principle (considered later in this chapter) whereby easements can be acquired by long use. A particular difficulty is that prescription is generally thought to be based on acquiescence: the owner of the burdened land acquiesces in the use made of it. *Dalton v Angus & Co*[16] involved a prescription claim to a right of support. How can there be said to be acquiescence when there is no practical way not to accept the pressing on the land (support)? Nevertheless, the House of Lords recognised prescription of rights to support. Similarly, the owner of the burdened land cannot stop the exercise of rights to light, save by putting up hoardings to block light. Such extreme and anti-social activity has been rendered unnecessary by legislation[17] whereby registering a notice stops time running (20 years' use is required for prescription). It applies only to rights of light.

What should we make of negative easements today? Though there are good reasons for treating negative rights as restrictive covenants,[18] the distinction between positive and negative rights is not easily drawn. The fact that some negative easements are recognised makes it virtually impossible to bring coherence to the area. This is reflected in the Law Commission's untidy compromise that express negative rights should operate as covenants ('land obligations') and implied/prescriptive negative rights as easements.

No positive obligation on the servient owner

We can now turn to the third additional requirement for easements. Although an easement must normally be positive in the sense that it must enable the holder to do something, it cannot be positive in the sense of requiring the owner of the burdened land to do anything. There is a semantic trap here in the dual use of the word 'positive'. Positive *rights* are recognised (indeed, usually required); positive *obligations* are not. This requirement mirrors the principle that positive covenants are not proprietary.[19] There is an exception for easements to fence.[20] This is anomalous, but it provides useful certainty (especially for farmers) as to who is responsible for the maintenance of fences.

Usually, it will be clear when a right is positive – the test is whether the right requires any form of activity or expenditure. However, suppose that there is a right to a supply of water or electricity. Water and electricity can flow through pipes and cables without the servient owner having to do anything. However, their use by the benefited land owner may result in the burdened land owner, through whose meter they flow, having to pay

---

[16] (1881) 6 App Cas 740.
[17] Rights of Light Act 1959.
[18] Discussed in the next chapter (pp. 291–2, Chapter 17).
[19] Confirmed by the House of Lords in *Rhone* v *Stephens* [1994] 2 AC 310 (Extract 20.2.2); see below (pp. 278, 287–9).
[20] *Crow* v *Wood* [1971] 1 QB 77; the Law Commission recommends abolition of this exception.

the water or electricity supplier. In **Rance v Elvin**[21] (Extract 19.1.6), the Court of Appeal accepted the right to water as an easement, characterising it as an obligation not to interfere with the flow of water. Even though the servient owner may have to pay the water supplier, no obligation is owed to the benefited land to pay. If payment is not made and the supply is cut off as a result, the holder of the easement cannot object. In practice, there will usually be a single supply for both the benefited and burdened plots; the burdened owner will have no choice but to pay in order to continue to have a water supply. However, there is a right to recoup the cost from the owner of the benefited land. The result is convenient, even if it stretches the principles a little.

It is not clear how far the **Rance** principle extends. Recently, Lord Scott stated[22] that the right to use a swimming pool might fail because of the expenditure required to maintain the pool. The possibility of using a **Rance** analysis (a right so long as the pool was usable) was not explored.

Creation of easements

Nothing need be said regarding express creation, save that registration is required for legal status (for registered titles).

Implied easements

CRITICAL ISSUE

Easements and profits are readily implied when land is sold. Even though both contract and conveyance may be silent, it is quite possible that a purchaser will acquire, for example, a right of way over the seller's adjoining land. One reason for having generous implication rules is that easements can be very beneficial rights, being much more valuable to the benefited land than harmful to the servient land. This means that it is economically beneficial to recognise easements. Nevertheless, some easements can seriously restrict the use of the burdened land and many (including the Law Commission) argue that the law has gone too far in implying easements.

Easements are implied when the seller (or lessor) of one plot owns an adjoining plot. Almost always, the claimed right is being exercised before that sale. This use might be by the seller, the buyer (typically as tenant of the plot sold) or a third party (often an earlier tenant of the plot sold). We call the right a *quasi-easement* – it is not a true easement but a use which looks rather like an easement. If exercised by the seller it cannot be an easement because one cannot have an easement over one's own land. If it is exercised by the buyer or a tenant, this will normally be by simple permission (licence).

Where the implication rules apply, the easement is implied into the transfer or lease. Because the easement is implied into a deed, it can exist as a legal interest. Furthermore, it is usually an overriding interest and exempted from registration requirements.[23] More

---

[21] (1985) 50 P&CR 9; applied to electricity in *Duffy v Lamb* (1997) 75 P&CR 364.
[22] *Moncrieff v Jamieson* [2007] 1 WLR 2620 at [47] (Extract 19.1.11).
[23] See above (p. 132).

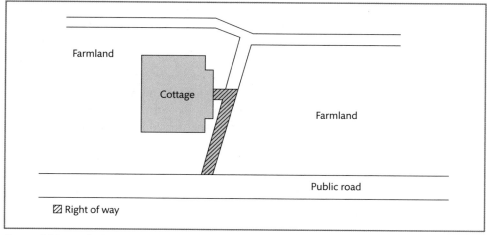

Figure 16.1 Hayley's right of way to her cottage: an easement

rarely, an easement may be implied into a contract for a transfer or lease – that will not of course create a legal easement.

Figure 16.1 is an illustration of an easement already encountered in Chapter 1. Suppose the farmer had built the cottage for himself and has been living in it. His access over the shaded track constitutes a quasi-easement (right of way). If the farmer sells the cottage, it is very likely that an easement for the purchaser to use the track will be implied into the transfer.

The difference between grant and reservation

A crucial point to grasp is that easements are much more readily implied as grants than as reservations. In this section, we consider what is meant by grants and reservations and the reasons for distinguishing them. The implication rules for each of reservations and grants are considered in the following sections.

As explained above, the context for implication involves a person (the grantor) who sells land and retains other land in the vicinity. When we refer to implied grants, we are dealing with grants by the seller in favour of the purchaser or lessee (the grantee). The seller is granting an easement that will burden his or her retained land. Reservation operates when a right is implied in favour of the seller: this burdens the land being sold.

Although this distinction between grant and reservation is clear, how does it apply to multiple sales?

> Chloe transfers part of her land to Davina and then another part to Emily. It is easy to say that both Davina and Emily can take advantage of implied grant rules to claim rights over any other land retained by Chloe, but can they claim rights by implied grant over each other's land? So far as Davina is concerned, the clear answer is yes: the land later sold to Emily had already been burdened by an implied grant in Davina's favour. However, it

appears that Emily cannot claim an easement over Davina's land. It follows from first principles that the sale from Chloe to Emily cannot create new rights over Davina's land: nobody can create rights over a neighbour's land. For Emily to have an easement, it should have been reserved when Chloe sold to Davina. Then the benefit of an existing easement would pass to Emily.

This is the conclusion when there are entirely separate sales to Davina and Emily. However, if the sales are at the same time – the most obvious example is at the same auction – then each sale is treated as coming first. This means that each can take advantage of the more generous implied grant rules. Both Davina and Emily can claim rights by implied grant over the other's land.

The very sensible approach just described has been applied for many years. However, it is not enough that the sales are close together. In *Wheeldon v Burrows*[24] (Extracts 19.2.6, 19.2.1), one of the properties failed to sell at auction and was sold some four weeks later. This was held to be outside the contemporaneous sales rule. Auctions feature in nearly all the cases, but the rule probably applies to properties that are marketed together, even though sales may be agreed a few days or weeks apart.

Why is the law more favourable to buyers (grantees) than sellers (reservation)? A general principle (not limited to easements) is that a grantor is not allowed to derogate from a grant.[25] This means that the grantor must respect what the grantee expects to receive from the deed. It is based upon the perception that the grantor generally determines the scope of the grant and is well able to insert necessary terms for his or her protection. Accordingly the court favours the grantee, who is perceived to be in a relatively weak position and less able to appreciate what rights might be required by the land purchased. Derogation from grant underpins the *Wheeldon v Burrows* rules on implied easements, to be discussed shortly.

Easements are also implied by section 62 of the Law of Property Act 1925 (LPA) (Extract 19.2.11). This is usually the more generous form of implication. Its wording makes it applicable to grants but not to reservations. It is a word-saving provision, designed to put in statutory form words that were almost invariably found in nineteenth-century conveyances. In other words, the idea is that easements are implied when experience shows that sellers and buyers want them. Word-saving provisions render it unnecessary to insert lengthy standard terms into every conveyance.

An obvious danger is that perceptions and practice may change, so that section 62 might not represent current intentions. In that case, parties will exclude it; conveyances will be lengthened rather than shortened. Does section 62 reflect current views? These are probably best evidenced by the modern form of contract for the sale of land, in which standard terms have been refined through frequent updating. The current contract[26] has only a minor effect on the grants implied by section 62. More importantly, it broadens

---

[24] (1879) 12 Ch D 31.
[25] Discussed in the leases context, above (p. 212).
[26] *Standard Conditions of Sale* (4th edn), 2003.

reservation so that it operates as widely as implied grants. This shows that limiting section 62 to implied grants no longer fits what the parties usually want.

Implied reservation

Implied reservation (in favour of the seller or landlord) is quite rare. *Wheeldon v Burrows*[27] established that it operates only when an easement is necessary for the land to be used, rejecting suggestions of a more liberal regime. *Nickerson v Barraclough*[28] (Extract 19.2.3) holds that the implication is based on the intentions of the parties, rather than policy. It follows that the parties are free to exclude it, though this would be unusual.

Necessity has been restricted to rights of access. The presence of an alternative means of access, however inconvenient, will be fatal to a claim for necessity. The only exception is helicopter access – the rules were developed long before helicopters became common! So long as land can be reached, the courts do not treat other rights, however beneficial to its use, as being necessary. This was illustrated by *Union Lighterage Co v London Graving Dock Co*[29] (Extract 19.2.4), in which a dock required tie rods on the grantee's land to secure its sides. This was held to fail the necessity test. Stirling LJ limited the category to 'an easement without which the property retained cannot be used at all, and not merely necessary to the reasonable enjoyment of that property'.

Sometimes a more generous approach is taken. If a particular use of the land is shown to be intended by the transaction, then an easement will be implied if it is necessary to give effect to that intention. Here, it should be noted, the necessity relates to fulfilling the intended use. High authority is found in *Pwllbach Colliery Co Ltd v Woodman*,[30] where Lord Parker said: 'The law will readily imply the grant or reservation of such easements as may be necessary to give effect to the common intention of the parties to a grant of real property, with reference to the manner or purposes in and for which the land granted or some land retained by the grantor is to be used.'

As these dicta indicate, this applies to both reservations and grants. Most of the best examples of it are grants. *Wong v Beaumont*[31] (Extract 19.2.5) involved the lease of land for use as a restaurant. The tenant was held to have a right to attach ventilation ducting to the landlord's retained land: this was essential for lawful use of the restaurant.

Few cases of reservation on the *Pwllbach* basis can be found, though *Lyttleton Times Co Ltd v Warners Ltd*[32] provides a good example. When a building was rebuilt as a printing house, the landlord agreed to lease part of it to the claimants for use as a hotel. It was held that the landlord was entitled to make the amount of noise inevitable for printing houses, even though it would otherwise have constituted a nuisance.

However, it is unusual for the facts to support such a reservation. In particular, the fact that rights are currently and openly being exercised by the seller or landlord will be quite insufficient to attract the rule. Thus in *Re Webb's Lease*[33] the landlord had

[27] (1879) 12 Ch D 31.
[28] [1981] Ch 426.
[29] [1902] 2 Ch 557 at p. 573.
[30] [1915] AC 634 at pp. 646–7.
[31] [1965] 1 QB 173.
[32] [1907] AC 476 (PC).
[33] [1951] Ch 808.

advertisements on a wall of the leased premises. Despite this open exercise of the 'right' before the lease, the Court of Appeal refused to find an implied reservation. It was, of course, difficult to assert that the advertisements were necessary for the landlord's use of the retained land. Further, there was no 'definite and particular manner' of use of the land as required by Lord Parker in *Pwllbach*. This is a very tough rule and there is something to be said for the contrary view of Danckwerts J at first instance in *Re Webb's Lease* that the parties really intended the landlord to be able to maintain the advertisements.

Implied grant

In cases of necessity, grants as well as reservations are readily found. However, implied grants operate in a much wider range of circumstances. These implications are based upon two grounds. The first is the common law proposition that a grantor shall not derogate from his grant. This is the rule in *Wheeldon v Burrows*.[34] The second is the 'general words' implied by statute (LPA, section 62) into virtually every transfer. It is wider in its application and we shall start with it.

The general words: LPA section 62

The overall purpose of section 62 is to include words into conveyances in order to define exactly what was sold – it isn't limited to easements. It reads:

> A conveyance of land shall be deemed to include and shall by virtue of this Act operate to convey, with the land, all buildings, erections, fixtures, commons, hedges, ditches, fences, ways, waters, watercourses, liberties, privileges, easements, rights, and advantages whatsoever, appertaining or reputed to appertain to the land . . .

As mentioned above, this wording means that section 62 operates in favour of the grantee: it does not permit implied reservation. It may be added that 'conveyance' includes transfers of registered land and leases.

It is quite clear (and unremarkable) that the benefit of existing easements passes to the purchaser. Much more interesting, however, is the impact of the words 'reputed to appertain'.

Andrew is a tenant of a house owned by Brenda and is allowed to use a secondary access over her adjoining land to the rear of his house. If Andrew (or somebody different) later buys the house, an easement of secondary access can be said to be 'reputed to appertain' to the house – Andrew's actions make it look as if there is an easement. The result is that an easement may be created by section 62.

It is a remarkable effect of the section that it converts the mere permission (or licence) originally held by Andrew into a permanent easement. This effect of section 62 has been firmly established ever since the judgment of Farwell J in *International Tea Stores Co v Hobbs*[35] (Extract 19.2.12) (the facts were similar to the example involving Andrew).

---

[34] (1879) 12 Ch D 31.
[35] [1903] 2 Ch 165, supported by earlier authorities.

The effect of the section is very wide indeed. It has been applied to rights as varied as rights of way, rights to use a coal shed and rights to access for property maintenance. We will consider several points on the operation of the section.

Nature of the right

It is obvious that the right must be a recognised form of easement. However, the point to stress is that not just the right claimed, but also the right as exercised before the conveyance must possess the characteristics of an easement. This is well illustrated by *Green v Ashco Horticulturist Ltd*[36] (Extracts 19.2.13, 19.2.15), in which the claimant had requested permission each time an access route was used. Although what was claimed – a right of way – was plainly capable of being an easement, the facts were not such that an easement was 'reputed to appertain'. A right to use an access route only when the servient owner agrees does not look like an easement. It is not a problem that the servient owner has given permission for a continuing use; what is fatal is getting permission each time the use occurs.

The nature of the permission and the user

Giving permission for a limited period excludes section 62. In *Goldberg v Edwards*[37] (Extract 19.2.14), a landlord gave permission to use an access route through the servient land. The Court of Appeal considered that the crucial question was whether the permission was given so long as the servient land was owned by the landlord. Though *International Tea Stores* shows that a permission granted indefinitely, in the knowledge that it can be withdrawn at any time, leads to the operation of section 62, a permission given for a particular period does not attract section 62. It is not a distinction that makes obvious sense!

Section 62 operates whether the prior exercise of rights is by the purchaser or by a third party (typically a previous tenant). How does *Goldberg* operate if the limited permission has been given to such a third party? Perhaps a purchaser who is unaware of that limit should be able to assume that the exercised rights will continue. On the other hand, a purchaser who is aware that a right is intended to last only as long as the permission continues has a less meritorious claim. However, this distinction is quite difficult to extract from the words 'reputed to appertain'. There is no authority on the point.

Must the use of the land be obvious to a purchaser? Cases such as *International Tea Stores* and *Goldberg* show that there is no need for the layout of the premises to indicate that a right of way exists. However, an easement which is not obvious from the layout will not be reputed to appertain to the land if it is exercised covertly or extremely rarely. This was discussed as regards a right of access for maintenance in *Ward v Kirkland*[38] (Extracts 19.1.10, 19.2.8). The problem was that a wall of a cottage was on the boundary with the servient land; it could be reached (for window cleaning and other exterior maintenance) only from the servient land. Ungoed-Thomas J accepted that intermittent and non-apparent rights would not qualify. However, section 62 applied on the facts because it was obvious from looking at the premises that access was essential.

[36] [1966] 1 WLR 889.
[37] [1950] Ch 247.
[38] [1967] Ch 194; above (p. 257).

The use of the land need not continue right up until the grant. Many cases involve use by tenants. Suppose the tenant leaves (so that the use ceases) and the land is then sold. It would be overly technical for section 62 not to apply in such cases and Cross J in *Green* held it applicable so long as there is a 'pattern of regular user'. One would expect the result to be different if the use had ended because the grantor had prohibited it.

Diversity of occupation

For section 62 to apply, the benefited and servient plots must normally be occupied by different persons (diversity of occupation). The fact that an owner of two plots of land walks over one of them as an alternative access to the other is not really indicative of there being an easement – it is the simple act of walking over one's own land! Although section 62 does not explicitly establish the rule, it seems correct to assert that no right is 'reputed to appertain'. The rule dates back to *Long v Gowlett*[39] (Extract 19.2.18) early in the twentieth century and was confirmed by the House of Lords in *Sovmots Investments Ltd v SSE*.[40]

This is a very important limitation upon the scope of section 62. It is justified as no purchaser could reasonably expect to do everything that had previously been done by the seller. Without the limitation, the section would have an unacceptably wide effect. However, there may be one very significant qualification on *Long v Gowlett*. *P&S Platt Ltd v Crouch*[41] states that diversity of occupation is not required if the easement is continuous and apparent. This means that, for example, rights based on pipes (either for fresh water or drainage) or tracks will be granted, regardless of diversity of occupation. On the other hand the diversity requirement was repeated, without the *Platt* qualification, in *Kent v Kavanagh*[42] (Extract 19.2.19). Neither case quotes all the relevant cases and the dicta in both are obiter: the question remains unsettled. The continuous and apparent test is central to the rule in *Wheeldon v Burrows*; it is further considered below.

Contrary intention

Section 62 does not apply if a contrary intention is expressed. Perhaps surprisingly, this has to be an intention that *the section* does not apply; this is more difficult to prove than an intention that there should not be an easement. However, an intention that there should not be an easement may trigger **rectification** of the conveyance, applying normal contract principles. In *Clark v Barnes*[43] (Extract 19.2.17), the parties had agreed that there should not be a right of way. The court rectified the conveyance and inserted a term excluding the right of way.

Application to contracts

Lastly, section 62 applies only to conveyances, not to contracts.[44] Usually, this will be material when the seller seeks to insert a term in the conveyance that section 62 is not

---

[39] [1923] 2 Ch 177.
[40] [1979] AC 144.
[41] [2004] 1 P&CR 242 at [42], [59]. See also *Alford v Hannaford* [2011] EWCA Civ 1099 at [36].
[42] [2007] Ch 1 at [46]; *Platt* was not cited in the judgments.
[43] [1929] 2 Ch 368.
[44] *Borman v Griffith* [1930] 1 Ch 493; see also below (p. 269).

to apply. It is plain that, given its wording, the section only applies to conveyances. More difficult is the argument that a term should be implied into the contract that the purchaser is entitled to a conveyance to which section 62 applies. Forbes J at first instance in *Sovmots Investments Ltd* v *SSE*[45] held that there was no such implication. This is surprising, as it sends the message that contracts should include all the terms implied by section 62 into conveyances. Otherwise, the purchaser runs the risk that the seller may exclude them when the conveyance is drafted.

The rule in Wheeldon v Burrows

Although the decision in *Wheeldon* v *Burrows* concerned implied reservation, the obiter dicta of Thesiger LJ on implied grant have proved most important:[46]

> . . . on the grant by the owner of a tenement of part of that tenement as it is then used and enjoyed, there will pass to the grantee all those continuous and apparent easements (by which, of course, I mean *quasi* easements), or, in other words, all those easements which are necessary to the reasonable enjoyment of the property granted, and which have been and are at the time of the grant used by the owners of the entirety for the benefit of the part granted.

Leaving aside section 62, this provides the basis for much of the modern law on implied grants. It marries together two very different ideas from the previous law. The 'necessary for reasonable enjoyment' test fits well with the traditional idea of grantors not being able to derogate from their grants. The 'continuous and apparent' test appears[47] to be derived from French law. What Thesiger LJ achieves is a marriage between these two ideas. The use of the phrase 'in other words' indicates that they are the same. Yet it is quite clear that they are different, not just in their origin but also in their application.

What is meant by continuous and apparent? The test clearly applies to easements with some continuous element, such as drainage rights, support and light. However, the courts have included discontinuous rights, if the land contains some permanent indication of their existence. A good example is that a track leading to the benefited land is indicative of a right to use it, as held in *Borman* v *Griffith*[48] (Extract 19.2.7). It may be more appropriate to describe the test as 'continuously apparent'.

The necessary for reasonable enjoyment test is much easier to satisfy than necessity in reservation. It is not enough, however, that the claimed easement is merely useful. Most problems have arisen in the context of secondary means of access. Simply providing a more convenient access will fail the test, as illustrated by *Goldberg* v *Edwards*[49] (Extract 19.2.14). An annexe to a house was reached by a passageway by the side of the house. A secondary right of access through the house failed the test. However, the courts have been prepared to find the test satisfied for easements which provide some important function. Examples are access for vehicles (where there is no other suitable access) and access to the rear of terraced houses, to avoid carrying things (such as coal for a coal shed at the rear) through the house.

[45] [1977] QB 411 at p. 442; the point was not argued when the case went on appeal.
[46] (1879) 12 Ch D 31 at p. 49.
[47] Simpson (1967) 83 LQR 240.
[48] [1930] 1 Ch 493.
[49] [1950] Ch 247. A claim based on s 62 succeeded.

It has been observed that the two tests (continuous and apparent; necessary for reasonable enjoyment) were equated in *Wheeldon* itself. Although differing views have been expressed, it is generally thought that both must be satisfied. In any event, it may be thought inappropriate to apply *Wheeldon v Burrows* as if it were an Act of Parliament. It may be preferable to see the tests as ones which guide the judge in deciding whether there is derogation from grant. If a right is continuous and apparent, then it might seem reasonable for the grantee to assume that the right will continue after the grant. On the other hand, many rights are relatively trivial and it would not be sensible to expect these to continue. This points towards saying that the necessary for reasonable enjoyment test should always be satisfied.

If a right is necessary for reasonable enjoyment, should that be enough to justify its implication? In *Ward v Kirkland*[50] (Extract 19.2.8) Ungoed-Thomas J thought that the continuous and apparent test always has to be satisfied. Yet other cases have placed more stress on necessity, especially because of its role regarding intended use of the land.[51] This might show that a high level of necessity might suffice by itself. Whether that really is the present law can be little more than speculation.

Section 62 and Wheeldon *compared*

The relationship between section 62 and *Wheeldon* may be explained in terms of diversity of occupation. In *Kent v Kavanagh*[52] (Extract 19.2.19), the Court of Appeal held that section 62 applies only if there is diversity and that *Wheeldon* applies only if there is no diversity. This neatly gives mutually exclusive spheres of operation to the two methods of implication.

Where there is diversity of occupation, section 62 offers a very simple route to implying easements. It was not clear prior to *Kent* whether *Wheeldon* could apply when there is diversity of occupation. The point is unlikely to be significant, as section 62 clearly applies. As section 62 requires neither continuous and apparent use nor reasonable necessity, any claimant will naturally rely on section 62.

Where there is no diversity, this seems to provide scope for *Wheeldon* to play an important role. However, it has been seen that there is controversy as to whether section 62 applies, even without diversity, to continuous and apparent rights. If it does, then again section 62 seems the obvious route to adopt, as it contains no necessity requirement.

If section 62 can apply even without diversity, this appears to leave *Wheeldon* without any role. There is one context in which *Wheeldon* clearly possesses an advantage. It has been seen that section 62 does not apply to contracts. Although non-derogation from grant, like section 62, applies to deeds, it is part of a more general implication rule. Maugham J in *Borman v Griffith*[53] (Extract 19.2.7) implied an easement into the contract on the basis of the principles in *Wheeldon*, despite having refused to apply section 62. Accordingly a purchaser who wants to rely on implying an easement into a contract will always have to rely on *Wheeldon*. Whether *Wheeldon* can apply to a contract where there is diversity is a question that has not been resolved: diversity was not mentioned in *Borman*.

[50] [1967] Ch 194 at pp. 224–5.
[51] *Pwllbach Colliery Co Ltd v Woodman* [1915] AC 634 at pp. 646–7; see above (p. 264).
[52] [2007] Ch 1 at [43]–[46].
[53] [1930] 1 Ch 493.

Reform

The Law Commission proposes radical reforms to the implication of easements. For a start, the distinction between implied grant and implied reservation would disappear. Though a central plank of the law ever since *Wheeldon*, the distinction can cause problems for those dealing with the land decades in the future. Should the owner of two adjoining plots sell one in 1920 and the other in 1921, the rights of the two purchasers as between each other may be very different (only the first can rely on implied grant). That may be acceptable as between those two purchasers, but it is less easy to explain to a person who purchases one of those plots in 2013.

Turning to the rules which would in future apply to both grant and reservation, section 62 would disappear. The amazing width of its operation has already been commented upon. Several cases[54] have expressed unease about it and it has also attracted sharp academic criticism. Any assumption on the part of a purchaser or tenant that all temporary permissions will be converted into permanent rights seems wildly optimistic and unjustified. Yet it must be recalled that section 62 was enacted because it was a term commonly inserted into conveyances; it is not an expression of statutory policy that it is desirable for such easements to be implied. It is instructive that the *Standard Conditions of Sale*[55] choose not to exclude the section, save for rights to lights. If section 62 really caused dismay for vendors and lessors, one would expect it to be routinely excluded.

Nor would *Wheeldon* survive unscathed from the reforms. The core of the proposed test is 'necessary for the reasonable use'. Though the continuous and apparent requirement would disappear, the test would be applied bearing in mind the use of the land (present or jointly intended), physical features on the land and the interference with the servient land that the easement would cause. The Law Commission observes that these factors 'replicate the most useful and practical features of the present law'. Though this might permit implication in some cases in which there is no continuous and apparent use, this relaxation of the present rules is easier to accept once section 62 no longer applies. One thing to remember in favour of a fairly generous basis for implying easements is that they are more likely to confer significant advantages to the benefited land than to cause significant loss or disturbance to the servient owner.

● Prescription

Easements and profits can arise from long use. This may be thought to be somewhat similar to adverse possession rules, whereby ownership can be gained by adverse possession of the land. However, the two doctrines operate very differently, so the comparison cannot be pushed too far. We will consider the material under three headings: the forms of prescription, the nature of the use required for prescription and the application of prescription to leases.

[54] These include *Wright* v *Macadam* [1949] 2 KB 744 at pp. 754–5 (Tucker LJ) and *Green* v *Ashco Horticulturist Ltd* [1966] 1 WLR 889 at p. 897 (Cross J).
[55] 4th edn, para 3.4 (2003).

CRITICAL ISSUE

Forms of prescription

The law in this area is complex and archaic. Prescription has been recognised for centuries: *common law prescription* operates where the use has taken place since 1189, the origin of legal memory. This is satisfied by proving use for 20 years (not necessarily the last 20 years). Nevertheless, a claim will fail if the right could not have existed as far back as 1189. Failure is likely as regards rights that benefit buildings. If the first building on the land was known to have been built no earlier than, say, 1850 then common law prescription will fail. Use for over 150 years will not suffice.

Statutory prescription under the Prescription Act 1832 was designed to avoid these problems, by concentrating on use for the immediate past 20 years. This will cover many cases, but problems remain. Many disputes arise after the owner of the **servient land** has prevented the exercise of the right. This does not bar reliance on the Act if legal proceedings are brought within a year of the interruption of the use. However, section 4 provides that longer interruptions are fatal if the interruption has been 'submitted to or acquiesced in'. Prescription operated despite a 13-month interruption in *Davies v Du Paver*,[56] but only because: 'The parties were breathing fury on each side of a newly erected fence.'

The defects with these methods of prescription led to the emergence of the curious fiction of *lost modern grant*. The fiction has been readily applied in modern cases where statutory prescription was impossible because of an interruption exceeding a year. If there has been use for 20 years, then the courts are prepared to presume that an easement has been granted, but that the deed of grant has been lost. Any 20 years will suffice – it need not be the last 20 years. Nobody any longer pretends that there was in fact a grant – it is a fiction and it is no answer to argue that there was not in fact any grant. Lost modern grant also applies to registered land, despite deeds not being effective without registration.

The nature of the use

It is said that the use must be 'as of right' – meaning that it must be the type of use that one would expect if there were already an easement. In particular, it must not be by force, stealth or permission (sometimes expressed in Latin as *nec vi, nec clam, nec precario*). These principles differ somewhat from those applying to adverse possession.

It is generally thought that prescription is based on ideas of acquiescence on the part of the owner of the burdened land; use as of right can be seen as spelling this out. In *Sturges v Bridgeman*[57] (Extract 19.2.24), the defendant was a confectioner whose work involved pounding sugar. The noise initially caused no interference with the claimant's use of the adjoining land. There was therefore nothing the claimant could complain about; he could not be said to acquiesce in the noise. When the claimant later built on his land close to the defendant's activities, the noise became a problem and the claimant sued in the tort of nuisance. Because there was no earlier acquiescence, the defendant had not acquired a prescriptive right to carry on his noisy activities.

[56] [1953] 1 QB 184.
[57] (1879) 11 Ch D 852.

The stress on acquiescence may make prescription look like estoppel, but there are many differences. Unlike estoppel, prescription does not require detriment. On the other hand, it does require an extended period of use.

Force has been given a wide meaning to include what is called 'contentious' use. If the owner of the burdened land makes it clear that the use is not allowed (this might be by putting up a notice), then prescription cannot operate. It is plain in such cases that there is no acquiescence. This can be a quite significant limit on prescription.

The meaning of permission has caused problems where the servient owner tolerates the use. Quite frequently, the owner of the burdened land is not inconvenienced by the use and so does not object to it. Subsequently, disagreements between the parties may develop – in particular, a purchaser of the burdened land may object to the use. Can there be prescription? At one stage, tolerating the use was thought to defeat prescription. There is some sense in this: why should the law condemn neighbourly conduct of an owner who does not object to a use which causes him or her no harm or inconvenience? Nevertheless, the courts have rejected this extension of permission. Indeed, it is difficult to think of situations where there isn't toleration of a use, unless that use is by force or stealth.

Prescription and leases

Prescription operates only to create easements that can last forever (equivalent to a fee simple estate). It follows that there cannot be prescription of an interest that will last for the duration of a lease. It should be stressed that an easement can be created (expressly or by implication) for the duration of a lease. Indeed, it is common for the tenant to enjoy an easement over the landlord's adjoining land. It is only prescription that poses problems.

So far as the benefit is concerned, prescription normally operates so that a tenant acquires the easement on behalf of the fee simple: no problem then exists. However, if the servient land is leased, then virtually every prescription claim hits a barrier. Prescription cannot operate against the lease alone, as the resulting right would be of limited duration. Nor can the prescription be effective against the fee simple. That would require acquiescence by the fee simple holder, which can virtually never be shown.

It is understandable that there is no prescription against the fee simple. However, the denial of prescription as against the lease (which could be a lease for 999 years) demonstrates unnecessary technicality and inflexibility.

Is prescription justified?

The complexity and oddity of many of these rules has led to suggestions that we should abolish prescription. In particular, the rejection of the toleration analysis has disadvantaged owners who do not object to presently harmless activities. It was seen (in Chapter 6) that the comparable area of adverse possession has been much reduced in scope. It may be thought that there are weaker reasons for recognising prescription than for allowing adverse possession, so that prescription should cease to operate. However, the Law Commission considers that the benefits of recognising long-standing activities and facilitating efficient land use justify retention of prescription, though with a new statutory structure that will replace the three present forms of prescription.

The extent of the easement

Changes in use

There is much litigation concerning the extent of easements, for example whether a right of way includes use by heavy lorries. This is generally a matter of construction; it raises few points of general interest.

What happens if a right becomes more onerous because the use of the land changes, perhaps from a large single home to a hotel? Express easements normally continue despite such changes. However, a less generous approach is taken as regards easements arising from implication or prescription. These are taken to be governed by the circumstances at the time the easement is created. A significant change of use of the land will terminate these easements, but only where it renders the easement much more onerous for the burdened land.

McAdams Homes Ltd v *Robinson*[58] (Extract 19.3.2) illustrates this for rights of foul water drainage. A bakery was changed into two houses, resulting in significantly more foul water (from toilets, baths, washing machines, etc.). Accordingly, the drainage right terminated. In contrast, rights of surface drainage (from rain) will vary little with a change of use and will be unaffected thereby.

Use for other land

An easement can be used only for the benefit of the **dominant land**.

Suppose that there is a right of way to a house. The owner of the house buys land at the back of it and builds an extra house there. Access to the new house is through the grounds of the original house. It is quite clear that the right of way cannot be used to gain access to the new house: it was created for access to the old house, not the new house on separate land. This has been clear at least since *Harris* v *Flower*[59] (Extract 19.3.3). A factory had been built partly on the dominant land and partly on other land. The court held that the right of way to the dominant land could not be used for access to the other land. Unlike the principles regarding change of use, this rule applies whether or not the easement is express.

The operation of the rule is not always clear-cut. The owner of the dominant land may purchase additional land which is incorporated into the original plot, perhaps as an extended garden. In those circumstances, it will often be realistic to say that access is to the original plot rather than to the extended area. However, this can lead to difficult questions. If the owner of the dominant land purchases an additional area which is used as a garage, can she drive her car through the dominant land to the garage? *Das* v *Linden Mews Ltd*[60] held not, though one might have thought that the garage was merely ancillary to the house.

[58] [2005] 1 P&CR 520.
[59] (1904) 74 LJ Ch 127.
[60] [2003] 2 P&CR 58.

Termination of easements

Easements can be terminated by agreement. They will also end automatically if both dominant and servient plots are owned by the same person. This is natural: one cannot have an easement over one's own land. How does this apply if there is a lease?

> Richard owns Blueacre, which has a right of way over Sarah's land, Greenacre. Richard leases Blueacre to Timothy for ten years and soon afterwards buys Greenacre. Although Richard now owns both dominant and servient plots, this does not affect Timothy's right to the easement (remember that a tenant can have an easement over the landlord's adjoining land). However, it will terminate when Timothy's lease comes to an end.

Abandonment is more interesting. Just as easements can be gained by long use, they can be lost by long periods of non-use. However, abandonment is difficult to prove. One problem is that even very lengthy non-use may not indicate a wish to abandon a right.

> Graham has two alternative rights of access to reach his land; one is over the lands of Harriet (the 'Harriet access') and the other is over Ivor's land (the 'Ivor access'). Access over Harriet's land is the more convenient and is the only access that Graham uses. This does not mean that Graham regards the Ivor access as irrelevant. Graham might contemplate building in the future, which would block the Harriet access. In that event, the Ivor access would become essential. Failure to use the Ivor access for decades (perhaps even centuries) proves nothing.

Two factors seem to be important in recognising abandonment. First, if the owner of the servient land has openly acted to their detriment on the basis that the easement doesn't exist, then it is likely that the easement will fail. An example would be building on the route of a right of way. This situation looks very similar to estoppel by acquiescence. Indeed, estoppel can be used to explain all successful claims to abandonment, though not all the cases employ the language of estoppel. The second factor is the pulling down (without replacement) of a building enjoying an easement. It is illustrated by *Moore* v *Rawson*[61] (Extract 19.4.2), which involved a right to light to a building. That building was pulled down and replaced by one without windows. Seventeen years later, it was held that the easement had been abandoned. However, it may have been very material (the judges do not express a uniform view) that the servient owner had subsequently built so as to block light.

It should be noted that there is no set period that can be relied upon as giving rise to abandonment. This would change if the Law Commission's proposals for a presumption of abandonment after 20 years' non-use are implemented.

[61] (1824) 3 B&C 332 (107 ER 756).

Questions to consider

1. What differences are there between easements and profits?

2. Why does the law limit what can be an easement? Are the present rules on this defensible?

3. Why should easements be implied? Are the present rules justified as regards rights implied in favour of (1) the seller/lessor and (2) the purchaser/tenant?

4. What is prescription? Does it play a useful role and, if so, could it be improved?

Further reading

Baker, A [2012] Conv 37: Recreational privileges as easements: law and policy.

Bridge, S (2005) 'Prescriptive acquisition of easements: abolition or reform?', in *Modern Studies in Property Law*, Vol 3, ed. E Cooke, Chapter 1.

Davis, C [1995] Conv 291: Abandonment of an easement: is it a question of intention only?

Dawson, I and Dunn, A (1998) 18 LS 510: Negative easements – a crumb of analysis.

Harpum, C (1979) 43 Conv 113: *Long* v *Gowlett*: a strong fortress.

Spark, G [2012] Conv 6: Easements of parking and storage: are easements non-possessory interests in land?

Sturley, M F (1980) 96 LQR 557: Easements in gross.

Tee, L [1998] Conv 115: Metamorphoses and section 62 of the Law of Property Act 1925.

Turner, P G [2012] Conv 19: Prescription by and against lessees.

Visit **www.mylawchamber.co.uk** to access tools to help you develop and test your knowledge of land law, including interactive multiple choice questions, practice exam questions with guidance, weblinks, glossary flashcards, legal newsfeed and legal updates.

Use **Case Navigator** to read in full some of the key cases referenced in this chapter with commentary and questions:

Wheeldon v *Burrows* [1874–80] All ER Rep 669

Wright v *Macadam* [1949] 2 KB 744

17 Covenants

Nature and importance

Covenants (obligations in deeds) are, like licences, on the dividing line between contract and proprietary interests. Covenants need not involve land at all – I could simply covenant to pay Catriona £3,000. It is where covenants benefit land (I covenant to maintain the river banks of land belonging to Daniel) or are made by a landowner (I covenant to paint my house every five years) that we begin to be interested in them.

Because covenants are obligations, there is always one party with the benefit and another with the burden (or obligation). We are interested in the passing of the benefit or burden when the benefited or burdened land is sold. The transfer of the benefit is not surprising, as the benefit of contracts can be assigned. Thus Catriona could assign the benefit of the £3,000 covenant to Emily, who could then sue me. Of more importance to land law is whether the benefit passes automatically, without express assignment, when benefited land is sold. This question has given rise to a surprisingly large body of technical law.

Burdens of contracts generally cannot be transferred.

> If I owe Catriona £3,000 I cannot simply say that I am transferring that obligation to Andrew. It would take a tripartite agreement between Andrew, Catriona and myself to achieve that result. However, land law does recognise the transfer of burdens of obligations where the obligation constitutes an interest in land. An estate contract provides a good example. If I contract to lease my house to Bella, then a purchaser of my house may be subject to Bella's claim.

It was observed above that covenants may benefit or burden land. Frequently, there will be both benefited and burdened land.

> I own two adjoining houses, Blue Lake and Green Lawn. I sell Green Lawn to Lara, requiring her to covenant not to use Green Lawn for commercial purposes. That covenant is intended to maintain the tranquillity of Blue Lake, which I retain. Green Lawn is the burdened land and Blue Lake is the benefited land.

As we shall see in more detail below, the burden of a *restrictive covenant* (an obligation not to do something, as in the example above) can bind purchasers. In contrast, the burden of a *positive covenant* (an obligation to do something) almost never binds purchasers.

Restrictive covenants are similar to easements: both involve one plot of land having a burden and another having a benefit. Another comparison is with leasehold covenants. We have seen that the benefit and burden of covenants in leases affect purchasers, without any distinction being drawn between positive and restrictive covenants. These comparisons are discussed as a Critical Issue.

When and how are covenants created? Nearly always, covenants are entered into when land is sold and the seller retains adjoining land: the covenant is inserted into the deed of transfer. The example involving Blue Lake and Green Lawn is very typical. Covenants are always express; unlike easements, they are never implied.

A final introductory observation is that the Law Commission[1] has proposed a new land obligations scheme to replace covenants; this impacts on many of the issues discussed in this chapter. Although we will not look at the proposals in detail, some of their most important elements will be mentioned as we look at the relevant issues.

Restrictive covenants

Restrictive covenants have bound purchasers of the burdened land ever since the decision in *Tulk v Moxhay*[2] (Extract 20.2.1) in 1848. The case involved the sale of Leicester Square garden, with a covenant to 'keep and maintain [it] in sufficient and proper repair as a square garden and pleasure ground, in an open state, uncovered with any building, in neat and ornamental order'. When a later purchaser of the garden proposed to build on it, the court ordered compliance with the covenant.

What induced Lord Cottenham LC to promote the restrictive covenant from a contract to a proprietary interest binding the purchaser? He gave two reasons. The first was that it would otherwise be impossible to sell part of one's land without running the risk of the remainder becoming worthless. Encouragement to landowners to sell was important in the 1840s, when land was required for industrial use and cities were developing fast. His second reason was that it would be unjust if a purchaser, having accepted an obligation, could remove that obligation from the land by the simple expedient of selling it on. This is unconvincing. It would allow any obligation to be recognised as proprietary. Unless the courts are willing to go that far (they never have), it is too broad an argument to carry much conviction. The initial purchaser in any event remains liable for breach of contract.

Requirements

What is required for a valid restrictive covenant? The basic rules were sorted out in the century following *Tulk*; today the law is quite straightforward. It was soon clarified that

---

[1] Law Com No 327.
[2] 2 Ph 774 (41 ER 1143).

Tulk applies only to restrictive (not positive) covenants.[3] A frequently quoted comment of Jessell MR[4] is that 'The doctrine of [*Tulk* v *Moxhay*], rightly considered, appears to me to be either an extension in equity of the doctrine of *Spencer's Case* [on leasehold covenants] to another line of cases, or else an extension in equity of the doctrine of negative easements'. The comparison with easements is instructive, as easements do not generally involve positive obligations. The exclusion of positive covenants was confirmed by the House of Lords in *Rhone* v *Stephens*[5] (Extract 20.2.2), which will be discussed in the context of positive covenants.

When is a covenant restrictive? A frequently cited test is whether the covenantor (the party with the obligation) has to 'put his hand in his pocket', i.e., pay to comply with the obligation. If the answer is yes, then it is a positive covenant. Covenants often employ a mixture of requirements. Thus in *Tulk* itself, the obligation to keep in proper repair looks positive, whereas the obligation not to build is clearly restrictive. It is clear that the courts will enforce the restrictive aspects of such mixed covenants.

A separate requirement is that there must be benefited land.[6] This fits both the comparison with easements and also the policy justification of encouraging sale of part of a larger plot. Unsurprisingly, one cannot simply designate benefited land; it really has to benefit. So long as the plots are reasonably close, this is quite easily shown for obligations not to build or not to use for commercial purposes (two common forms of covenant).

What was probably not anticipated in 1848 was the use of restrictive covenants to avoid competition with the benefited land. Suppose Brian runs a hairstyling business. He sells three plots of land a hundred metres away with a covenant that they should not be used for a hairstyling business. Breach of the covenant would not have such a direct effect on the benefited land as in *Tulk*. Rather, it would impact on the profitability of Brian's business and the value of the land and business combined. Although some unease has been expressed, the courts appear to recognise this as a sufficient benefit. Indeed, it would be impractical to exclude competition benefit, as such covenants can benefit the land in a more conventional manner. Thus a covenant not to sell alcohol might benefit adjoining land because it will limit the risk of nuisance from rowdy conduct. However, the covenantee may own a neighbouring pub, the real purpose being to protect his business.

Competition covenants may pose particular problems because benefit can still be argued despite the plots being separated by a considerable distance. With other types of covenants, benefit is difficult to prove once a fairly small distance separates the plots. The cases provide little specific guidance as to what distance is acceptable, but it is likely to be no more than a few hundred metres.

---

[3] *Haywood* v *Brunswick Permanent Benefit BS* (1881) 8 QBD 403; *South Western Railway Co* v *Gomm* (1882) 20 Ch D 562.

[4] *South Western Railway Co* v *Gomm* (1882) 20 Ch D 562 at p. 583.

[5] [1994] 2 AC 310.

[6] *Formby* v *Barker* [1903] 2 Ch 539; *LCC* v *Allen* [1914] 3 KB 642 (Extract 20.2.3).

Running of the burden

Provided that the requirements above are satisfied, the running of the burden is straightforward. Provided that the covenant is registered, any successor in title will be bound.

Running of the benefit

This topic has caused the courts much difficulty; it is the most litigated issue in covenants. This is very surprising. Passing the benefit of obligations shouldn't really be a problem: in the similar area of easements it has been relatively trouble-free.

There are two types of point to consider. The first is whether a neighbour of the covenantee can claim on the covenant. The second point is whether a purchaser (or other successor in title) from the covenantee can claim.

On neighbours, LPA section 56 (Extract 20.1.3) permits such third parties to claim as long as the covenant purports to be with them.[7]

> Richard purchases land from Sufiya and enters into a restrictive covenant with her. Section 56 will operate if the covenant provides: 'I promise Theresa, Sufiya's neighbour, that I will comply with the covenant': Theresa can claim on the covenant. What does not suffice is a promise to Sufiya for the benefit of her neighbour: the promise has to be *to* the neighbour. This is a very fine distinction.

However, a more general right to sue may be based on the Contracts (Rights of Third Parties) Act 1999 (Extract 20.1.5). The application of that Act to freehold covenants has yet to be litigated.

Most problems, however, concern purchasers from the covenantee. Before looking at the rules, is there any reason why the issue should give rise to difficulties? A practical point is that the benefited land will very frequently not be identified.

> Andrew owns a large area (it could be several thousand acres) and sells a quarter-acre plot to Brenda, imposing a restrictive covenant that no more than one house will be built upon the plot. It may be noted that covenants are usually imposed on purchasers, not sellers. The natural wording of the obligation will not define Andrew's retained (and benefited) plot. This example shows that we normally know what land is burdened (the plot sold), but frequently it isn't made clear what land is benefited.

Does it matter if it is not obvious from the transfer what land is benefited? Any problems will be most acute as regards purchasers of the two plots.

---

[7] *Amsprop Trading Ltd* v *Harris Distribution Ltd* [1997] 1 WLR 1025 (Extract 20.1.4), based on *Beswick* v *Beswick* [1968] AC 58.

Let us assume further facts in the previous example: Andrew has sold the benefited land to George and Brenda has sold the burdened land to Hayley. George will have no difficulty in proving that he owns Andrew's retained plot. As regards Hayley, it may be argued that she simply shouldn't breach the covenant: it doesn't matter if she is not sure who can sue. These arguments overlook one important point. It cannot be assumed that covenants will always be enforced so as to prevent breach. If Brenda had wanted to build a second house, it might have been possible for her to do a deal with Andrew so that he receives a cash payment in return for not enforcing the covenant. If the breach were less serious, Andrew might simply agree to it. These are examples of the principle that the holders of the benefit can agree to modify or terminate the covenant.

If the benefited land is not obvious from the transfer, how can Hayley discover who holds the benefit? There may be numerous plots of land around the burdened land: how is the successor to know which of them was owned by Andrew? There wouldn't be a problem if Andrew were still the owner, as he could be contacted. However, it is troublesome if he has sold. There is then a real danger that Hayley's desirable land development or use may be thwarted by the risk of an unexpected person seeking to enforce the restrictive covenant. These factors justify rules that ensure certainty as to the identity of the benefited land. They were stressed by the Court of Appeal in **Crest Nicholson Residential (South) Ltd v McAllister**[8] (Extract 20.2.9), discussed below.

It is commonly said that there are three ways in which the benefit may run: annexation, assignment and schemes of development.

Annexation

This is the permanent linking of the covenant to the land. Once a covenant has been annexed, the benefit will pass automatically to future purchasers of the land. **Annexation** requires wording which links the benefit of the covenant to specified land, so as to become part of that land. The most commonly quoted case is *Rogers* v *Hosegood*,[9] in which a covenant with the vendors, 'their heirs and assigns, and others claiming under them to all or any of their lands adjoining or near to the said premises' was effective to annex. It may be contrasted with a covenant with the 'vendors, their heirs and assigns',[10] which makes no reference to successors in title and, indeed, no reference to any land; it fails to annex.

For much of the twentieth century, it was assumed that annexation requires express words. However, some commentators argued that annexation could be implied from LPA, section 78. This deems covenants 'to be made with the covenantee and his successors in title'. Initially, this was treated as a word-saving provision, intended to show only that the benefit was not personal to the covenantee and *could pass* to a purchaser; it did not mean that it in fact *did pass*. To the surprise of many,[11] the Court of Appeal in

---

[8] [2004] 1 WLR 2409 at [34].
[9] [1900] 2 Ch 388.
[10] *Reid v Bickerstaff* [1909] 2 Ch 305; *Renals v Cowlishaw* (1878) 9 Ch D 125; (1879) 11 Ch D 866.
[11] See the convincing criticism by the leading practitioner and author in the area: Newsom (1981) 97 LQR 32.

Federated Homes Ltd v *Mill Lodge Properties Ltd*[12] rejected this word-saving interpretation and held that section 78 itself effected annexation. This was a radical change, as it meant that the parties no longer had to insert careful wording. It seemed that annexation would virtually always operate.

It was soon observed that section 78 contains no provision for contrary intention (unlike section 79, a similar provision relating to the burden of covenants). If section 78 could force unwanted annexation on the parties, this would be inexplicable. Fortunately, the Court of Appeal in *Crest Nicholson Residential (South) Ltd* v *McAllister*[13] has held that the wording of section 78(1) ('land . . . intended to be benefited') shows that intention is relevant, so that a contrary intention precludes annexation.

More significant is a second question considered in *Crest Nicholson*: does section 78 effect annexation only if the benefited land is identified by the covenant? The section is silent as to this. Because section 78 has been held to effect a statutory annexation, it might be thought that no such requirement exists. However, *Federated Homes* deliberately left the question open. When the issue later arose in *Crest Nicholson*, the Court of Appeal stressed how important it is for purchasers of the burdened land to be able to identify the benefited land. This is essential for identifying the persons presently holding the benefit, with whom negotiations about the covenant may need to be undertaken. This is a very good point. Identification was held to be required.

How important is statutory annexation following *Crest Nicholson*? If the benefited land is identified, then it is quite likely that the wording will suffice to annex under the pre-*Federated Homes* rules. In other words, the section will apply when its use is least necessary! It may help to avoid any technical objection that inappropriate wording has been used, but it would be unsafe to assume that annexation will nearly always apply.

Should this narrowing of annexation be welcomed? This is not an easy question. On the one hand, the stress on the needs of people dealing with the land is very welcome and provides a powerful argument. If *Crest Nicholson* really provides greater certainty for purchasers, then surely it is the right answer. Unfortunately, certainty remains elusive. The first problem is that the purchaser will not know whether there has been an assignment (discussed below). Assignment does not require the covenant to identify the benefited land, so the purchaser of the burdened land has no idea who may be able to enforce the covenant.

The second problem is that the *Rogers* v *Hosegood* formula for annexation, approved in *Crest Nicholson*, fails miserably to provide the necessary certainty. The wording 'all or any of their lands adjoining' tells us virtually nothing. If we were to guess what land is benefited when the covenant is silent we would naturally say that it is the vendor's retained adjoining land – exactly the same as the *Rogers* v *Hosegood* formula.

It may be unfair to criticise *Crest Nicholson* for these problems. They may be too ingrained within the cases for any court (at least below the House of Lords) to make the necessary changes and provide the necessary certainty.

The Law Commission's proposed land obligation scheme involves identification of the benefited land. Though identification would not be an integral part of a land obligation,

---

[12] [1980] 1 WLR 594.
[13] [2004] 1 WLR 2409 at [34], approving the result in *Roake* v *Chadha* [1984] 1 WLR 40.

land obligations would operate as legal interests. Just as with easements, registration will require entry of the benefit; this necessarily requires identification of the benefited land. This may be seen as accepting and expanding upon the approach in *Crest Nicholson*.

A quite different question comes from our having two forms of annexation. The first is called annexation *to the whole*. Its essence is that it treats the land of the covenantee (the party with the benefit of the covenant) as a single entity. It may be illustrated as follows.

Charles owns a large estate of 3,000 acres, which we will call the Eastminster Estate. He sells ten acres to Diana, subject to a restrictive covenant, the benefit being expressly annexed to the Eastminster Estate. Subsequently, Charles transfers a one-acre plot out of the Eastminster Estate to Camilla and then the remainder of the estate to William. In this example, Camilla cannot be said to own the Eastminster Estate (the 'whole') and so cannot enforce the covenant. William, however, does own the Eastminster Estate and can sue; we do not require ownership of literally all the original land, so long as William can fairly be said to own the Eastminster Estate.

Alternatively, there can be annexation *to each and every part*. In that event, an owner of any part of the benefited land is able to sue[14] – a much simpler outcome. Many potential problems have been avoided since the Court of Appeal in *Federated Homes Ltd v Mill Lodge Properties Ltd*[15] introduced a presumption that annexation was to each and every part.

That presumption has been widely welcomed, but are there any problems or disadvantages with annexation to each and every part? One point is that it will have to be shown that the relevant part is in fact benefited by the covenant; this could be difficult if it is a large estate and the relevant part is distant from the burdened land. In annexation to the whole, it is relatively easy to conclude that the whole *as a single unit* is benefited.[16]

A quite different point is that the covenantee may positively wish that later purchasers of parts should *not* be able to sue on the covenant. This is explained by the following example.

CRITICAL ISSUE

Alison sells a field (part of her farm) to Brian for £300,000, subject to a covenant to use it for farming purposes only. This arrangement is made against the background that, as they are aware, the field could be worth up to £5 million if planning permission for building were obtained. Alison later sells a small part of her retained land (the benefited land) to Charles. Brian now wants to build on the field and is offering Alison £3 million to be released from the covenant. Alison decides to accept this offer. It would be disastrous for her if Charles could enforce the covenant. Either Charles could block the projected building or he could claim a share of the £3 million in return for his agreement. Of course, if Alison really wants to stop building in any circumstances then she will be happy for Charles to share the benefit: annexation to each and every part then works well.

---

[14] *Marquess of Zetland* v *Driver* [1939] Ch 1.
[15] [1980] 1 WLR 594.
[16] One example is *Marten v Flight Refuelling Ltd* [1962] Ch 115.

Assignment

The covenantee can assign the benefit of a restrictive covenant to a successor in title. Assignment differs from annexation in a number of respects. First, it takes effect at a different time: annexation takes place on setting up the covenant, whereas assignment operates when the benefited land is subsequently sold. Next the parties are different: annexation is an act of the covenantor and covenantee, whereas assignment is a transaction between the covenantee and a later purchaser of the benefited land (the covenantor is not a party).

What suffices for an assignment? No specific words are required, but there must be some reference to the purchaser obtaining the benefit of the covenant – assignment cannot be implied from simply selling the land.[17] The covenant need not identify the benefited land: it suffices if extrinsic evidence identifies the benefited land with reasonable certainty.[18]

It remains to make three final observations. The first is that, despite some earlier uncertainty, it seems necessary to have an assignment every time the land is sold, sometimes called a 'chain of assignments'. An argument that assignment constitutes 'delayed annexation' has not been adopted by more recent cases.[19] The second point is that assignment is essentially a contract-based concept. Rules that make sense in a contractual setting may look out of place in the property context. We have seen that assignment doesn't fit well with the stress on certainty of benefited land in *Crest Nicholson*.

Lastly, it is difficult to see any role for assignments of land obligations, as the benefit will run automatically. However, an unregistered land obligation will still operate as an equitable interest. How the benefit of equitable land obligations will pass is not made clear. There might be a role for annexation and assignment here, though the treatment of the equitable land obligation as analogous to equitable easements might point to a fresh start.

Schemes of development

It is common in large developments to sell all the plots subject to identical covenants. These covenants are used to ensure a cohesive development, so that all the houses (schemes are usually found in the housing context) are used in a similar manner. There is no reason why the normal restrictive covenant rules should not apply, but there are special rules applicable to schemes of development, sometimes called building schemes. We need to examine when there will be a scheme of development and what its effects are.

The effect of schemes

We start with the effects of a scheme, as this will help explain the requirements for a scheme to exist. As a contrast with the normal rules, the benefit of the covenant will pass to purchasers without any need for annexation or assignment. The essential idea of a scheme is that there is a form of 'local law' binding all houses within the scheme –

[17] *Roake* v *Chadha* [1984] 1 WLR 40 (Extract 20.2.11), rejecting an argument based on LPA, s 62 (Extract 19.2.11).
[18] *Newton Abbot Co-operative Society Ltd* v *Williamson & Treadgold Ltd* [1952] Ch 286.
[19] It might, however, be revived by *Cygnet Healthcare Ltd* v *Greenswan Consultants Ltd* [2009] EWHC 1318 (Ch) at [14].

everybody buying a house within the scheme should expect to be both benefited and burdened by the covenants.

The following example shows how schemes operate.

Developers plc has set up a scheme of development for a 50-house development. Developers sell, say, ten houses and are now selling a house to Lucy. Each sale is subject to identical restrictive covenants. Who has the benefit of Lucy's covenants? It is easy to see that the benefited land includes the plots retained by Developers and that the benefit will pass to later purchasers of these plots. But what about the ten plots already sold? The effect of a scheme is that they also obtain the benefit; there is no need to rely on LPA, section 56 (Extract 20.1.3).

A separate point concerns the land retained by Developers. Suppose that Developers find that the houses sell slowly and decide to build a factory instead of the last 25 houses. Reciprocity is treated as a crucial element of a scheme of development. Even though the covenant may concentrate only on what the purchaser should not do, all land within the scheme (sold or unsold) is burdened as well as benefited. It follows that Developers cannot build that factory.

A quite different element of schemes of development is the consequence of two plots becoming owned by the same person.

In the above example, suppose Lucy later buys an adjoining plot within the scheme for her elderly father to live in. After her father dies, that plot is sold to Malcolm. Assuming that the sale makes no reference to the covenants, can Malcolm and Lucy enforce the building scheme covenants between each other? Normally, covenants (just like easements) terminate if the benefited and burdened plots become owned by the same person. However, the rule is different for schemes of development: the idea of a local law binding the area is too strong for covenants to terminate in this manner. Once the plots are separated again, the scheme springs back into action between them.

This rule avoids what Megarry J[20] has described as 'haphazard islands of partial immunity within the area of the scheme'.

When is there a scheme?

The ideas of 'local law' and reciprocity mentioned above go far to explain the requirements for schemes of development. The traditional requirements were established a century ago in *Elliston v Reacher*[21] (Extract 20.2.11), Parker J required proof of four factors:

1. that both the claimant and defendant derive title from the same common vendor;

2. that previously to selling the land the vendor laid out the estate for sale in lots subject to restrictions intended to be imposed on all the lots; the restrictions may vary in

---

[20] *Brunner v Greenslade* [1971] Ch 993 at p. 1004, approved in *Texaco Antilles Ltd v Kernochan* [1973] AC 609 (Extract 20.2.14).

[21] [1908] 2 Ch 374 at p. 384, approved by the Court of Appeal [1908] 2 Ch 665.

details as to particular lots, but must be consistent only with some general scheme of development;

3. that these restrictions were intended by the common vendor to be and were for the benefit of all the lots intended to be sold, whether or not they were also intended to be for the benefit of other land retained by the vendor; and

4. that the lots were purchased from the common vendor upon the footing that the restrictions were to operate for the benefit of the other lots included in the scheme.

These tests are notoriously difficult to satisfy. However, cases in recent decades have relaxed the requirements: it suffices to show that reciprocity of obligation is intended throughout the area of the scheme.[22] If this reciprocity is explicit on the face of the documents, that is sufficient. In other cases, the traditional *Elliston* criteria are employed to discover whether that reciprocity is present. Even then, the criteria should not be employed in too technical a manner. For example, there is no reason why there should not be a scheme if two adjoining landowners together set up a scheme applying to the land of both of them – despite there being no single common vendor.

Land law students commonly make the mistake of assuming that there is a scheme whenever similar covenants are imposed on purchasers. Similar covenants are doubtless necessary for there to be a scheme, but countless cases demonstrate that more has to be proved. The most revealing question is whether it is apparent to the first purchaser that all future plots will be sold on a similar basis, such that the seller cannot thereafter change his or her mind about their use. Unless that is the case, there will be no scheme.

Land obligations

It is difficult to see how schemes of development could have any special effect as registered land obligations;[23] this area of law might wither away.

Privity exceptions?

Is it possible for the covenantor and covenantee simply to agree (without annexation) that a purchaser of the benefited land should be able to sue? The standard answer is that the purchaser is not in privity of contract with the covenantor (let alone purchasers of the burdened land).

In looking at neighbours, we saw that LPA section 56 (Extract 20.1.3) and the Contracts (Rights of Third Parties) Act 1999 (Extract 20.1.5) sometimes enable neighbours to sue. Could these provisions apply in favour of purchasers of the benefited land? Although it is settled that section 56 cannot be applied in this way, there seems to be no reason why the 1999 Act should not operate (it explicitly applies even though the third party is not in existence at the time of the contract). The question is likely to be whether there is a sufficient promise to benefit successors in title. The language of LPA section 78 (discussed above as part of annexation) may well assist in proving this. Though the covenantor

---

[22] *Baxter v Four Oaks Properties Ltd* [1965] Ch 816 (20.2.13) and *Re Dolphin's Conveyance* [1970] Ch 654 are the seminal cases.

[23] The rule whereby a covenant survives temporary common ownership of two plots within a scheme (p. 284 above) will become applicable to all easements and land obligations.

might be liable on this basis (contract-based liability), it is more difficult to argue that a successor in title is liable (land law-based liability).

The operation of restrictive covenants

Two very different points will be mentioned. First, there is a statutory discretion[24] to modify or terminate restrictive covenants that are obsolete or are otherwise disproportionate (compensation for the benefited owner may be ordered). Restrictive covenants last indefinitely and may become seriously out of date as the nature of the locality changes. A covenant not to use land for commercial purposes may make sense when all the adjoining properties are houses. A century later, all the adjoining houses may have been converted into shops or pulled down and rebuilt as offices. Continuing to enforce the covenant is pointless and may prevent necessary redevelopment or changes in use.

This may be an appropriate stage at which to mention that restrictive covenants play a similar role to **planning permission**. Planning permission is required (from local authorities) before buildings are built or their use is changed. The system was introduced after the Second World War and at one stage it was thought that it would replace restrictive covenants. That has not happened: restrictive covenants are as popular as ever. Planning permission exists to serve the public interest as regards what land development should be permitted. The private interest of owners of adjoining land may be very different. A planning authority might think it a very good idea that a house be converted into a restaurant serving the locality, whereas the owner of the adjoining house may have very different ideas! That is not to say that the position of neighbours is ignored within the planning process, rather that a wider set of interests come into play. One consequence is that an application for modification or termination of a covenant may fail despite planning permission having been granted.

The second point for discussion concerns enforcement. It is unusual for breach of a restrictive covenant to cause really significant financial losses. Most owners of benefited land are more concerned with loss of amenity than with reduction in land values. It follows that claimants nearly always seek an injunction to prevent breach, rather than damages. It will be fairly easy to obtain an injunction to prevent future breaches.

More difficult are situations in which the breach has taken place, especially where a building has been built. Will there be an injunction to pull it down? The courts are reluctant to allow such wanton waste of resources, though an injunction is likely if the burdened owner has built in full awareness of the covenant and the opposition of the claimant. More frequently, the builder believes either that there is no breach of covenant or that there is nobody able to enforce it. In such cases, the court is likely to refuse an injunction. However, damages will be awarded so that the builder has to share with the claimant some of the profit from the new building: often around a third. That sum is likely to far exceed any financial loss caused by the breach. It is usually explained as what could have been negotiated by the claimant (before the breach) as a payment for giving permission for the building.[25]

---

[24] LPA, s 84 (Extract 20.2.15).
[25] *Jaggard* v *Sawyer* [1995] 1 WLR 269 (Extract 20.3.1).

Positive covenants

● Passing the burden

The courts have consistently refused to allow the burden of positive covenants to run with the land. Unlike restrictive covenants, they have never been admitted to the list of recognised proprietary interests. The law on this point is well settled. It had been decided early in the nineteenth century and, despite some initial doubts, has been held to be unaffected by *Tulk v Moxhay*. Most significant today is the confirmation of the earlier cases by the House of Lords in *Rhone v Stephens*[26] (Extract 20.2.2), which involved an obligation to keep a roof in repair.

Justifications for the contrast with restrictive covenants

In *Rhone*, Lord Templeman argued that to recognise positive covenants would be inconsistent with privity of contract ideas. This is unconvincing. Recognising a proprietary right is almost invariably equivalent to accepting that the normal privity rules no longer apply. His reasoning essentially assumes what he is seeking to prove.

Five lines of argument are more convincing.

1. The first is that any change in such a clear legal principle would run counter to the assumptions of those drafting covenants in millions of transfers. It would be difficult to avoid the criticism that any change would impose obligations on those who have been told (with impeccable legal advice) that they are not bound by covenants. The law might be changed prospectively without such objections, but that is better undertaken by Parliament.

2. Next, it can be argued that need for positive covenants to run is less convincing than for restrictive covenants. For the latter, it is easy to see that irreparable harm can be done to adjoining land by inappropriate development of the burdened land. A landowner might well be inhibited from selling part of a large landholding if restrictive covenants did not bind purchasers of the part sold. If Agatha covenants to repair Bertha's river banks (a positive covenant), matters are quite different. If Agatha fails to repair, then Bertha can do the work herself. She faces financial loss rather than irreparable damage to her land; this loss can be adequately compensated by a damages award against Agatha. However, this reasoning does not apply to all positive covenants. If the covenant is to do something on the covenantor's own land, then the covenantee really needs the covenant to be performed. The facts of *Rhone* provide a good example. The covenantor's roof extended over part of the covenantee's cottage; the covenant was to keep the roof in repair. Obviously, failure to repair the roof would cause great problems for the cottage.

   Rhone is illustrative of problems that apply whenever properties are dependent upon each other, most especially within a block of flats. Take the roof of a block of flats as an example. It is necessary to establish who is to maintain it and how the costs

[26] [1994] 2 AC 310.

are to be shared. Later purchasers of the flats cannot be sued on such obligations; this rendered freehold flats unworkable. Fortunately, **commonhold** (see Chapter 3) can now be used in such cases.

3. A third argument concerns enforcement. Restrictive covenants are usually easy to enforce: in a typical case there will be an order prohibiting breach. Enforcement of positive covenants is more problematic: mandatory orders to do something are more difficult to draft and to police. In general, the courts are more reluctant to issue mandatory injunctions.

4. Next, positive obligations are more intrusive upon purchasers. One reason for having a limited range of property interests is to avoid the ownership of land becoming too burdensome: it encourages a ready market in land and ensures that prospective purchasers are not put off by the spectre of extensive liability. On the other hand, the recognition of liability on positive covenants in leases does not seem to have had any disastrous effect on the willingness of people to take assignments from landlords or tenants.

5. Finally, the running of the burden of positive covenants would involve difficult practical issues. Thus Lord Templeman noted in *Rhone* that problems in the enforcement of some leasehold covenants had required legislation to prevent abuses. A good example of a practical issue for freehold covenants is whether tenants should be bound. This poses no problem for restrictive covenants. If the owner cannot use the premises as a shop, nor can a tenant. It is very different for positive covenants. An obligation to repair could be very onerous for a tenant who has taken a lease for a few months – students leasing a house for a year would be a good example. However, to exempt tenants altogether would enable simple avoidance by the expedient of granting a long lease. The obvious solution is to distinguish between long and short leases. Such a distinction can be readily made by legislation, but not by the courts.

These arguments go far to explain the current state of the law, though the first and last have little relevance to statutory reform. It is plain that the failure to recognise positive covenants looks anomalous and can cause problems, especially where commonhold is inappropriate. There are ways in which the rule can be circumvented,[27] but these are clumsy and inadequate. The Law Commission had little hesitation in concluding that its new land obligations scheme should include both positive and restrictive obligations. However, what qualifies as a positive obligation is restricted to work on the burdened land or payments for benefits to the burdened land. These are thought to be the most important obligations; they would not include undertaking work on the benefited land.

Circumventing the rule: can purchasers be made liable?

A number of possibilities have been discussed over the years, but three will be mentioned here. The first is that it is possible to place a restriction on the register of the burdened land, requiring the consent of the proprietor of the benefited land to be obtained before the land is transferred (we saw in Chapter 10 that restrictions can be entered despite the

[27] See below.

absence of any proprietary interest).[28] The idea is that consent will be given if the new purchaser promises to comply with the covenant. There is then a direct contractual link with the new purchaser. Technically, it isn't a case of a proprietary interest binding a purchaser, but a new obligation freely undertaken by the purchaser. There will be a fresh restriction on the purchaser's registered title, so the process continues indefinitely.

However, the most common route is through the so-called 'chain of covenants'.

> Marilyn covenants with Norman (a neighbour) to keep her land in repair. Marilyn later transfers her land to Olive. LPA, section 79 presumes that a covenantor makes a covenant 'on behalf of himself his successors in title and the persons deriving title under him'. This does not mean that Olive is bound (that argument was rejected in **Rhone**), but that Marilyn is herself liable for breaches by successors in title such as Olive. This potential liability encourages Marilyn to insist on a term being inserted in the transfer that Olive will comply with the covenant. Norman has (most likely) no action against Olive, but there is a fair chance that Olive will comply with the covenant in order to avoid liability on her promise to Marilyn. If she fails to do so, then Norman can sue Marilyn, who in turn can sue Olive.

The principal weaknesses in the chain of covenants are that it depends on the covenantor's remembering to impose an obligation on the purchaser and that the whole edifice collapses if there is a flaw in any link in the chain. If Marilyn sells the land and moves away (or dies), then it may be impossible to trace and sue her. The risks increase the more frequently the land is sold. There remains, however, a possibility that a promise by the current owner (Olive, for example) could be enforced by the original covenantee (Norman) under the Contracts (Rights of Third Parties) Act 1999 (Extract 20.1.5). This legislation allows contractual obligations to be enforced by non-parties, for whose benefit they have been entered into. The problem in the present context is as to whether Olive's covenant is intended to benefit Norman as well as Marilyn. There is no authority on the question.

Finally, it is sometimes possible to use the benefit and burden doctrine (discussed towards the end of Chapter 8) to enforce positive obligations. This is most common where there is an obligation (the positive obligation) to pay for certain benefits received. A person who chooses to take advantage of the benefits has to accept to make the corresponding payment.

Passing the benefit

The benefit of most contractual obligations can be assigned. The question to consider is whether the benefit passes automatically if the benefited land is transferred.

Positive covenants have never been bedevilled by the complexity encountered with restrictive covenants. So long as the positive covenant affects the land ('touches and concerns'), the courts have allowed the benefit to pass automatically.[29] LPA section 78 (the basis of annexation in many restrictive covenants) is sometimes cited as authority.

---

[28] See above (p. 123).
[29] *Kumar* v *Dunning* [1989] QB 193 (Extract 16.3.9).

Whether or not section 78 is really needed, it abrogates the inconvenient rule that the successor in title had to have the same estate as the covenantee. This means, for example, that a tenant of the covenantee can sue.[30]

It is difficult to say why the benefit of positive covenants is passed more readily than restrictive covenants. Indeed, it isn't clear whether the distinction is between passing at law and passing in equity or between positive and restrictive covenants. Whatever the distinction, is there a good reason why restrictive covenants attract a tougher rule?

Even though *Federated Homes Ltd* v *Mill Lodge Properties Ltd*[31] (Extract 20.2.8) has made it easier for the benefit of restrictive covenants to run, we have seen that the benefited land must be identified. There is no such requirement for positive covenants.[32] Can this be justified? We saw that a good reason for identifying the benefited land is that it may become necessary to negotiate about the covenant and that identifying the benefited land can be a real problem for purchasers of the burdened land. For positive covenants, purchasers of the burdened land are not bound. The original covenantor is fairly likely to be aware of the land owned by covenantee, so there is less need to insist upon identification in a positive covenant.

Comparisons

In this section, we shall see how covenants principles compare with leasehold covenants and easements and draw some conclusions.

Leasehold covenants

Covenants run in leases regardless of whether they are positive or negative. We need to consider how this relates to the very different rules for freehold covenants.

One point is that a lease is commonly used instead of a freehold transfer when it is regarded as essential that positive covenants should run. As seen above, this is very common for blocks of flats. Where it is a substitute for a transfer, there will be a long lease, providing almost as much economic protection and value as the fee simple. Nevertheless, many people who buy flats want the fee simple and this led to the introduction of commonhold in 2002.

Does this use of leases achieve the same results as if positive freehold covenants could be enforced? If the burden of positive covenants were to run, then the flat owners could sue each other. Leases permit the enforcement of covenants as between the landlord and the tenant. In a block of flats, only the landlord can enforce the covenants – not the other flat dwellers. The landlord might be independent of the tenants (typically the developer of the flats) or might be a company controlled by all the tenants. Especially in the latter case, the covenants are intended to protect not so much the landlord's

---

[30] *Smith and Snipes Hall Farm Ltd* v *River Douglas Catchment Board* [1949] 2 KB 500 (Extract 20.1.2).
[31] [1980] 1 WLR 594.
[32] *Smith and Snipes Hall Farm Ltd* v *River Douglas Catchment Board* [1949] 2 KB 500 at p. 508.

interest but those of the other tenants. It is a distinctly artificial use of the leasehold structure, even though leasehold covenants can be made to work.

Why does the law allow positive leasehold covenants to run, when freehold covenants currently do not? The only rational answer can be that leases involve a continuing relationship. When there are two parties sharing rights to a single property, that relationship must be made to work. Take one simple example. A tenant pays rent. To say that this is a positive obligation, not binding on an assignee of the lease would make the relationship non-viable. Obviously, leasehold covenant rules ensure that the assignee is liable for rent. Such a continuing relationship is less likely for freehold covenants, though flats (for which commonhold is available) provide one clear exception.

Covenants and easements

This comparison is timely, as the Law Commission did give brief consideration to adopting a single structure covering both interests. This is discussed in the section 'Conclusions' below.

An initial point is that neither covenants nor easements recognise positive proprietary obligations. The two are often regarded as very similar property rights affecting adjoining landowners. Looked at in this way, the failure to recognise positive covenants fits in quite neatly. That does not of course mean that it makes sense. If future legislation recognises positive covenants as binding purchasers, then a right which fails as an easement might be reworded so as to constitute a land obligation. An example would be an obligation to maintain a boundary wall.

Given that restrictive covenants and easements have many similarities, how and why do we distinguish between them? When considering easements,[33] we saw that easements normally confer rights to do something: a right of access along a track, for example. There are some old examples of negative easements (rights to light and support are the best known), but these are regarded as anomalous. Novel negative claims are not recognised: they have to fit within the restrictive covenant rules.

Easements may originally have been regarded as the more important rights, with restrictive covenants not being regarded as sufficiently significant to constitute property interests until the nineteenth century. That would not justify continuing to distinguish between them today. A slightly more convincing argument is that easements are usually legal interests. That they bind purchasers automatically is justified because of their practical importance (rights of access, for example) and because they can often be discovered from physical clues on the land. By contrast, restrictive covenants are less important and are rarely (if ever) obvious from looking at the land. Requiring the purchaser to have notice of them establishes a reasonable balance between the needs of claimant and purchaser. However, that argument is of minimal weight now that land registration applies to the huge majority of titles. Express easements and restrictive covenants both have to be entered on the register. Neither will bind a purchaser unless that entry is made.

---

[33] See above (p. 259).

Much more important is that easements can be implied or arise from long use (prescription). There are many examples of such easements in the cases. There are no examples of implied covenants, such as an implied obligation not to build on land. In part, this may be justified because it is easier to draw inferences from the current exercise of positive rights (easements) than from the simple failure of a landowner to do something (restrictive covenant). However, the more convincing explanation is that easements are frequently important for efficient land use, whereas restrictive covenants are less important. There is little reason for the law to lean over backwards to imply a covenant when the parties have not regarded the issue as important enough to address it themselves. If we were to amalgamate easements and covenants, it is unlikely that we would wish there to be implied or prescriptive covenants.

Other differences can also be identified. The passing of the benefit causes much more difficulty for restrictive covenants than for easements. This may be explained because, in easements, the extent of the benefited land will usually be obvious. Where an easement benefits a purchaser, the deed will identify the land sold. In any event the nature of a positive right is that both the documentation and the physical state of the land will normally show what land is benefited. Accordingly, it is the nature of the restrictive covenant as being negative in kind and normally benefiting the seller that justifies rules which require identification of the benefited land.

A final difference is that the statutory jurisdiction to modify (or terminate) restrictive covenants does not apply to easements. One reason for the legislation is that restrictive covenants are frequently based on the nature of the neighbourhood, which can change over time. Easements are less likely to inhibit useful development of land. Even so, it might be argued that some easements are out of date and that a similar jurisdiction to modify would be valuable, even if it would be less frequently invoked.

CRITICAL ISSUE

Conclusions

The analyses in this chapter demonstrate the ambivalent position of covenants. Their origin is obviously contractual, but then that is true of nearly all property interests! We have not finally sorted out how far they should be incorporated into property law and how far contractual principles (assignment is the best example) should continue to operate. Fortunately, the Law Commission's proposals go some way in pushing the land obligation into property law.

Should land law continue to recognise freehold covenants as a separate category of proprietary interests – or should they form part of a category of land obligations, which would include easements? This was considered by the Law Commission and ultimately rejected.[34] Three principal reasons may be identified. First, easements are substantively different. They form a relatively restricted group of rights to use another's land, whereas land obligations are obligations with no limit as regards the nature of the obligation. Next, we have just seen that there are significant differences in, especially, their modes of creation. Finally, the Law Commission had no wish to codify the law of easements.

[34] See the 2008 Consultation Paper 186.

Though the new land obligations regime will replace the present law on covenants, a similar exercise for easements is not 'a necessary or proportionate response' to present problems. This does not mean that each area cannot adopt rules from the other. Thus the new land obligation will be treated for registration purposes in the same way as easements. Meanwhile, the modification jurisdiction will be extended (suitably fine-tuned) from covenants to easements.

Questions to consider

1. Is there any good reason why obligations in freehold transfers should bind later purchasers of the burdened land?

2. Is there any need for rules limiting when the benefit of a covenant will pass to a purchaser of the benefited land? Are the present rules optimal?

3. Should positive covenants be treated in the same way as restrictive covenants?

4. Would covenants be radically changed by the Law Commission's 2011 proposals for land obligations?

Further reading

Gardner, S (1982) 98 LQR 279: The proprietary effect of contractual obligations under *Tulk* v *Moxhay* and *De Mattos* v *Gibson*.

Hayton, D J (1971) 87 LQR 539: Restrictive covenants as property interests.

Martin, J [1996] Conv 329: Remedies for breach of restrictive covenants.

Newsom, G H (1981) 97 LQR 32: Universal annexation?

O'Connor, P [2011] Conv 191: Careful what you wish for: positive freehold covenants.

Turano, L [2000] Conv 377: Intention, interpretation and the 'mystery' of section 79 of the Law of Property Act 1925.

Visit **www.mylawchamber.co.uk** to access tools to help you develop and test your knowledge of land law, including interactive multiple choice questions, practice exam questions with guidance, weblinks, glossary flashcards, legal newsfeed and legal updates.

Use **Case Navigator** to read in full some of the key cases referenced in this chapter with commentary and questions:

Tulk v *Moxhay* 2 Ph 774 (41 ER 1143)

18 Mortgages

Nature and importance

Mortgages are of tremendous social and economic importance. There are around 7.5 million households with mortgages: 35 per cent of the total in England and Wales. Indeed, 80 per cent of houses are bought with mortgage loans. The burden of mortgage expenses is significant – between a fifth and a quarter of all household income of first-time buyers is spent on mortgage payments. The situation in the example below is quite typical.

Catherine and David are buying their first home together; it costs £150,000. Unless they are remarkably fortunate, they will have nothing like that amount of savings and will have to borrow, say, £120,000. Lending that sort of money to a young couple without security would be an extremely risky business; it wouldn't happen. Any lender is going to be troubled by the question of what happens if money is short because, for example, Catherine loses her job or becomes pregnant and chooses to be at home with her young family. Sometimes it is possible to obtain personal security: David and Catherine's parents may have savings and be prepared to guarantee repayment of the loan. In most cases, that will not be viable. What the lender requires is security over the land being bought: a mortgage. This means that if Catherine and David find it impossible to meet the mortgage instalments, the lender can sell the house. So long as the value hasn't dropped significantly, the lender can be assured of getting its money back. This means both that lenders are prepared to lend and that the rate of interest can be relatively low. Sale of the house may be a disaster for Catherine and David, but without a mortgage the house could not have been bought. Even if a lender could be found to lend £120,000 unsecured, a very high interest rate would have to be charged to cover the real risk of the capital not being repaid.

Catherine and David are likely to be paying £7,500 to £10,000 a year on mortgage instalments (assuming a repayment mortgage). It should not be assumed that lenders look only at the value of the property: they will rarely lend unless they think the borrowers can afford repayments. Though security is vital, lenders do not want to get into the position of having to sell homes if it can be avoided. If Catherine is earning £25,000 and David £20,000, then they should be able to borrow around £200,000 (this depends on other financial commitments).

At this stage, it may be worth stressing terminology. The borrower is the person who grants a mortgage: the mortgagor (or chargor). People often refer to 'getting a mortgage'. Technically, this is inaccurate. What the borrower obtains is a loan: the mortgage is the security interest which the borrower grants to the lender. The lender is called the mortgagee (or chargee). To aid comprehension, this chapter normally refers to lenders and borrowers.

In this chapter, we consider the various forms of mortgage and the rights they confer on lenders. Because borrowers tend to be in a weak position (they are often in desperate need of money), there have long been protections against terms which may restrict rights to recover the land or which are unfair. A more modern problem has involved landowners who mortgage their land to guarantee others' debts. This is common in a family setting. There are many cases in which wives have mortgaged family homes as security for bank loans to their husbands' business, without appreciating the risks being taken. The home will be lost if the business becomes insolvent, though the family will benefit if the business prospers. This last area will be discussed as a Critical Issue.

Types of mortgage

Until 1925, mortgages took the form of a transfer of the fee simple to the lender, with the borrower getting it back once the loan was repaid. The security is obvious: the lender owns the land, though the borrower would be in possession. This structure looks odd to modern eyes: borrowers naturally regard themselves as owners. Indeed, this was recognised by the courts, which treated the lender as having a security interest rather than normal ownership. Accordingly, the courts insisted that the borrower always had a right to redeem (to get the fee simple back on repayment), even if there was no contractual right.

Because this was so well known, mortgages frequently provided for repayment after six months, though nobody expected repayment then. This retains some significance today: the lender has a statutory power to sell the land only when 'the mortgage money has become due'. The six-month clause ensures that there are no problems in satisfying that requirement, though sale is very unlikely unless the borrower has defaulted in making payments.

This transferring of the legal fee simple to and fro is unnecessarily complex. The 1925 legislation prohibits it, instead giving the lender a 3,000-year lease (though still with power to sell the fee simple). This lease seems even more strange than transferring the fee simple, though at least borrowers could proclaim themselves as owners.

The 1925 legislation also introduced the modern form of mortgage: the legal charge. The **charge** constitutes a security interest, without creating any conventional property interest (fee simple or lease) in the lender. The charge was an alternative to the 3,000-year lease, though it soon became used in nearly all transactions. Since the Land Registration Act 2002[1] (Extract 10.2.4), it has been the only way of mortgaging a registered

[1] Section 23(1).

legal estate. Unfortunately, this does not mean that we can forget the 3,000-year lease. The rights of lenders under legal charges are those of a 3,000-year tenant. In particular, this explains the lender's right to possession. There is a strong argument that it is time to ditch the long lease completely and for statute to clarify the rights of the lender.

Mortgages can be either legal or equitable. There will be an equitable mortgage if there is no deed, or a mortgage of an equitable interest. Another security interest is the charging order (described in Chapter 12[2]). It may be seen as part of the remedies of lenders as much as part of the law of mortgages.

Mortgages are sometimes distinguished according to the arrangements for repayment. In an instalment (or repayment) mortgage, a constant monthly payment will pay off both interest and capital over the life of the mortgage, which might be up to 25 or 30 years. Other mortgages will involve interest only payments to the lender. Most purchasers will wish to ensure that the loan is paid off, at the latest before they retire. As an alternative to a repayment mortgage, this may be achieved by linking some form of investment to the mortgage. Endowment mortgages were very common until a few decades ago: the borrower entered into a linked endowment life insurance policy. Unfortunately, these policies often failed to provide enough money to pay off the loan; they have fallen out of favour. Another distinction is between mortgages with an interest rate fixed for a specified period (often up to five years) and those with a variable rate mortgage. Especially when interest rates are low, the borrower may find it cheaper to have a variable rate mortgage. It is unusual for one party to be allowed to change the terms of a contract. However, it has been a very common form of mortgage and the courts have held it valid, though they may imply a term that the right to change interest rates must be exercised reasonably.[3]

CRITICAL ISSUE

Vitiating factors

These are factors which prevent there being a valid mortgage in the first place. The normal contract rules (mistake, misrepresentation) apply. However, many problems have arisen in recent decades when a charge to a bank has been procured by the misrepresentation or undue influence of a family member (not the bank).

Mortgages often aid the funding of small businesses. Although we may think about mortgages as being about the funding of house purchases, they can provide security whenever money is owed. Many small businesses possess insufficient assets for use as security. The only assets belong to the individuals running the company. The most common asset is a family home, which is frequently jointly owned with a spouse or partner. For a loan to the business to be feasible, the family home will have to be mortgaged and the spouse or partner will need to join in the mortgage. In other cases, parents or children may have assets that can be charged.

---

[2] See above (p. 174).
[3] *Paragon Finance plc v Nash* [2002] 1 WLR 685 at [36]–[41]; it is not difficult for the lender to satisfy that requirement.

There is nothing wrong with any of this. Finance is crucial to most small businesses and relatives are often happy to assist. For spouses and partners, their family prosperity is often dependent on the success of a business run by one of them. The courts have recognised that it would be harmful for the law to make it difficult for small businesses to raise money in this way. It is only from a narrow financial angle that the charge looks disadvantageous to the chargor. To overemphasise it risks endangering both the availability of finance and the free will of the parties involved, as well as the likely long-term financial benefit of the chargor.

On the other hand, problems do arise. Two will be mentioned. The first is that the charge may make no sense at all. This might be because the business is clearly going to fail, so that the charge will bring at best temporary relief. Alternatively, little benefit may be gained in return for extensive liability. These are circumstances in which few rational landowners, even if fully willing to assist family members, would enter into charges. The second problem is where the borrower exerts undue influence on (or makes a misrepresentation to) the chargee. The borrower is frequently desperate to get money to advance the business, the more so if its financial position is weak. Pressure may be put on the spouse/partner/family member to go ahead with the charge.

There is no general duty on lenders to advise chargors: they are expected to be aware of what they are doing and to take their own decisions.[4] The principal legal developments are based upon the second of the above problems. Misrepresentation and undue influence are vitiating factors which enable a contract to be set aside. However, mortgages involve an awkward tripartite relationship: lender, borrower and chargor. The charge is between lender and chargor, while the misrepresentation is between borrower and chargor.

Erica and Fred are living together and jointly own the family home. Erica runs a business and Fred is willing to charge the family home to secure a new loan to the business by Grasping Finance plc. Erica, knowing that Fred is worried about the extent of liability, tells Fred that just £10,000 is involved. She fails to say that the charge also covers existing debts owed by the business, which amount to £25,000. Grasping is wholly unaware of Erica's misrepresentation.

Should Grasping be affected by Erica's conduct? Arguments that Erica should be treated as the agent of Grasping in getting Fred's agreement have been rejected as artificial. Instead, in **Barclays Bank plc v O'Brien**[5] (Extract 21.3.1) the House of Lords held that the lender (Grasping) will be affected if it has notice of Erica's misconduct.

It is now accepted that *O'Brien* uses the doctrine of notice in an unconventional manner. The doctrine usually applies where a purchaser has notice of a claim to the land. Here, the question is all about Fred's claim not to be bound by the charge he has signed, not about any claim to Erica's land. Furthermore, we shall see that Grasping will be

---

[4] *National Westminster Bank plc v Morgan* [1985] AC 686 rejected arguments based upon inequality of bargaining power between lender and chargor.
[5] [1994] 1 AC 180.

protected if it takes specified steps to ensure that Fred is given appropriate advice. The *O'Brien* rules make sense, but they are not a conventional application of the doctrine of notice.

The principles established in *O'Brien* gave rise to a mass of litigation and the House of Lords returned to the question in *Royal Bank of Scotland plc v Etridge (No 2)*[6] (Extract 21.3.3). Today, we can turn directly to the rules laid down by *Etridge* in 2001. An opening comment is that they were articulated in a detailed fashion which reads more like statute than case law.

The wrong

Nothing special need be said about misrepresentation. However, in *Etridge* the House of Lords redefined the requirements of undue influence. This is principally a contract issue and will be considered briefly. Some relationships (such as lawyer and client) give rise to a presumption of undue influence, but this has little relevance for us. Otherwise, there are two requirements. The first is a relationship of trust and confidence and the second is that the transaction is not readily explicable by the relationship of the parties. The required relationship is readily shown in the present context – the mere fact that one person guarantees another's debt (without payment) will usually suffice.

The nature of the transaction is more important. It is enough that there is 'a disadvantage sufficiently serious to require evidence to rebut the presumption that in the circumstances of the parties' relationship, it was procured by the exercise of undue influence'.[7] This test is not easily applied. Though a charge is superficially detrimental, it is exactly the sort of transaction that family members often enter into willingly. The House of Lords recognises that it is not enough to prove simply that one spouse has guaranteed the other's debts: this is not indicative of wrongful conduct. On the other hand, supporting a plainly failing business may well call for explanation. It remains to be seen how far the approach in *Etridge* will limit undue influence.

Putting the lender on inquiry

When will the lender be put on inquiry, so that further steps must be taken to counter any wrongful conduct? *Etridge* recognised that the courts had a choice between two approaches in dealing with this. One is to identify circumstances in which there is a very real risk of wrongful conduct by the borrower and then to provide onerous controls over the charge. If such onerous controls were applied too widely, this would make charges unworkable and give rise to the adverse economic results mentioned above. The alternative is to cast the net of suspicion far more widely, but to provide a lighter touch control based upon advice for the chargor; this still goes some way to providing protection for chargors.

It is extremely difficult to identify those charges which involve a very real risk of wrongful conduct, so the House of Lords opted for the second approach. The result is

---

[6] [2002] 2 AC 773. The following analysis is based on Lord Nicholls, with whom all the Law Lords agreed.
[7] *Etridge* at [25].

that the lender will be put on inquiry in most cases. Lord Nicholls appears to consider that a lender is put on inquiry whenever there is a non-commercial surety arrangement:[8] this will include all family relationships. It possesses the merit of catching cases such as *Credit Lyonnais Bank Nederland NV v Burch*[9] (Extract 21.3.4) (discussed below), in which an employee guaranteed her employer's loan. The rules will not apply, however, if there is a joint loan to the borrower and chargor. There are many situations in which family members borrow money for a joint enterprise, whether to pay for an extension of the house or other substantial expenditure.[10] On the other hand, a loan to a husband's company, where the chargor wife is a director or shareholder, is not treated as a joint loan, with the result that the lender is put on inquiry.

Consequences of being put on inquiry

In *Etridge*, the House of Lords recognised the need to establish procedures whereby the effect of any wrongful conduct practised on chargors could be countered, while providing lenders with some certainty that the charge is effective. A lender who does not faithfully follow the procedures is at great risk. In assessing these procedures, it must be remembered that lenders are put on inquiry in vast numbers of charges, most of which will involve no wrongdoing.

In *O'Brien*, it had been contemplated that the lender would interview and advise the chargor. This did not work: experience showed that lenders preferred to leave this role to lawyers. The House of Lords in *Etridge* recognised that it would be lawyers who would be advising the chargor. At the time of *Etridge* there was a widespread impression that the quality of advice was frequently poor; the House of Lords set out to counter this problem.

Selection of solicitor

A crucial element of the new rules is an emphasis on the duties of the solicitor to the chargor. A first stage is that the lender must write to the chargor, explaining that legal advice is essential and will preclude any later objection to the charge. The chargor must be asked to nominate a solicitor. The lender will then provide the solicitor with details of the loan and the borrower's current indebtedness. In the rare case in which the lender suspects wrongdoing by the borrower, the solicitor must be told about the relevant circumstances.

The most controversial issue is whether it is appropriate for the borrower's solicitor to give this advice. From one point of view, an independent solicitor is necessary for impartial advice to be given. It is difficult for the borrower's solicitor to divorce the duty to the chargor from the pre-existing role as solicitor for the borrower. This factor probably explains many earlier examples of perfunctory and unsatisfactory advice. However, two arguments persuaded the House of Lords that use of the borrower's solicitor is

[8] At [87].
[9] [1997] 1 All ER 144.
[10] *CIBC Mortgages plc v Pitt* [1994] 1 AC 200 (paying off a small existing mortgage and the purchase of a second home).

acceptable. First, that person will frequently already be known to (sometimes acting for) the chargor. This is likely to be the person whom the chargor most trusts to give advice. Indeed, that solicitor will know more about the circumstances and usually be in a better position than an outsider to give the best advice. Second (not to be minimised), it will cost considerably more to bring in an outside solicitor who will have much work to do before being in a position to give advice. It may be thought that the present law is not ideal, but provides the best compromise.

A related question is whether the lender's solicitor can be used. This seems to be accepted if the solicitor's role relative to the lender is simply settling the formalities of the charge, but not if providing more substantial legal services to the lender.

What the solicitor must do

Again, it is central that the solicitor owes the chargor a quite independent duty. A solicitor who feels constrained by a conflict of interest should decline to act. An important minimum requirement is that there must be a personal meeting with the chargor in the absence of the borrower. This is obviously important when attempting to counter any wrongdoing by the borrower.

The solicitor must explain the role of legal advice and obtain confirmation that the chargor wishes him or her to act. Advice has to be given as to the nature of the documents and the effects of default (loss of the home). Some assessment of the commercial situation is required, though there are obvious limits on lawyers' skills in this context. Plainly, if the borrower's business is failing, then it would be pointless for the chargor to guarantee debts. It needs to be stressed that the chargor has a choice. Finally, the chargor must give authority for the solicitor to confirm to the lender that appropriate advice has been given.

These steps should go some way to avoiding hasty or ill-advised decisions to enter into charges. How far will they counter misrepresentation or undue influence? The nature of the advice should correct at least some misrepresentations, but undue influence is more problematic. It is stressed that the solicitor has no duty to search out undue influence. To do that would require probing questions about the nature of relationships; these would offend most chargors and be more appropriate to a police investigation.

The greatest difficulty arises when the solicitor advises against entering into a charge and yet the chargor is determined to proceed. In some cases this will be because the chargor has a different set of priorities. The solicitor may believe that a 75 per cent risk of business failure does not justify a charge. The chargor (usually the wife of the borrower) may accept that risk, reasoning that financial hardship will follow anyway if the business fails and the borrower is bankrupt as a result. As expressed by Sir Richard Scott V-C:[11] 'But the purpose of advisers is to advise. The recipient of advice does not have to accept it.' Yet there is a real danger that the undue influence that has been practised may be such as to make the chargor impervious to legal advice. We cannot be confident that, just because good advice has been given, the effects of undue influence have been countered.

[11] *Banco Exterior Internacional SA v Thomas* [1997] 1 WLR 221 at p. 229.

The difficulty facing the solicitor is that there is no sure way of knowing whether the chargor has taken a truly independent decision or is subject to overbearing undue influence. Some guidance comes from the pre-*Etridge* decision of the Court of Appeal in *Credit Lyonnais Bank Nederland NV v Burch*.[12] An employee had guaranteed repayment of her employer's loan. What made this particularly harsh was that the charge covered all sums owed by the employer (potentially up to £270,000; £60,000 was actually claimed) when the extra money borrowed was just £20,000. The court had no hesitation in holding that there was undue influence and that the bank, aware that the chargor was an employee, could not enforce the charge. Millett LJ expressed the opinion (obiter) that the result would be the same even if legal advice had been received: any lawyer should in the circumstances have refused to continue to act for the chargor in the face of such an inexplicable transaction. But why should an employee be prohibited from assisting an employer for whom they have worked for nearly a decade, in circumstances in which their life revolved around their work and they enjoy a close friendship with the employer? Few of us would do so, but should it be outlawed?

Does this survive *Etridge*, which takes a less paternalistic approach? There are indications that a solicitor who believes that there has been wrongful conduct should either make further inquiries or withdraw from the transaction. Merely feeling that it is a most disadvantageous transaction would not be enough to impugn the transaction (or make the solicitor liable).

The solicitor's certificate

The final piece in the jigsaw is that the solicitor gives the lender a certificate that the charge has been properly explained. This is conclusive in favour of the validity of the charge, at least unless the lender has reason to believe that proper advice has not been given. If the appropriate advice has in fact not been given, it is the solicitor who will be liable to the chargor.

Assessing *Etridge*

Does *Etridge* provide adequate protection for chargors and lenders? It is difficult to answer this with confidence, as there are few post-*Etridge* cases. If we accept that charges of the family home are very important to both the national and family economies, then some risks have to be run. It would be unrealistic to expect that any system would spot every example of wrongdoing. But do we do enough to protect chargors? This involves asking whether it is appropriate to use lawyers to give what is fundamentally economic advice, as well as whether allowing the borrower's solicitor to advise the chargor takes too much of a risk. As so often in assessing legal rules, it is all a question of balancing differing objectives: each lawyer (and reader) will have his or her own answer.

A rather different point flows from the successful use of *Etridge* to defeat a lender's claim. The chargor may have won a battle rather than the overall war. The chargor's

---

[12] [1997] 1 All ER 144.

overall objective will be to keep the family home. Yet when lenders seek possession and sale, this is invariably because the borrower cannot afford the mortgage instalments. If the land cannot be sold, then the borrower will almost certainly be bankrupt. If the home is jointly owned, then the **trustee in bankruptcy** can usually obtain a court order for sale under the Trusts of Land and Appointment of Trustees Act 1996.[13] The chargor will lose their home, though at least they will receive their share of the proceeds of sale. This outcome was established in *Alliance and Leicester plc v Slayford*[14] (Extract 21.3.6). The point to stress is that the lender's remedies are cumulative: if one (sale as mortgagee) proves useless, then others (sale on bankruptcy) can still be pursued.

Rules protecting borrowers

There is frequently great inequality of bargaining power between borrower and lender. The danger is that borrowers will agree to virtually any terms when they are in desperate need of money in order to buy property or (in the older cases, especially) stave off financial disaster. This has led to a series of controls over terms in mortgages. We will put them into three categories: rules relating to **redemption**, common law rules relating to fairness of terms, and statutory controls. Other rules specific to lenders' powers of possession and sale are considered later.

Redemption

Because the courts view mortgages as security rights, they insist that it should always be possible to redeem: to pay off the mortgage loan and get the property back in its original state. Three types of term may fall foul of this principle.

Preventing or postponing redemption

Any attempt to preclude redemption will be struck down. This made good sense when the lender obtained the fee simple. It is entirely possible, however, for the mortgage agreement to postpone redemption. We should bear in mind the economics of mortgages. For example, entering into a secured loan transaction may involve the lender in significant expenses. Although these expenses are sometimes charged to the borrower, in other cases they are recovered by a slightly higher interest rate over the life of the mortgage. To allow immediate redemption in the latter case might be unfair on the lender.

In *Knightsbridge Estates Trust Ltd v Byrne*[15] (Extract 21.4.1), there was an unusually long postponement for 40 years. The borrower had sought this in order to obtain a reduction in the interest rate. The Court of Appeal upheld the postponement. It was material that the borrower was a company and there was no hint of pressure or wrongful conduct by the lender. This seems right, though an exceptionally lengthy postponement may be treated as equivalent to losing the property.

---

[13] See Chapter 10, above (p. 176).
[14] (2000) 33 HLR 743.
[15] [1939] Ch 441.

This last point has caused problems for charges over leases, as some leases last for relatively short periods. In *Fairclough v Swan Brewery Co Ltd*[16] (Extract 21.4.2), a 17-year postponement would end within weeks of the end of the lease. As the lender would get virtually nothing back on redemption, the postponement was struck down.

Fairclough is difficult to justify. The real significance of postponing redemption is to prevent repayment of the loan. No convincing reason was given in *Fairclough* for attacking a freely negotiated 17-year loan arrangement. Is it meaningful to say that the lender will get nothing much back at redemption? After all, after 17 years the lease ends anyway! The image one gets is that the land belongs to the lender for 17 years and that is why the borrower gets virtually nothing back. However, that imagery is quite inappropriate in the modern structure of legal charges. The borrower still owns and occupies the charged property (fee simple or lease) and the only significant question is whether a long-term loan can be repaid early.

Options

Occasionally, a mortgage may give the lender an option to purchase the charged property. If this involves purchase at market value, it seems harmless. Yet such an option was struck down by the House of Lords in *Samuel v Jarrah Timber & Wood Paving Corporation Ltd*[17] (Extract 21.4.3). The reason is that it prevents the borrower from getting the property back. It is true that this is inconsistent with the right to redeem, but there seems nothing wrong or unfair in the transaction.

The *Samuel* principle has long been criticised. It will not be applied if the option is in a transaction after the mortgage and genuinely separate from it.[18] More recently, it has been held that it does not apply if the option can properly be seen as part of a separate transaction. In *Warnborough Ltd v Garmite Ltd*[19] (Extract 21.4.10) land was sold; the purchaser borrowed the purchase money from the seller, secured by a charge on the land. On the same day, the purchaser gave the seller an option to repurchase the land. It was held that the option was part of the sale rather than the mortgage, though the transactions were contemporaneous. This is an approach more generous to lenders than *Samuel*, though it seems eminently justifiable.

The property after redemption

The courts have insisted that the borrower should not just get the property back, but also get it back in its original condition. A good example is provided by the decision of the House of Lords in *Bradley v Carritt*[20] (Extract 21.4.8). The mortgage was over shares in a tea company and the lender was a tea broker. The mortgage required the borrower, both before and after redemption, to use his best endeavours as shareholder to ensure that the broker should act as agent for the sale of the company's tea.

[16] [1912] AC 565.
[17] [1904] AC 323.
[18] *Reeve v Lisle* [1902] AC 461. Simply using two documents on the same day does not work: *Lewis v Frank Love Ltd* [1961] 1 WLR 261.
[19] [2003] EWCA Civ 1544; [2004] 1 P&CR D18.
[20] [1903] AC 253.

The House of Lords held (by a three to two majority) that the property would not be redeemed in its original state: the borrower would still have to use the votes attached to the shares to benefit the lender. Accordingly, the term could not be enforced after redemption. From a practical point of view, there doesn't seem anything wrong with the arrangement: there was no unfairness or taking advantage of the borrower. However, the majority considered that the rule that the property must be redeemed in its original state was central to the law of mortgages.

Although supported by earlier cases, *Bradley* was controversial. Nor was it the last word on the matter. In *Kreglinger v New Patagonia Meat & Cold Storage Co Ltd*[21] (Extract 21.4.9), the House of Lords considered a right of pre-emption (a right to purchase if the seller chooses to sell) over part of the mortgaged property. Because this right could apply after redemption, *Bradley* might be thought to strike it down. However, the House of Lords in *Kreglinger* was far more influenced by ideas of freedom of contract; the right was upheld. It has always been difficult to explain the precise basis of the decision. The approach of Viscount Haldane VC is generally thought to embody the preferable approach: there was a 'collateral undertaking, outside and clear of the mortgage'.

This 'collateral undertaking' does not require a wholly separate agreement. The analysis is that there is a security agreement and a pre-emption agreement. In truth, the courts are saying little more than that they will treat some benefits as collateral. The analysis may be seen as little more than a fig leaf hiding the courts' embarrassment in departing from the *Bradley* reasoning. Nevertheless, there will sometimes be a genuine collateral agreement. This was true of *Warnborough*, in which *Kreglinger* was relied upon heavily. The option in *Warnborough* was rightly seen as part of the sale agreement rather than the mortgage agreement.

There are two difficult questions consequential upon *Warnborough*. The first is whether *Kreglinger* is narrowed so that it applies only if there is such a genuine separate agreement. That would make *Kreglinger* more comprehensible, though it runs against the trend to limit *Bradley* and to recognise the parties' freedom to contract as they wish. The second question is whether, if the wider effect of *Kreglinger* survives, it extends to options. This is difficult: options are more obviously inconsistent with the right to redeem. However, the modern approach is to deride the option rule. As Lord Phillips MR has stated, it 'no longer serves a useful purpose'.

Fairness of terms: common law rules

The ability of the courts to strike down unfair terms goes far to explain the disenchantment with the redemption rules discussed above: they are no longer necessary to protect the disadvantaged borrower.

The law is best illustrated by two twentieth-century decisions. In *Cityland & Property (Holdings) Ltd v Dabrah*,[22] there was a loan of £2,900, the borrower promising to repay £4,533 over six years. No interest was specified, though the repayment equated to annual interest of 19 per cent over the six years. As is common, the mortgage provided

[21] [1914] AC 25.
[22] [1968] Ch 166.

that the capital would become due if the borrower defaulted on making payments. However, the unusual wording of the mortgage meant that a default even early in the mortgage would lead to the full £4,533 being payable (not the much smaller sum of £2,900 plus interest, as would normally follow). On the facts, there was early default; the lender's claim to £4,533 represented 38 per cent interest. Goff J rejected the claim to £4,553 and substituted £2,900 plus interest at seven per cent.

The second case, *Multiservice Bookbinding Ltd v Marden*[23] (Extract 21.4.12), again had unusual facts. A loan of £36,000 was calculated in Swiss francs and repayable over ten years. Even though the borrower had repaid £24,000, massive depreciation of sterling meant that the original loan had grown to £63,000. Overall, the mortgagor's obligations were equivalent to annual interest of 33 per cent over the life of the mortgage: much more severe than 38 per cent for a year or so in *Cityland*. Nevertheless, Browne-Wilkinson J held the terms valid: this was a deal negotiated between businessmen who fully understood what they were doing. That it turned out very disadvantageous to one of them was a risk they took.

What exactly is the test applied in these cases? Some of the dicta in *Cityland* support a reasonableness requirement. Counsel relied upon this in *Multiservice*, where the agreement was unreasonable because the lender got the twin benefits of a safe currency (Swiss franc) and a high interest rate appropriate for a weaker currency (sterling). However, Browne-Wilkinson J rejected reasonableness as the test. For the courts to intervene, the term must be 'unfair and unconscionable'. He explained this as requiring that the offending terms must be imposed in a 'morally reprehensible manner'. This will usually involve unfairly taking advantage of the borrower. It will be very difficult to prove if the borrower has independent legal advice.

A very different principle is that covenants in unreasonable restraint of trade will be struck down. This applies to all agreements, not just mortgages. It most commonly applies when the lender is also a provider of goods. There may be a 'solus tie', an agreement to sell only the lender's goods for a stipulated period. A good example is *Esso Petroleum Co Ltd v Harper's Garage (Stourport) Ltd*[24] (Extract 21.4.11), in which Esso lent money; the mortgage required the purchase of their petrol for periods of 5 and 21 years. The House of Lords held that ties are void if they are unreasonable, whether as between the parties or as regards the public interest. On that basis, the 5-year tie was upheld, but the 21-year tie struck down. One important limitation on the principle is that it applies only if the borrower is already trading from the premises: it will not apply to the funding of a purchase.

● Fairness of terms: statutory rules

Loans to individuals are covered by the Consumer Credit Act 1974, section 140A (Extract 21.4.13). This provision applies to any 'unfair' term or exercise of powers (or other conduct) by the lender. The court has wide powers to strike down terms, amend them and generally correct the unfairness. Section 140A was inserted by the Consumer Credit Act 2006,

[23] [1979] Ch 84.
[24] [1968] AC 269.

replacing control over extortionate terms. Until we have cases, it is difficult to say what difference there is between 'extortionate' and 'unfair' and whether the 'unfair' test is much different from the common law test.

The Unfair Terms in Consumer Contracts Regulations 1999[25] also apply to loans to individuals, acting in a non-business capacity. However, they do not apply to all terms (they are unlikely to apply to objections to the interest rate, for example) and it seems unlikely that they will be significant now that we have an unfairness test in the consumer credit legislation.

Rights and remedies of the lender

This topic is vitally important, as it concerns the lender's ability to enforce the security. We will consider three areas. **Foreclosure** applies once the mortgage money is due (likely to be soon after the loan); the right to possession applies immediately on entry into a mortgage; sale applies once there has been default. It is confusing that they are triggered in such different ways. It may be noted that these rights and remedies can be amended by the agreement between the parties.

Foreclosure

Foreclosure is the termination by the court of the borrower's right to redeem. It has the drastic result that the lender becomes the absolute owner of the property. It was the traditional remedy for lenders, but today it is rare and so is considered very briefly. It will be ordered only after the borrower has been given an extended period to come up with the money.

The real vice of foreclosure was that the lender became owner even if the property was worth a lot more than what was owed. For many years, the courts have had jurisdiction to order a sale rather than foreclosure, so that risk is minimised. Even where foreclosure has been ordered, it can be set aside if the borrower later finds the money. Even apart from these disadvantages, few modern lenders want to end up owning the property.

Possession

The right to possession is much more important. We now consider four aspects of the right: (a) the reasons for taking possession; (b) when the right to possession arises; (c) statutory control over the right; and (d) obligations flowing from taking possession.

Reasons for taking possession

In the great majority of cases, possession is taken as a prelude to selling the land. In practical terms, it is virtually impossible to sell land unless the purchaser is given vacant

---

[25] SI 1999 No 2083.

possession (excepting land sold subject to a lease). It follows that a lender has to take possession in order to get purchasers interested.

In fewer cases, possession may be sought in order that the lender can manage the property. This may be relevant if the borrower fails to take proper care of it, such that the lender fears that the value of the security may be endangered. Alternatively, the lender may want to lease the property and apply the rent to cover interest payments (this is rare for residential property). Such cases are exceptional: most lenders are large financial institutions, for whom the idea of managing thousands of properties is unattractive.

The right to possession

Borrowers expect to have possession and this is the normal position. A couple buying a home with a building society loan do not expect the lender to possess their new home! It is a strange feature of the present law that the borrower's possession has no clear legal basis, though modern charges quite commonly contain terms permitting possession until default; occasionally, the courts have implied this.

By contrast, the standard legal analysis is that lenders have an immediate right to possession. This is a direct result of the fiction of a 3,000-year lease. A tenant is entitled to possess and so therefore is a chargee. As Harman J observed, the right arises 'before the ink is dry on the mortgage'.[26]

It is surprising that this right to possession is not linked to any default by the borrower. There may be a good case for allowing possession occasionally where there is no default, but the lender should prove good cause to a court. Furthermore, there is no general common law control over exercising the right. The borrower is given the opportunity to pay off the capital within a very short period, but otherwise possession will be ordered pretty well automatically.[27] It may well be thought that the law fails to reflect the legitimate expectations of borrowers. In practice, however, it is unusual for possession to be sought without default. In nearly all cases, the mortgage lender is seeking possession in order to sell the land; we shall see later that sale requires default.

Statutory limits

Given these criticisms, it is unsurprising that the Administration of Justice Act 1970 (AJA) section 36 (Extract 21.4.19) introduced a discretion to adjourn proceedings or delay possession. We should note that this applies only to dwelling houses; there is no similar protection for other property.

Nearly all mortgages provide that the entire capital shall become due if there is default in paying interest. This is part of the armoury of weapons available to the lender in the event of default, though chances of payment are minimal. AJA section 36 provides that a court order may be made if the 'mortgagor is likely to be able within a reasonable period to pay any sums due'. The words 'any sums due' will include the entire capital

[26] *Four-Maids Ltd* v *Dudley Marshall (Properties) Ltd* [1957] Ch 317 at p. 320.
[27] *Birmingham Citizens Permanent BS* v *Caunt* [1962] Ch 883 (Extract 21.4.17).

CRITICAL ISSUE

because of the provision just described. It will virtually never be the case that a borrower, let us call her Betty, struggling with paying interest (perhaps £600 monthly on a £120,000 loan) will be able to repay capital (£120,000 plus arrears) within a short period. This threatened to make the protection illusory: Parliament had overlooked the problem and the result was clearly unintended. Fortunately AJA 1973 section 8 (Extract 21.4.20) amends section 36 so that such accelerated liability is ignored. If Betty has missed four payments, the question is whether she can afford £600 a month plus (over a reasonable period) arrears of £2,400.

There are two types of issue that have dominated the cases: what types of mortgage are covered and how readily the courts will refuse possession. In addition, we will investigate a couple of further problems in the application of the legislation.

Types of mortgage covered

We have seen that there may be instalment mortgages (where capital is paid off over the life of the mortgage), endowment mortgages (where a linked endowment insurance policy pays off the capital) and interest only mortgages – as well as the nineteenth-century form of mortgage which was silent as to duration. AJA section 36 (Extract 21.4.19) applies to all of these. The single form of mortgage held to be outside the protection is a charge to secure a bank overdraft. Without considering the technical reasons for this, it may be observed that bank overdrafts are of an essentially temporary nature. The purpose of AJA section 36 is to deal with short-term problems in long-term arrangements.

The exercise of the discretion

If the borrower can pay the arrears (plus current instalments) within a reasonable period, then the court can intervene. It seems that Parliament had in mind problems such as unemployment or ill health, which would have a short-term effect on ability to make repayments. The Payne Committee, which recommended the statutory discretion, thought that postponement for six months would normally suffice.

For several years, it appeared that the question for the court was whether the arrears could be paid off within, at most, around two years. This was radically changed by *Cheltenham & Gloucester BS v Norgan*[28] (Extract 21.2.24), probably the most important AJA case. The Court of Appeal held that the 'reasonable period' allowed in AJA section 36 (Extract 21.4.19) can extend to the intended life of the mortgage. This is tremendously important. If there is a 25-year loan of (say) £150,000, it is easy for arrears of £30,000 to accumulate before the case comes for final decision. Paying £30,000 over two years will be a hopeless task for somebody who has had difficulty in paying interest (£750 per month is typical for a loan of this amount). However, over the 25 years of the mortgage, the extra monthly instalments may be no more than £150 per month. If the borrower has significant earnings, paying a monthly total of £900 may be entirely feasible. In practice, it appears to be common for repayment to be required over a shorter period

[28] [1996] 1 WLR 343.

than the entire mortgage – at least when that is a long time.[29] However, this will still be much longer than a couple of years and so remain a real benefit to borrowers.

It is apparent that *Norgan* represents a more generous approach. However, the borrower has to produce a budget showing earnings that will enable the new instalments (£900 in the above example) to be paid: the court will not accept vague promises. There are other elements of the decision that could work to the borrower's disadvantage. In the past, it was common for several postponements to be ordered and for the borrower to fail to pay the sums agreed in any of them: years would pass by while arrears mounted. In *Norgan*, it was said that the new approach should be to allow just one chance; thereafter the land should be sold if there were further default.

Whatever the period, how does the court decide whether to exercise its discretion? Crucial factors are the extent of the arrears and the earning power of the borrower. Problems frequently arise when relationships break down. Two incomes may have enabled payments to be made in the past, but are often insufficient when two homes have to be supported. Social security benefits may sometimes assist, but often the financial position is hopeless. In these cases, the courts will give possession to the lender. This is illustrated by *First National Bank plc v Syed*[30] (Extract 21.4.25), in which the borrowers had failed to make payments (about £100 per month) for several years. The borrowers now offered to pay £150 per month, but because of large arrears the monthly interest now exceeded that sum. In other words, the debt would further increase even if the borrower was able to afford the £150. The court had no hesitation in holding that there was no jurisdiction to postpone possession.

How does the prospect of capital repayment affect the statutory discretion? The borrower may argue that the entire loan will be paid off by selling the property and making a capital payment (rather than monthly instalments, as in the *Norgan* context). This is nicely illustrated by *Bristol & West BS v Ellis*[31] (Extract 21.4.27). The borrower owed around £77,000 (plus costs). She wished to postpone sale for three to five years while her children were completing their education. She was willing to repay £5,000 immediately and had valuations of £80,000 and £85,000 for the house. Even though the only monthly payments she could afford would be of interest (paid by social security), she argued that the sale proceeds would more than cover the debt.

The Court of Appeal thought it possible, in principle, to postpone sale for the period the borrower had in mind. Their major concern was with the safety of the security. If the lender could be assured of being repaid, then a delay of a few years would be acceptable. On the facts, the amount due was far too close to the valuation of the land for the court to be confident that the loan would be fully repaid if the land were sold within a few years. The court was well aware that valuations are sometimes unrealistically high, quite apart from the risks of land values dropping over a short period. There are also, of course, costs involved in selling land and a danger that future default in making interest payments might cause the debt to grow.

---

[29] *Bank of Scotland plc v Zinda* [2012] 1 WLR 728: suspension for 9½ years when 23 years left. The period of suspension was not challenged in the Court of Appeal, but drew no adverse comment.
[30] [1991] 2 All ER 250.
[31] (1996) 73 P&CR 158.

In some cases the court may doubt whether a future sale will materialise: the borrower may be grasping at a straw to stave off the evil day when the home is lost.

> Sandra has borrowed £120,000 from Big Bank and her house is worth £140,000. Sandra has lost her job and accepts that she cannot afford the monthly payments. When Big Bank seek possession, her defence is that she should sell the land (without any delay, unlike the proposal in **Ellis**). There is some merit in this. Sales by owners in possession often attract higher prices than sales by lenders: the property can be better presented by a person living there. But the danger is that Sandra may in fact delay sale. Asking, say, £180,000 for the house will be effective in putting off most likely buyers. The chances are that the house will not be sold and that the arrears will mount up.

A borrower who really wants to sell will have had plenty of opportunity to do so before possession proceedings start. In some cases, the land has been on the market for some time; again, this indicates that a sale by the borrower is unlikely to materialise.

A related point is that lenders generally regard it as essential to take possession before advertising the land for sale. What if the borrower says that they will stay there and co-operate while the lender markets the property? This is attractive for the borrower because it delays the time at which possession has to be given up and may result in a higher price being received. Unfortunately, life is not so simple. There is a real danger that the borrower will fail to support a sale, knowing that the sooner a sale results then the sooner the home will be lost. Even with a co-operative borrower, prospective purchasers may well be put off. They may foresee the risk of the borrower refusing to move out, which at best would delay the sale. The result would be difficulty in selling and, probably, a lower price. Conventional wisdom is that it is almost essential for the person in charge of the sale (whether it be borrower or, as here, lender) to be in possession.

Problems in the ambit of the protection

Two factors are assumed by AJA, section 36 (Extract 21.4.19). The first is that court proceedings for possession will always precede sale; the second is that there are always arrears. Both these assumptions have been shown to be false.

Asserting possession normally requires a court order: criminal law prohibits violence to property or person (or threats) to secure entry.[32] However, as shown by *Horsham Properties Group Ltd* v *Clark*[33] (Extract 21.4.33), sale can be effected without taking possession. The purchaser was held to be entitled to possession. The AJA was inapplicable to the purchaser's claim, as the mortgage no longer bound the land. This result seems wholly inconsistent with the statutory policy, though it is an inevitable consequence of the legislation. Counsel tried to avoid it with a human rights argument, but this failed. The court regarded it as hopeless to attack the long-standing power of sale, especially as it is an implied term in the agreement between lender and borrower.

---

[32] Criminal Law Act 1977, s 6.
[33] [2009] 1 WLR 1255.

The reason why sales without possession are uncommon (save where the house has been let to tenants) is that few people are interested in purchasing land occupied by the borrower. Any sale is likely to be at a sharply reduced price. It remains to be seen whether a sale in these circumstances breaches the lender's obligation to take care to obtain a proper price.

In any event, the Ministry of Justice is consulting on a proposal to require a court order before most sales of owner occupier housing, where the loan was for its purchase.[34] It is not thought that the problem revealed by *Horsham* is likely to be exploited before this proposal is implemented. Though the property in *Horsham* was occupied by the borrower, the facts involved a buy-to-let mortgage; this probably explains how the sale came about.

Turning to the issue of arrears, the discretion operates only if arrears can be paid off within a reasonable period. What happens if there are no arrears, or they have already been paid off? The right to possession does not, of course, depend on there being arrears. If there are no arrears, the result could be that (1) the powers do not apply; (2) (the opposite conclusion) there is an automatic right to have possession postponed; or (3) there is a true discretion.

This problem surfaced in *Western Bank Ltd* v *Schindler*[35] (Extract 21.4.23). Defective drafting meant that no interest was payable until the repayment of the mortgage. The lender became justifiably worried when interest payments ceased. Possession was the only viable remedy: it meant that the lender could obtain rental income from the property and thus prevent the overall debt from increasing. A majority of the Court of Appeal held that the AJA powers were applicable. They reasoned that it would be 'irrational and unfair' for the powers to apply only if there are arrears. Whatever the wording of the section, this point seems entirely valid.

However, the court went on to reject the argument that section 36 (Extract 21.4.19) meant that the discretion had to be exercised so as to deny possession. Instead, the court has (as in the normal cases when there are arrears) a true discretion. On the facts, possession was required to protect the security and accordingly the lender was given possession.

Do the statutory powers work well?

Leaving aside the problems revealed by *Horsham*, the law establishes a reasonable balance. It protects the borrower where there is a reasonable chance of the loan being repaid over the intended lifetime of the loan; the lender will obtain possession in other cases.

Three factors, which often occur together, explain many of the problems faced by defaulting borrowers:

1. First, there may be a long-term loss of income so that payments cannot be made; quite often this is a result of relationship breakdown. Despite some help from social security payments, these circumstances are very likely to lead to the lender gaining

[34] Mortgages: Power of Sale and Residential Property CP55/09.
[35] [1977] Ch 1.

possession. In the difficult economic conditions of 2011, the annual number of repossessions was around 37,000, with around 70,000 court applications (and around 160,000 mortgages in arrears). To put this into context, even the mortgage in arrears figure is less than 1.5 per cent of all mortgages.

2. Next, increases in interest rates may ruin financial plans. Many loans have variable interest rates (usually the interest rate is adjusted in line with national interest rates). Even fixed interest loans are usually fixed for two to five years and are susceptible to increases when the fix ends. Indeed, a large sudden increase in a fixed interest loan may be less manageable than a series of small increases to a variable interest loan. Large numbers of repossessions have often coincided with higher interest rates.

3. Finally, it is crucial that arrears are not allowed to mount up. Particularly in the years before *Norgan*, arrears mounted quickly. This was partly because of high interest rates at the time and partly because there were repeated and costly court applications when payments were missed. Once the arrears have reached a high level, the chances of repayment (even on the more generous *Norgan* basis) are much reduced.

The statutory discretion is of immense importance, but we should never forget that its impact may be eclipsed by general economic developments and the benefits to borrowers of effective debt management.

The economic difficulties experienced over the past few years have threatened a large increase in the number of possession applications. This has caused the law regarding possession to come under increased scrutiny. Though the basic legal structure has been kept in place, there is a protocol[36] governing the steps which mortgage lenders should take before seeking possession of residential property. These are designed to encourage discussion between the parties, the obtaining of advice and, where appropriate, rescheduling the loan payments. A very different protection (for up to two months) is provided for tenants of defaulting borrowers by the Mortgage Repossessions (Protection of Tenants etc) Act 2010.

Obligations on lenders in possession

The law does not allow the lender to benefit from both interest on the loan and possession. If the lender receives rent from the property then this must be paid (less unpaid interest) to the borrower. How do the rules work if the property is kept by the lender?

Adrian has charged his shop to Basil as security for a £150,000 loan. Basil takes possession and runs the shop himself, making a profit of £50,000 a year. Had the shop been leased, a rent of £15,000 a year could have been achieved. Basil has to pay Adrian £15,000 a year (less any unpaid interest). The rest of the profit (£35,000) can be kept by Basil: it represents Basil's skill and work in running the shop.[37]

---

[36] http://www.justice.gov.uk/civil/guidance/courts-and-tribunals/courts/procedure-rules/civil/contents/protocols/prot_mha.htm
[37] *White v City of London Brewery Co* (1889) 42 Ch D 237 (pub) (Extract 21.4.30).

The above example shows that the lender cannot view possession as a route to making a quick profit. Indeed, the lender in possession has an obligation to obtain income from the land. However, no liability is incurred where possession is taken in order to sell: nobody expects the land to be leased for a short period until the sale goes through.

Sale

If the borrower defaults on loan repayments, such that it becomes apparent that future payments are unlikely to be made, then the lender may well wish to sell the charged land. This is the most effective way of realising the security. As has been noted, there is no need for court approval of sale. However, possession will nearly always have to be sought to make sale feasible. If possession is contested, then almost inevitably there will be a court application in order to avoid the potential for criminal liability. For dwelling houses, this will activate the court's discretion to protect the borrower who has a reasonable prospect of paying arrears.

Unlike foreclosure and possession, the power of sale is statutory (originally it was a very common express power). There are two tests for when the land can be sold. The first establishes when the power *arises*. Normally, this is all that the purchaser is concerned with. The second establishes when a power is *exercisable*. This is primarily of importance as between the lender and borrower: any sale when the power is not exercisable constitutes a breach of duty by the lender. A borrower who acts in time can stop the sale. If the sale has been completed, then the borrower can claim against the lender for any loss caused. The purchaser is under no obligation to check that the power is exercisable and is free from liability, unless aware that there is a problem.[38]

When does the power arise? LPA section 101 (Extract 21.4.31) gives the answer: when the mortgage debt is due. It is common for mortgages to state that the money is due after six months. This is distinctly fictitious: this is not when the sum is expected to be paid. A modern mortgage may state that the money is due solely for the purposes of section 101. In any event, the practical point is that the power arises at a very early stage, which purchasers can easily ascertain.

The power is exercisable only when there has been real default. This is the province of LPA section 103 (Extract 21.4.31). There are three possibilities:

1. three months' notice requiring capital repayment has been given (assuming the lender is entitled to repayment);
2. interest is in arrear for two months; or
3. some other breach has occurred.

These are matters that it would be awkward for purchasers to go into. For example, looking closely at the payment record of a borrower (the details of which might be contested) is the last thing a purchaser wants to get involved with. Most cases involve failure to pay interest. It may be noted that the power does not disappear because the

---

[38] LPA, s 104(2); *Bailey v Barnes* [1894] 1 Ch 25.

arrears have been paid off, although possession of dwelling houses is unlikely to be obtained in such cases.

A vitally important aspect of sale is that the lender can keep only the money owed (including arrears of interest and costs of selling). The entire balance has to be paid to the borrower. There is no question of the lender making a profit: this makes sale more acceptable than foreclosure. If the sale price does not cover the amount due, then the borrower can be sued for the difference. Often, of course, there will be insufficient assets to make this viable.

The fact that the lender keeps only what is due reduces the incentive to sell for the best price, so long as the debt is covered. Yet the borrower has a crucial interest in the best price being received. What duties are owed by the lender? For a start, the lender is not a trustee of the power: it is exercised for the lender's benefit. It was settled in the 1970s in **Cuckmere Brick Co Ltd v Mutual Finance Ltd**[39] (Extract 21.4.36), that the lender owes a duty of care to obtain the proper price. On the facts, the sale publicity failed to mention the existence of **planning permission**, which would enhance the value of the land. The lender was not personally at fault: it was the estate agent who was to blame, but the lender was held responsible for that.

Subsequent cases have denied the existence of a more general duty of care – that would sit uneasily with power's being exercised for the lender's benefit. This is illustrated by the more recent decision of the Court of Appeal in **Silven Properties Ltd v Royal Bank of Scotland plc**[40] (Extract 21.4.39). Here it was argued that planning permission should have been sought for the land prior to selling it, in order to enhance its value. That argument was rejected by the Court of Appeal. The lender can choose when to sell, even if this involves selling at the 'worst possible moment'. This necessarily meant that there was no need to delay to seek planning permission: there is no obligation to improve the property or increase its value. The only duty is to get the proper price at the time it is decided to sell. Once a decision to sell has been taken, then the land must be marketed in such a way as to attract a proper price – insisting on sale within an unreasonably short period (a week, for example) is very likely to constitute a breach of duty.

A final and rather different point is that the court has jurisdiction to order sale at any time[41] (Extract 21.4.42). Though a lender's decision not to sell is not a breach of duty, the court can still order sale. An example is provided by **Palk v Mortgage Services Funding plc**,[42] where the debt exceeded the value of the property ('negative equity'). The lender wanted to delay sale, in the hope that the value would increase in the future. The property would be leased in the meantime, though the rent would be insufficient to cover all the interest. The borrower wanted the property sold in order to avoid what was seen as an open-ended personal liability to pay the mounting difference between the property value and what was due. The Court of Appeal sided with the borrower, regarding the lender as taking a one-way bet on the future of property prices: they benefited if prices increased, whereas the borrower would face liability if prices were to fall or stay constant.

[39] [1971] Ch 949.
[40] [2004] 1 WLR 997 at [15].
[41] LPA, s 91.
[42] [1993] Ch 330.

Accordingly, sale was ordered. This may be regarded as a rather harsh outcome as regards the lender. The burden on the borrower is only realistic if the borrower has (or will have) sufficient funds to pay off the balance of the debt. Those circumstances will not be common; usually, the real risk in delaying sale will be incurred by the lender.

Questions to consider

1. What is a security interest? How does a 'legal charge' differ from a traditional mortgage?
2. How does the law protect individuals against the risk of being pressurised (by borrowers) into mortgaging their land?
3. What control is there over the terms the parties can insert into a mortgage? Does the law establish a reasonable balance between (i) the need to protect weak parties to transactions and (ii) freedom of contract?
4. Are there effective controls over mortgagee lenders who wish to sell the land?

Further reading

Bamforth, N [1996] CLP Pt 2, pages 207–244: Lord Macnaghten's puzzle: the mortgage of real property in English law.

Brown, S [2007] Conv 316: The Consumer Credit Act 2006: real additional mortgagor protection?

Robinson, S [1989] Conv 336, 412: Mortgages – care and protection.

Rudden, B (1961) 25 Conv 278: Mortgagee's right to possession.

Thompson, M (2003) 'Mortgages and undue influence', in *Modern Studies in Property Law*, Vol 2, ed. E Cooke, Chapter 7.

Watt, G (2007) 'The lie of the land: mortgage law as legal fiction', in *Modern Studies in Property Law*, Vol 4, ed. E Cooke, Chapter 4.

Whitehouse, L (1997) 'The right to possession: the need for substantive reform', in *The Reform of Property Law*, eds. P Jackson and D Wilde, Chapter 9.

Visit **www.mylawchamber.co.uk** to access tools to help you develop and test your knowledge of land law, including interactive multiple choice questions, practice exam questions with guidance, weblinks, glossary flashcards, legal newsfeed and legal updates.

 **mylaw**chamber

Use **Case Navigator** to read in full some of the key cases referenced in this chapter with commentary and questions:

Cheltenham & Gloucester BS v *Norgan* [1996] 1 WLR 343

Glossary

*Words that are **emboldened** are themselves described in this glossary. Where a term is defined or described in the book, the relevant pages have been inserted after the entry.*

Adverse possession The acquisition of ownership by long use, inconsistent with the rights of the **true owner**. (p. 39)

Annexation The linking of the benefit of a **restrictive covenant** to land, so that the benefit of the covenant passes automatically to a purchaser of that land. (p. 280)

Assignment The transfer of the benefit of a right, commonly applied to the transfer of leases. The person making the transfer is the *assignor* and the person to whom the right is transferred is the *assignee*. (p. 222)

Beneficial owner The person who is entitled to land as the beneficiary under a **trust**. (p. 130)

Benefited land Land which is benefited by an **easement** or **covenant**. (p. 9)

Burdened land Land over which an **easement** is exercised or whose holder is obliged to comply with a **covenant**. (p. 9)

Charge A right enabling its holder (the *chargee*) to sell the land to ensure payment of a debt (or performance of any obligation). It is a form of **mortgage**. (pp. 64, 126, 173, 295)

Commonhold A system for the ownership and management of flats and other properties that require active management. (pp. 21, 188, 288)

Completion The final stage of buying land, when the purchase price is paid and there is a transfer of ownership to the purchaser. (p. 59)

Concurrent interests The interests of two or more people who have rights to enjoy property at the same time. They are called *co-owners*. The most common example is where a couple own their house together. (pp. 6, 145)

Constructive notice Where a purchaser ought to be aware (from looking at the **title deeds** and the land) that somebody other than the seller has an interest in the land. (p. 116)

Constructive trust A trust imposed by the court to avoid unconscionable (unfair) conduct. (pp. 55, 72)

Conveyance The formal transfer (usually by **deed**) of land. For **registered land**, we more simply refer to transfers. (p. 59)

Covenant An obligation entered into by a deed. The person entering into the obligation is the *covenantor* and the person with the benefit of the covenant is the *covenantee*. (p. 272)

Deed A formal written document that is signed and witnessed. It is required for many land transactions. A person transferring an interest by deed is usually described as the *grantor*. The person to whom the interest is transferred is the *grantee*. (p. 62)

Derogation from grant The principle whereby a grantor in a **deed** is not permitted to act in such a way as to deny or devalue what the grantee expects to receive. (p. 212)

Discontinuous lease A **lease** that can be exercised on certain dates every month or year, so that there is no single continuous period of occupation. (p. 122)

Disposition The transfer of an **estate** or the creation of any interest (including **leases** and **mortgages**) by the holder of an estate. (p. 55)

Dominant land Land which is benefited by an **easement** or **covenant**. The holder of the dominant land is the *dominant owner*. (p. 273)

Easement A right over neighbouring land, which benefits the land of the person holding that right. An example is a right of access (right of way). This is useful if the owner of the **dominant land** has no other access, or else an inconvenient access. Most easements involve a right to do something on the **servient land**. (pp. 8, 253)

Electronic registration (e-conveyancing) The transfer or creation of interests by direct electronic contact with the land registry (not yet implemented). The register will be instantaneously updated to effect the transfer or creation. (p. 5)

Equitable lease A **lease** recognised by **equity**. It usually arises when a legal lease has failed because it does not comply with **formalities** requirements. (p. 204)

Equity A system of rights and remedies (including **proprietary interests**) originally developed by the Court of Chancery. (p. 12)

Estate contract A contract to acquire a legal **estate** in land. It constitutes a **proprietary interest**. (pp. 10, 118)

Estates Rights to enjoy land, analogous to ownership at their most extensive. Estates are measured by time, so that a right to land for life is a **life estate**. An interest that may last forever is a **fee simple** estate. (p. 6)

Estoppel The principle (more fully, proprietary estoppel) applicable if an owner encourages a person to assume that an interest exists, whether by representation or acquiescence in a mistake. A remedy may be given if that person has acted to their detriment. (p. 75)

Fee simple An **estate** in land that may last forever. A fee simple absolute **in possession** is virtually the same as ownership. It is *absolute* if it cannot be artificially cut short. (p. 6)

Fine A capital sum paid by a tenant at the time a **lease** is entered into (usually reducing the rent otherwise payable). (p. 63)

Fixture An object fixed to land such that it belongs to the owner of the land and ceases to exist as a separate object. (p. 50)

Foreclosure The termination of a mortgagor's (borrower's) right of **redemption**, so that the mortgagee (lender) becomes the owner. It is rare today. (p. 306)

Forfeiture The cutting short of an interest. It is most important as a means of terminating a **lease** when the tenant is in breach of its terms. (p. 216)

Formalities Requirements that certain interests or transactions have to be created in a certain way: by writing, a **deed** or entry on a register. (pp. 5, 55)

Four unities The unities of possession, interest, title and time must be present before a **joint tenancy** can exist. A **tenancy in common** requires only unity of possession. (p. 149)

Freehold estates Those estates that are not **leases**. It is often used as a synonym for the fee simple absolute in possession. (p. 6)

Future lease A lease that will commence in the future, as where a lease is entered into on 1 April for occupation on 1 August. (p. 122)

Indemnity Compensation payable by the land registry when a mistake has been made on the register, regarding **registered titles**. (p. 139)

Intestacy Dying without making a will. Legislation provides for the assets of the deceased person to pass to a spouse or close relatives. (p. 159)

Joint tenancy A form of **concurrent interests** whereby each joint tenant is regarded as owning the whole. On death of one joint tenant, the survivors own the land; the deceased's share does not pass under his or her will. (p. 148)

Land charges A system of registration of specified interests in land, but not of **estates**. It will become obsolete when **land registration** is completed. (pp. 20, 118)

Land registration See **registered land**. (p. 64)

Lease An **estate** whereby land may be enjoyed for a fixed period. The period may be as short as a day or last hundreds of years. The person who grants the lease is the *landlord*, or *lessor*. The person to whom the lease is granted is the *tenant*, or *lessee*. (pp. 7, 187)

Legatee A person who is entitled to property under a will.

Licence A right to enter or do something on (or having an effect on) land. It applies to situations as diverse as living in a friend's house and visiting a cinema. It is a residuary category, covering rights that are not **leases** or **easements**. It is thought not to be a **proprietary interest**. (p. 239)

Life estate An **estate** giving a right to enjoy land for the holder's lifetime. (p. 6)

Mortgage A property interest that exists to ensure payment of a debt, most commonly by selling land if the debt is unpaid. Modern mortgages are frequently described as **charges**. We say a debt is *secured* if it is protected by a mortgage or charge. The lender (the person to whom the security is given) is the *mortgagee*. The borrower is the *mortgagor*. (p. 294)

Notice (doctrine of) In traditional analyses, a purchaser is bound by an existing equitable interest only if there is actual or **constructive notice** of it. Notice is of little significance for **registered land**. (p. 116)

Numerus clausus The law recognises a *closed list* of interests in property; the owner is not allowed to create novel forms of proprietary interests in the property.

Option The right to purchase land (or an interest in it) if the holder of the option chooses to do so. It is a form of **estate contract**. (p. 10)

Overreaching When land held on **trust** is sold, the interests of the trust beneficiaries are transferred from the land to the proceeds of sale. Overreaching ensures that trustees can sell land without the purchaser having to investigate the beneficial interests. (pp. 17, 162, 182)

Overriding interests Interests that bind purchasers of **registered land** despite their not being protected on the register. (pp. 20, 124)

Partition When two or more people have **concurrent interests** in land, sometimes it may be physically divided between them.

Periodic tenancy A form of **lease** which superficially lasts for a period such as a week or year, but which continues unless either party gives notice to end it. (p. 201)

Perpetuities Rules designed to ensure that an interest cannot be made to **vest** too far in the future. (p. 148)

Personal representatives The persons who administer the property of a deceased individual, paying debts and passing it to those entitled under the will. (p. 26)

Planning permission A system whereby permission must be sought before any building or change of land use is undertaken. (p. 286)

Positive covenants Covenants that require the expenditure of money or work to be undertaken. Unlike **restrictive covenants**, they are not **proprietary interests**. (p. 4)

Possession (in) An interest is said to be in possession when it is presently being enjoyed. (p. 6)

Prescription The acquisition of **easements** by long use, without the permission of the owner of the **servient land**. (p. 270)

Priorities A system for working out which of two competing interests wins. Suppose an owner of land **leases** it to Brian on day one and **mortgages** the same land to Charles on day two. Priority rules tell us whether Brian can enforce his lease against Charles. (p. 115)

Privity of contract The principle (amended by legislation) that only the parties to a contract can sue and be sued on it. (pp. 73, 225)

Profit The right to take something from somebody else's land, such as fish from a river. It is analogous to **easements**, though it need not benefit neighbouring land. (p. 254)

Proprietary interests Interests that affect **successors in title** to the person who creates them. (p. 3)

Proprietor The term used for the owner of a **registered title**. (pp. 5, 29, 121)

Rectification (1) of documents The amendment of documents by the court to correct mistakes made in their drafting. (p. 14, 117, 138, 267)

Rectification (2) of registered titles The amendment of the register under statutory powers to correct mistakes on the register. (p. 138)

Redemption The termination of **mortgages** and **charges** by the repayment of sums due to the lender. (p. 302)

Registered land (or title) A system whereby fees simple and leases are registered by the land registry. Other rights (such as **mortgages** and **restrictive covenants**) are entered on the register of the **fee simple** or **lease** affected. The register is guaranteed to be accurate and replaces **title deeds**. (p. 115)

Remainder (in) An **estate** that does not give present enjoyment of land, usually because somebody else has a life interest **in possession**. (p. 6)

Restrictive covenants Covenants that require no expenditure of money and no work to be undertaken. An example is an obligation not to build on land. (pp. 9, 277)

Resulting trust Where property is transferred to another, the transferee holds on resulting trust for the transferor unless a gift was intended. A similar trust arises if a person provides money for the purchase of property: the purchaser holds on trust for the person who provided the funds. (p. 69)

Servient land Land over which an **easement** is exercised or whose holder is obliged to comply with a **covenant**. The holder of the servient land is the *servient owner*. (p. 271)

Settlement An arrangement whereby **successive interests** are created in land. The term *settled land* is used more specifically to describe a system, now obsolescent, of statutory regulation of settlements. (pp. 52, 146)

Severance Converting a **joint tenancy** into a tenancy in common. (p. 152)

Specific performance A court order requiring a party to carry out an obligation (usually contractual). (pp. 14, 204)

Sublease A **lease** created by somebody who is a tenant rather than owner. (pp. 222, 229)

Successive interests Estates that are enjoyed one after another, as where one person is entitled for their life and thereafter the land will go to another person. (pp. 6, 146)

Successor in title Somebody whose right to land derives from a specified person. The term includes purchasers, tenants and those taking title under a will.

Survivorship The principle that when one **joint tenant** dies, the survivors own the land. The deceased's share does not pass under his or her will. (p. 148)

Tenancy in common A form of **concurrent interests**, under which the shares can be of whatever nature and size the parties choose. There is no survivorship: the interest passes under the will of a deceased tenant in common. (p. 148)

Title deeds Documents shown by a seller of **unregistered land** to the purchaser, proving that the seller owns the land. They are usually successive conveyances of the land going back at least 15 years. (p. 116)

Trespass Wrongful entry on land. (p. 45)

True owner The person who is shown to be the owner of land by the title deeds or register. To be contrasted with the adverse possessor. (p. 39)

Trust An arrangement whereby a *trustee* manages property for the benefit of a *beneficiary*. The trustee and beneficiary both have **proprietary interests** in the property (legal and equitable interests respectively). Some trusts are imposed by the courts to ensure that the holders of property cannot keep it for themselves: **constructive** and **resulting trusts**. (p. 12)

Trust for sale A **trust** under which the trustees have an obligation to sell, though invariably they have power to postpone sale. (pp. 162, 184)

Trust of land Any **trust** over land. The term possesses particular significance because the Trusts of Land and Appointment of Trustees Act 1996regulates trusts of land. (pp. 18, 162)

Trustee in bankruptcy The person to whom the assets of a bankrupt person pass. The trustee in bankruptcy will sell those assets in order to pay the debts of the bankrupt. (p. 154, 302)

Undivided shares Another name for a **tenancy in common**. (p. 150)

Unregistered land Land where the **fee simple** or **lease** is not **registered**. (p. 19, 115)

Vesting An interest is vested when there is nothing to stop the holder from enjoying the property other than a prior interest. If there is a prior interest, the interest is said to be *vested in interest*. An interest is not vested if the identity of the holder is not settled or some qualification (such as attaining a specified age) has yet to be satisfied. (p. 147)

Index

Page references in **bold** refer to Glossary entries.